Anarchism in the
Chinese Revolution

Anarchism in the Chinese Revolution

Arif Dirlik

UNIVERSITY OF CALIFORNIA PRESS
Berkeley · *Los Angeles* · *London*

Chapter 3 is a revised version of an article that first appeared in *Modern China* 12, no. 2 (April 1986); chapter 4 is a revised version of an article (coauthored with Edward Krebs) that first appeared in *Modern China* 7, no. 2 (April 1981); chapter 5 is a revised version of an article that first appeared in *Modern China* 11, no. 3 (July 1985); chapter 6 is a revised version of an article that first appeared in *International Review of Social History* 1 (1989); chapter 7 first appeared in *Modern China* 15, no. 4 (October 1989). I am indebted to these journals and to Sage Publications.

University of California Press
Berkeley and Los Angeles, California

University of California Press, Ltd.
London, England

© 1991 by
The Regents of the University of California

Library of Congress Cataloging-in-Publication Data

Dirlik, Arif.
    Anarchism in the Chinese revolution / Arif Dirlik.
        p.   cm.
    Includes bibliographical references and index.
    ISBN 0-520-08264-8
    1. Anarchism—China—History—20th century.   2. China—
    History—20th century.   [1. Revolutions—China—History—20th
    century.]   I. Title.
HX950.D57   1991   90—21407
320.5'7'09510904—dc20   CIP

Printed in the United States of America

The paper used in this publication meets the minimum requirements of American National Standard for Information Sciences—Permanence of Paper for Printed Library Materials, ANSI Z39.48-1984. ⊚

For Roxann

Contents

Acknowledgments

This work is a preliminary one, an attempt to lay the groundwork for further study of anarchism in China. The substance of the study is based on articles on Chinese anarchism that I have published over the last decade. I have added several new chapters and revised already published ones extensively, both to incorporate new materials and to rework them into a historical narrative. In the process, I have also brought to the foreground an interpretation of the place of anarchism in Chinese radicalism that was present only implicitly in my previous work.

Several people have contributed to this work significantly, both with their own work and with the materials they have uncovered. I should like to mention five scholars in particular who, in the best spirit of scholarship (and anarchy) have shared with me their work and research: Professor Lu Zhe of Nanjing University, an "Old Comrade," whose own manuscript on Chinese anarchism has just been published; Diane Scherer, who generously kept me informed of her findings over the course of a long trek of research into Chinese anarchism that took her around the world; Edward Krebs, who was my coauthor in the writing of the original article that was the basis for chapter 5; Marilyn Levine and Peter Zarrow, who shared with me their dissertations. Zarrow's *Anarchism and Chinese Political Culture* (New York: Columbia University Press, 1989) and Lu Zhe's *Zhongguo wuzhengfu zhuyi shi* (History of Chinese anarchism) (Fujian: Renmin chubanshe, 1990) have already added much to our understanding of anarchism in China. I look forward to the publication of the studies by Krebs, Levine, and Scherer.

Unfailingly stimulating conversations with Harry Harrotunian (friend, colleague, and former professor) helped me think out the ideas that have gone into the theoretical underpinnings of this study. The study also benefited from careful readings by Irwin Scheiner, Larry Schneider, and Peter Zarrow. I acknowledge their contributions while relieving them of any responsibility for what appears here.

I should like also to acknowledge a long-standing debt to a former teacher, Dr. Ercument Atabay of Bosphorus University, Istanbul (formerly Robert College), who had much to do with my interest in history while I was still an engineering student. Dorothy Sapp, of the Department of History at Duke University, as usual gave her all to seeing this manuscript through to its completion (and to catching the errors that rarely escape her sharp eyes).

I first seriously got into the collection of materials for this study in 1978–79, with a generous grant from the National Endowment for the Humanities for the study of Chinese political thought. Over the years I have received support from the Duke University Research Council, as well as a summer grant from the Hoover Institution and the Stanford Center for East Asian Studies, which have enabled me to keep up with new materials pouring out of the People's Republic of China. A grant from the American Council of Learned Societies in 1985–86 for writing up the study ended with a diversion to a study of the origins of Chinese communism; this study shows, I hope, that the diversion was not whimsical. Finally, I should like to thank the staff of the Hoover Institution's East Asian Collection (where I have spent a good deal of research time over the years), in particular its curator, Ramon Myers, for their gracious hospitality over the years.

I dedicate the study with love to my spouse, colleague, and comrade, Roxann Prazniak. Roxann's "animism" has influenced the way I look at anarchism. I leave it to her, however, to delve into the question of the relationship between anarchism, Buddhism, and Saint Francis!

CHAPTER ONE

Introduction

Anarchism and Revolutionary Discourse

Anarchism is not the easiest subject to think, speak, or write about within a cultural context that takes hegemony for granted as a principle of social and political integration. The most consistent and thoroughgoing of all modern radical social philosophies in its repudiation of this principle, anarchism has also for that reason suffered the greatest marginalization. Other radicalisms, too, have invoked fear and ridicule, but they have acquired respectability to the extent that they have come to share in the premises of organized power. The fear of anarchism, in contrast, is built into the word itself, whose meaning ("no rule") has been suppressed in everyday language by its identification with disorder. To take a pertinent recent example, in the television coverage of the tragic events in China in 1989, what Chinese leaders spoke of as "great disorder" (*daluan*) was consistently rendered in the reporting as "anarchy." (This is not to suggest that Chinese leaders themselves are incapable of the identification.) But fear may not be as effective as ridicule in the marginalization and distortion of anarchism; to dismiss anarchism as irrelevant works better, since it is thus removed from the domain of "serious" political dialogue— and historical attention.

This study deals with a historical occasion when anarchism fared better, indeed was central to speculation on politics: China in the early part of the century, when anarchism held a place in the center of revolutionary thought. I argue not only that the revolutionary situation created by China's confrontation with the modern world gave birth to a radical culture that provided fecund grounds for anarchism, but also that anarchists played an important part in the fashioning of this radical culture. The significance of anarchism, however, went beyond the roughly two decades (1905–1930) when anarchism was a highly visible current in the revolutionary movement. At a time when a revolutionary discourse was taking shape, anarchist ideas played a crucial part in injecting into it concerns that would leave a lasting imprint on the Chinese revolution, reaching beyond the relatively small group of anarchists into the ideologies of other revolutionaries. For the same reason, the history of anarchism offers a perspective from which to view the subsequent unfolding of the revolution and the ways in which the revolution, in order to achieve success, was to suppress the very social ideals that initially gave it meaning.

With the success of the October Revolution in Russia and the consequent diffusion of Leninist Marxism worldwide, Eric Hobsbawm has written,

> It became hard to recall that in 1905–14, the marxist left had in most countries been on the fringe of the revolutionary movement, the main body of marxists had been identified with a *de facto* non-revolutionary social democracy, while the bulk of the revolutionary left was anarcho-syndicalist, or at least much closer to the ideas and the mood of anarcho-syndicalism than to that of classical marxism. Marxism was henceforth identified with actively revolutionary movements. . . . Anarchism and anarcho-syndicalism entered upon a dramatic and uninterrupted decline.[1]

This could serve equally well as a description of the situation of Chinese radicalism in the early part of the century, with two qualifications. There was no "marxist left" to speak of in China until 1920–21; non-Marxist social democratic currents that appeared in Chinese radical thought early on were not necessarily inimical to anarchism but, on the contrary, willing to recognize it as a common, if remote, ideal. While in China, too, anarchism fell into decline with the appearance of Leninist Marxism in 1920–21, and was repudiated by the revolutionary Left, which thereafter identified with Marxism, the relationship of Marxism to anarchism retained some ambiguity. I have argued elsewhere that most of those who were to emerge as leaders of the Communist movement in China went through an anarchist phase before they became Marxists.[2] I will endeavor to show here that these anarchist origins may be important to an understanding of how they became Marxists, and also of some features of Chinese Marxism

1. Eric Hobsbawm, *Revolutionaries* (New York: New American Library, 1973), 61.
2. Arif Dirlik, *The Origins of Chinese Communism* (New York: Oxford University Press, 1989), esp. chapters 3 and 8.

(especially in its Maoist version) that diverged from the Leninist interpretation of Marxism that they espoused formally.

That anarchist ideas may have survived the decline of anarchism suggests, in turn, that anarchism had a different relationship to revolutionary discourse in China than in Europe. The fortunes of anarchism in China paralleled (indeed, were part of) the situation that Hobsbawm describes. But Chinese anarchism was bound up from the beginning with an incipient revolutionary discourse that was ultimately the product of China's confrontation with the modern world, and anarchists were to play some part in the formulation of that discourse. While anarchism in China was also the ideology of the revolutionary Left, which identified itself with what it took to be the most advanced radical ideology of the contemporary world, it was phrased (especially initially) within the language of this discourse. For the same reason, anarchist ideas entered this discourse as its constituent elements. I will argue that anarchism derives its significance in Chinese radicalism, at least in part, from the diffusion of anarchist ideas across the ideological boundaries that divided radicals.

Nevertheless, the anarchist origin of these ideas was forgotten as anarchism gradually retreated before Leninist Marxism in the 1920s. It is important to recall these origins (the subject of this study), for both historical and political reasons. Anarchism was important historically in a contextual sense: as the ideology of the radical Left in China for more than two decades at the beginning of the century. Because this was also the period when a revolutionary discourse emerged that was to shape Chinese radicalism in ensuing years, the anarchist contribution to the formulation of this discourse must be part of any account that seeks a comprehensive grasp of Chinese radicalism.

The recalling of anarchism also has obvious political implications for our understanding of the past and present of socialism in China. The repudiation of anarchism with the ascendancy of Leninist Marxism also meant the suppression of certain questions crucial to socialism as a political ideology—in particular the question of democracy. The Communist regime in China is in a crisis today, which not only has thrown into question the continued viability of socialism, but has shaken the credibility of the socialist revolution. Although the crisis is ideological, part of it lies unquestionably in the failure of the regime to deliver the democratic promise of socialism, a failure that has caused a new generation of radicals to look outside of socialism for alternatives in the creation of a democratic society.

I would suggest here that to recall anarchism, which Leninist Marxism suppressed, is to recall the democratic ideals for which anarchism, among all the competing socialisms in China's revolutionary history, served as the repository. It is a reminder that the socialist tradition in China, released from the ideological boundaries within which it has been confined, may serve as a source of democratic inspiration and social imagination. Whether the kind of democracy anarchists envisioned is feasible is beside the point; what is important is that it affords a critical perspective upon the claims to democracy of competing socialist and bourgeois alternatives of the present—and makes it possible to imagine the future in new ways. The challenge of the anarchist notion of democracy has been swept under the rug both by capitalism and by socialism as it exists: how to be both ethical (and therefore deeply mindful of social relationships) and rational (and therefore able to overcome the hierarchical bind of conventional social relationships). This was ultimately the challenge that anarchists introduced into revolutionary discourse in China, even if none stated it with the directness with which I have expressed it here. At a time of social breakdown and individual alienation, anarchists imagined a society where individual freedom could be fulfilled only through social responsibility, but without being sacrificed to it, which is the essence of socialist democracy and may be central to any conception of democracy. The challenge was to resonate with key questions of Chinese politics, which may account for the refusal of anarchism to disappear, even when it has had little to say about practical politics.

Over the past decade there has been a surge of interest in China in the history of Chinese anarchism. Scholarly journals regularly publish discussions of the place of anarchism in the Chinese revolution. Two major (and thorough) compilations of anarchist writings from the first three decades of the century were published in 1984, which have made available to contemporary readers scattered (and rare) documentation on Chinese anarchist thinking and provided direct encounter with a long-forgotten phase in a (still) unfolding revolutionary discourse. Even a biography of M. Bakunin and a translation of P. Kropotkin's *Conquest of Bread* appeared at about the same time. As if in answer, a voluminous collection appeared and made available extensive Marxist criticisms of anarchism. A history published in 1989 has provided a detailed coverage of the unfolding of anarchism, and other works are in preparation.[3]

3. Ge Maochun, Jiang Jun, and Li Xingzhi, eds., *Wuzhengfu zhuyi sixiang ziliao xuan* (Selection of materials on anarchist thought [hereafter *WZFZYSX*]), 2 vols. (Beijing: Beijing daxue chubanshe, 1984); Gao Jun et al., eds., *Wuzhengfu zhuyi zai Zhongguo* (Anarchism in

What this activity adds up to is difficult to say. Especially problematic is the question of whether interest in the history of anarchism in China is a sign of interest in anarchism itself. We can only safely deduce that interest in the history of anarchism is part of a surge of interest in the history of socialism in China. Anarchism is not the only socialism to enjoy renewed attention in contemporary China among historians, political ideologues, and the general reading public alike, but it does appear as one prominent crest in a broad wave of interest in the past of Chinese socialism, which includes, among other things, an interest in long-forgotten aspects of the history of the Communist party itself.

Anarchism has a contemporary relevance to the extent that it is implicated in the current crisis of Chinese socialism—and of the historical consciousness of socialism. I refer here to the crisis created by the repudiation of Mao Zedong and of Maoist communism, which has created a profound uncertainty in Chinese consciousness concerning not only the future but the past of socialism in China. For the past four decades, the history of socialism in China has been thought and written around the paradigm of Mao's personal biography—in China and abroad. The Cultural Revolution in particular was responsible for elevating Mao's biography to paradigmatic status in the conceptualization of Chinese socialism, although the process was already under way in the 1940s, even before the victory of the Communist Party in 1949. The repudiation of the Cultural Revolution following Mao's death in 1976 was rapidly to call into question Maoist historiography of the socialist revolution as well. The crisis in the historical consciousness of socialism that has ensued presents a predicament as well as novel opportunities. Predicament because the history of socialism has been deprived of its reference in Mao's biography and needs to be relocated in time (the Communist party does not provide a ready substitute, because in repudiating Mao it has also deprived itself of the claim to historical infallibility). Opportunity because the repudiation of Mao has burst open the ideological closure in which socialism had long been restricted, which has made possible new ways of seeing its history.

China) (Changsha: Hunan renmin chubanshe, 1984); Lu Zhe, *Zhongguo wuzhengfu zhuyi shi* (History of Chinese anarchism) (Fujian: Renmin chubanshe); Xu Shanguang and Liu Liuping, *Zhongguo wuzhengfu zhuyi shi* (History of Chinese anarchism) (Changsha: Hunan renmin chubanshe, 1989); *Makesi Engesi lun Bakuning zhuyi* (Marx and Engels on Bakuninism) (Beijing: Renmin chubanshe, 1980); Li Xianjong, *Bakuning pingzhuan* (Biography of Bakunin) (Beijing: Xinhua shudian, 1982); Kropotkin, *Mianbao yu ziyou* (Bread and freedom) [*sic*] (Beijing: Shangwu yinshuguan, 1982). For a listing of articles on anarchism, see *Makesi zhuyi zai Zhongguo* (Marxism in China), 2 vols. (Beijing: Qinghua daxue chubanshe, 1983), 2:573–74.

Anarchism has had a significant part to play in this crisis. In the
immediate if brief atmosphere of ideological freedom that followed upon
the official repudiation of the Cultural Revolution, critics of Maoism
from the Left in the ill-fated Democracy Movement of 1978–1980 called
for a more democratic socialism, on the model of the Paris Commune of
1871.[4] The Paris Commune is not to be claimed for anarchism, of course,
because it holds an equally venerable place in both anarchist and Marxist
revolutionary traditions. But I suggest that as an instance of a democratic
and self-governing social organization, the Commune stands at the inter-
section of anarchist and Marxist revolutionary ideals, where the historical opposition between anarchism and Marxism is blurred into an authentic social revolution in which the opposition is dissolved in the common
vision of which they are alternative products. Although, as far as I am
aware, the leftist socialists of the Democracy Movement did not use the
word "anarchism" in their discourse, the use of the Commune as a model
recalled anarchism, or if not anarchism, then that area of Marxism which
overlaps with anarchism and is especially problematic from the perspective of Leninist Marxism.

To make matters worse, the Paris Commune had also provided a
model for the Cultural Revolution at its more radical moments.[5] It is
not surprising, therefore, that when the first writings on anarchism
began to appear in Chinese publications in the early 1980s, they cast
anarchism in a negative, pejorative mold to attack "bourgeois" individualism, often confounding the anti–Cultural Revolution demands of the
Democracy Movement with the Cultural Revolution "perversion" of
correct Marxism. It was ostensibly the urge to find the key to this
perversion, ultimately, that was to sustain the surge of interest in anarchism. Some have argued that the Cultural Revolution was a product of
the persistence of "anarchist" influences that had entered the Communist party at its very origins through the founding fathers of the party,
many of whom had gone through an anarchist phase before they became Marxists, and stubbornly survived the party's repeated efforts to
purge itself of its anarchist beginnings.[6] While the use of "anarchism"
in such writings is often vulgarly simplistic, equated with a "petit-
bourgeois" propensity to mindless individualism and disorder, it has

4. A collection of Democracy Movement writings is available in Gregory Benton, ed.,
Wild Lilies and Poisonous Weeds (London: Pluto Press, 1982).
5. John Bryan Starr, "Revolution in Retrospect: The Paris Commune through Chinese
Eyes," *China Quarterly*, no. 49 (January–March 1972): 106–25.
6. Li Zhenya, "Zhongguo wuzhengfu zhuyide jinxi" (Past and present of Chinese anarchism), *Nankai xuebao* (Nankai University journal), no. 1 (1980).

nevertheless provoked a search for anarchism at the origins of Chinese communism and, by extension, in the early part of the century. The result has been the rediscovery of the crucial part anarchism played in the Chinese revolutionary movement in the first three decades of the century.

On the surface, this rediscovery has merely confirmed the superiority of Marxian communism (or Bolshevism) to anarchism. As the editors of the compilation of anarchist writings conclude from the decline of anarchism in the late twenties: "No bourgeois or petit-bourgeois thinking or theory can carry the Chinese revolution to victory; only Marxism-Leninism can save China. Marxism-Leninism has uninterruptedly gained in power in its struggles with bourgeois and petit-bourgeois thinking."[7] There is in this statement, however, a sense of unease, as if it were addressing unnamed antagonists who might think that a "petit-bourgeois" ideology such as anarchism might provide an alternative to Marxism-Leninism. And while it would be an exaggeration to suggest that there are those in China today who promote anarchism as an integral social philosophy, it is possible to read in the advocacy for a democratic socialism, such as during the Democracy Movement, the persistence of anarchist "influences." It is also difficult to avoid the impression that the interest in anarchism, even in this particular compilation, has gone beyond the urge to discover the sources of Marxism's perversion during the Cultural Revolution, in order to find out more about this early alternative to Marxism.

The intellectual context for the surge of interest in the history of anarchism is, ultimately, not just the repudiation of the Cultural Revolution but the disillusionment with Marxism-Leninism that it has brought in its wake. In this sense, the revival of interest in anarchism may be compared to a similar revival in Europe following the events of May 1968 in France and the consequent repudiation of Stalinist communism. There may also be a comparison in the ideological content of the interest, which rests on anarchism, not so much as a self-contained substitute for Marxism, but as a source of inspiration for a democratic socialism and of insights with which to complement a Marxism that has become insufficient to explain the world and to correct for its ills. Anarchism, in other words, must be reintroduced into revolutionary discourse if it is to be released from the ideological closure imposed by Marxism, especially

7. *WZFZYSX* 1:iii.

Marxism-Leninism, and redirected toward a democratic socialism better able to account for the problems of the contemporary world.[8]

The contemporary Chinese interest in anarchism points, therefore, in two directions. In a negative sense, it points to anarchism as an explanation of the perversion of Marxism whose ultimate manifestation was the Cultural Revolution, and it seeks in recalling anarchism a means to put Marxism back on the right track. In a positive sense, it points to anarchism as a means of breaking out of the ideological closure imposed by a Marxist-Leninist past, which views anarchism not as a source of perversion of Marxism-Leninism but as a corrective to the antidemocratic tendencies that are implicit in the latter. The one sense is "reconstructive," the other "deconstructive." The one seeks to restore authoritarian politics; the other points toward a more democratic socialism.

It is the "deconstructive" sense that guides the perspective I bring to this discussion of the history of anarchism. My evaluation here is the opposite of those Chinese writers on anarchism who present a negative portrayal of the part anarchism played in revolutionary discourse. No matter what we may think of individual anarchists, anarchism was a source of democratic ideals in the socialist revolutionary discourse, and if anarchist influences did indeed survive to lead to negative consequences during an event such as the Cultural Revolution, it may be because they were put to uses unintended by the anarchists and within a political context of the kind that anarchists rejected. Whatever may be the shortcomings of anarchism as a social philosophy, the unconditional repudiation of anarchism by a Marxist-Leninist Communist party was to deprive it of an important source of democratic ideals.

Recognition of the significance of anarchism in the Chinese revolutionary movement has two broad consequences, at least so long as we recognize a positive function to anarchism in the socialist movement. First, we are compelled to rewrite the history of socialism in China, which may no longer be conceived simply as a progressive evolution of a correct socialism under the guidance of Mao Zedong or the Communist party, as Chinese historians would have it; it must be seen also as a series of suppressions: not simply as the evolution of a strategy and a set of policies that brought socialism to power, but also—in the course of those very formulations—a suppression of the ideals and the democratic vision

8. Daniel Guérin, *Anarchism*, trans. M. Klopper (New York: Monthly Review Press, 1970). See also Anthony Arblaster, "The Relevance of Anarchism," *Socialist Register* (1971), 157–84.

that had initially motivated the revolution. Political victory may be important, but it is not proof of the "correctness" of the strategy that made victory possible—not in terms of the ideological premises of the revolution. There was also a price to be paid for victory in the attenuation of the revolutionary vision in whose name the revolution was conducted. Recognition of a historical presence to anarchism brings into full relief what the price would be.

Second, the history of anarchism in China, no less than elsewhere, draws our attention to the problematic relationship between Marxism and anarchism. An important anarchist criticism of Marxism in the twenties was that in its urge to establish a center to history, either in the proletariat or in its "representative," the Communist party, Marxism reproduced the very power structures that in theory it rejected. As I view it, this urge to decenter power does not necessarily call for a repudiation of Marxism but is, rather, a reminder to Marxists of their own revolutionary premises. It certainly is a crucial issue of the day not just in China but worldwide, where voices other than that of the proletariat are calling upon Marxism to recognize forms of oppression that are not restricted to the oppression of the working class by the bourgeoisie—oppression by the bureaucratic state, and gender, racial, and national oppression immediately come to mind. A single-minded preoccupation with class and capitalism inevitably results in total or partial blindness to these other forms of oppression. Similarly, an unwavering commitment to modernism (a unilinear view of history and its material basis in industrial and technological progress), which is characteristic of mainstream Marxism and most certainly of existing socialist states, makes for a blindness to contemporary questions related to ecology, community, and alienation, which may no longer be blamed simply on capitalism, but are products of a modern culture of which Marxism partakes. Anarchism, in surprising ways, may have a "decentering" effect on Marxist modernism (which does take capitalism as the central datum of modern history) and thus may enable us to think about socialism in new ways without necessarily abandoning Marxism, which stands to this day as the most thorough critique of capitalism while sharing its modernist premises. As recognition of the history of anarchism in China may have a deconstructive consequence in our appreciation of Chinese socialism by decentering Marxism-Leninism and releasing us from the ideological closure imposed upon history by the Communist victory in China, so may the anarchist critique of Marxist-Leninist efforts to establish a new center to history, as one episode in the global history of socialism, bring that history closer to

the present in the contemporary effort to release socialism from the ideological closure that its history has imposed on it globally.

I will now elaborate on the significance of anarchism to an understanding of the revolutionary discourse in twentieth-century China and draw
out further its historiographical as well as its political implications.

THE ANARCHIST PRESENCE
IN THE CHINESE REVOLUTIONARY MOVEMENT

The heyday of anarchism in China were the years between 1905 and
1930. Expressions of interest in anarchism were heard first in 1903–4.
And anarchists would remain active after 1930. But it was in 1906 that
the first anarchist association came into existence, and concentrated anarchist activity for all practical purposes would cease after 1930. During
these two-and-a-half decades, however, anarchism was to play a central
part in articulating an emerging social radicalism in the Chinese revolution.

What Hobsbawm has observed of anarchism worldwide is also applicable, I think, to the case of anarchism in China. Hobsbawm suggests
that anarchism has enjoyed the greatest popularity at moments of spontaneous revolutionary mobilization when revolutionaries, rather than making revolution or preparing the conditions for it, have been able to share
in the possibilities offered by a revolutionary situation. He distinguishes
between revolution as a "happening" and revolution as a product of
revolutionary activity:

> The test of greatness in revolutionaries has always been their capacity to
> discover the new and unexpected characteristics of revolutionary situations
> and to adapt their tactics to them. Like the surfer, the revolutionary does not
> create the waves on which he rides, but balances on them. Unlike the surfer—
> and here serious revolutionary theory diverges from anarchist practice—
> sooner or later he stops riding the wave and must control its direction and
> movement.[9]

The distinguishing feature of the Chinese revolutionary movement
during these years, especially during 1915–1925, was a mass mobilization to which political (if not social) organization was largely irrelevant
and which brought into the radical movement entire social groups (students, women, laborers) in pursuit of a new place for themselves in the
revolutionary reorganization of Chinese society. In contrast, when the

9. Hobsbawm, *Revolutionaries*, 89.

Guomindang restored political order after 1927, however superficially, and turned its back on its own revolutionary legacy in its suppression of mass movements, revolutionaries would depend for their success (and survival) on their ability to organize a social basis for revolution. The difference was between revolution as a "happening" and revolution as "made" by revolutionaries. Anarchists, we shall see, benefited from the former situation, but were unable—because of their own self-limitation—to cope with the latter.

This distinction is necessary, I think, to draw attention to the changing problematic of the revolutionary movement in China; but it needs some qualification if we are to overcome stereotyped notions of anarchism. Ultimately, the distinction is not between spontaneity and organization, but between different kinds of organization. What anarchists rejected was not organization per se but *political* organization, and if they appear to have insisted on a "spontaneous" social revolution, they conceived of spontaneity as social "self-activity" that would produce a new social organization in the course of revolutionary activity. The revolutionary movement during the earlier period was not spontaneous, it was also "made"—though in a radically different sense than after 1927—and anarchists played an important part in "making" it. The qualification enables us to see anarchist activity as something other than the haphazard activity of individuals, or as a diffuse radicalism without coherence.

Is it possible to speak of an anarchist movement in China? I think so, so long as the word "movement" is not understood just as activities whose motions are determined from an identifiable center—a restrictive stipulation that was *the* object of the anarchist challenge to the other social revolutionary movements of the time. In the ideological topography of Chinese radicalism in the first three decades of the century, anarchism was a pervasive presence without a center, concentrated around nodes of ideological dissemination and social activity whose location changed with changes in the fortunes of the revolutionary movement. Although it was a liability from the perspective of political effectiveness, this diffuseness of anarchism was an advantage in the dissemination of anarchist ideas. A revolutionary discourse on society that explicitly rejected politics, anarchism did not call for allegiance to an ideology or an organization as a condition of allegiance to its principles. Receptivity to anarchist ideas was most conspicuously a feature of Chinese radicalism when questions of social and cultural revolution were its foremost concerns; but anarchism could also infuse the thinking of those whose ideological convictions lay elsewhere, because it did not challenge them at the level of ideology. It was in this sense a revolutionary discourse that cut across ideological divides in the revolutionary movement.

The ideological diffuseness and organizational "decenteredness" of anarchism (the two were different sides of the same coin) make it difficult to identify anarchists or to define the contours of anarchism as a movement. The appeals of anarchism in China were varied. While all anarchists shared a common social idealism that expressed itself in the repudiation of authority, especially of the state and the family, what they found in anarchism is another matter. For different anarchists, anarchism expressed everything from trivial acts of antiauthoritarianism to rebellion against the suffocating authority of the family, of the oppression of women by men and of youth by their elders, to an aesthetic promise of individual liberation, all the way to the pursuit of a social and economic equality that was barely distinguishable from that of the Communists. Even among the "social anarchists," the main concern here, anarchism provided a refuge for modernists who identified it with the truth of modern science and uncompromisingly rejected a prescientific past, as well as for antimodernists who, in their frustration with modern society, sought in the past the promise of a good society. In the early twenties, anarchist ideals were diffused broadly in radical thinking; even those who in 1921 would establish the Communist party of China shared the outlook of anarchism before that time, if they did not actually identify themselves as anarchists, and would retain anarchist affinities after their conversion to Bolshevism. Some of the most distinguished anarchists were also members of the Guomindang, even though in theory they rejected politics, and would play an important part in the Guomindang suppression of Communists (and of anarchists) in the late twenties. Anarchist commitments had such an evanescent quality that even anarchists were on occasion unsure of the seriousness of commitment, not just of rank-and-file, fly-by-night anarchists, but of those with leadership roles in the movement.

Anarchist attitudes toward organization compounded (we might even say were responsible for) the problem. Strict organizational affiliation, which quickly disciplined a comparable ideological diffuseness among Marxists in the early 1920s, is of no help in delineating the anarchist movement because anarchists repudiated the subjection of the individual to the organization and of the peripheries of the movement to a center; jealous of local autonomy (localized ultimately at the individual level), anarchists were at one in rejecting centralized regulation of their thinking and activities. Anarchist organizational rules, rather than requiring members to subscribe to a well-defined set of rules, often stipulated only that they "do not oppose" the revolutionary goals of anarchism, which were often very vaguely stated.[10] According to one writer, there were in the early twenties "several thousand" anarchists in China (an estimate that probably included fly-by-night anarchists).[11] These anarchists had their own local organizations and pursued their own localized activities, which not only differed from one another but were, in some cases, antithetical. Between 1919 and 1925, ninety-two anarchist organizations came into existence in China (some only short-lived).[12] Evidence of the widespread popularity of anarchism, the proliferation of anarchist organizations is indicative also of the absence of a center to anarchist activity. In the absence of organized direction, individual loyalty and seriousness had to assume the burden for ideological integrity and consistency of purpose. Not only was anarchism individualized, it also made great demands upon individuals, which in the end only a few were able to meet.

It does not follow, however, that there was no logic or pattern to anarchist activity. Though the movement lacked a center, it is possible to identify a number of "nodes" of ideological and social activity that were more "central" than the others (this was especially the case for the social anarchists under discussion). These nodes, and the individuals active in them, provided the anarchist movement with continuity over the years, as well as with some measure of ideological coherence and an identifiable pattern of activity. They were crucial in the dissemination of anarchist ideology. And they served both in organization and in activity as models for anarchists all over China. Certain individuals appear with regularity in anarchist publications and social activity and were given recognition in the movement as its leaders, not by organizational regulation but by the acclaim of their fellow anarchists.

The centers of Chinese anarchism in its origins lay outside of the physical boundaries of China, in overseas Chinese communities in Paris and Tokyo. One center was the Society for the Study of Socialism (*Shehui zhuyi jiangxi hui*), which was established in Tokyo in 1907 by the classical scholar Liu Shipei and his wife, He Zhen. The antimodernist, agrarian-oriented anarchism the Tokyo anarchists promoted in the two journals they published would have a lasting effect on the thinking of

10. "Shishede yiqu he dagang" (The goals and program of the Truth Society), *Banyue* (Half moon), 14 (15 February 1921). See reprint in *WZFZYSX* 2:529.
11. Xiao Xing, "Zemmayang xuanchuan annaqi zhuyi" (How should we propagate anarchism?), *Huzhu yuekan* (Mutual aid monthly) 1 (15 March 1923). See reprint in *WZFZYSX* 2:683.
12. See the listing in *WZFZYSX* 2:1061–66.

Chinese anarchists, but this society was in existence for only a brief period, and its impact on the anarchist movement per se was limited.

More important in this regard was the World Society (*Shijie she*), which was established in Paris in 1906 and would serve for decades as a conduit between European and Chinese anarchism. Its founders and leaders, Li Shizeng and Wu Zhihui, were among the doyens of Chinese anarchism. They were also close associates of Sun Yat-sen (Sun Zhongshan) and were important members of the Guomindang, in which capacity they would play important roles in the 1920s in anarchist anticommunism, as well as in the problematic relationship the anarchists would enter into with the Guomindang after 1927. The modernist, even scientistic, anarchism they promoted (inspired by Kropotkin) would fashion the thinking over the years of most Chinese anarchists. The "diligent-work frugal-study" program they initiated after 1912 to educate Chinese students in Europe was to serve as a recruiting ground for anarchists (though, ironically, among its graduates were some of China's most prominent Communists, including Zhou Enlai and Deng Xiaoping). This program, which not only sought to bring to Chinese intellectuals a consciousness of labor but also brought them together with Chinese laborers abroad (who were brought to Europe during World War I to work in European armies and factories, also through the intermediacy of Li and Wu) was to have a far-reaching impact on the Chinese revolution.

If anarchism in China appears at first sight to be primarily a southern Chinese, specifically Guangzhou (Canton), phenomenon, this impression, which is at least partially valid, is a product of the important role Guangzhou anarchists were to play for two decades, not just in the south but all over China, as well as in Chinese communities in Southeast Asia and as far away as San Francisco and Vancouver (Canada). The founding father of Guangzhou anarchism was Liu Sifu, better known under his adopted name, Shifu, who at his death in 1915 was to leave behind an image as *the* paradigmatic anarchist, as well as a devoted following determined to complete the task he had initiated. While there may have been anarchists in Guangzhou before 1911, the origins of Guangzhou anarchism go back to the Conscience Society (*Xinshe*), which Shifu had established soon after his conversion to anarchism. In 1914 he and his followers moved to Shanghai to escape government persecution. There he established, shortly before his death, the Society of Anarcho-Communist Comrades (*Wuzhengfu gongchan zhuyi tongzhi hui*). This society served as a model for similar societies established shortly thereafter in Guangzhou (led by Shifu's brother, Liu Shixin) and

Nanjing; Liu Shixin's group included Ou Shengbai, Liang Bingxian, Huang Lingshuang, and Huang Zunsheng, all of whom were to achieve prominence as leaders in the anarchist movement in the May Fourth period. The Society's journal, *People's Voice* (*Minsheng*), published until 1922 (irregularly after Shifu's death), was to provide much-needed continuity in the anarchist movement. Members or associates of Shifu's group were also responsible for initiating a syndicalist movement in China; in 1917 they were able to organize barbers and tea-house clerks in Guangzhou into China's first modern labor unions, and in 1918 they led the way in China's first May Day celebration in Guangzhou. According to one account, an associate of Shifu's group, Liang Bingxian, was the editor of the first labor journal to be published in China, *Labor* (*Laodong*), published in Shanghai in 1918. By 1921 anarchists had organized "at least forty unions" in Guangzhou.[13]

After Shifu's death there was no single figure to match him in stature in the anarchist movement. But Guangzhou anarchists continued to play leadership roles in the movement, both in Guangzhou and in other parts of China to which the student ferment of the late 1910s took them. In Guangzhou, Shifu's brother, Liu Shixin, and other members of the group, such as Huang Zunsheng, emerged as labor leaders. Anarchists from Guangzhou, most prominent among them Huang Lingshuang, Zheng Peigang, Yuan Zhenying, and Hua Lin, were to found the first anarchist group in Beijing, where they had congregated in 1917 as students and teachers at Beijing University. The society they established, Truth Society (*Shishe*), played an important part in infusing anarchist ideas into the New Culture Movement led by Beijing University professors and students. In early 1919 Truth Society merged with other anarchist societies in Guangzhou and Nanjing to establish an umbrella organization, Evolution Society (*Jinhua she*). The society's journal of the same name was edited by Chen Yannian, who wrote under a pseudonym articles critical of his famous father, Chen Duxiu, leader of the New Culture Movement and later the first secretary-general of the Communist party, who had little patience for anarchists (Chen Yannian would not convert to Marxism until 1923). In early 1920 we find Guangzhou anarchists in Zhangzhou in Fujian province, which thereafter served as a center for the dissemination of anarchism in its own right. Liang Bingxian was the editor of *Fujian Star* (*Minxing*), which the anarchists published in Fujian.

13. Huang Yibo, "Wuzhengfu zhuyizhe zai Guangzhou gao gonghui huodong huiyi" (Recollections of anarchist labor activities in Guangzhou), *Guangzhou wenshi ziliao* (Literary and historical materials on Guangzhou) 1 (April 1962): 3.

According to Liu Shixin, during these years anarchist ranks were swelled by splinter groups from the Chinese Socialist party (*Zhongguo shehui zhuyi dang*, established 1911 by Jiang Kanghu), who were inclined to anarchism and complemented the activities of the Guangzhou anarchists with anarchist associations of their own (such as the Masses Society, *Qunshe*, in Nanjing).[14]

The year following the May Fourth Movement of 1919 was a turning point in Chinese radicalism, as well as in the fortunes of anarchism. Though the movement was a product of patriotic resentment against the Versailles Treaty, the mass mobilization that accompanied it, especially the political emergence of Chinese labor, made socialism an immediate issue in Chinese politics. In an immediate sense, anarchists were beneficiaries of this turn in Chinese radicalism. Anarchism was the most popular and pervasive of all socialisms in China in 1919, as was evidenced by the rapid proliferation of anarchist societies all over China, and also by the diffusion of anarchist ideas in the thinking even of those who were not anarchists. Over the year following the May Fourth Movement of 1919, anarchist ideas became prevalent in the culture of radicalism, which among youth displayed itself in a flourishing "communal" movement, the so-called New Life Movement (*Xin shenghuo yundong*). In this communal movement, anarchist ideas appeared not so much as components of a formal ideology but as principles of everyday life. The effects on the consciousness of youth, I suggest, were all the more profound, for the new generation of youth assimilated anarchism, not as a set of fleeting ideas, but as part of quotidian culture. Among those engaged in the communal movement were those who within the year would participate in the establishment of the Communist party. The communal movement was to have a long-lasting effect on revolutionary consciousness, transcending questions of anarchist "influence."

Also at this time Chinese intellectuals began to show a genuine interest in Marxism as an ideology of revolution. Comintern initiatives to promote communism in China, starting in 1919, turned radicals to consideration of a political organization to guide the growing mass movement. This development would present the anarchists, with their opposition to politics, with an unprecedented challenge from the left.

To appreciate the significance for anarchists of these new developments, we must remember that there were no committed Marxists or

14. Liu Shixin, "Guanyu wuzhengfu zhuyi huodongde diandi huiyi" (Remembering bits and pieces of anarchist activity), in *WZFZYSX* 2:926–39.

Marxian Communists in China in 1919. A Communist political identity would not assume recognizable form among Chinese radicals until after the establishment of a Communist political organization in late 1920. As of 1919, Chinese radicals, including the later founders of the Communist party (with the sole exception of Chen Duxiu), displayed a diffuse radicalism in which anarchist ideas were most prominent; communism was still understood by most as anarcho-communism. Also, anarchists were still the most readily identifiable group on the social revolutionary Left, which may account for the eagerness of the Comintern to include anarchists in the political organization it sought to establish in China.

According to the anarchist Zheng Peigang, initial Comintern overtures bore fruit in late summer 1919 in the establishment of "socialist alliances" (*shehui zhuyizhe tongmeng*) in major cities.[15] In Beijing, Huang Lingshuang cooperated with his colleagues at Beida (and later leaders of the Communist party), Chen Duxiu and Li Dazhao, to establish the first of these alliances. Radicals in other parts of China followed suit. These alliances were to serve as the basis in 1920 for the Marxist study societies that sprouted in Chinese cities following the arrival in March of the Comintern representative Gregory Voitinsky, which initiated the founding of the Communist party. Anarchists were prominent in these societies; they constituted the majority in the Beijing Society for the Study of Marxist Theory. In Guangzhou, the "Marxist" group initially consisted entirely of anarchists and two Comintern advisers. Anarchists also assumed the responsibility in these groups for the crucial task of editing the labor journals which the groups started.

These societies were to provide the building blocks for the Communist party of China. During the fall of 1920, starting in Shanghai, Marxist study societies began their conversion into Communist cells. Although the Communist party was not founded officially until July 1921, by November 1920 an embryonic party organization had come into existence. The new organization adopted Bolshevik rules for its operation, and a Bolshevik program whose cornerstone was the creation of a "dictatorship of the proletariat." Anarchists, who were opposed both to hierarchical organization and to proletarian dictatorship, abruptly left the organization. At the same time, the organization of the party gave rise to the first polemics between Communists and anarchists, with the basic goal of drawing a clear distinction between the two philosophies of social revolution.

15. Zheng Peigang, "Wuzhengfu zhuyi zai Zhongguode ruogan shishi" (Some facts on anarchism in China), *Guangzhou wenshi ziliao* 1 (April 1962): 191–92.

The organization of the Communist party, with its demand for exclusive loyalty to the party and its ideology, inevitably split the social revolutionary alliance of the previous year. Nevertheless, the split was not final until sometime in the spring of 1922; even then, efforts to overcome differences between Communists and anarchists were not completely abandoned. Anarchists were among those invited to attend the Congress of the Toilers of the East in Moscow in spring 1922, and according to Huang Lingshuang, Chen Duxiu told him in the summer of 1922 that "anarchists and communists are the leaders of reforming society; they can only advance in unity, and should not divide to oppose one another."[16]

His invitation was probably not made out of open-mindedness. Anarchist popularity was still on the rise in 1922 (it would peak in 1922–23), and the first National Labor Congress, recently convened in Guangzhou, had just revealed the extent of anarchist influence in labor organizations in the South. Some among the anarchists continued to hope that Communists could be brought around to the anarchist cause, or at least persuaded to cooperate with anarchists. Anarchists who felt close to the Communist cause refused to abandon hopes of "anarchist-Bolshevik cooperation" (*anbu hezuo* or *anbu xishou*, literally, hand-in-hand), and as late as 1923, in the last installment of his polemics with Chen Duxiu, which had gotten under way in 1920, Ou Shengbai wrote: "Under the evil circumstances of present-day Chinese society, Marxists and Kropotkinists will both do. Let each seek in its own way to overthrow the forces of old society. We can resolve the question of social organization in practise when the time comes."[17]

Anarchists could see the writing on the wall, but they were reluctant to read it. Chinese anarchists were not much different in this regard from anarchists such as Emma Goldman and Alexander Berkman, who continued to hope, against all available evidence (which they witnessed at first hand), that the Bolshevik leadership would come around to the original promise of a popular social revolution once the crisis of the new Soviet state had been averted; anarchists, like other socialists, had invested a great deal in the October Revolution as the beginning of a new age in

16. "Lingshuang zhi mojun han" (A letter from Lingshuang), *Chunlei yuekan* (Spring thunder monthly), 1 (10 October 1923): 105.
17. Ou Shengbai, "Da Chen Duxiu junde yiwen" (Answering Mr. Chen Duxiu's doubts), *Xuehui* (Sea of learning), nos. 104–109 (February 1923). See reprint in WZFZYSX 2:664.

history and were unwilling to abandon hopes in its promise. Indeed, the final repudiation of Bolshevism by Goldman and Berkman had much to do with Chinese anarchists' loss of hope for an alliance with the Communist party in 1922. In the polemics against the Soviet Union and Bolshevism that Chinese anarchists launched after 1922, their writings were to play a crucial part. For their part, the Communists and their Comintern advisers would seem to have dropped their quest for converting anarchists once they had found more powerful allies in the Guomindang. The effort to convert individual anarchists never stopped, but anarchists were only a barely visible Communist concern after the party embarked on establishing a united front with the Guomindang in late 1922.

In early 1922 anarchists once again turned their attention to organizing an independent anarchist movement. With the rise in popularity of anarchism during the May Fourth Movement, anarchist societies had proliferated all across China. While Guangzhou anarchists retained a leading role in the anarchist movement, moreover, anarchists from other parts of China, especially from Hunan and Sichuan, increasingly distinguished themselves as leading voices.

The nationwide diffusion of anarchism even further decentralized the anarchist movement and made it more difficult for the historian to identify a center to Chinese anarchism. It is possible, nevertheless, to point to a number of anarchist societies at this time, if not as leaders, at least as clearinghouses in the propagation of anarchist ideology, and for the part they played in setting the tone for anarchist activity. These societies were distinguished for their longevity (and, therefore, the part they played in sustaining anarchist activity), the originality and intensity of their activities, and the general esteem in which anarchists across the country held the individuals who played leading roles in them.

In spring 1922 "more than fifty" anarchists met in Guangzhou to establish an "Anarchist Federation" (described simply as "AF"). Earlier prominent Guangzhou anarchists had met with Chen Duxiu and other Communist leaders in Guangzhou to discuss the possibility of cooperation; the federation may have been founded in response to the hopelessness of compromise between the two groups. The leadership of the federation included Ou Shengbai, Liang Bingxian, and Huang Lingshuang, the most prominent Guangzhou anarchists. A key role was played in the organization by a certain Russian who had recently appeared in Guangzhou, Dikebuo (Dikebov?), who apparently suggested the founding of a federation. The federation was organized as a secret conspiracy, complete with code names and passwords.[18] The federation did not last very long. The "barbaric" behavior of Dikebuo, who sought to assume dictatorial powers, and the fickleness of other members (by 1923 Ou Shengbai was in Paris and Huang Lingshuang at Clark University in Massachusetts) brought it to a quick end by fall 1922.

Anarchists, however, did not give up. By August 1923 they had established a new federation, based on the Reality Society (*Zhenshe*).[19] Founded by the anarchists Wang Siweng, Li Shaoling, Zheng Zhenheng, and Xie Juexian, Reality Society began publication in October 1923 of a new journal, *Spring Thunder* (*Chunlei*), which with some metamorphoses would serve for two years as an important organ of Chinese anarchism. The new federation had two important sections, general and propaganda. The latter was subdivided into three areas that reflected the concerns of federation work: peasant, worker, and education bureaus.

Closely associated with these activities was another Guangdong anarchist society that had come into existence in 1922, the People's Tocsin Society (*Mingzhong she*), led by Li Shaoling and Li Jianmin. At first a local society, this society had expanded its scope in response to the founding of the first federation in 1922. The journal that the society began to publish in July 1922, *People's Tocsin,* would be the longest-lived (uninterrupted) journal in the history of Chinese anarchism. It was published for five years to the month, mostly in Guangdong until it was moved to Shanghai in the spring of 1927. In later years, Bi Xiushao, Fan Tianjun, and Li Taiyi played important parts in both the society and the journal. The contributors to the journal included the most important of Chinese anarchists in the 1920s: Ou Shengbai, Huang Lingshuang, Liang Bingxian, Li Feigan (Bajin), Qin Baopu, Jing Meijiu, Wei Huilin, and others, whose names appeared frequently in anarchist publications but are not identifiable beyond the pseudonyms they employed (Kuli and Zhiping). Its special issues on Kropotkin in 1923 and Shifu in 1927 were landmark events for anarchists and drew contributions not only from those listed above but from the doyens of anarchism, Li Shizeng and Wu Zhihui. It was not only an important organ for the anarchist criticism of communism, it was also at that time the foremost source for the writings of

18. "Benshe zhi gedi tongzhi han" (A letter from this society to comrades everywhere), *Chunlei yuekan,* 1 (10 October 1923): 92–95, for this account. Also see Zheng Peigang, "Wuzhengfu zhuyi," 202.
19. This could also be translated as Truth Society. I use Reality Society here to distinguish it from the Shishe, which I have translated as Truth Society.

European anarchists such as Proudhon, Bakunin, Kropotkin, Jean Grave, and Varlaam Cherkezov.[20]

When the Anarchist Federation was established in 1922, it sent Huang Lingshuang to Shanghai to bring anarchists there into the federation. The group in Shanghai (which was involved mainly in the teaching of Esperanto) included two Guangzhou anarchists, Zheng Peigang and Liu Wudeng (Shifu's sister and Zheng's lover), as well as Deng Mengxian and a woman anarchist from Hunan, Zhou Dunhu, a labor organizer and associate of Huang Ai and Peng Renquan, who had recently been murdered for their labor activities. In 1923 this group started publishing its own journal, the short-lived *Mutual Aid* (*Huzhu*), edited by Deng Mengxian, as part of federation activity. They also participated in the revival of *Freedom* (*Ziyou*), edited by Jing Meijiu, which had been suspended by the authorities in 1922. Freedom Society would also serve in ensuing years as a source of anarchist literature.[21]

The Anarchist Federation also corresponded with the Paris anarchist journal, *After Work* (*Gongyu*), which between 1922 and 1925 was an important anarchist organ in the polemics against the Communists in France. It was edited at first by Chen Duxiu's sons, who, until their conversion to communism in 1923, led the polemics against their father's party (represented in Paris by *Youth* [*Shaonian*], in which Zhou Enlai defended Bolshevism against the anarchists). After 1923 Li Zhuo and Bi Xiushao played an important part in this journal. In 1925, when Bi returned to China, *After Work* was merged with *Free People* (*Ziyou ren*), edited by Shen Zhongjiu, who, like Bi, was from Zhejiang province.[22] (Bi also became the editor, briefly, of *People's Tocsin* when it was moved to Shanghai.)

Three other societies, which were at best loosely connected with Guangzhou anarchists and the federation, were to play important roles in the anarchist movement, either as disseminators of anarchism or as nodes of anarchist activity. First was the Free People Society founded in Shanghai in 1924, led by the Zhejiang anarchist Shen Zhongjiu and one Chinu (a pseudonym). The importance of this society derived above all from its involvement in the syndicalist movement in Shanghai. Members of the society were active in the syndicates and in labor education. They were

20. "Fangwen Fan Tianjun xianshengde jilu" (Account of a visit with Mr. Fan Tianjun), in *WZFZYSX* 2:1039.

21. Zheng, "Wuzhengfu zhuyi," 202.

22. Bi Xiushao, "Wo xinyang wuxhengfu zhuyide qianqian houhou" (Account of my anarchist beliefs), in *WZFZYSX* 2:1025.

involved in, if they did not initiate, a syndicate periodical, *Labor Ten-daily* (*Laodong xunkan*). Shen worked closely with Hunanese anarchists, who were an important force in the Shanghai Federation of Syndicates (*Shanghai gongtuan lianhe hui*). He was also a teacher at the experimental Lida School, established in Shanghai at this time by the Hunanese anarchist Kuang Husheng. It was possibly out of this association that a plan emerged at this time to establish a Labor University (*Laodong daxue*), which was realized three years later. The Free People Society corresponded with *Spring Thunder* in Guangzhou and would, in 1925, merge with *After Work* (of these activities, more below).[23]

A second important society in Shanghai was the People's Vanguard (*Minfeng*) Society, in which the Sichuan anarchists Lu Jianbo and Mao Yibo played leading roles. The society was established in Nanjing in 1923 and published there a journal of the same name before moving to Shanghai in 1925. Lu had earlier been active in anarchist activities in Sichuan and had some association in Shanghai with his more famous fellow provincial, Bajin, who also had moved to Shanghai in the mid-twenties. Lu was responsible for founding two societies in 1927 that played some part in anarchist activity in Shanghai, the Society for the Study of Syndicalism (*Gongtuan zhuyi yanjiu hui*) and the Federation of Young Chinese Anarcho-communists (*Zhongguo shaonian wuzhengfu gongchan zhuyizhe lianmeng*). He had to leave Shanghai in 1928 to escape persecution by the Guomindang because of his criticism of anarchist-Guomindang cooperation (he was accused by Guomindang-related anarchists of being a "Bolshevized-anarchist"). In the late thirties he was back in Sichuan, publishing another anarchist periodical.[24]

Finally, the most active anarchist society in northern China was the Sea of Learning Society (*Xuehui she*), which published a supplement of the same name to the *National Customs Daily* (*Guofeng ribao*), edited by the Shanxi anarchist Jing Meijiu. One of the elders of Chinese anarchism at the time, Jing had converted to anarchism in Tokyo in the days before the 1911 Revolution. Jing possibly had been influenced by the agrarian anarchism that the Tokyo anarchists had propagated. In addition to

23. "Tongzhi xiaoxi" (News of comrades), *Jingzhe* (Spring festival, literally "the awakening of insects"), 1 (1924). This journal was a continuation of *Chunlei* after the latter was shut down. See also Zheng Peigang, "Wuzhengfu zhuyi," 204–6.

24. Jiang Jun, "Lu Jianbo xiansheng zaoniande wuzhengfu zhuyi xuanchuan huodong jishi" (An account of Mr. Lu Jianbo's anarchist activities in his youth), in *WZFZYSX* 2:1009–22. "Fangwen Fan Tianjun," 1041–43, discusses some activities of this radical group.

disseminating anarchism in the North, members of the Sea of Learning Society were also active in the promotion of anarchism in rural areas.[25]

Further research may reveal that other anarchist societies played equally, possibly more, important roles in the anarchist movement in the 1920s. Anarchists were active everywhere, involved in their own organizations as well as organizations of others, who nevertheless gave the anarchists room in their own publications (such as the supplement to the *Current Affairs Daily* [*Shishi xinbao*] of the antirevolutionary Research Clique, *Light of Learning* [*Xuedeng*], an important forum for anarchist writings on the Soviet Union). Their activities ranged from the distribution of anarchist pamphlets to more sustained ideological activity as well as organizational activities among labor and the agrarian population.[26]

The dispersed nature of these activities makes risky any generalizations about these societies or their relationship to one another. The societies were distinguished by the sustained nature of their activities, which made them somewhat more visible as centers of activity. In spite of their assumption of such appellations as "federation," these societies were largely independent of one another in their activities. What gave them some semblance of unity was the correspondence in which they engaged and the relatively frequent contact between those who played leadership roles within them. In the end, for these societies, as well as for numerous others in both rural and urban China, anarchism became a movement through the motion of individual anarchists, often but not always along the same general direction.

One thing that unified the anarchists in the 1920s was their opposition to Bolshevism. The question of anarchists' relationship to the Guomindang, however, was a divisive issue. The doyens of Chinese anarchism, such as Li Shizeng and Wu Zhihui, had also been members of the Guomindang since its establishment, and with the party "reorganization" of 1924 (whereby Communists were allowed to become members of the Guomindang), they assumed powerful albeit "unofficial" roles in the party. The younger, more radical among anarchist activists were initially opposed to any involvement with the Guomindang. Nevertheless, with the Guomindang suppression of Communists in 1927, the latter suspended their opposition to the Guomindang and followed the lead of Li and Wu to enter

25. Jing Meijiu, "Zuian" (Account of crimes), in *Xinhai geming ziliao leipian* (Materials on the 1911 Revolution), ed. Chinese Academy of Social Sciences (Beijing, 1981), 54–157.

26. These activities may be gleaned from the "News of Comrades" sections published in anarchist journals. For a sampling from *People's Tocsin*, see *Wusi shiqide shetuan* (Societies of the May Fourth period), ed. Zhao Chonghou et al. (Beijing, 1979), 4:275–80.

the party, hoping thereby to recapture mass movements—in particular labor—for anarchism.

The result was a short-lived but significant anarchist alliance with the Guomindang. Most important in the alliance were the Guomindang anarchists and radical activists from Sichuan and Zhejiang who had been active during preceding years in the syndicalist movement in Shanghai. The alliance was not restricted to them, however. In other parts of China, such as Guangzhou, anarchists made an attempt to recapture the labor movement under Guomindang auspices; even the brother of the venerable Shifu, Liu Shixin, was willing to collaborate with the Guomindang in the late twenties.

The institutional centers of anarchist collaboration with the Guomindang were the Labor University (*Laodong daxue*) established in Shanghai in the fall of 1927, and a journal the anarchists published weekly in conjunction with the university, *Geming zhoubao* (Revolution, hereafter, simply *Geming*). Labor University, which was to last for nearly five years, was intended to fulfill the long-standing anarchist dream of creating a new kind of Chinese, "whole persons" equally adept at mental and manual labor, upon whom anarchists continued to rest their hopes for the solution of the most profound cultural and social problems (which they took to be identical) facing China. The immediate purpose was to train a new kind of labor leader in China, who would be able to guide labor movements without subjection to political parties. *Revolution*, which was to be the last important anarchist journal in China, publicized these goals of Labor University.

The collaboration lasted only about a year. By 1928 the Guomindang had completed its task of unifying the country once again and was no longer interested in the continuation of mass movements, in which it perceived a challenge to its new status quo. Mass movements were suspended in the spring of 1928. For the activist anarchists, this was a major blow, and even as they continued to collaborate with the Guomindang, they now turned their criticisms from the Communists to the Guomindang leadership, including their anarchist leaders in the party. In response, the Guomindang curtailed anarchist activity within Labor University and in fall 1929 proscribed *Revolution*.

The proscription effectively brought to an end the anarchist movement in China. Individual anarchists continued to be active in the thirties, but after this proscription it becomes difficult to speak of anarchism in China as a "movement," or even as an effective voice in the Chinese revolution. Anarchism had flourished during the previous two decades under circumstances of political disintegration and mass mobilization. The establishment of a new political order, ironically under a revolutionary party, was to deprive anarchists of space for activity. After 1927 the revolutionary movement in China was to pass into the hands of those who were willing to "make" revolution, if necessary by armed force, which required the kind of organization that anarchists were unwilling to condone and unable to put together. The days of anarchism as a force in the Chinese revolutionary movement were over.

During these years Chinese anarchists viewed themselves as part of a worldwide anarchist movement. The first Chinese anarchists owed their conversion to anarchism to contact with foreign anarchists. Li Shizeng, founder of the World Society in Paris, converted to anarchism as a consequence of his close relationship with the family of the famous French anarchist Élisée Reclus; the Reclus family would in ensuing years retain a close association with the anarchist movement in China. A similar part was played in Tokyo by the Japanese anarchist Kotoku Shusui, who was the keynote speaker at the first meeting of the Society for the Study of Socialism. In the mid-teens, the anarchist Hua Lin even called upon Kropotkin himself in London.[27] The socialist alliances founded in 1919 were products of a conference of "Far Eastern" socialists held in Shanghai, in which the Japanese anarchist Osugi Sakae was a participant (a police report even reported erroneously that Emma Goldman was in Shanghai).[28] Chinese anarchists in the Soviet Union in the early twenties established contact not only with Russian anarchists, but also with foreign anarchists in Russia, such as Emma Goldman and Alexander Berkman; out of these contacts would emerge the lifelong association between Goldman and the anarchist writer Bajin. Osugi Sakae, just before his murder in Japan in 1923, briefly visited China again on his way to an international anarchist conference in Europe.[29] Meanwhile, anarchists in France retained their relationship with leaders of the European anarchist movement, such as Jean Grave; and when Mme Kropotkin met European anarchists in Paris after leaving the Soviet Union in 1923, Chinese anarchists were among them. In the late twenties, as anarchists in Fujian prepared for a rural insurrection, they were joined by anarchists

27. Hua Lin, "Tan annaqi sixiang" (Discussion of my anarchism), in Hua Lin, *Bashan xianhua* (Idle words from Bashan) (Shanghai, 1945), 49.
28. Thomas A. Stanley, *Osugi Sakae: Anarchist in Taisho Japan* (Cambridge: Harvard University Press, 1982), 132–35.
29. Bi Xiushao, "Wo xinyang wuzhengfu zhuyi," 1023.

from Japan and Korea who believed that Fujian could serve as the base for an East Asian anarchist insurrection.[30]

These contacts suggest that the fortunes of anarchism in China were tied in, not only with the particular conditions of Chinese society and politics, but with the fortunes of anarchism as a global movement. Anarchism flourished in China when it was also the foremost ideology of social revolution globally. Anarchists in China drew both their vitality and much of their intellectual inspiration from anarchism as a global movement. Likewise, the decline of anarchism in China in the late twenties corresponded to a worldwide recession of anarchism as Marxism, now in a Leninist guise, once again took over from anarchism as the foremost ideology of social revolution in the aftermath of the October Revolution.

These intimate ties with the fortunes of global anarchism were also reflected in subtle shifts in the anarchist argument for revolution. Throughout, the anarchism of P. Kropotkin, as refracted through the interpretations of Reclus and Grave, was the foremost source for Chinese anarchism. But a Tolstoyan anarchism also found its way into Chinese anarchism through the agency of the Tokyo anarchists. In the 1920s Russian anarchists' writings provided much of the basis for anarchist criticism of Marxism. In the late twenties P-J. Proudhon's ideas briefly acquired prominence in the anarchist collaboration with the Guomindang. In the late thirties, long after the heyday of anarchism, Spanish anarchism provided some inspiration before the Spanish revolution was extinguished by the forces of fascism. Whereas Chinese anarchism was largely derivative of these foreign sources, the ideas that gained currency in China were closely bound up with the particular concerns of the Chinese revolution.

THE ANARCHIST CONTRIBUTION
TO RADICAL IDEOLOGY

During the period 1905–1930 anarchism served as a source of revolutionary ideas that placed anarchists in the forefront of the revolutionary movement or reinforced important elements in revolutionary thinking, which were not necessarily of anarchist origin but in their coincidence with basic anarchist ideas enabled the anarchists to play a central part in "mainstream" radical activity. From 1907 until well into the twenties, of

---

30. "Fangwen Fan Tianjun xiansheng," 1046.

all the competing radical philosophies imported into Chinese thinking, only anarchism was available in any comprehensive coverage and enjoyed widespread distribution among the reading public. Most of the classics of anarchism were already available in Chinese translation by the early 1910s (which could not be said of *any* important Marxist work until 1920), and some made their way beyond radical periodicals to mainstream journals and newspapers. These translations served as the medium through which central concerns of European radical thinking were transmitted to China, including problems of political and economic democracy, economic equality and justice, the relationship of the individual and society, the place of the family in society, the place of women in society, the relationship between education and democracy, science and social thought, and so forth. Anarchists were in the vanguard of the calls for a universal education, for the transformation of the family and the culture that sustained the old family, and for the emancipation of women and the liberation of the individual, which by the mid-1910s were commonplaces of radical thinking in China. They could also claim a few important "firsts" of their own, which prefigured the turn the revolutionary movement would take as it assumed a social character in the 1920s. Anarchists were the founders of the first modern labor unions in China (in 1917). They also spearheaded the transmission of the revolutionary movement to rural areas. They were the first to experiment with new forms of education as well as new forms in the organization of production. Finally, whether with these experiments or with organizational activities in the city or the countryside, they established patterns of activity that would in the long run provide models for other revolutionaries: the creation of an educational and institutional context whereby individuals and social groups (students, women, workers, or peasants) could engage in social activity.

Both anarchist activity and the patterns that it followed were direct offshoots of the anarchist conception of revolution and the philosophical outlook that underlay it. To clear up two basic misconceptions concerning the anarchist outlook: anarchists did not elevate the individual above society—they only repudiated social arrangements that ignored the individual; they did not reject all social institutions—they rejected only those that were coercive. They believed that coercive institutions distorted the essential sociability of human beings, set them against one another in the pursuit of individual or group interests, turned society from a realm of authentically social existence into a realm of conflict between partial interests, which then could be overcome only through the further use of coercion. The goal of revolution was to break into this vicious cycle. The liberation of the individual was intended to free the individual, not from any social restraint, but from this particular social condition, which rendered impossible a truly social existence by alienating both the rights *and* the obligations of individuals to coercive institutions—which converted individuals into individualists and then called upon coercion to contain their activities. The elimination of coercion was, therefore, a precondition for the assumption by individuals of their social birthright as well as of their social obligations; the goal of individual liberation, in other words, was the restoration to the individual of his or her essential sociability. This meant the reorganization of society on the basis of voluntary association. Only free people could establish authentically social institutions; and only those institutions founded on freedom could nurture authentically sociable individuals. The anarchist repudiation of politics, the state, and other institutions of authority was intended to remove the structures that intermediated in the relationships between individuals so as to give free play to the dialectic between the individual and society.

This required a two-pronged revolutionary strategy: a social revolution to remove authoritarian structures, and a cultural revolution to purge individuals of habits of authority and submission which had become second nature in a long history of living under coercion. The two were not separate operations but part of the same revolutionary process; for authoritarian structures could not be abolished so long as habits of authority and submission persisted, and those habits would be perpetuated so long as authoritarian structures lasted.

This insistence on the inseparability of the social and the cultural was the distinguishing feature of the anarchist idea of social revolution. Anarchists could justifiably claim, I think, that they were the first within the revolutionary discourse in China to raise the issue of cultural revolution, with far-reaching implications in the unfolding of that discourse. Those implications are not clear, however, unless we look more closely at the consequences for revolutionary thinking of the relationship they established between the social and the cultural.

The relationship, in the first place, made for an acute consciousness of the relationship between the ends and means of revolution. Since the goal of revolution was not just to substitute new institutions for old, but to change the cultural habits that informed all institutional structures— which ultimately meant changing the language in which people spoke and thought about society—those institutions that perpetuated old habits could not serve as a proper means to achieve revolutionary goals:

revolution could not be achieved through methods that contravened its goals. The question was not simply a moral one (that is, the rejection of immoral means to achieve moral ends), or even a matter of revolutionary authenticity—though both were present in anarchist thinking. More important are its implications for revolution as a process of change. The urge to make revolutionary methods consistent with revolutionary goals brought those goals into the very process of revolution. The anarchist "utopia" was not somewhere out there in the future, it was an informing principle of the revolutionary process—a different way of saying that anarchists utopianized the revolutionary process itself. This is not to suggest that anarchists at all times lived up to their own premises, for they did not. But the utopianization of revolution (a faith in the ability of revolution to create revolutionary institutions in its very processes) was to be a dynamic element of revolution in China.

Second, and even more basic, the relationship anarchists established between the social and the cultural presupposed a perception of the problem of revolution as a discursive problem: meaningful revolution implied the transformation of the social discourses—ways of thinking and talking about society—that constituted society. Anarchists were the first in China to call for a cultural revolution; more important, they conceived culture socially, as quotidian culture that constituted social relations at the level of everyday interactions and was itself reproduced daily.

It is not surprising then that anarchists took education to be the cornerstone of revolution—education not in a formal sense but as a process of transformation of everyday habits. Whether in the educational experiments they initiated, or in labor and peasant organization, the guiding principle of anarchist revolutionary activity was to create spaces wherein people could think differently about society by living differently. The dialectic between the individual and society, the fundamental premise of the anarchist conception of revolution, was articulated at the level of revolutionary practise in two ideas that anarchists introduced into Chinese education, which may also be the most important anarchist contributions to revolutionary discourse. One was the creation of "whole individuals," which concretely meant the combination of labor and learning in the education process. Anarchists perceived in the separation of mental and manual labor not only a cause of the impoverishment of the individual but the fundamental basis of social inequality as well; overcoming the distinction was, therefore, the key to the creation of a different way of life—and a different way of thinking about society. The second idea was the creation of social spaces in which this basic division of labor could be overcome, and the individual in voluntary participation in the group could realize his or her social potential. Anarchists were the first advocates in China of communal organization that would abolish the division between city and country, industry and agriculture, manual and mental labor. The abolition of the distinction between manual and mental labor at the level of the individual had its counterpart at the social level in the organization of student communes, village associations, and labor syndicates; change at the one level was the condition of change at the other.

These are ideas that are familiar to students of China as key elements in Mao's Marxism that became particularly prominent during the period of the Cultural Revolution.[31] In pointing to their anarchist origin, I do not suggest that Mao or anyone else who upholds these ideas is, therefore, an anarchist, or that anarchism has an exclusive claim upon them. Similar ideas are to be found in the works of Marx, and it is arguable that Marxism (at least the Marxism of Marx) is quite cognizant of their basic premise: that social revolution ultimately entails a transformation of consciousness because the structures that give form to society are reproduced at the level of everyday social interactions—and even within language, which Marx referred to on one occasion as "practical consciousness."[32]

While it is important to recognize the overlap between anarchism and Marxism where these ideas are concerned, it is also necessary to distinguish them on both historical and theoretical grounds. Historically, it was through the agency of anarchism that these ideas entered the revolutionary discourse in China, and, at least initially, they were identified with anarchism. When a Marxian communism entered the revolutionary movement, it established its identity by repudiating these ideas for being irrelevant to immediate problems of revolution. Furthermore, during the ideological struggles that accompanied the political conflicts of the twenties, these same ideas provided intellectual ammunition for the opponents of Marxism. That these ideas should survive the anarchist movement to be lodged in locations as diverse in revolutionary consciousness as Mao's Marxism and the Guomindang shows that they had become significant components of a revolutionary discourse that cut across party or ideological boundaries; but their origin historically is traceable to the anarchists.

More important, that the same ideas are to be found in both anar-

31. The editor of a reissue of P. Kropotkin's *Fields, Factories and Workshops of Tomorrow* (New York: Harper Torchbooks, 1974), Colin Ward, found in the Chinese communes established after 1958 (abolished in 1983) "the nearest thing to Kropotkin's industrial villages" (188).

32. Karl Marx, *The German Ideology*, ed. R. Pascal (New York: International Publishers, 1947), 19.

chism and Marxism does not imply that they carried the same meaning within the two ideological contexts; it only points to the area of Marxism that overlapped with anarchism, with disruptive consequences for its theoretical structure. Whatever the resemblance between anarchist and Marxist ideas of social revolution, the two ideas arranged the priorities of revolutionary practise differently. While education and cultural transformation held a place of primary significance in the anarchist conception of social revolution, Marxists gave priority to the transformation of structural relations in society. The difference may be illustrated by reference to another concept that was central to both ideas of social revolution: the concept of class. While Marxists perceived the nurturing of class consciousness as the key to revolution, anarchists believed that only the abolition of consciousness of class could yield to genuinely revolutionary change in society. Whether the Marxist idea of ideology may be reduced to an endowment of class will be discussed later; I suggest here that while Marxism, too, recognizes culture and consciousness as a problem of quotidian life, this recognition is shaped by another conception of culture as a function of social structure to which class is central—which possibly accounts for the theoretical richness of Marxism against the "theoretical primitivism" (in Hobsbawm's words) of anarchism. I suggest, nevertheless, that the theoretical complexity of Marxism (often to the point of forgetting the revolutionary goals of theoretical activity) has also blinded Marxists to the rich insights contained in the seemingly simple anarchist premise that revolution must take as its ultimate goal the transformation of social discourses—of the very language of thinking about society. If anarchism has not paid sufficient attention to structural transformation, the Marxist preoccupation with structural transformation has diverted Marxism from the equally crucial task of transforming social discourses—indeed has obstructed the latter by erecting further structures inimical to this goal. Hobsbawm, for instance, misses the point about this problem when he states that Marxists may have something to learn from anarchist "spontaneity": "The very organizational feebleness of anarchist and anarchizing movements has forced them to explore the means of discovering or securing that spontaneous consensus among militants and masses which produces action."[33] This is to miss what the anarchists clearly recognized: that there is nothing "spontaneous" about the masses. There is, rather, a different discourse about society, which radicals must assimilate in their very efforts to transform the masses. It is not accidental

33. Hobsbawm, *Revolutionaries*, 90.

that anarchists were the first to compile a dictionary of popular language, which they believed might enable them to communicate with the masses more effectively. And anarchists did not turn to this endeavor because their activities were organizationally "feeble"; on the contrary, they believed that organization was undesirable to the extent that it created an obstacle to such communication (or, more precisely, because it turned communication, which must be two-way if it is to be genuinely revolutionary, into the imposition of the will of the revolutionaries upon the masses, which from the beginning doomed revolution to a betrayal of its own premises).

Before Chinese revolutionaries. faced this problem of two-way communication as a practical task, which they would in the 1930s when the revolution was forced to move to the countryside, anarchists had introduced it into the revolutionary discourse as a central problem of revolution. This awareness brought anarchists considerable success in revolutionary activity—but only at the local level. It was at the level of more comprehensive political organization that anarchists failed as revolutionaries. On the other hand, the success of other revolutionaries at this other level would in its consequences bear out anarchist fears of the fate of revolution that subjected the crucial task of discursive transformation to goals formulated at the level of politics.

ANARCHISM AND REVOLUTIONARY DISCOURSE

Whether we recognize in anarchism a lasting significance in the Chinese revolution depends largely upon whether we recognize the importance of the idea of the social in revolutionary discourse. The significance of anarchism rests ultimately upon its insistence on the priority of the social in the revolutionary discourse that took shape during the years when anarchism enjoyed its greatest popularity in Chinese thinking on revolution. Anarchists were not the first in China to raise the question of the social, nor were they the only ones in ensuing years to insist on the essentialness of a social component to revolution. The question was a product of an emerging nationalist consciousness, which at the turn of the century first raised the question of the relationship between state and society, pointing to social transformation as the essential moment of building a nation-state that, unlike the monarchy it was to replace, could claim no transcendental or transhistorical moral sanction but depended for its legitimacy on its ties to the society it claimed to represent. Calling society into the service of the state as its legitimating principle revealed not only a new problematic of politics, but problematized the notion of society as well. While this was to become, and has remained, the essential question of Chinese politics, it was through socialism—which over the years was identified with social revolution—that the problem was articulated with the greatest explicitness and consistency. The insistence on a "social revolution" was a common feature of all socialist discourse and spilled over to nonsocialist advocacies of change as well. Different groups meant different things by "social revolution," depending on the sources for the idea but more importantly on their conception of the social. By the early twenties most prominent in addition to anarchist ideas of the social were Communist and Guomindang ideas of social revolution.

It is precisely this pervasiveness of the idea of the social that endows with historical significance the anarchist advocacy of social revolution, which otherwise would have been condemned to a quaint marginality. I mean this in two senses. First, the discourse on the social in its unfolding nourished off a number of competing (and conflicting) ideologies of social revolution, which, nevertheless, intersected on the terrain of the discourse, with considerable interchange among them. Hence we find that in spite of significant differences in the "social revolution" they advocated, there was also significant overlap among anarchist, Communist, and Guomindang notions of the social. That the discourse drew on European socialism in its language guaranteed such overlap because, in spite of its disintegration into numerous factions by the turn of the century, socialism in Europe retained the common language of its origins and was even blurred at its edges into liberal or bourgeois ideas of social change.[34] Within the Chinese context, moreover, discursive conflicts were contained within a national revolutionary movement which, especially in the first three decades of the century, rendered heterogeneous ideas of the social into different aspects of a common revolutionary project; hence discursive overlap expressed a revolutionary situation in which different revolutionary groups were participants in the same revolutionary movement: not only ideas were interchangeable—so was actual membership in different revolutionary groups. As a constituent of this discourse, anarchist ideas acquired a wide currency beyond the

34. Indeed, China's first socialists (Sun Yat-sen and his followers) derived their socialism from Euro-American social reformers who sought to incorporate socialist programs into a liberal political agenda to prevent the social revolution that socialists espoused. See Dirlik, "Socialism and Capitalism in Chinese Thought."

relatively small number of radicals committed to anarchism as an integral ideology.

Second, given the pervasiveness of the concern with the social within the revolutionary discourse, the particular anarchist conception of the social that unequivocally asserted the claims of society against the state (and politics in general) drew its significance from its implications for the revolutionary discourse as a whole. Among all the advocates of social revolution, anarchists were distinguished by their uncompromising (and exclusive) insistence on the social: a "true" revolution could be nothing but social; a revolution that was not social could not qualify as a revolution; and a revolution that compromised the social by subjecting it to political considerations compromised itself as a revolution. In an immediate sense, within the historical context in which the revolutionary discourse took shape, this uncompromising insistence on the social disrupted the boundaries of political debate by underlining the limitations—indeed, the ideological oppressiveness—of politics against the horizon of the social; against the prospect of total social transformation politics, any politics, appeared as so much ideological closure to contain the social. The result was to force the discourse on revolution out of its political boundaries onto the uncertain terrain of the social. Whether they subscribed to anarchist ideas, or even found anything of worth in the anarchist idea of social revolution, all advocates of social revolution in China had to come to terms with this idea of the social. That many also internalized anarchist ideas of the social or social revolution in the process may not be as important as their implicit or explicit admission that these ideas pointed to an irreducible horizon of revolutionary discourse, which could be denied only by resorting to an argument based on necessity: that revolution could succeed historically only by suppressing its historical origins, by containing within politically acceptable limits the vision that was its motivating intention in the first place. The Communists admitted to this restriction of vision when they argued against the anarchists that before the social revolutionary ideal could be realized, which was the common goal of both anarchism and Marxism, a political dictatorship of the proletariat must be interposed in the history of revolution, even if it meant a temporary suspension or even betrayal of revolutionary aspirations. So did Sun Yat-sen, who was no anarchist, when he declaimed in 1924 that the ultimate goal of his Principle of People's Livelihood was "communism, and anarchism," although he insisted that people's livelihood must serve as the means to fulfill the goals of revolution. The relegation of anarchism to a distant future rationalized the reassertion of the primacy of politics in the immediate historical context, but not without an acknowledgment that the revolution thus achieved would be an incomplete revolution so long as it did not keep its sight fixed on that future. In a crucial sense, then, anarchism extended the frontiers of revolutionary discourse by pointing to a social project that negated the boundaries established by a political conception of society; and its very presence in the revolutionary discourse rendered problematic any effort toward an ideological closure of the social by the political. Similarly, in historical perspective, recognition of the anarchist presence in revolutionary discourse is a reminder of the ideological appropriation of the discourse on the social as social revolution was harnessed in the service of political goals. This perspective calls into question the claims on history of successful revolutionaries—whose success, therefore, may not be viewed simply as a fulfillment of the social aspirations of the revolution but must be understood simultaneously as the suppression (if not the total elimination) of the social imagination that motivated its history.

This evaluation of anarchism's significance presupposes a certain conception of the problem of ideology—in this case a specifically socialist ideology—that needs to be spelled out briefly before we discuss the concrete contributions of anarchism to revolutionary discourse in China. Of special importance is a distinction I should like to draw between ideology and discourse, "a certain way of talking about a specific set of objects."[35]

The central problem concerns the relationship of ideology to its broader social and intellectual context. The distinction between ideology and discourse is intended to overcome the dilemma presented by a reductionist conception of ideology, which reduces ideas to expressions of class or other group interests and is the point of departure for most post-Marxist discussion of ideology. If ideas or sentiments are expressions of class or other interests, how do we account for the fact that they are shared widely by those outside of the class or group whose interests they are purported to express? While the debate touched off by this question is too complex for summary here, I think that the answers have unfolded in two broad directions. First is the substitution of a totalistic for a reductionist conception of

35. I owe this cogent phrasing of the sometimes turgid idea of discourse to Harry Harootunian, *Things Seen and Unseen: Discourse and Ideology in Tokugawa Nativism* (Chicago: University of Chicago Press, 1988), 25. Harootunian's formulation of the problem of discourse and ideology (not to mention our chats by Lake Michigan) played an important part in stimulating the reasoning I offer below, though I absolve him of all responsibility for the specific issues I raise. What I say of anarchism in its relationship to a revolutionary discourse became most evident in Chinese anarchism in the 1920s, especially in anarchist polemics against the Marxist Communists.

ideology; the seminal example is to be found in the work of Clifford
Geertz, who stresses the "integrative" function of ideology as a set of
"symbolic formulations" that are shared commonly in a "cultural system"
across class and other partial interests.[36] Second are those attempts to
reintroduce into this integrative conception of ideology a critical Marxist
perspective by uncovering within the "symbolic forms" of "ideology as a
cultural system" the patterns of authority and domination that characterize most known social systems, which constitute the ideology. As Paul
Ricoeur puts it in a recent work, "While ideology serves . . . as the code of
interpretation that secures integration, it does so by justifying the present
system of authority."[37] This post-Marxist debate has also brought ideology much closer to problems of everyday life and culture by repudiating
the "reflective" notion of ideology implicit in the reductionist base-
structure model of ideology that renders ideology epiphenomenal to material existence. Ideology is to be sought not in abstract, formally articulated
ideas, but in everyday speech and activity. While the debate has repudiated
a reductionist Marxist notion of ideology, in other words, it also represents
a return to an alternative conception of ideology in the work of Marx
implicit in Marx's description of language as "practical consciousness."

The problem, then, is twofold: (1) how to reconcile the two notions of
ideology—the integrative notion that renders ideology as a commonly
shared set of symbols and ideas, and the dissimulative notion in which
these commonly shared symbols and ideas conceal relationships of power
and domination—both of which have compelling plausibility; and, (2)
where to look for ideology. An additional problem is that of class (or
other social interests). John Thompson has argued that to achieve a genuinely critical conception of ideology, it is necessary to reintroduce class
into the discussion.[38] It is fair to say, I think, that Ricoeur, for example,
while he restores the relationship between ideology and power in pointing out that "ideology as a cultural system" also justifies the "present
system of authority," does not make the issue of class or social interest a
central concern of his analysis. This not only ignores how the structure of
social interests in different contexts impinges upon the particular forms
assumed by the structure of authority and, therefore, of ideology, but,

36. The most explicit statement is to be found in his "Ideology as a Cultural System."
See Clifford Geertz, *The Interpretation of Cultures* (New York: Harper Torchbooks, 1973),
chap. 8.
37. Paul Ricoeur, *Lectures on Ideology and Utopia,* ed. George H. Taylor (New York:
Columbia University Press, 1986), 13.
38. John B. Thompson, *Studies in the Theory of Ideology* (Berkeley and Los Angeles:
University of California Press, 1984), 34.

even more serious, renders ideology into a seamless entity against a conception of it as an arena of conflict between social interests who share in the ideology and also seek to interpret (or appropriate) it in accordance with their own interests. It is curious that Ricoeur's discussion of ideology, while comprehensive, ignores the work of the one Marxist thinker whose work not only foreshadowed many of these problems but also has had enormous influence in shaping recent conceptualizations of ideology, Antonio Gramsci, whose concept of "hegemony" sought to account for ideology not only in its double sense of integration and dissimulation, but also as conflict between different social interests, whereby these interests (primarily classes in his presentation) sought to appropriate a common ideology. The Gramscian notion of hegemony, while it points to conflict as a permanent condition of all class society, is particularly important for dealing with revolutionary situations when conflict (including the conflict over language) assumes an acute form, when the challenge to the existing system of authority presupposes for its success the appropriation of "hegemony" by revolutionaries, whereby they assimilate to their own ideology the interests of classes and groups outside of their own class.[39]

From this brief discussion we may infer that in confronting the problem of ideology, we need to account for two questions: (1) ideology as the articulation of class or other social interests; (2) ideology as the articulation of a broader system of authority structured by the interaction of these more narrow interests from which ideology as an "integrative cultural system" derives its form.

Because of the confusion created by the application of the term "ideology" to both these articulations, which are related and yet distinct, I would describe the latter as "discourse" and reserve "ideology" for the former. Discourse, a way of thinking and talking about things, common to society as a whole and evident at the most basic level in everyday speech and culture, is integrative because of a common language and also dissimulative because embedded in the common language are relationships of power and domination, as Michel Foucault and Raymond

39. For a comprehensive discussion of Gramsci's ideas in this regard, see *Gramsci and Marxist Theory*, ed. Chantal Mouffe (London: Routledge & Kegan Paul, 1979), esp. Mouffe's own essay, "Hegemony and Ideology in Gramsci." Although Gramsci's notion of hegemony yields a complex appreciation of the problem of ideology, Gramsci's own goals were rather limited and prevented him from pursuing the logic of the problem to its end (as it has his followers, who often present him, wrongly in my opinion, as the key to a democratic socialism). Gramsci was, after all, a Leninist, and while his concept of hegemony pointed the way to exposing the problem of social discourses as distinct from ideology, his goal was to substitute the hegemony of revolutionaries for the hegemony of the bourgeoisie, rather than to recognize social discourses as a problem for ideology.

Williams have reminded us; it is also, therefore, the arena for ideological conflict whereby different social groups seek to assimilate the discourse to their own way of life and interests.[40] This appropriation of discourse is where ideology becomes manifest as a social and historical phenomenon. As Harry Harootunian has put it, in reference to the unfolding of nativism in Japan, "when the interaction of knowledge and interest . . . displaced base/superstructure, form and content, knowledge, or discourse—a certain way of talking about a specific set of objects— became ideological."[41] The procedure is one that Fredric Jameson has described as a "strategy of containment," which he perceives as the goal of ideological activity.[42] In other words, the ideological appropriation of discourse appears as a "containment" of the discourse in accordance with specific social interests or outlooks. Containment is also primarily a procedure of exclusion, a silencing of those elements of the discourse that are inimical to the interests of the group. But it may also mean, I suggest, a rearrangement of the terms of the discourse so as to define its priorities in keeping with such interests.

The critical conception of ideology, which has evolved out of analysis of the use of ideology within the context of established systems (capitalism in particular) to perpetuate the system, is equally applicable, I think, to the problem of ideology in socialism as a radical movement, as intimated in the distinction I have drawn with reference to the socialist movement in China between "revolutionary discourse" and ideology. The discourse is what socialist revolutionaries (and not *just* socialist revolutionaries) shared in common. The discourse on the social, as I have already observed, drew on disparate ideological sources in European socialism (even on liberal ideologies that sought to come to terms with the socialist challenge, from which China's first socialists drew their inspiration). Nevertheless, within the revolutionary movement in China, these ideological sources were integrated, however uneasily, into the language of a common discourse on revolution, and this explains the overlap between otherwise conflicting notions of the social. For the same reason, we may also view the efforts of different groups of revolutionaries— anarchists, Bolsheviks, Guomindang socialists, among others—to appropriate the discourse, a way of talking about social revolution, as alterna-

40. Raymond Williams, *Marxism and Literature* (London: Oxford University Press, 1977); Michel Foucault, *Power/Knowledge: Selected Interviews and Other Writings, 1972–1977*, ed. Colin Gordon (New York: Pantheon, 1977).
41. Harootunian, *Things Seen and Unseen*, 25.
42. Fredric Jameson, *The Political Unconscious: Narrative as a Socially Symbolic Act* (Ithaca: Cornell University Press, 1981), 52–53.

tive "strategies of containment," as different ways of interpreting the discourse by rearranging its terms, through which they sought to constitute the problem of social revolution in accordance with their political and organizational interests, which in turn were conceived in relationship to broader national and social interests. The process of ideological appropriation ultimately involved the question of hegemony over the revolutionary movement.

While the importance of revolutionary hegemony for revolutionary success is self-evident, the critical question for the future of revolution is whether hegemony is more desirable because it is revolutionary—especially since revolution, if successful, establishes itself as a new order. Is it not likely that a revolution that takes as its premise the hegemony of revolutionaries will result in a new structure of authority, reproducing in its very hegemony that hidden relationship between ideology and power to overthrow which was the goal of revolution in the first place, against which the only guarantee is the good will of the revolutionaries or their claim to a scientific discovery of the path to liberation? Is this not the point in revolutionary discourse at which revolution, which seeks to dispose of ideology, itself becomes ideological because it dissimulates in its discourse its relationship to power?

At its most basic, anarchism in China derived its significance from the fact that anarchists were the only ones among social revolutionaries to raise these questions consistently. Their insistence that revolution could not achieve its goals through methods contrary to its aspirations was a constant reminder of this basic problem of revolutionary discourse. The questions offer a critical perspective on the course the revolutionary movement would eventually take in China. They also remind us of the links between the Chinese revolutionary movement and the most fundamental problems of revolutionary discourse in general.

In one sense, anarchists were as ideological as any of their social revolutionary competitors. They not only sought to adjust their conception of social revolution to the exigencies of power in China, with a consequent suspension of their own revolutionary premises, but in some cases displayed considerable ideological opportunism in doing so. Some of the major figures in Chinese anarchism were also members of political parties, in particular the Guomindang, betraying in practise their formal repudiation of politics; worse, they were willing to instrumentalize anarchism in the service of political power. More fundamentally, in claiming for anarchism the status of scientific truth (following Kropotkin), anarchists, like their counterparts in the social revolutionary movement, sought to appro-

priate the discourse on the social for anarchism, thereby excluding from
consideration crucial issues of social revolution. If they were not successful
in doing so, it was because their organizational diffuseness undercut their
efforts to formulate a coherent "strategy of containment," which ideological appropriation of the discourse presupposed.

And yet this inability to appropriate the discourse by "containing" it
was not accidental, or the product of intellectual failure, but the result of
a conscious refusal to do so, which was bound up with the most fundamental premises of anarchism, which were deconstructive rather than
reconstructive. It is this other, deconstructive, aspect of anarchism, which
has been suppressed in historical memory, that points to its significance
in the discourse on revolution. My concern here is not to chronicle what
the anarchists achieved or did not achieve, or to evaluate their sincerity in
upholding the ideas they professed, but to recall from the history of
anarchism the anarchist critique of ideology and its implications for revolutionary discourse. Although of considerable significance both in its
immediate context and in the themes it contributed to the Chinese revolution, anarchism from a political perspective was in the long run irrelevant, and it can be dismissed as a transient intellectual fad that owed its
passing popularity to a naive utopianism that prevailed for a brief revolutionary period. It is precisely this issue of the sufficiency of a political
perspective on revolution that anarchism raised, however, by uncompromisingly repudiating politics and pointing to the realm of the social as the
only proper object of revolutionary discourse. In doing so, anarchists
opened up a perspective on revolution that was foreclosed by the political
and suppressed even in the thinking of revolutionaries, who insisted on a
social revolution but could not conceive of the social apart from the
political tasks of revolution. To affirm the fundamental significance of
anarchism in revolutionary discourse is not to privilege anarchism per se,
but to reaffirm the indispensability of an antipolitical conception of society in raising fundamental questions about the nature of domination and
oppression, which are otherwise excluded from both the analysis of ideology and historical analysis in general. In declaring politics—all politics,
including *revolutionary* politics—to be inimical to the cause of an authentic social revolution, anarchists pointed to the politicization of the social
as an ideological closure that not only disguised the fact that revolutionary hegemony itself presupposed a structure of authority that contradicted its own goals, but also covered up areas of social oppression that
were not immediately visible in the realm of politics (the family and
gender oppression were their primary concerns). More fundamental, anar-

chists explained that the revolutionary urge to restore political order was a consequence of the "naturalization" of politics—the inability, therefore, to imagine society without politics—as one of the most deeply ingrained ideological habits that perpetuated relations of domination in society. The explanation moved them past the realm of ideology to the realm of social discourses as the location for habits of authority and submission that sustained both political and social oppression. Hence in the anarchist argument the project of social revolution was inextricably bound up with cultural revolution (rather than a political revolution, as with their competitors): the goal of revolution was, at its most fundamental, to transform the social discourses that constituted society on a daily basis.[43] The eradication of habits of authority and submission from social discourses was the key to achieving the liberating promise of the revolutionary project. The way anarchists conceived it, the goal of revolution was not to create a new hegemony, which implied the continuation of social division and conflict, but to abolish altogether the notion of hegemony. They saw social division as the consequence of structures of authority that distorted the "natural" propensity of human beings to cooperation and sociability; the elimination of authority would, therefore, eradicate social division as well. Revolution was not just a liberating project; in eliminating ideology from social discourse, it would also create the conditions for human integration on a new basis of equality.

The affinity of the anarchist perspective on the social with that underlying post-Marxist criticism of ideology implies only equivalence, not sameness; to suggest otherwise would be not only reductionist but also circular. Each nevertheless has something to tell us about the other. So long as Marxism is bound to premises of economic determination or to a political project that makes class the central datum of history, it views anarchism as a vacuous utopianism that has little to say about the processes of revolution. Utopianism is not to be dismissed so cavalierly, for it may have something essential to say about revolution. Reflecting on the meaning of the term "nowhere," Ricoeur has observed recently that "perhaps a fundamental structure of the reflexivity we may apply to our social

43. This is where the problem of ideology appears as the problem of social discourses, "the practical consciousness" that is unconscious of itself as ideology because it is embedded in the language of everyday life. For a discussion of the problem of ideology as a problem of language, see John Thompson, *Studies in the Theory of Ideology*. The anarchist appreciation of the problem of social revolution as a problem of cultural revolution sounds very contemporary because of a contemporary tendency, in reaction to the seeming futility of politics (socialist or otherwise), to focus on the realm of culture as the site where solutions to contemporary problems of domination are to be found.

roles is the ability to conceive of an empty place from which to look at ourselves."[44] To conceive the possibility of a "nowhere" implies an ability to free social imagination; and does not revolution negate its own undertaking when it denies this freedom?

But anarchism was not merely utopian and appears so only because it is weakly theorized. Anarchists rested their case on the assumption of the "natural" sociability of human beings; therefore, they took social division and conflict to be a consequence of the distortion of humanity by structures of authority. The task of social (and therefore cultural) revolution was to peel off layers of accumulated oppression to reveal the human core within, and to create the social conditions that would enable humanity to realize its "natural" propensity to cooperation. Cultural revolution was the key to restoring to humanity consciousness of its essential nature. The anarchist argument proceeded less by social analysis than by analogy between nature and society, which obviated the need for extensive theorization. Nevertheless, *because* anarchists took nature rather than society as the point of departure for their criticism of power and authority, they had a more comprehensive grasp than their Marxist competitors of the problem of oppression; for rather than seek out key social relationships or institutions as explanations for power, they focused on the social totality as the realm of oppression: all social relationships were artifices of power and, therefore, equally complicit in oppression, even though the state as the embodiment of the social totality had a particularly important role to play in perpetuating the structure(s) of authority. Hence their appreciation of social discourses as the ultimate realm of authority because the social totality drew its plausibility from the reproduction of structures of authority and submission in quotidian encounters. The apparently metaphysical juxtaposition of nature and society became in the process the source of a comprehensive social criticism, including the criticism of society for its antagonism to its natural roots.

It is also true, however, that this criticism was buried within moralistic protests against society for its deviation from nature, and in the absence of a rigorous theoretical elaboration of their insights, anarchists suffered from a social ambiguity that in practise frustrated their efforts to agree

44. Ricoeur, *Ideology and Utopia*, 15. If ideology in our day has become "invisible," in Lefort's words, because of a dissolving of the distinction between the real and its representation, utopia (an "empty place," but primarily a place outside of society) may be more important than ever in cultivating a consciousness of ideology. For "invisible ideology," see Claude Lefort, *The Political Forms of Modern Society,* ed. John B. Thompson (Cambridge: MIT Press, 1986), 224–36. Lefort in describing anarchism as a version of bourgeois ideology, overlooks the possibilities it offers in this regard (205).

upon procedures of revolutionary activity and made anarchism a gathering place for the socially disaffected, ranging from the most serious advocates of radical change to atavistic nihilists in personal rebellion against society.

Ironically, it is the highly rigorous and complex theoretical procedures of post-Marxist criticism of ideology, much of which draws upon Marxism, that enables us to grasp the theoretical import of the anarchist argument. Anarchism in turn may help us grasp the social and political conditions that have made this criticism possible. From an anarchist perspective, Marxism in its political guises appears as another form of ideological closure on the social, not only incapable of grasping the anarchist argument but inimical to it. The very affinity of post-Marxist criticism of ideology with the anarchist perspective (which enables it to grasp the significance of the latter) may suggest that it has brought Marxism closer to anarchism, not in a formal sense—for it draws on diverse intellectual sources and is informed by the history of Marxism since Marx—but in prying open this ideological closure that long has cut off the Marxist idea of the social from that of anarchism. Two developments in particular have been of the utmost importance. First is the reopening of the question of the relationship between politics and society in response to the political experiences of Marxist-led revolutions, which have not fulfilled their liberating promise. The second is the intrusion upon the consciousness of oppression of a whole set of problems that are not readily reducible to class oppression; the increasing importance, in other words, of forms of oppression that have come to overshadow class oppression. That these developments have revived interest in anarchism is not to be disputed, as the following statement by a contemporary ecofeminist illustrates: "Many of us who began the ecofeminist movement were strongly influenced by anarchism, and accepted the anarchist critique of Marxism, for its economism, opportunism, anti-ecological viewpoints, and a radical separation of means and ends."[45] The question is whether the reintroduction of anarchism offers anything in the way of a better grasp of the post-Marxist criticism of ideology and power.

This question may be answered in the negative; for it is possible to argue that the Marxist tradition contains within it all that is necessary for a critique of the historical unfolding of Marxism, to pry open the ideological closure that historical Marxism has imposed upon the discourse in Marx's texts. It is arguable that Marx himself did not hold a reductionist

45. Ynestra King, "Ecological Feminism," *Zeta Magazine* (July/August 1988), 125.

concept of ideology that reduced ideology to class interest, but rather perceived it in its discursive guise (for example, language as "practical consciousness") in everyday relations of domination that took a different form within the context of different social relationships. It is also arguable that Marxism itself is a discourse on the social, which not only gave priority to the social over the political but also shared with anarchism the common goal of abolishing politics. Certainly in the revolutionary discourse in China there were broad areas of overlap between anarchist and Marxist conceptions of the social and social revolution that make it difficult to identify some ideas as Marxist or anarchist.

This strategy of privileging text over history, and certain parts of the text over others, however, disguises in its references to the text its own interpretive undertaking, which is informed by its own historical situation. While it is indeed necessary to separate Marx from subsequent Marxist traditions (which is but a recognition of *their* historical situations), to portray the latter as denials of Marx or deviations from an authentic Marxism is to deny the multiplicity of interpretations that Marx's texts offer. Leninism may not be a necessary product of Marxism, but as Lenin himself understood, it is one possible product. Likewise, to suggest that Marx had anticipated in his texts the discursive assumptions of post-Marxist criticism of ideology is to draw attention to those aspects of his texts against others that yield different conclusions.

If we examine the relationship between anarchism and Marxism from this perspective, it is possible to argue that while Marxism and anarchism may coincide on certain basic issues, Marxism calls for a different arrangement of the elements of the discourse on social revolution than does anarchism, that even as Marx recognized the multifaceted character of domination he assigned the strategic priorities of revolution differently (with a primary emphasis on class) and assigned to politics a central part in revolution, which together endow Marxism with an ideological visage different from anarchism. The same Marx who recognized language as "practical consciousness," who found in the Paris Commune a paradigm of democratic revolution (as did the anarchists), and who looked to the abolition of the state as the ultimate goal of revolution could say of Bakunin that "this ass cannot even understand that any class movement, as such, is necessarily . . . a political movement."[46] Even more fundamental, it is necessary to remember that whereas Kropotkin—the major

46. Paul Thomas, *Karl Marx and the Anarchists* (London: Routledge & Kegan Paul, 1985), 347.

source of anarchist theoretical discourse—composed his *Mutual Aid* to disprove Darwinian notions about nature and society, Marx found in Darwin a confirmation of the "scientificity" of his social theory. Unlike the anarchist repudiation of social division and conflict, the point of departure for Marxism is the social system as a realm of conflict, which is to be comprehended not in contrasts with nature but by reference to its own history. Power, instead of being an "unnatural" intrusion upon society of something that is extrinsic to it, is an instrument of social conflict that may be understood only historically, in the different forms it assumes in different historical contexts. To moralize against it, or even to speak of it, is meaningless, therefore, except in relation to its social context. Until conflict has been eliminated from the social system (which requires abolition of social interests embedded in economic organization, whose agent is to be the proletariat), power may have an integrative role to play in society, which may otherwise break apart under the pressure of conflicting social interests. Unlike the anarchist argument where liberation (the abolition of power) and integration appear as parts of the same process, Marxist revolutionary strategy sets them apart in the immediate future of revolution in antagonism to one another: power is necessary to secure the integration that liberation threatens. The immediate problem, therefore, is not to abolish power but to reorganize it in order to achieve its ultimate abolition.

Hence, whereas the anarchist problematic of social revolution was shaped by the problem of cultural revolution—the transformation of social discourses—Marxism has placed the primary emphasis on the restructuring of power, to which the transformation of class relationships is essential. The need to restructure power, as the point of departure for theoretical activity, accounts for the complexity of Marxist and post-Marxist criticism of ideology, which has a much more sophisticated appreciation of the relationship between power and ideology than the anarchists had, with their propensity to dismiss the problems it presents because they were interested mainly in abolishing power, not restructuring it, which they thought could be achieved through cultural revolution. Ironically, as Marxism has gained in complexity with the problematization of politics and a consequent recognition of power as a problem not merely of politics or class but rather of culture (in the sense of culture as social discourse), it has moved once again closer to the anarchist criticism of power as an endowment of the structure of authority of the social totality. Anarchism helps us understand why. The ideological closure implicit in a political or class-based notion of social revolution also implied, as anarchists insisted, a reproduction in different guise of the structures of authority that the revolution sought to abolish. The decentering of these conceptions in post-Marxist criticism of ideology has opened up this closure and turned attention to the social totality as the realm of authority. The deconstructive consequences of this decentering recalls the deconstructive implications of the anarchist insistence on the social against the political. This does not mean that anarchism and Marxism have become one; but it is not incidental that the deconstruction has returned Marxism to those texts of Marx that have the most in common with anarchism.

My reading of Chinese anarchism in the following pages then is guided by two considerations beyond the historical. Within the specifically Chinese context, anarchists demand our attention, not for who they were or what they accomplished, but because against revolutionary strategies that presupposed a necessary compromise of revolutionary goals in order to confront the exigencies of immediate necessity they reaffirmed a revolutionary consciousness (or should we say, conscience) that provides an indispensable critical perspective from the Left on the unfolding of the Chinese revolution. Second, though the Chinese anarchists are remote in time or space (although not so remote as they once seemed), what they had to say about revolution in one of the most important revolutionary historical contexts of the twentieth century may have much to tell us about revolution at a time when the crisis of socialism (and society) is deeper than ever—or at least as deep as it has ever been.

CHAPTER TWO

Nationalism, Utopianism, and Revolutionary Politics

Anarchist Themes in the Early Chinese Revolutionary Movement

Anarchism appeared in China at a moment of national crisis. In 1906–7 Chinese intellectuals abroad established two societies, within months of each other, devoted to the propagation of anarchism, one in Paris, the other in Tokyo. At a time when a revolutionary discourse was taking shape, with origins in a new national consciousness, the anarchism these societies promoted introduced into the discourse dissonant themes that would have a lasting effect. In spite of their basic conflict with nationalist goals, these themes would display a remarkable staying power in the revolutionary discourse fueled by the pursuit of political forms to give coherence to a nation in the making. Their echoes are audible to this day as the pursuit continues.

The receptivity to anarchism at a moment of nascent national consciousness seems anomalous. Mainstream Chinese political thinking during the first decade of the century revolved around the question of how to make China into a nation, to forge a cohesive political system out of the loosely organized power structure of a bureaucratic monarchy, and to ward off the threat to the country's existence in a new world where the competition for power of expansive nation-states promised to consume those societies unable to emulate their example. The urgent questions of the day were what to do with the "alien" Manchu dynasty that continued to rule the majority Han people that constituted China and seemed to be less concerned with the nation's welfare than with its own; how to transform the political system so as to extend political participation to larger numbers of Chinese in order to secure the people's loyalty to the state;

and how to develop the country economically to establish a material foundation for national strength—and the conditions for political sovereignty in a world where national political power seemed to be contingent upon the control of global economic resources. The pursuit of national "wealth and power" seemed to rule the world. The "static" society of China must be dynamized by this same pursuit if it was to survive—and reassert the glory to which it was entitled by a glorious past.[1] Building a nation was essential to this end.

The very presence of anarchism in Chinese thought might be taken as evidence that these concerns were not shared as widely as they first appear to be—were it not for the fact that anarchists themselves were intimately involved with the revolutionary movement nationalism spawned, and anarchist ideas first made their appearance within a new discourse that took as its point of departure China's reconstitution as a nation. Rather, the anarchist presence suggests that this discourse is not reducible to a one-dimensional defensive or parochial search for "wealth and power," that it was multidimensional in the possibilities it produced—including, ultimately, the negation of the premise that lay at its origins—which made it authentically revolutionary. It is not in the immediate political concerns of Chinese nationalism, but rather in the intellectual problematic the new national consciousness (or, consciousness of the nation) presented, that we must seek for clues to why anarchism, despite its basic contradiction of nationalist goals, acquired a significant place in intellectual discourse.

This new consciousness was to play a crucial part in the articulation, in the words of Thomas Metzger, of a "modern Chinese intellectual *problematique*."[2] This is not to suggest that modern Chinese thought is but an account of the problems presented by national consciousness, or that all problems of Chinese thought from this point on must be referred back to a national consciousness and the political questions it raised. In his recent study of Chinese intellectuals at the turn of the century, Chang Hao has argued plausibly against the limitations of an exclusively political formulation of the problems that faced Chinese intellectuals, which were not just political, social, or even broadly cultural but ethical and existential as

1. Benjamin Schwartz, *In Search of Wealth and Power: Yen Fu and the West* (Cambridge: Harvard University Press, 1964).
2. Thomas A. Metzger, "Developmental Criteria and Indigenously Conceived Options: A Normative Approach to China's Modernization in Recent Times," *Issues and Studies* (February 1987), 72.

well.[3] Metzger shares Chang Hao's view in his identification as a central concern of modern Chinese thought the establishment of "a moral language with which to envisage the good society."[4]

At its broadest, this problematic entailed the reconstitution of both self and society in a discourse of modernity, which called forth questions not only of social and political form but, ultimately, of the meaning and ends of individual existence. The intellectual and ethical postulates of modernity, which forced themselves on the consciousness of Chinese intellectuals in the encounter with the West, were to provoke a rethinking of received traditions in their totality in the new possibilities they suggested. While Chinese intellectuals have continued over the years to draw upon these traditions as a source for an autonomous critique of Euro-American modernism, they have been able to do so only by rephrasing earlier problems in a new discourse that is unmistakably modern in its premises and sensibilities; even where the answers are old, the questions that produced them have been phrased in the problematic of a new historical situation. The problem was especially acute for the first generation of intellectuals to become conscious of this new historical situation, who, as products of a received ethos, had to remake themselves in the very process of reconstituting the problematic of Chinese thought. Anarchism, as we shall see, was a product of this situation. The answers it offered to this new problematic were not just social and political but sought to confront in novel ways its demands in their existential totality. At the same time, especially in the case of the first generation of anarchists, these answers were couched in a "moral language" that rephrased received ethical concepts in a new discourse of modernity.

Although this new "intellectual *problematique*" is not to be reduced to the problem of national consciousness, that problem was important in its formulation, in two ways. First, essential to the new problematic is the question of China's place in the world and its relationship to the past, which found expression most concretely in problems created by the new national consciousness. Second, national consciousness raised questions about social relationships, ultimately at the level of the relationship between the individual and society, which were to provide the framework for, and in some ways also contained, the redefinition of even existential questions. For the universalistically oriented among Chinese intellectuals, consciousness of the nation created some discomfort, which was to serve

3. Chang Hao, *Chinese Intellectuals in Crisis: Search for Order and Meaning* (Berkeley and Los Angeles: University of California Press, 1987). Introduction.
4. Metzger, "Developmental Criteria," 72.

as a source of existential problems as well as of an urge to transcend the limitations imposed by national consciousness. I will also argue that nationalism itself pointed to a new kind of universalism that pushed against the boundaries imposed by a national reorganization of society. In either case, this new consciousness provided the premise even of its own negation. This was true as well of the anarchists who took national consciousness as the greatest obstacle to the realization of the kind of society they advocated. Perhaps more important, the new discourse that emerged at the turn of the century coalesced around the problem of national consciousness, which, therefore, provided the conceptual conditions of the discourse, and delineated for those who were uncomfortable with the new national consciousness the ideological horizon they would have to transcend in order to overcome the limitations it established.

My concern is not with the alternative directions nationalism assumed in China from the very beginning, but rather with identifying the terms of the problematic it produced, which was to provide the discursive context within which consciously anarchist ideas first made their appearance in Chinese thought.

NATIONALISM AND REVOLUTION:
GLOBAL CONSCIOUSNESS AND
THE RECONCEPTUALIZATION OF POLITICAL SPACE

To see Chinese nationalism only in its immediate political aspirations is to see only part of it and to ignore a new global consciousness that was its precondition and a new consciousness of political space that informed it. Nationalism as a political ideology may be most striking for its exclusionary parochialism, for the physical and ideological boundaries it seeks to establish to separate those within the nation from those without. In the face it presents to the outside, it may be no different than other forms of parochialism except in the scope of the territory it claims for itself. Nationalism, however, is also a revolutionary political ideology that is unmistakably modern in its premises concerning global organization, externally, and political space, internally. Internally, it presupposes a new conception of political space, which is reorganized to bring the state closer to the society over which it rules, for the nation-state claims legitimacy not in some external source but in its ability to represent the nation—which inexorably entitles those who constitute the nation to make claims upon the state, for they are no longer merely subjects but citizens. Externally, by its very logic if in spite of itself, nationalist consciousness extends the same entitlement to others, who are perceived no longer merely as aggregates of people but as other nations, and who are therefore entitled to *their* own claims upon their political fate, and a state of their own to realize that fate. As Liang Qichao wrote in 1901: "Nationalism is the most promising, upright, and unbiased idea in the world. It does not allow other people to infringe my freedom, nor does it let me impose on other people."[5]

Imagined the national community may be, as Benedict Anderson has argued,[6] but it may be all the more revolutionary for being imaginary, for nationalist political ideology since its origins in Europe in the sixteenth and seventeenth centuries has called forth the reorganization of societies globally into nations. This in turn has provoked a revolutionary reconceptualization of political legitimacy and a reconstitution of political space internally to create nations. We need only to remember that over the last two centuries, even the most despotic states have excused their despotism by recourse to national interest, which those who have struggled against despotism have countered by asserting their rights as citizens—and alternative conceptions of national interest.

Such a change of consciousness accompanied the articulation of a nationalist political ideology in China at the turn of the century. If we perceive nationalism in terms of its global revolutionary premises rather than its parochial manifestations, it is not surprising that the first Chinese to raise the question of China's reorganization as a nation were not the conservative defenders of the Confucian political order, who continued to insist that China was a world unto itself and that the Chinese world contained all the necessary institutions for a civilized world. They were those Chinese who, having discovered other societies with *their* own institutions, were willing to recognize alternative claims to civilization— and even that those claims were more suitable to the age than the claims of the Confucian political order, which had been designed for circumstances when China's civilization had no competitors.[7] Once the rude shock of military defeat by European powers had been overcome, and Chinese intellectuals had acquired some familiarity with Europeans in China, especially through direct contact with European societies in the 1870s and 1880s, some at least were willing to recognize that the Europe-

5. Quoted in Tang Xiaobing, "History Imagined Anew: Liang Ch'i-ch'ao in 1902." Unpublished paper (1990), 7.
6. Benedict Anderson, *Imagined Communities: Reflections on the Origin and Spread of Nationalism* (London: Verso, 1983).
7. Paul Cohen, *Between Tradition and Modernity: Wang T'ao and Reform in Late Qing China* (Cambridge: Harvard University Press, 1974).

ans' strength resided not just in superior weapons or military power but in their political and economic institutions. They may have been interested primarily in uncovering the secret of the "wealth and power" of Europeans, but what is important is that they were willing to recognize the institutions they discovered as the keys to "wealth and power," not as the fortuitous products of barbaric societies, but as the very endowments of an alternative civilization with its own claims to history. What impressed them most about this civilization was its dynamism, which rested upon a close relationship between rulers and ruled—which accounted for the responsiveness of the rulers to the ruled and the willingness of the ruled to make common cause with their rulers.

The new consciousness of the globe lies at the origins of the emergence of a national consciousness in China with varied responses. For those committed to the existing order, nationalism took the form of strengthening existing institutions to ward off the challenge presented by these alternative models of civilization; this response implied the closing off of the new world in a parochial reaffirmation of the superiority or sufficiency of the ideological bases of Chinese civilization, which needed little from the outside world except those techniques that might contribute to strengthening native institutions.

The radical alternative came from those who felt uncomfortable with the parochialism of a politics that took the nation as its own end. This response took the form of projecting upon the new global situation a native idealism and utopianism that now took the nation as its point of departure, but perceived in the future the realization of universal ideals, which had formerly taken Chinese society as their locus but in the new consciousness became attributes of a society conceived globally. The inscribing of native ideals (predominantly Confucian and Buddhist in origins) upon the new global situation expressed a new cosmopolitanism that would ultimately rephrase those ideals in the language of a global political discourse.

In an immediate sense, this new cosmopolitanism had two implications: (1) bringing a new sense of space and time into the discourse on ideal society, and (2) incorporating into the procedures for achieving an ideal society lessons learned from the experiences of others, with the consequence that the emerging revolutionary discourse extended to the past its cosmopolitan vision of the future and drew upon the pasts of other societies as much as on China's past in charting a future course. The recognition of alternative claims to civilization, as Joseph Levenson has argued, meant the inevitable shrinking of Confucian claims to possession of *the* civilization; Chinese civilization was only one among others, and not necessarily the one best suited to survival in the contemporary world.[8] Survival, indeed, demanded reconstitution of that civilization institutionally and ideologically, which meant remaking China from a universal empire into a nation. For that is what the new models of "wealth and power" implied: states that derived their legitimacy not from a higher power or an abstract morality but from their representation of their constituents, and people who for the same reason were committed to national goals.

The shrinking of the Chinese world, implicit in the recognition of the historical legitimacy of other civilizations, was accompanied by a sharp awareness that, if China was to survive and flourish under such novel circumstances, Chinese politics must be reorganized in accordance with the models provided by these civilizations. Nationalism as it emerged in China was intended to ward off the threat to China's existence; but in its very premises it presupposed the recognition of the claims of that world, not that it would be closed off. And it was revolutionary because entry into the world called for the recognition of China as a political entity that was its own end rather than an institutional complex that expressed transcendental norms. Such recognition required a shift in the tasks of politics from preserving the purity of inherited institutions to preserving the territory and the people that constituted the nation—which could be accomplished only by bringing the people into politics.[9] Those who first spoke timidly of other civilizations in the 1880s were hounded out of office by their fellow Confucians; within years, a revolutionary movement was under way that called for a republican reorganization of China, to which Manchu rule was unacceptable because one nationality must not be subject to rule by another.

National consciousness was revolutionary at the turn of the century because it compelled Chinese intellectuals, in the words of Chang Hao, "to do something they probably had not done since the axial age of the late Chou, namely, to reexamine the institutional foundation of the Chinese sociopolitical order."[10] Examination of the intellectual premises of the new national consciousness reveals that the revolution in Chinese political consciousness extended beyond the "reexamination" of "the

8. Joseph Levenson, *Confucian China and Its Modern Fate* (Berkeley and Los Angeles: University of California Press, 1968) 1, chap. 7.

9. For the conversation between Kang Youwei, the reformer who made this statement, and the Emperor Guangxu, see Hsiao Kung-ch'uan, "Weng T'ung-ho and the Reform Movement of 1898," *Tsing Hua Journal of Chinese Studies* 1, no. 2 (April 1957): 175–76.

10. Chang Hao, *Chinese Intellectuals in Crisis*, 6.

institutional foundation of the Chinese sociopolitical order," and implied a transformation in the spatial and temporal conditions of politics. In his *Autobiography at Thirty*, Liang Qichao, prominent reformer and intellectual "clearing-house" for his generation,[11] who would do more than any of his contemporaries to articulate the new conception of the nation, wrote:

> I was born January 26 of the twelfth year of Tongzhi (1873), ten years after the Taiping Kingdom was defeated in Jinling (Nanjing), one year after the Qing scholar Zeng Guofan died, three years after the Franco-Prussian War, and the year that Italy became a nation in Rome. When I was a month old, my grandmother Li died.[12]

The statement is remarkable for the new sense of space and time that informs it. Unlike earlier authors, but like his contemporaries, Liang took as the reference for his autobiography not just events in China but worldwide events. This consciousness at the personal level was paralleled at the political level by an incipient awareness that China was no longer *the* world, but part of a larger world. The same awareness was reflected in the transformation of historical consciousness: that Chinese history, once taken to be *the* history of civilization, was little more than the history of one civilization among many, and, judging by contemporary results, it was not a history of success. It was urgent to relocate Chinese history in world history and to transform China accordingly, if Chinese society was to be guaranteed a future.

Historians long have noted the crisis in Chinese consciousness created by this realization, and the contradiction that it created for Chinese intellectuals: that in order to ward off the Euro-American powers that threatened the existence of Chinese society, China must adopt the ways of the very powers that threatened it. The repeated defeat of China at the hands of these powers confirmed for Chinese the predictions of the social Darwinian ideology that entered Chinese thinking at about the same time: that only those nations would survive that could adjust to the demands of the contemporary world. Hence the Chinese revolution appears from its origins in its defensive motivations: as a means to guarantee China's survival in a world of competition and conflict. Chinese "internationalism"—the willingness to adopt Western ways—appears accordingly as part of this strategy of survival.

11. The description is Philip Huang's; see *Liang Ch'i-ch'ao and Modern Chinese Liberalism* (Seattle: University of Washington Press, 1972).

12. Quoted in Wendy Larson, "Literary Authority and the Chinese Writer," unpublished ms., 57. I am grateful to Professor Larson for sharing this ms. with me.

While the validity of this view is not to be denied, it is somewhat one-sided. If Chinese nationalism did not mean merely closing out the world, but presupposed for its very emergence a new sense of time and space, it becomes possible to comprehend another phenomenon that accompanied the first stirrings of national consciousness: an internationalist utopianism. Charlotte Furth has noted the appearance of a pervasive utopianism in Chinese thinking at the turn of the century.[13] This utopianism, though expressed in a native vocabulary that owed much to Confucianism and Buddhism, was the counterpoint to the new national consciousness and expressed hopes in a "new China," in Hsiao Kung-ch'uan's felicitous words, in a "new world."[14] The ideal of world unity, once encompassed within the claims to universality of Chinese civilization but no longer contained within the conception of a spatially and temporally limited Chinese nation, was now projected upon the new world of nations as a historical project in whose realization China was to be a participant. It may not be coincidental that Kang Youwei, the leader of the first serious reform movement in modern China in 1898, who in the name of national survival mounted the fatal challenge to the claim to universality of the Confucian imperial order, should also have authored a utopian treatise, *The Book of Great Unity (Datong shu)*, which depicted the material and moral features of a future society that had once again transcended nationalism.[15] Kang's society of Great Unity represented the final stage of human progress, following stages of familism and nationalism, in that order. The utopia drew its name and virtues from a native Chinese utopian tradition, but already its inspiration came from the future—a future, moreover, that transcended China's own world and took as its scope the global society of which China had just become an integral part.

What is most significant here is that the very condition that necessitated the redefinition of China as a nation in a world of nations elicited as its dialectical counterpoint a new vision of a world in which nations would once again disappear and humankind would discover a world of unity. Others were to follow Kang. The urge to a new universalism was also expressed at about the turn of the century in a Buddhist revival, as well as in the universalization of Confucian values, which were alienated

13. Charlotte Furth, "Intellectual Change: From the Reform Movement to the May Fourth Movement, 1895–1920," in *The Cambridge History of China*, ed. John K. Fairbank, vol. 12, pt. 1 (New York: Cambridge University Press, 1983).

14. Hsiao Kung-ch'uan, *A New China and a New World: K'ang Yu-wei, Reformer and Utopian, 1858–1927* (Seattle: University of Washington Press, 1975).

15. K'ang Yu-wei, *Ta T'ung Shu: The One World Philosophy of K'ang Yu-wei*, tr. L. G. Thompson (London: Allen and Unwin, 1958).

from their association with institutions particular to the Confucian socio-political order to become potential endowments of humanity as a whole.

Within the context of this utopianism that was its dialectical counter-point, the emerging Chinese national consciousness appears not merely as a defensive parochialism, but as a step in an idealistic project whose ultimate goal was the transformation of humanity globally. China, more-over, must participate in this global project, not just as its object but as a subject that had much to contribute to its realization. The utopianism hinted at a discomfort with nationalism as an end in itself; and it was this discomfort that was revolutionary, for it looked beyond the achievement of national goals to a global transformation. Kang Youwei, whose reinter-pretation of Confucianism was to establish the intellectual premises of nationalist ideology, nevertheless expressed in his utopia a profound dis-comfort with all institutions that divided people from one another, includ-ing nationalism, to which he traced the causes of human suffering. The discomfort was not his alone. Kang's disciple Tan Sitong expressed it even more cogently in a statement that may well be taken as a prelude to the anarchist resolution of the problem:

> The earth must be governed in such a way that there is only one world but no states. . . . To enable everybody to enjoy freedom, people would not have to belong to any state. If there were no states, there would not be any boundaries, wars, suspicion, jealousy, power-struggles, distinction between the self and others, and equality would emerge. Even if the world exists, it would be as if there were no world at all. When rulers are all deposed, then there will be equality between the higher and lower; when universal principles are fol-lowed, then there will be equality between the rich and the poor. For thou-sands and thousands of miles, the entire world will be like one family, one man. Homes will be looked upon as guest houses, and people, as compatriots. There will be no need for fathers to apply their paternal love, and for sons to exercise their filial piety. Elder and younger brothers can forget about their friendly respect, and husbands and wives their mutual harmony. It would be like the man mentioned in a Western story book, who wakes up after dream-ing for a hundred years, and finds that the atmosphere of One World is almost like that described in the chapter on the "Evolution of Rites" in the *Book of Rites*.[16]

Tan's book was named after the central virtue of Confucianism, "hu-maneness" (*ren*), and he drew heavily on Buddhist ideals in describing his vision of the future. He also establishes an equality here between the ideal

---

16. Tan Sitong, *An Exposition of Benevolence: The Jen-hsueh of T'an Ssu-t'ung*, tr. Chan Sin-wai (Hong Kong: Chinese University Press, 1984), 215–16. I have changed "benevolence" to "humaneness."

of "great unity" (*datong*) in the *Book of Rites* and what would appear to be a reference to Edward Bellamy's *Looking Backward*. He was one of the first martyrs of the Chinese revolution.[17]

This utopian dimension to Chinese nationalism suggests one reason why anarchism, for all its opposition to nationalism, found a receptive audience in China in the midst of a tide of nationalism. Another reason lies in the questions raised by the nationalist demand to bring state and society closer in the reorganization of Chinese politics. Here, too, the problem must be perceived in ways more complex than is allowed for in the interpretation of Chinese nationalism merely as a quest for "wealth and power."

In practical terms, the most conspicuous aspect of the urge to remake China as a nation was to find ways to bring society close to the state so as to motivate the people to pursue national goals actively. Chinese thinkers at the turn of the century believed that through centuries of political rule that had denied popular political participation the people had become passive subjects who cared little for the fate of the nation as a whole. In advocating greater political participation, their immediate goal was not to make the state an instrument of social interests, or to foment conflict between state and society, but to unify the two into a whole, capable of acting as one. Liang Qichao, who enunciated this problem most clearly, conceived of the nation, in the words of Chang Hao, as a "moral *gemeinschaft*," which in turn presupposed an organic conception of the relationship between state and society.[18]

Once again, while this view of initial nationalist aspirations (a continuing problem of Chinese politics) is valid, it is only part of a complex picture. The questions raised by nationalism also legitimized division in a political system that had hitherto refused to address as legitimate the question of social interest. Specifically, if nationalism presupposed a state that represented the interests of the nation, how was it to be determined that the state did indeed represent the nation's interests? Even if the state could be made to represent the nation, how were those interests to be determined, since the nation itself was a composite of social relationships that articulated divergent, and conflicting, social interests? I suggest that

17. Chan suggests in his footnotes that the Westerner in question is Rip Van Winkle. The "hundred-year" sleep makes it more likely that it was the hero of Bellamy's *Looking Backward*, which was already translated into Chinese at this time and made a great impression on Kang Youwei and his disciples. For Bellamy and the Chinese, see Martin Bernal, *Chinese Socialism to 1907* (Ithaca: Cornell University Press, 1976).

18. Chang Hao, *Liang Ch'i-ch'ao and Intellectual Transition in Modern China* (Cambridge: Harvard University Press, 1971).

the nationalist demand for the reorganization of political space in the first decade of the century, in giving rise to such questions, represented the emergence of politics in China by transforming a ritual conception of political order as the administration of society into a political conception where order was to be created out of the harmonizing of conflicting interests between state and society, as well as of divergent social interests. Liang Qichao's was one solution among others, one that sought to resolve the predicament created by nationalism by asserting the priority of the nation conceived as an organic entity. In practise, however, the question of legitimacy raised by the new nationalist conception of China produced, almost immediately, social and political conflicts, which found expression in divergent conceptions of the nation. Given a situation where the ruling dynasty was ethnically different from the majority of the population, the legitimacy of the state came under attack first from those preoccupied with the fate of the nation, and quickly turned into a critique of despotism in general—in other words, an assertion of the rights of society against the state. It was accompanied almost immediately by conflicts over who was to be included in the new political arrangement and whose interests were to take priority in the definition of national interest. By 1905, against Liang Qichao's pleas for organic national unity, the Revolutionary Alliance (*Tongmeng hui*) under the leadership of Sun Yat-sen had already incorporated in its republican program a call for social revolution, to safeguard the interests of the majority against the minority of economic and political power holders. The following year, anarchists would propose their own version of social revolution, this time intended not as the basis for a new state but against the state and politics in general.

In raising the question of the relationship between state and society, the nationalist argument, contrary to its intentions, also raised the possibility of opposition between state and society. The state, now dependent for its legitimacy on its ability to represent the nation, could no longer identify the latter with its own will. The same argument legitimized the right of revolutionaries to speak against the state in ways that had been impossible so long as the Chinese order had refused to recognize society as an autonomous source of political legitimacy.

The problem of state and society appeared at the level of the individual as a problem of morality: public morality (*gongde*) versus private morality (*side*). The nationalist problematic was to give a new twist to this long-standing problem in Chinese political thought. The problem was how to reconcile a private morality (expressed in personal relationships and loyalties) with a public morality (expressed in obligations to a more abstract political order). Political orthodoxy in China, following the injunction in the canonical text *The Great Learning*, presented the relationship as a continuum: the perfection of private morality was a prerequisite to, and found its fulfillment in, the achievement of public morality. Politics did not always live up to its own ideological premises, however, and Confucian theorists were always acutely aware of the potential conflict between private and public, between particularistic loyalties and the universalistic obligations necessary to the sustenance of public order; thinkers of the early Qing dynasty (1644–1911), whose writings would deeply impress the first generation of Chinese nationalists, had been particularly explicit in their condemnation of rulers who gave priority to private over public interest and, therefore, undermined the political order.

Two aspects of this problem had appeared in Confucian thinking. First was its scope: while public obligation was incumbent upon everyone, it was truly significant only for those who carried the responsibility for public order—the ruler and those who participated in ruling functions. Second, while private interest might be tolerated to the extent that it was not inimical to the public order, ultimately it carried no legitimacy, and the web of particularistic relationships that constituted the individual were prized only to the extent that they prepared him for public responsibility in a patrimonial and patriarchal political order. It is not that the theory did not allow for individual conscience, for it did, but that the political order made no room for those whose conscience led them to radical dissent.

The nationalist problematic was to recast this problem. To put it bluntly, the reconstitution of China as a nation presupposed the reconstitution of the subjects of the Confucian order as citizens who were the ultimate source of political legitimacy and whose active participation in politics was essential to the creation of a new national order. The theoretical implications of this new assumption are obvious. Everyone, not just the ruler or the ruling class, was equally obliged under the circumstances to cultivate the public morality that was the essential condition of a cohesive national community. At the same time, however, the possibility of public morality was even more of a predicament for nationalist discourse than it had been for the Confucian, because of its recognition of, or demand for, the individual as citizen—as the autonomous source of public values. The question for nationalist discourse was not whether Chinese should be transformed from subjects into citizens, but how soon they could be expected to make the transformation. This is quite clear in

Liang Qichao's classic statement of the problem in 1902 in his "On the New Citizen."[19] Liang, already fearful of the possibility of revolution and deeply committed to the national idea as a "moral *gemeinschaft*," recognized the crucial importance of turning Chinese into autonomous citizens. He believed that because most of the people were ill-prepared to undertake the burden, a period of education in the new political system was required of them; while they were richly endowed with "private morality," they were lacking in "public morality," which in this case meant loyalty to the abstraction that was the nation, and had to learn to reconcile the conflicting demands of public and private obligations. Liang did not deny the autonomy of the citizen, or the legitimacy of private morality, but offered a strategy for reconciling them with the demands of the national community.

Others were to go further. While Liang sought to contain individual autonomy within his ideal of a national community, the very recognition of legitimacy to private space within a public realm also created the possibility of opposition between the two. Hence the subjection of individual to public interests and needs could appear as a perpetuation of the social and political oppression of the individual, which obstructed the creation not only of autonomous citizens but of a nation, and which could be resolved only by the lifting of political *and* social restrictions on the individual. In its positing of the individual as an autonomous source of national values, nationalist discourse opened the way to an opposition not only between the individual and politics but between the individual and society as well. The predicament appeared on the surface as primarily a political problem; as Chang Hao has argued, however, it was also felt by those involved as a deeply existential one. It also was revolutionary because the possibility of individual autonomy opened up the possibility of radical dissent as the legitimate prerogative of individuals.

The adoption of Western ideas and institutions in order to ward off the West; the transformation or abandonment of native institutions and ideas in order to preserve a Chinese identity; a practical quest for national "wealth and power," which results in a utopian repudiation of nationalism; demands for closer integration of state and society that open the way to the opposition of society to the state; the desire to create loyal citizens, which ends up with the affirmation of individual autonomy against both

19. "Xinmin shuo," in *Xinhai geming qian shinianjian shilun xuanji* (Collection of essays from the decade before 1911) (Beijing: Sanlian shudian, 1978) 1:118–57. For an extensive discussion of the "new citizen," see also Chang Hao, *Liang Ch'i-ch'ao.*

state *and* society—such were the contradictions embedded in the seemingly transparent and one-dimensional problematic of Chinese nationalism. In its origins the nationalist impulse was simple enough: to protect China's integrity and to create a wealthy and powerful nation. *How* to create such a nation was another matter. From the moment of its articulation, the nationalist discourse revealed itself to be far more complex than the impulse that had given it birth; indeed, some of the alternatives it called forth promised to negate the very impulse that lay at its origins.

The contradictions were those of the "overdetermined" milieu from which Chinese nationalism sprang, which was no longer *just* Chinese, but a Chinese society in the process of transformation and incorporation into a broader world economically, politically, and culturally. Chinese thinkers had already begun to derive their political inspiration, and even political models, from Euro-American modernity, which not only dominated the present but seemed to hold the key to the future. At the same time, however, while Chinese nationalism as it appeared at the turn of the century set itself against the received Confucian tradition, the problems that occupied it, as well as the language in which it phrased those problems, derived from that same tradition. Nationalist discourse broke with the received political tradition, not by purging it from memory or language, but by recasting it in a new problematic, which added to the contradictions already implicit in its ambivalent relationship to its Euro-American inspiration. Central to the nationalist problematic was a new conception of China's place in the world, which was to raise further questions concerning the basis of political legitimacy and organization, as well as the ethical obligations of the individuals who constituted the nation. While prenationalist traditions persisted into the new discourse, basically through the medium of a social and political language that kept alive older conceptions and associations, they were problematized, acquired new meanings, and were placed now in an intellectual context that not only opened the way to new questions that demanded new answers but also rephrased old questions so as to yield answers that had been foreclosed earlier. As late as the middle of the nineteenth century, Chinese thinkers facing a novel situation in the confrontation with the West had been able to interiorize the problems presented by this situation within an inherited problematic, which, they believed, could contain these problems in the alternatives it offered. By the turn of the century, Chinese history had already been inscribed upon a history that transcended it, and the crucial question for Chinese thinkers was how to make China a sustainable component of a new world. The utopian strain in Chinese

thinking, which accompanied the new national consciousness to the forefront of Chinese thought; the call for a revolutionary transformation of
the political order, which grew directly out of demands to reconstitute the
imperial order as a nation; and the radical culture that arose simultaneously with new conceptions of the ethical obligations of individuals as
citizens—all were products of this question. The "modern Chinese intellectual *problematique*," which appears with the nationalist reformulation
of China's place in the world, has been dynamized by successive reformu-
lations of this same question as changes in internal and external circumstances have added to it new dimensions; but the problematic retains its
vitality.

The reformulation of China's place in the world within the nationalist
discourse had one other important consequence: the incorporation into
political discourse in China of other traditions external to Chinese history.
I refer here, not merely to the "influence" on China of political discourses
that had originated elsewhere, but to the discursive appropriation in Chinese politics of revolutionary traditions, which then appear as part of the
process of political transformation in China. As I noted above in the case of
Liang Qichao, already in the early twentieth century worldwide events
appear as markers in a historical consciousness that is no longer bound in
its conceptions of time and space by a specifically Chinese past. Liang's
autobiographical statement points to this new consciousness as personal
and existential; and indeed as Chinese intellectuals confronted the world,
either as students or as political exiles abroad, their experiences of the
world opened up their consciousness to alternative ideas and values, which
became part of their very intellectual and emotional constitution. The
same was true on a broader political level. Nationalist discourse from the
beginning called upon the experiences of others in making its case for
political transformation and the political vision that informed arguments
for political transformation. The English, American, French, and other
revolutions were on the minds of Chinese nationalists, and the ideas that
had brought about those revolutions, as well as the examples they provided, were to contribute significantly to the formation of a radical discourse in China. In later years, other examples would be added to these
original ones. What is remarkable is not that Chinese radicals would continue to draw upon China's past, but rather that the past now appeared as
only part of a political discourse that was global in its inspiration and
political formulations.

The two by-products of the emerging national consciousness—a utopianism that sought to transcend the nation, and the establishment of the

nation as the source of political legitimacy—produced an explosive mixture that quickly revolutionized Chinese society. In 1903, in a classic of the Chinese revolution, *The Revolutionary Army*, the young author, Zou Jong, combined the two in what may best be described as a utopianization of revolution itself: "Ah, revolution, revolution! If you have it, you will survive; but if you don't, you will die. Don't retrogress; don't be neutral; don't hesitate; now is the time."[20]

A product of China's plight at the turn of the century, nationalism was to produce an intellectual orientation that discovered in revolution the key to China's survival—and the creation of a new world. It was in the context of this emerging radical culture that Chinese intellectuals first discovered anarchism. Though anarchism may have been inimical to the predominantly nationalistic orientation of Chinese politics, it owed its initial appeal in China to its resonance with themes that owed their origins to the new nationalist consciousness. For the same reason, the nationalist political discourse provided the language in which anarchism was phrased, especially in its initial phase.

INITIAL RECEPTION OF ANARCHISM

Anarchism was the first of the alternative currents in European socialism at the turn of the century to make a significant impact on Chinese radical thinking and behavior. Although a distinctively anarchist social revolutionary program was not enunciated until 1906–7, when with the founding of the groups in Paris and Tokyo some of the revolutionaries openly declared an anarchist identity to distinguish themselves from fellow revolutionaries, the burgeoning revolutionary movement after 1903 had already found in anarchism an outlook akin to its own and a vocabulary to express its radical concerns. There was considerable confusion concerning anarchism in these early years; Chinese had no direct access to anarchist works, and what they knew of anarchism was derived from Japanese discussions of European socialism or from translations in Japanese of general histories of socialism, which presented anarchism as an "extremist" (*guoji*) current in socialism (an "extreme revolutionism"), often confounding it with Russian nihilism or populism.[21] The very diffuseness

20. Zou Rong, *The Revolutionary Army*, tr. John Lust (The Hague: Mouton, 1968). This translation is in *The Chinese Revolution, 1900–1950*, ed. R. Vohra (Boston: Houghton Mifflin, 1974), 19.

21. Chinese radicals derived this view of anarchism, as well as much of their information on it, from an influential book by the Japanese author Kemuyama Sentaro, *Modern Anarchism*. Though Kemuyama distinguished anarchism and nihilism, his book may ac-

in the understanding of anarchism, however, reveals the resonance of anarchist ideas with the radical orientation—as much in mood as in intellect—created by the new national consciousness.

In these earliest discussions, anarchism appears in three guises: first, as a critique of despotism, anarchism was conflated with Russian nihilism, since the struggle against despotism appeared to Chinese radicals to be the distinguishing feature of both anarchism and nihilism. Second, anarchism expressed a longing for a unified and cosmopolitan world in whose creation China would participate. Finally, anarchism appears as the expression of a mystical vision, a philosophical nihilism, as it were, that promised a cosmic unity by abolishing the very consciousness of sentient existence.

Discussions of anarchism in this early phase invariably juxtaposed it to despotism, more often than not focusing attention on Russia, where anarchism was more prevalent than elsewhere, it was believed, because of the unparalleled severity despotism had reached there. One author, in comparing Russia and China, observed: "I have heard that despotism is a factory that manufactures the anarchists who promote the overthrow of despotism; the better equipped a factory is with machinery, the more it produces; the deeper the despotism, the more numerous are the anarchists it produces." China at the present, he continued, did not have as many anarchists as Russia because despotism there had not yet reached the depth it had in Russia. Against those who despaired of the increasing despotism of the Chinese government, he suggested with "optimism" that despotism sharpened the sensibilities of the people and was sure to create a greater number of anarchists.[22]

What most impressed this author, Ma Xulun, and some of his contemporaries was the anarchist pursuit of "natural freedom" (*tianran ziyou*). In primeval times, humankind had enjoyed a "natural freedom," deriving all its needs from nature and enjoying peace and happiness. "Ever since kings and governments had arisen, they had established politics and manufactured laws. Presently, religion, education, and all kinds of institutions that curtailed natural freedom had come into existence, humankind had been

count partially for confounding the two, as two-thirds of the book was devoted to the revolutionary movement in Russia. See Don Price, *Russia and the Roots of the Chinese Revolution, 1896–1911* (Cambridge: Harvard University Press, 1974), 122–24.

22. Ma Xulun, "Ershi shijizhi xin zhuyi" (The new ideology of the twentieth century) (1903). See reprint in *Wuzhengfu zhuyi sixiang ziliao xuan* (Selection of materials on anarchist thought [hereafter *WZFZYSX*]), ed. Ge Maochun et al., 2 vols. (Beijing: Beijing daxue chubanshe, 1984), 1:13.

restricted within the confines of such institutions, and natural freedom had disappeared like tobacco burning out." Anarchists took as their general guideline the destruction of such institutions and "returning humankind to this pristine state of natural freedom."[23]

According to Ma, while everyone spoke of civilization, what ruled the world was "not universal principle (*gongli*) but force (*shi*)." Among the chief manifestations of this was nationalism, which had reached the stage of imperialism. Anarchism sought to destroy this world of force; and while Russia did not appear as civilized as other countries, the flourishing of anarchism there promised that it would be pivotal in the struggle against "force" in the twentieth century:

> The twentieth century has a new ideology (*zhuyi*); it is the anarchism of Russia. The anarchism of Russia guarantees that it will be pivotal to civilization in the twentieth century. Why? The aims of the anarchists are high, their understanding broad, their hopes are great; imperialism steps back and nationalism retreats before it.[24]

What the practical appeal of anarchism might be under China's circumstances was enunciated in 1904 in an essay by Zhang Ji, entitled "Anarchism and the Spirit of the Anarchists" (*Wuzhengfu zhuyi ji wuzhengfu dangzhi jingshen*), which was also important for its brief history of anarchism in Europe. Zhang agreed with Ma in emphasizing the importance to the twentieth century of the anarchist pursuit of freedom:

> People value self-government (*zizhi*) and are unwilling to be ruled by others; therefore, anarchism was born. The twentieth century is the battleground for anarchism.

Zhang was most impressed, however, by the anarchist affinity with terrorism (*kongbudang*):

> Terrorists have declared openly: "the end justifies the means." What this means is that whatever the means may be, if it helps achieve my goals, I may use it. If my means may bring security to the people of the nation, even if it entails killing, I may use it. The theory of the anarchists is similar to this; hence they advocate assassination.[25]

In defense of terrorism, Zhang cited Danton to the effect that "violent measures are necessary to achieve the peace and security of the people." Most important about terrorism, however, was the spirit of daring it embodied, which (he quoted from Kropotkin) was "more effec-

23. WZFZYSX 1:8.
24. WZFZYSX 1:9, 7.
25. Ziran sheng (Zhang Ji), "Wuzhengfu zhuyi ji wuzhengfu dangzhi jingshen" (1904). See reprint in WZFZYSX 1:25.

tive than thousands of periodicals and newspapers." A few people could, with such a spirit of daring, create an atmosphere of fear and awaken others to action. The spirit of daring derived its power to move others from the spirit of self-sacrifice it embodied: "There is nothing more awesome than the spirit of sacrifice for humanity, which spreads with the speed of an infectious disease."[26]

Both essays were richer in content than these brief descriptions suggest; I have singled out these aspects because they dominated the two authors' interpretations of anarchism, and because these were the aspects of anarchism that caught the imagination of early Chinese revolutionaries. Before I explain why this might have been so, I shall describe briefly the two alternative visions of anarchism that appeared at the time, the one offered in an interesting utopian fantasy by the later prominent intellectual leader and educator, Cai Yuanpei, the other tagged on to the end of Ma Xulun's essay to provide a metaphysical context for his discussion of despotism. Though highly abstract, these alternative visions of anarchism offer some clues to the underlying mentality of Chinese radicals that rendered them receptive to the anarchist message, and also point to a connection between anarchism and preanarchist native utopianism that characterized the Chinese understanding of anarchism, at least initially.

There is nothing evidently anarchist about the utopian plea for cosmopolitanism that Cai Yuanpei wrote in 1904, "The New Year's Dream" (*Xinnian meng*).[27] The word *anarchism* does not appear in the "story," and there is little in Cai's career then or later to suggest that he was an anarchist in any strict sense of the word. Yet he would associate with anarchists closely in later years, and in the twenties was one of the foremost promoters of educational ideals inspired by anarchism. Zhang Binglin, who was a close associate of Cai's in the early revolutionary movement, testified on one occasion that "Cai was an anarchist."[28] It is possible to suggest at least that, however abstractly, he shared some of the philosophical premises of anarchism and its vision of a cosmopolitan world. If his contemporaries did indeed view him as an anarchist, as Zhang's statement suggests, his story would have appeared to them as of anarchist inspiration, whether or not he explicitly described it as anarchist. Most important, the content of the story provides a link between preanarchist native utopianism (some of its themes overlap with Kang

26. *WZFZYSX* 1:28, 27.
27. Reprinted in *WZFZYSX* 1:41–51.
28. See Cai Shangsi, *Cai Yuanpei xueshu sixiang zhuanji* (An intellectual biography of Cai Yuanpei) (Shanghai: Lianying shudian, 1950), 167.

Youwei's utopia) and the explicitly anarchist utopias of the post-1907 period. There is sufficient reason to place it within the anarchist canon in China.[29]

The story begins with the words "Congratulations! Congratulations! It's the New Year, a new world has arrived. Truly joyful! Truly joyful!" The words are spoken by the hero of the story to a friend. The occasion is New Year's Day, 1904, which also signals the birth of a new world.

The hero is described merely as "some Chinese" (*Zhongguo yiren*). He had left home at the age of sixteen to travel in China and the world. By the time he was done with his travels (at the age of thirty), he had been to most countries in Europe and North America and learned all the major foreign languages. He had become a believer in "cosmopolitanism" (*shijie zhuyi*) and "loved equality and freedom." He had also decided that the problems of the world, especially humankind's continued subjection to nature, were due to its division into nations and families. In the "civilized" countries of Europe and North America, people expended half their energy on their families and half on their nations. In the less "civilized" Slavic and Chinese societies, they had "families and no nation." To create a new society in China should not be difficult, "if only the energies people presently expended on their families could be turned to the public cause." Once they had achieved this, then through the same process a world society could be created out of nations.[30]

The story is an account of the hero's efforts to achieve this end. It proceeds in two stages. In the first stage, Chinese society is reorganized and China is genuinely unified into a nation. The hero in his wanderings in China comes upon a meeting of representatives from all parts of the country who are organized, not according to province, but according to location vis-à-vis the major rivers (e.g., east of the river, west of the river). He submits to the meeting a plan for reorganization, which is passed after much debate. Basic to the plan is the reorganization of the population according to age and professional groupings. Most interesting is the allocation of labor. When children reached the age of seven, they would begin their education, which would last till the age of twenty-four. Between the ages of twenty-four and forty-eight, everyone would engage in publicly valuable professional tasks of one kind or another. After forty-

---

29. In including this piece in their collection on anarchist thought, Ge Maochun and the coeditors of *Selection of Materials on Anarchist Thought* obviously agree with this observation.

30. "Xinnian meng," 42.

eight they would retire and engage in the education of youth. The plan even specified the allocation of the hours of the day: eight hours of work, eight hours of reading, talking, and other activities, and eight hours of sleep. To those who objected that such a plan would be unworkable because of people's unwillingness to work, or that the curtailing of the pursuit of self-interest would be inimical to progress, the hero countered with an organic metaphor—that each would perform tasks in society as the five sensory organs and the four limbs did for the body—which quickly convinced everybody.[31]

With this reorganization, China would quickly become "civilized" and strong, revive the northeastern provinces (Manchuria), and retrieve the foreign concessions, and foreign powers would be made to realize that they should give up reliance on "naked force" (*qiangquan*) over "universal principle" (*gongli*). The country would develop rapidly, using the capital that Chinese had in abundance but were unwilling to invest under the present system (instead, they hid it). It would be built up politically from model villages (*mofan cun*) at the locality through a series of representative institutions all the way to the national level, so that the whole country would become as one (literally, of one heart, *quanguo yixin*).[32]

The hero then turns his attention to the international scene. He goes to Russia to participate in the activities of the people's party (*mindang*), which quickly manages to acquire political power. China then allies with Russia and the United States (where people's sovereignty was already strongly established) to convince other powers to abandon national aggression and create a new world government.

Cai describes the then existing society as follows:

> Civilization had reached its highest point. Speaking of mores and customs, people no longer used names or surnames but were simply identified by number; there were no longer any designations of ruler or minister, and as the conduct of affairs had been rendered rational, none of the uncertainties of election or appointment; there were no longer any designations of father and son, the young were educated by the public, the old were taken care of, and the sick cured; there were no longer any designations of husband and wife; once men and women had agreed to become mates they would conclude it with a ceremony in a public park from where they would proceed to their assigned quarters, hence adultery would disappear.[33]

31. Ibid., 42–45.
32. Ibid., 46, 48.
33. Ibid., 51.

The congress to establish the new government is planned for New Year's Day, 1904. It is at this point that the hero, now ninety years old, is awakened by the sound of bells, and in spite of his awareness of the darkness of the existing world (*heiande shijie*), utters the words "Congratulations! Congratulations! It's the New Year, a new world has arrived."[34]

In its historical premises, Cai's fantasy was reminiscent of the idea of progress of Kang Youwei, who had earlier established as a universal principle the progression from the family through the nation to the world. In his prescriptions for China's reorganization Cai anticipated the explicitly anarchist utopia that Liu Shipei would propose only three years later, and the themes he raised we encounter in later years in other utopias—and social experiments. Whether we are justified in describing it as anarchist, it provides us with a link to the cosmopolitan ideal that accompanied the emergence of Chinese nationalism and anarchism.

Ma Xulun provides us with a third, and the most intriguing, aspect of anarchism's appeals in China in this early period: anarchism as a means to recovery of a natural state of affairs. Ma agreed with Cai that anarchism offered a means of unifying the globe and creating a world society, but he placed this goal within a cosmic vision of the unity of nature and humanity.

In Ma's view, government (and other state institutions) had curtailed the "natural freedoms" enjoyed by humanity in its primeval condition. In the concluding section of his essay, he turned this to a critique of the Chinese political legacy, focusing on a distinction Confucian thought had drawn between "humane government" (*renzheng*) and "tyranny" (*baozheng*), associated respectively with the government of Confucian sages and the despotic government proposed by the Legalists and practised by the likes of the First Emperor of Qin. He saw no significant difference between humane government and tyranny, between the sage-rulers and the despots:

> I say that Yao, Shun, Yu, Tang, Wen and Wu [the sage rulers] are the ancestors of the First Emperor of Qin, emperor Wu of Han and Tai Zu of Ming. Had there been no Yao, Shun, Yu, Tang, Wen and Wu, there would have been no First Emperor, no emperor Wu of Han, no Tai Zu of Ming. Conversely, if the First Emperor, Wu of Han, Tai Zu of Ming had been born first, and Yao, Shun, Yu, Tang, Wen and Wu later, the world would have sung the praises of the former and cursed the latter. The terms humane government and tyranny persist out of habit, not because they are natural (*xiguan er ran, fei ziran er*

34. Ibid.

ran). I wish to get rid of these terms . . . and restore nature. . . . To restore its way, we must start with what the anarchists promote.[35]

The problem of politics, in other words, appeared to Ma as a problem of culture (i.e., habit), and the problem of culture resided in the very language of politics, which must be abolished if one was to discover what was natural to humanity.

Ma went even further. Anarchism to him ultimately represented a negation, as in the Chinese word *wu,* not just of government, as in *wuzhengfu,* but of the sentient world in general. In a phraseology reminiscent of the first lines of the Daoist classic *Daode jing,* he continued:

> That which exists (*you*) is the beginning of all things; that which does not exist (*wu*) is the mother of existence. The nonexistent is born of nature, what exists ends up in nonexistence, hence nature. Nature cannot be described, cannot be pictured, cannot be named; if it can be described, it is not nature; if it can be pictured, it is not nature. To name nature the nature that cannot be named is to force a name on it. . . . Can the minds of humanity be liberated from their predicament? Anarchism offers a precious raft to find the correct ford to cross the stream. I want to present it to humanity so that it can return to its mother.[36]

Whether the philosophical nihilism implicit in these lines, which owed much to the vocabulary of Daoism and Buddhism, had anything to do with the association of anarchism with the Russian nihilists (*Xuwu dang,* in Chinese) in practise is difficult to say. It does suggest a connection between anarchism and a basic premise of Chinese utopianism at the turn of the century that, because distinctions between people were the ultimate cause of suffering in the world, the abolition of all distinctions was key to the creation of a new world.[37] It was on those grounds that anarchism, in

35. Ma, "Ershi shijizhi xin zhuyi," 15.

36. Ibid., 15–16.

37. This was the basic premise of Kang Youwei's *Datong shu.* See chapter 1, where Kang describes distinctions (including those of nation, race, gender, family, and age) as the cause of all suffering in the world. Kang's discussion had a strongly Buddhist tone, as did an essay that the prominent intellectual and revolutionary, Zhang Binglin, wrote in 1907, "Wu-wu lun" (Essay on the five negations). To achieve the "supreme good," Zhang proposed "five negations": no government (*wuzhengfu*), no fixed abode (*wujulo*), no humankind (*wurenlei*), no living creatures (*wu-zhongsheng*), no world (*wushijie*). By the latter he did not imply extermination of humankind or the world; rather, he meant overcoming the illusion of endowing them with a reality they did not have, much in the manner of Buddhism. For a discussion of this essay, see Michael Gasster, *Chinese Intellectuals and the Revolution of 1911* (Seattle: University of Washington Press, 1969), 210–13. This also suggests that "negation" (*wu*) and even "nihilism" (*xuwu*) did not have the negative connotations in China that they had in Europe, that they appeared positive from a Buddhist perspective, which perceived in the annihilation of consciousness a means to end suffering—and achieve salvation. This subject awaits study in its own right.

the interpretation of someone like Ma, was conjoined with the Buddhist ideals that enjoyed a revival at about the same time. The connection would persist into the early Republic.

Although the Chinese access to materials on anarchism may have been limited, there was enough in available writings to indicate that anarchism was not reducible to Russian nihilism. In the preface to his translation of Thomas Kirkup's *A History of Socialism,* Ma Junwu wrote:

> The French have the highest intellect of any people in the world. Saint-Simon's disciples have spread socialism [i.e., communism] all over the world; its power increases daily. In the nineteenth century, in England Darwin and Spencer invented [*sic*] the principle of evolution. Out of these two theories arose a new ideology (*zhuyi*). This new ideology is called "anarchism."[38]

Similarly, Zhang Ji's discussion of anarchism traced it to the history of European socialism, whose origins he located in the French Revolution.[39] Chinese intellectuals were also already well aware that anarchism was not simply a critique of despotism (as with nihilism), but sought to abolish government and all the institutions connected with it; as Ma Xulun's essay indicates, they were also cognizant of the antinationalist thrust of anarchism.[40] Above all, however, scattered throughout these discussions are references to anarchism as a philosophy of social transformation, one that sought to put an end to the inequality of "rich and poor, noble and mean, young and old, and men and women"; Zhang Ji's discussion in particular emphasized the role anarchism played in Europe in the struggles of labor against capital.[41]

These fundamental aspects of anarchism would come to the fore when anarchism acquired an identity of its own after 1906. The reception of anarchism in this early period suggests, however, that what most impressed Chinese intellectuals initially were those aspects which anarchism seemed to share with Russian nihilism. In his study of the Russian influence on Chinese intellectuals at this time, Don Price has suggested that the identification of anarchism with nihilism went beyond what was justifiable in the sources available to Chinese intellectuals.[42] Young

38. Ma Xulun, "Ilosi da fengchao" (Great storm in Russia) (1902). See reprint in *WZFZYSX* 1:1–2. This statement is somewhat puzzling. Ma presumably meant that anarchism rose in response to the theories of Darwin and Spencer, as a socialist reaction to them. This was the meaning associated with anarchism in later years.
39. "Wuzhengfu zhuyi ji wuzhengfu dangzhi jingshen," 28–31.
40. "Ershi shijizhi xin zhuyi," 6.
41. "Wuzhengfu zhuyi ji wuzhengfu dangzhi jingshen," 33.
42. Price notes that Chinese used Kemuyama's book on anarchism primarily as a source on Russian revolutionaries. See *Russia and the Roots of the Chinese Revolution,* 122.

Chinese radicals who were attracted to anarchism in the years 1902–
1907 read anarchism through nihilist political practise: the struggle
against despotism whose most prominent feature was individual political action, especially assassination.

This reading of anarchism was possibly facilitated by the commonly
held image of anarchism (in Europe itself) at the turn of the century as a
source of terrorism. In Price's words, "nihilism and anarchism were linked
in the public eye . . . by connotations of violence, a fanatical hostility to the
existing order, and ruthless idealism."[43] After 1906 Chinese anarchists
would draw a clear distinction between anarchism and other seemingly
"anarchist" approaches to politics, and would also downplay (even renounce) the use of terrorism in favor of long-term strategies of social
transformation. Though Chinese intellectuals were aware early on of the
social dimension of anarchism, the awareness was at best marginal in their
appreciation of anarchism, which they understood as an "extreme revolutionism," the use of violent methods to overthrow despotism. The association with nihilism, furthermore, would persist in later years; in the 1920s
the anarchist writer Bajin (Ba Jin) still would include the Russian nihilists
within the heroic tradition of anarchism.[44]

The confounding of anarchism and nihilism among early Chinese revolutionaries was not fortuitous, nor may it be ascribed simply to the confusion created by the literature to which they had access. And it was not a
simple matter of a superficial resemblance between anarchist and nihilist
political tactics. Anarchism may not be reducible to nihilism; on the other
hand, it shared with nihilism a conception of politics that was deeply
moralistic, that allowed a perception of political action as the assertion of
individual moral authenticity. Chinese radicals of the early part of the
century, who made high moral purpose the measure of revolutionary
authenticity, discovered in anarchism a kindred political philosophy, and
in the nihilists the most striking models of its practise.

The radical movement that emerged in China in 1902–3 took as its
main object the overthrow of the Manchu despotism, which, in its resistance to the inclusion of the people in politics in a common struggle
against the forces that threatened the country, promised national extinc-
tion. As Mary Rankin and Don Price have demonstrated in their separate
studies of this radicalism, although its origins lay in a sharp sense of

---

43. Ibid.
44. Li Feigan (Ba Jin), in *Gemingde xianqu* (Vanguards of revolution) (Shanghai, 1928).

national crisis, once it came into existence the movement acquired a life of its own in generating an opposition to despotism beyond immediate nationalistic considerations: despotism must be opposed, not only because Manchu despotism sapped the strength of the nation but, more important, because it was contrary to "universal principle" and confined the "natural freedom" to which humanity was entitled.[45] Chinese radicals identified with the Russian nihilists, not because of a commonality between China's situation in the early twentieth century and the Russia of the 1860s, but because they shared the common goal, embedded in "universal principle," of overthrowing despotism. If assassination appeared in either case to be the most effective weapon in the struggle against despotism, we must remember that in both cases political despotism was very real and permitted few alternatives of political expression.

Nevertheless, there were alternatives (as was exemplified by the reformist movement of the constitutional monarchists and by Sun Yat-sen's revolutionary movement); and the political condition of despotism does not explain the attraction to assassination among young radicals or their sense of kinship with the Russian nihilists. The radical movement also generated a morality of its own, to which self-sacrifice in the struggle against despotism represented the highest embodiment of revolutionary authenticity. The heroic daring necessary in risking one's life in assassination attempts appears among this first generation of radicals to go hand in hand with a will to self-extinction apparent in the resort to suicide as a form of expression; the most celebrated example may be that of the woman revolutionary Qiu Jin who, following the assassination of a provincial governor in which she was implicated, refused to listen to those who urged her to flee, but stayed to be arrested and executed.[46] Wu Zhihui, who after 1907 would emerge as one of the most prominent of Chinese anarchists, in the early 1900s attempted suicide to protest against the government.[47] What assassination and suicide shared in common was what Zhang Ji in his essay described as the "spirit of self-sacrifice."

Beyond offering one of the few options of effective political expression in an environment that did not allow for politics, assassination represented to Chinese radicals not merely a practical means of political action

45. Price, *Russia and the Roots of the Chinese Revolution;* Mary B. Rankin, *Early Chinese Revolutionaries: Radical Intellectuals in Shanghai and Chekiang, 1902–1911* (Cambridge: Harvard University Press, 1974).
46. Rankin, *Early Revolutionaries,* 185.
47. Richard Wang, "Wu Chih-hui: An Intellectual and Political Biography" (Ph.D. diss., University of Virginia, 1976), 42.

but, in the suicidal risks that it entailed, an affirmation of individual moral commitment and revolutionary authenticity; or, as Price has noted, proof of "purity of motive" in political activity: "Since the revolutionary effort was one which imposed an obligation of self-sacrifice and which could not succeed without it, he [Ch'in Li-shan] felt it extremely important that revolutionaries eliminate the self-seeking considerations that produced timidity and dissension." Individual acts of political expression, even when their political futility was evident, served to affirm just such "purity of motive." The heroic tradition in Chinese politics provided one model for this kind of behavior; the Japanese samurai on the eve of the Meiji Restoration of 1868 (the *shishi,* or men of will) provided another. This was also the source of the affinity Chinese radicals felt for the "extreme revolutionism" of Western revolutionaries, in particular in Russia where

> hundreds of educated and privileged youth sacrificed their ease and status to propagandize the benighted peasantry and workingmen. And when this failed, there was the grim turn to violence—"the blood-and-iron tactic" of assassination but still in a spirit of self-sacrifice. Sofia Perovskaya almost epitomized the history and character of the revolutionary movement. She had "gone to the people," suffering all the hardships of a village schoolteacher and then conspired in the plots which ultimately killed Alexander II. At her trial she was particularly impressive, demanding that she be shown no clemency on the grounds of her sex; and she mounted the scaffold as calmly as any of her comrades.[48]

This moralistic dedication to self-sacrifice in the cause of revolution deeply impressed Chinese revolutionaries, whose own approach to revolution made a suicidal resignation to self-extinction preferable to living to fight another day. Anarchism, with its own preoccupation with authenticity, resonated with their "politics of authenticity" at a deep moral level. This attitude toward revolution, which left its imprint on Chinese anarchism at its very origins, would persist in later years, after Chinese radicals acquired a more sophisticated grasp of anarchism as a social philosophy and came to view terrorism as only a marginal tool of an anarchist revolution. Paris anarchists in 1907 glorified the actions of Qiu Jin (and her associate, Xu Xilin) for their selflessness. They themselves continued to insist that they were not concerned with success or failure but with truth. One of their number, Chu Minyi, went so far on one occasion as to suggest that assassination was justified if only because it had a purifying effect on the revolu-

---

48. Price, *Russia and the Roots of the Chinese Revolution,* 199.

tionary.[49] This may not be very surprising; the first generation of anarchists in China, including Wu Zhihui, Zhang Ji, and Shifu, were all graduates of the radical movement during the last decade of the Qing dynasty.

Ironically, this same spirit of self-sacrifice may provide a clue to understanding the association of anarchism with Buddhism. Disassociated from terror and violence, the spirit of self-sacrifice resonated with the "Bodhisattva ideal" in Buddhism. As we shall see, Buddhism provided an emotional space (as well as a literal one in the form of a Buddhist monastery) for the conversion to anarchism of the famous anarchist Shifu and his followers; and the Bodhisattva ideal was very much in their consciousness in their daily practices.[50] Buddhist monks were also visible among China's first anarchists; others preferred adopted names with Buddhist connotations.

ANARCHIST THEMES IN THE EARLY
REVOLUTIONARY MOVEMENT

The sparse literature available to Chinese radicals in the early part of the century was sufficient to indicate that anarchism was an integral current in the socialist tradition in Europe and, as such, encompassed much more than the antidespotism struggles of the nihilists in Russia, with their conspiratorial style of political action. Anarchism included an essential social dimension; as Zhang Ji put it in his essay, "anarchists trace all matters back to society."[51] This might have suggested, however abstractly, that the individualized mode of politics that characterized anarchist activity should be placed within the context of a broader social philosophy.

There is little evidence that an awareness of the broader social goals of anarchism had any significant immediate effect on revolutionary activity in this early phase. Rather, Chinese radicals read anarchism through the interpretation suggested by Russian nihilism. And where they associated it with broad goals, they perceived it through a moral utopianism, more often than not assimilating it to a native utopianism in which recognition of the new world situation of China was blended inperceptibly into a metaphysical cosmic vision. If the two readings of anarchism coincided, it was on the ground of a moralistic conception of politics that focused on

49. Chu Minyi, "Puji geming" (Universal revolution), *Xin shiji* (New era), no. 18 (19 October 1907): 3.

50. Edward Krebs, "Liu Ssu-fu and Chinese Anarchism, 1905–1915" (Ph.D. diss., University of Washington, 1977), 252–55.

51. "Wuzhengfu zhuyi ji wuzhengfu dangzhi jingshen," 36.

the individual as the harbinger of new values. In Cai Yuanpei's utopian fantasy, no less than in the activities of the bomb-throwing activists, it was the committed individual armed with a new vision who brought about political change.

This was consistent with the image of anarchism that prevailed at the turn of the century—in the West no less than in China. It was an image in whose propagation governments played a crucial role in representing anarchists as dangerous "extreme revolutionists." Yet it was not the only available image. Japanese radicals, from whom Chinese learned much of their radicalism at the time, already spoke of the social dimension of politics, and there were those in China who drew attention to the social problem in politics.

Ultimately, the social dimension in anarchism was irrelevant at this time because anarchism exerted the greatest appeal among radicals whose own conception of politics was highly moralistic and who rejected politics as the realm of selfishness against which they sought to establish their own public commitment in acts of selfless, or self-sacrificing, revolutionary endeavor. It is true that the impossibility of political action under the conditions of government despotism left them few choices. And at this time, society in a concrete sense was largely absent from politics, even from the politics of those who spoke of social change and social revolution. But there was an additional element in their case, a reaction to the emergence of politics that found its expression in the disassociation of the conception of the public from that of the political, and a tendency to view them as being antithetical to one another. The separation was one that would nourish anarchism over the years; for anarchism suggested that an authentically public existence could be achieved only outside of, and in opposition to, politics.

The new situation created by nationalist ideology provides the context for an understanding of the appeals of the "politics of authenticity" of anarchism to early Chinese revolutionaries. Not that nationalism fed anarchism, for it did not; but nationalism raised questions about politics, and about China's place in the world, that made for a receptivity to anarchism. The utopianism that appeared as the counterpoint to nationalist parochialism provided fecund grounds for anarchist cosmopolitanism. Ma Xulun's statement on the origin of anarchism also offers some support for James Pusey's suggestion that an appeal of anarchism at this time was the argument it provided against the Darwinian notions of conflict underlying nationalist fears; this would become more evident after 1906 when Chinese anarchists became familiar with Kropotkin's idea of "mutual aid" against "the survival of the fittest."[52]

Nationalism also raised the question of politics. In positing that the strength of the state was proportional to its ability to express social interests, nationalist ideology legitimized a notion of politics as the articulation of interests. The same nationalist ideology also called for the creation of an organic order in which social and state interests were harmonized in the interests of the whole. The contradiction was expressed in the disassociation of the public from the political, of the realm of organic unity from the realm of private interest. The contradiction could be resolved by asserting the priority of the state over society. Or it could be resolved by a reconstitution of society from the bottom up to achieve an organic (public) unity. Cai Yuanpei's utopian fantasy suggests that in anarchism Chinese radicals suspicious of politics may have discovered a guide to the latter. Its full articulation, however, would come after 1906 when anarchists established their own identity in their assertion of the priority of society over the state—indeed, against the state.

52. James Pusey, *China and Charles Darwin* (Cambridge: Harvard University Press, 1983), 370–433.

CHAPTER THREE

Science, Morality, and Revolution

Anarchism and the Origins of Social Revolutionary Thought in China

Anarchism emerged as a distinctive current in Chinese revolutionary thought when, in 1906–7, Chinese intellectuals studying abroad launched, almost simultaneously, two openly anarchist societies in Paris and in Tokyo. Before 1907 Chinese intellectuals had little appreciation of anarchism as an integral social philosophy. Rather, anarchist themes had been assimilated to the orientation of revolutionary thinking by intellectual dispositions that had originated in the revolutionary situation created by a new national consciousness. These dispositions were to persist in anarchist thinking. With the founding of these societies, however, they were rephrased within an anarchist language of revolution. Fundamental to this language was the idea of social revolution. Anarchist advocacy of social revolution was to open up new channels of lasting import in revolutionary thinking.

What brought about this change is more difficult to say. One change was in the access to anarchist literature. Intellectuals in Paris, in particular, discovered an anarchist tradition that was not to be subsumed under Russian nihilism, but had a history of its own as part of European socialism. The European anarchists they encountered had, moreover, an orientation that was significantly different from that of the early Chinese (or, for that matter, Japanese) radicals. The very organization into anarchist clusters gave an integrity and coherence to the anarchism they advocated; unlike their predecessors, who had viewed anarchism but as one weapon among others in the struggle against despotism, the intellectuals who organized the anarchist groups in Paris and Tokyo now promoted anarchism as an integral philosophy of global social transformation.

The political context, too, had changed. After 1905 the Manchu monarchy in China had decided to proceed to a constitutional form of government, which altered the conditions of political activity in China. The revolutionary struggle was no longer a struggle against a despotic government that allowed for no political expression; it was against a government that sought to recapture political legitimacy by making room for some measure of political representation. Radicals bent on overthrowing the Manchu government found that the enemy was no longer simply despotism; they had to come to terms with a state that sought to assimilate society to its own ends.

A new departure in the Chinese revolutionary movement had been announced in 1905 with the founding of Sun Yat-sen's Revolutionary Alliance (*Tongmeng hui*), which advocated a republican revolution against the constitutional monarchy that the Manchu government and its reformist supporters preferred. Based on Sun's own experiences in Europe, the Revolutionary Alliance had also incorporated in its political agenda a program of social revolution (the first advocacy of socialism in China), which added a social dimension to a revolution that had hitherto been conceived primarily in political terms.[1] The founders of Chinese anarchism were already members of this organization, which indeed was little more than an "alliance" born of the diffuse currents in the struggle against despotism. However ineffective it may have been politically, the Revolutionary Alliance did create a new space in which to think of issues of revolution in new ways. Anarchism represented one of those new ways.

ANARCHISM AND SOCIAL REVOLUTION

Anarchists were not the first to advocate social revolution in China, but they introduced seminal new elements into Chinese thinking on social revolution. The Revolutionary Alliance conception of social revolution was political in its orientation; it proposed to achieve social revolution through the agency of the state.[2] Anarchists, in their rejection of the state,

1. Earlier, Liang Qichao had toyed with the idea of socialism, but abandoned it when the Revolutionary Alliance began to advocate social revolution. For a discussion, see Arif Dirlik, "Socialism and Capitalism in Chinese Thought: The Origins," *Studies in Comparative Communism* 21, no. 2 (Summer 1987): 131–52.
2. Ibid.

challenged this conception and offered an alternative idea of social revolution that focused on the problem of cultural transformation and took the individual as its point of departure. The anarchist conception of social revolution was authentically social, moreover, in its focus on society (in contrast to the state) and in its insistence on popular participation in the process of revolution.

Anarchism was to make a lasting, if ambiguous, contribution to social revolutionary thought in China. As much the expression of a mood as a philosophical critique of politics, anarchism represented an antipolitical strain, a mistrust of political institutions and of politics in general, whose power was revealed in the diffusion of anarchist ideals over a broad spectrum of Chinese political thought over the next two decades. The anarchist message was a revolutionary one. Radicals intent upon the realization of a good society through an immediate revolutionary upheaval discovered a source of inspiration in the anarchist vision of community and a new humanity. In the 1920s Sun Yat-sen was inspired to remark on one occasion that anarchism was the ultimate goal of his Three People's Principles, a sentiment echoed by other Guomindang theoreticians. Critics of the Cultural Revolution of the 1960s have argued in recent years that the Cultural Revolution was inspired by anarchist ideas and attitudes that, having entered the Communist party in the early twenties, survived the long years of revolution to pervert Marxism in the party. It is possible to argue, I think, that some of the themes that emerged during the Cultural Revolution may indeed be viewed as faint echoes of themes in the Chinese revolution that had first been enunciated by anarchists.

The appeal of anarchism, however, was not restricted to revolutionaries. Conservatives who defended social and political order against the threat of revolution were also able to find in anarchism ideals on which to focus their yearning for a good society. This ambivalence, to the point of ideological schizophrenia, was reflected in the history of anarchism in China. The most radical current in Chinese socialist thought until the early twenties, anarchism was to end up in the service of Guomindang reaction in the late twenties. To be sure, anarchist relationship with the Guomindang went back to personal and political relationships that the early anarchists (many of whom were Revolutionary Alliance members) had established with later Guomindang leaders, relationships that existed independently of their ideology. Nevertheless, anarchist ideology, in its peculiar formulation of questions of interest and conflict in society, lent itself to counterrevolution almost as easily as to revolution.

The ambivalence that was to characterize Chinese anarchism was already apparent in the backgrounds of the two groups among the early anarchists and in the different anarchisms they propagated. The Paris group was organized as the New World Society (*Xinshijie she*) in 1906. It started publishing in 1907 a journal that lasted for a remarkable three years and over one hundred issues. This journal, the *New Era* (*Xin shiji*), was subtitled *La Tempoj Novaj* in Esperanto, probably after *Les Temps Nouveaux*, published by Jean Grave. The names of the society and its journal were indicative of the inclinations of the Paris anarchists, a group of intellectuals who had been baptized into revolutionary activity in the early 1900s. Li Shizeng, the moving spirit of the group intellectually, had been living in Paris since 1902. He had evidenced an internationalist orientation very early on, studied biology, and had become close friends in Paris with members of the family of the French anarchist-geographer Élisée Reclus, which probably launched him on the path to anarchism. Wu Zhihui, who had the major responsibility for publishing the *New Era,* had been involved in the early 1900s in radical patriotic activities in Japan and China. It was Li, according to Richard Wang, who persuaded Wu of the virtues of anarchism when they met in Paris in 1906. The group's activities were financed by the enterprises of its third important member, Zhang Jingjiang, which included a *dofu* factory and a restaurant–tea shop. They were all from elite families and, after 1905, members of the Revolutionary Alliance. From the beginning, they seemed to have little difficulty in reconciling their anarchist philosophy with their political involvements in China and abroad. In the 1920s, as unofficial Guomindang "elders," they would be involved in the Guomindang suppression, first, of the Communists and, then, of their own young anarchist followers. The importance of their ideological contribution to social revolutionary thought in China lies in the consistency of the ideology they propagated, not in the consistency with which they lived up to their own ideals.[3]

The Paris anarchists advocated a revolutionary futuristic anarchism,

3. For further information on the Paris anarchists, see Robert Scalapino and George T. Yu, *The Chinese Anarchist Movement* (Berkeley: Center for Chinese Studies, 1961); Peter Zarrow, "Chinese Anarchists: Ideals and the Revolution of 1911" (Ph.D. diss., Columbia University, 1987); Richard Wang, "Wu Chih-hui: An Intellectual and Political Biography" (Ph.D. diss., University of Virginia, 1976); Li Wenneng, *Wu Jingxian dui Zhongguo xiandai zhengzhide yingxiang* (The influence of Wu Jingxian [Zhihui] on modern Chinese politics), Taibei, 1973; Shao Kelu (Jacques Reclus), "Wo suorenshide Li Yuying xiansheng" (The Li Yuying [Shizeng] that I knew), tr. Huang Shuyi (Mme J. Reclus), *Zhuanji wenxue* (Biographical literature) 45, no. 3 (1983); Zhu Chuanyu, ed., *Li Shizeng zhuanji ziliao* (Materials for a biography of Li Shizeng), Taibei, 1979.

which introduced into Chinese socialist thought an unequivocally radical current in Western revolutionary thinking. Over the three years of its publication as a weekly, the *New Era* serialized long translations from European anarchists, such as Kropotkin, Bakunin, Malatesta, and Reclus. These translations, reprinted over and over in anarchist journals and special compendia after 1911, provided a major source of radical literature in China until the early twenties; by 1920 anarchist literature available in Chinese was unmatched in scope and comprehensiveness by any other social and political philosophy of European origin. Students of Chinese anarchism have pointed out that anarchism provided not only radical literature but a language of radicalism that facilitated the efflorescence of socialism in China in the twenties. The Paris anarchists played a major part in making this language available.

At about the same time that the *New Era* started publication in Paris, Chinese anarchists in Tokyo established a Society for the Study of Socialism (*Shehui zhuyi jiangxihui*), which published its own journals, *Natural Justice (Tianyibao)* and the *Balance (Hengbao)*. Intellectually, the moving spirits behind both the society and its journal were the classical scholar Liu Shipei and his spouse, He Zhen, who was probably responsible for the more radical aspects of Tokyo anarchists' ideology. *Natural Justice* and *Balance* were very revolutionary in tone and in their analyses of the plight of women and the lower classes in China, which were more concrete than anything to be found in the *New Era*. Nevertheless, Tokyo anarchists propagated an antimodernist anarchism that stressed the virtues of agrarian society and preferred the "freedom" from political interference that prevailed under the imperial state in China to the "despotism" of the modern nation-state. Whereas *New Era* writers discovered the archetypal anarchist vision in Kropotkin, Tokyo anarchists gave the greatest prominence among foreign anarchists to Tolstoy.[4]

Natural Justice lasted for one year. After Liu's return to China in 1908, he apparently served as an agent provocateur for the monarchy and was prominent after 1911 as one of China's foremost conservatives. Although *Natural Justice* did not have the long-term influence of *New Era,* it was very influential in its time because of the large number of Chinese students in Japan and because of its proximity to China, which gave it an edge over the *New Era* in terms of accessibility. Liu's antimodernist anarchism, moreover, sensitized him to certain important

4. For the Tokyo anarchists, see Zarrow, "Chinese Anarchists." For the earlier period of Liu's activities, see Martin Bernal, "Liu Shih-p'ei and National Essence," in *The Limits of Change,* ed. C. Furth (Cambridge: Harvard University Press, 1976).

questions in Chinese society; some of his analyses of the problems of modernity in China anticipated themes that were to become prominent in Chinese radical thinking in later years.

THE PLACE OF ANARCHISM IN LATE QING POLITICS

The rise of interest in anarchism at this time has prompted Martin Bernal to observe that 1907 marked "the victory of anarchism over Marxism" in China under the influence of a similar shift of interest among Japanese radicals at the same time.[5] There is no question that, as with all Chinese socialism, Japanese sources and radicals played a significant part in Chinese anarchism (the term for anarchism, *wuzhengfu zhuyi*, first used in Chinese in 1903, was of Japanese derivation). Nevertheless, this view is misleading, and not only because it is erroneous to describe as "Marxist" the socialism of the Revolutionary Alliance, which is what Bernal has in mind in referring to "marxism." The major center of Chinese anarchism before 1911 was Paris, and shifts in Japan had little to do with the anarchism of the Paris anarchists. While some Revolutionary Alliance members began to show interest in assassination activities after 1907, it is not correct to read this as an interest in anarchism, even though assassination was associated in some circles with anarchism. The change in revolutionary methods can be more concretely explained by the political dilemma which the Qing dynasty's constitutional reforms presented revolutionaries, who were now faced with deflation of their revolutionary ardor. Revolutionary Alliance socialists, moreover, did not abandon the kind of socialism they had advocated in 1905–1907, for these ideas persisted in their thinking in later years. Anarchism may have added new themes to their conception of social revolution, but the best that can be said is that the proliferation of new ideas of social revolution complicated social revolutionary thinking and possibly added to ideological confusion over socialism. A clear distinction would not be drawn between anarchism and socialism until 1913–14; nor between anarchism and Marxism until the early 1920s.

It is futile, I think, to look for a single, all-encompassing explanation for the attraction anarchism had for the Chinese intellectuals who in these years engaged in "anarchist" activity or professed belief in anarchism. In explaining why anarchism has remained alive as a revolution-

5. M. Bernal, "The Triumph of Anarchism over Marxism," in *China in Revolution*, ed. M. C. Wright (New Haven: Yale University Press, 1971).

ary faith in the West in spite of the failure of anarchists to achieve any important results, James Joll has observed that a basic strength of anarchism has been its offer of something for everyone; the diffuseness of anarchist ideology—its weakness as a practical radical ideology—has been its strength as a social philosophy.[6] This offers insights into the appeals of anarchism in China as well. Converts to anarchism in early-twentieth-century China ranged from disciples of revolutionary terrorism, who found in anarchism justification for their activities, to modernists attracted to anarchist scientism, to Buddhist monks, who discovered in the anarchist message of love something akin to Buddhist ideals, to esthetes, who perceived beauty in the anarchist ideal of a beautiful society. Not everyone who found something of value in anarchism upheld, therefore, a coherent philosophy of anarchism.

Such profusion of appeal militates against easy explanations, especially explanations based on vague notions of outside "influence" that ignore the dispositions of the influenced. Foreign sources were important for anarchism, as they were for all Chinese socialism, but it was the intellectual and emotional needs generated by a society in revolutionary crisis that ultimately endowed anarchism with meaning for Chinese intellectuals. For all their contradictoriness, the varied reasons for attraction to anarchism shared a common ground in the anarchist vision of social revolution, which, however abstract and utopian, spoke to the immediate concerns of Chinese intellectuals who, in the midst of the political and ideological crisis of Chinese society, were uncertain about their place in their society and the place of their society in the world. In its affirmation of the essential unity of human beings, anarchism provided a counterpoint to the division of humanity into nations, races, and classes, which in the early part of the century confronted Chinese intellectuals as the reality of their world. And in its affirmation of the irreducible significance of the individual, anarchism provided a counterpoint to the preoccupation with the state that sought to expand its powers at the cost of social autonomy.

It was the anarchist view of the individual as a social being, a basic ontological premise of anarchism, that pointed to possibilities beyond social alienation.[7] Although anarchism was still associated with individ-

---

6. James Joll and D. Apter, eds., *Anarchism Today* (New York: Anchor Books, 1972), 248.
7. For a discussion of this point, see Richard Saltman, *The Social and Political Thought of Michael Bakunin* (Westport, Conn.: Greenwood Press, 1983), chaps. 1 and 2.

ual action and assassination after 1907, the social and cultural implications of the anarchist ideal of revolution would gradually move to the forefront of Chinese thinking on anarchism and leave a lasting impression on Chinese social revolutionary thought. China's most respected anarchist, Shifu, started his career with assassination activities, then moved away from assassination as he became familiar with anarchist philosophy. After the republican Revolution of 1911, anarchists distinguished themselves in educational and social mobilization activities, including the establishment of the first modern labor unions in China. In the midst of the wave of individualism that swept Chinese youth in the late 1910s, it was the anarchists who, in their insistence on the essential sociableness of human beings, kept alive social issues and played a major part in the emergence of widespread concern with society and social revolution in the aftermath of the May Fourth Movement of 1919.

These social concerns, as well as the anarchist vision of a world free of division, place anarchism at the heart of the emergent political discourse in China in the late nineteenth and the early twentieth century. The reconsideration of the relationship between public and private, between the individual and society, society and the state, all provoked by a reconsideration of China's place in the world, were central to this discourse. An emergent nationalism lay at the root of all these questions. Revolutionary Alliance socialism was an integral component of the search for national integration. Anarchism, likewise, may be seen as part of the utopian cosmopolitanism that emerged with, and as a counterpoint to, Chinese nationalism. On the other side of the political spectrum, as we have seen, Liang Qichao, like his teacher Kang Youwei before him, was dissatisfied with institutions that divided people, and saw in the creation of an organic society the ultimate fulfillment of the human promise. This promise was also central to anarchism, although the additional considerations anarchists brought to the quest had revolutionary implications that distinguish their views from those of Liang and others. The centrality of the concern to contemporary political discourse, nevertheless, suggests why anarchism might have seemed much less peripheral to contemporary politics than it does in hindsight.

Anarchism is ultimately a philosophy of the individual, not of individualism as an end in itself, as is assumed by those who confound anarchism with libertarianism, but of the individual in his or her relationship to society. The preoccupation with the self had already emerged by the early part of this century as a feature of Chinese thinking in the activities of young radicals who believed that in selfless activity lay the salvation of

their society. Anarchism provided a systematic philosophical explanation
for the problem of the self: politics, in the anarchist view, was the realm
of oppression, authority, and division; the hope of community rested
with the self purged of the accumulated corruption of institutions of
power. The message had a powerful appeal among intellectuals who had
already become uncertain of their relationship to existing social institutions. It is not surprising that the message had the greatest influence
among members of the Chinese elite who felt deeply their alienation from
the institutions of power on which they had been nourished. Anarchism is
by no means restricted in its appeals to the elite, but it has everywhere
found its most cogent spokesmen among the elite for the simple reason
that the alienation of the self from power is more an elite than a popular
problem. In the years after 1911 anarchists would take the lead in popular mobilization. Nevertheless, from the beginning, anarchism's most eloquent proponents were members of the Chinese elite who, having been
alienated from existing social relations, turned to new ideas of community to redefine their relationship to society—the almost exclusive concern of the first generation of Chinese anarchists.

The lasting contribution of anarchists to Chinese social revolutionary
thought would be a redefinition of the relationship between intellectuals
and society, however abstractly the latter was conceived. Indeed, the
significant impact of anarchist philosophy on Chinese intellectuals lay
not in its justification of individual acts of violence, but in its turning
them to the articulation of this relationship. Anarchism provided Chinese intellectuals with their first genuinely social conception of social
revolution, which not only pointed to society as the proper realm of
change but placed the responsibility for changing society upon social
activity. This conception led to a reading of the problems of changing
China that anticipated questions that would assume increasing importance in Chinese social thought in later years. For reasons I shall explain, the logic of the anarchist idea of social change brought to the
surface early on the problem of cultural revolution, the moral and intellectual transformation of individuals. In raising questions about individual transformation, anarchists also raised questions about the social
institutions that obstructed individual transformation; they were the
first Chinese intellectuals to point unequivocally to problems of women
and the family, which continue to be central problems of Chinese social
thought. They were the first to point to the need to bridge the gap
between classes, especially intellectuals and laborers, by turning intellectuals into laborers, and laborers into intellectuals. To resolve all these

problems, finally, they called for a social revolution that made revolution itself a utopia, which would have dramatic consequences for the Chinese revolution in the twentieth century.

Within Chinese socialism, then, anarchism provided the counterpoint to state-oriented strategies of change. The Revolutionary Alliance argument had proposed to use the state to prevent the devastation of society by conflicting interests. That argument had addressed the prospects of capitalism for China. The anarchist argument addressed the second important issue of the day, the state. Anarchists envisaged the abolition of interest in society through a total revolutionary transformation whose basic premise was the destruction of the state. Convinced of the essential sociableness of human beings, they believed that a genuine human community could be realized if institutional obstacles to free association could be abolished. Such institutions included the family and the capitalist economy; but the state, as the mightiest of these institutions and the protector of all partial interests in its defense of the political order, was the chief enemy of human society. As interest in socialism had accompanied the initial realization that capitalism was not only a means to economic development but also a primary source of the problems of modern society, anarchism expressed a parallel apprehension that the modern nation-state not only reflected the will of the people but also served as a dehumanizing vehicle of control and oppression, an obstacle to the human liberation that revolution promised.

Both the Paris and the Tokyo anarchists subscribed to these basic premises of anarchism. Since they differed widely in their vision of anarchist society in history, their views are best discussed separately.

THE PARIS ANARCHISTS

Whereas Revolutionary Alliance socialists had proposed social revolution as a supplement to the task of political revolution, anarchists made it a substitute for the latter. In one of the earliest statements of the Paris anarchists' position on revolution, Wu Zhihui drew a clear distinction between social and political revolutions:

> Those of old who advocated revolution spoke only of the political aspect of revolution but did not emphasize society. They desired to abolish despotism to extend people's sovereignty, sought legal freedom but not freedom of livelihood, political but not social or economic equality. They sought the happiness and welfare of one country or some of the people, not the happiness and welfare of the masses of the world.

"Socialist revolution" (*shehui zhuyizhi geming*) would

> seek equality, freedom, happiness and welfare for society, make justice
> (*gongdao*) the measure of achievement, expunge whatever harms society, or
> runs contrary to this goal—such as despotism and classes, the roots of all
> calamity, institute scientific progress to achieve a real world civilization, and,
> ultimately, establish a humanitarian commonweal (*rendao datong*) and a
> paradisiacal world (*shijie jilo*).

Socialist revolution, Wu believed, would rid society of all the "poison"
inherited from the past and establish what was appropriate to social life.[8]

The anarchist social revolutionary idea differed from that of the Revolutionary Alliance both in goals and in method. The Revolutionary
Alliance conception of socialism had been an instrumental one: "social
revolution" as a policy tool for the state to achieve social harmony and
stability. The anarchist conception was a total one, which called for a
total reorganization of society in all its aspects to realize an all-
encompassing vision. In his long essay "Anarchism," Chu Minyi described four goals of anarchism: (1) to abolish authority (and its back-
bone, the military) to establish humanitarianism, (2) to abolish laws to
institute freedom, (3) to abolish all inherited class distinctions (as embodied in the teachings of the sages) to establish equality, (4) to abolish
private property and capital to establish communism (*gongchan*).[9] A
major essay, written by Li Shizeng and Chu Minyi, describing the anarchist view of revolution, made even more explicit the ethical objectives
underlying anarchist goals. The eight "meanings" of revolution, the
essay stated, were freedom, fraternity (*boai*), public-mindedness, reform,
equality, universal unity (*datong*), truth, and progress.[10] These goals
were to be achieved through the abolition of marriage, property, family
and familial relations, the private ownership of land, and racial and
national boundaries.[11]

For the anarchists, social revolution was different from political, not
only in its goals but also, even more fundamentally, in its means. Whereas
political revolution was revolution of the "few," social revolution was
the revolution of the many—the common people (*pingmin*). Anarchists

8. Qian Ye (Wu Zhihui), *Jiu shehui zhuyi yizheng gemingzhi yilun* (Clarifying the
meaning of revolution through socialism), (Paris: Xin shiji congshu, 1906), 2, 4.

9. Min, "Wuzhengfu shuo" (Anarchism), *Xin shiji* (New era [hereafter *XSJ*]), no. 60
(15 August 1908): 8. This was part of a long article that ran in *XSJ*, no. 31 (25 January
1908) through no. 60.

10. Li Shizeng and Chu Minyi, *Geming* (Revolution), (Paris: Xin shiji congshu,
1907), 7.

11. Min, "Wuzhengfu shuo," *XSJ*, no. 38: 4. Also see "Liyun datong shiyi" (Explanation of great unity in the *Evolution of Rites*) in the same issue.

believed that "overthrowing the government must have the recognition and the consent of the majority."[12] To this end, they specified five methods of revolution: propaganda (books, magazines, lectures), mass associations, mass uprisings, popular resistance (opposition to taxes and conscription, strikes and boycotts), and assassination (propaganda by the deed).[13] Anarchists themselves were not always consistent on the question of methods; to appreciate their preferences, it is necessary to keep in mind their general perception of social revolution. Anarchists rejected not only political institutions but politics as well, even though an editorial in *New Era* referred on one occasion to the revolution they advocated as "a political revolution of pure socialism" (*chuncuide shehui zhuyizhi zhengzhi geming*).[14] They believed, however, that authentic social revolution could not be imposed from above, through inherently authoritarian institutions.[15] Even though they were members of the Revolutionary Alliance, their idea of social revolution was counterposed explicitly to the social revolutionary program of Sun Yat-sen, both because of the reliance of the latter on the state and for its ambiguities concerning the role of the "many" in the revolution.

Anarchists themselves conceived of social revolution as a process of social activity, a "revolution of all the people" (*quantizhi geming*).[16] The revolutionary methods they proposed were all intended to stimulate such social activity. Neither the Paris nor the Tokyo anarchists engaged actively in assassination activity or social mobilization, but they looked favorably upon others who did so. They alluded with enthusiasm to the Pingxiang uprising in Hunan in 1906 and to its leader, Ma Fuyi.[17] They wrote with approval of the self-sacrificing spirit demonstrated by Xu Xilin and Qiu Jin.[18] Assassination undertaken in the spirit of self-sacrifice and with a clear commitment to "universal principle" (*gongli*), the anarchists believed, furthered the cause of revolution and humanity.[19] This notion that the beau geste may be more important than living to fight

12. Min (Chu Minyi), "Puji geming" (Universal revolution). *XSJ*, no. 17 (12 October 1907): 2. This long article ran through five issues.
13. Li and Chu, *Geming*, 8.
14. "Yu yourenshu lun Xin shiji" (Discussion of the *New Era* in response to a letter from a friend), *XSJ*, no. 3 (6 July 1907): 1.
15. Min, "Puji geming," *XSJ*, no. 17 (12 October 1907): 4.
16. Min, "Wuzhengfu shuo," *XSJ*, no. 34 (15 February 1908): 4.
17. *Pingxiang gemingjun yu Ma Fuyi* (The Pingxiang revolutionary army and Ma Fuyi) (Paris: Xin shiji congshu, 1907).
18. Zhen (Li Shizeng), "Xisheng jishen jili yiqiu gongdaozhi daibiao Xu Xilin" (Xu Xilin who sacrificed his body and his interest in the pursuit of the public way), *XSJ*, no. 12 (7 September 1907).
19. Min, "Puji geming," *XSJ*, no. 18 (19 October 1907): 2.

another day revealed the ethical impulse that underlay the anarchists' idea of revolution, and distinguished them from latter-day revolutionaries in China, to whom the success of revolution would be far more important than gestures of personal authenticity. "Give me liberty or give me death," Chu Minyi was to declaim in his defense of violence as a revolutionary method.[20] The rebels they lauded were not anarchists, nor were their activities intended to achieve anarchist goals; what counted was the act, the struggle itself, not its achievements. This does not mean that anarchists viewed violence as an end in itself; rather, they condoned violence only if it had a moral purpose. Chu Minyi observed in connection with Xu Xilin that violence was an expression of political desperation.[21] Wu Zhihui explained that violence was necessary because, under despotism, it was impossible otherwise to educate people to achieve humanitarian goals.[22] Anarchists agreed, moreover, that violence was effective only to the extent that it "moved people's hearts" and aroused mass support for the cause of revolution.

If violence without a clear moral and social sense would degenerate into mindless terrorism, the anarchists believed, revolution without education would turn into unconscious uprising.[23] Of all the methods of revolution the anarchists promoted, education was the most fundamental. Anarchists called for simultaneous destruction and construction. Violence could achieve destruction, but construction required education, which was the ultimate justification even for revolutionary violence.[24] If the masses could be won over to the revolution, then social revolution would take a peaceful course, and anarchist goals could be achieved gradually.[25] Education to the anarchists was not simply an instrument of revolution, it was the equivalent of revolution:

> Revolution will be effective only if, with the spread of education, people get rid of their old customs and achieve a new life. From the perspective of effectiveness, this means that if there is education for revolution before the revolution is undertaken, there will be nothing impossible about revolution. Therefore, anarchist revolution . . . is nothing but education.[26]

20. *XSJ*, no. 17 (12 October 1907): 3.
21. Ibid.
22. Wu, "Jiu shehui zhuyi," 8.
23. Ran (Wu Zhihui), "Wuzhengfu zhuyi yi jiaoyu wei geming shuo" (Anarchists make revolution through education), *XSJ*, no. 65 (19 September 1908): 11.
24. "Yu canzheng lixianzhi tongbao yitan" (A discussion with a compatriot who approves of constitution), *XSJ*, no. 16 (5 October 1907): 2–3.
25. Min, "Gemingzhi liuxue" (On revolution spilling blood), *XSJ*, no. 103:5–6.
26. Ran, "Wuzhengfu zhuyi yi jiaoyu wei geming shuo," 11.

As for the nature of the education necessary for anarchist revolution, Wu Zhihui explained that "there is no education aside from education in morality which encompasses truth and public-mindedness, such as reciprocal love, equality, freedom; all education is anarchist that encompasses truth and public-mindedness, including experimental science, and so forth."[27] Chu Minyi observed that while revolution (as an act) served a transient purpose, education lasted forever in its effects and transformed people endlessly. Unlike government-sponsored (*youzhengfude*) education, which taught militarism, legal-mindedness, religion, or, in short, obedience to authority, anarchist (*wuzhengfude*) education taught truth and public-mindedness, that is, freedom, equality, and the ability for self-government.[28]

Criticism of political revolution by anarchists yields further insights into the nature of the social revolution they advocated. Anarchists opposed political revolution because they believed that it only served to substitute new, and worse, inequalities for old ones. Political revolution, Wu stated, had "diminished misery in politics but increased economic misery."[29] In a more comprehensive statement criticizing proponents of democracy and the Republic, Chu Minyi observed:

> They do not know that freedom is the freedom of the rich, equality is the equality of the wealthy. The misery of the poor is the same as of old. What is freedom and equality to the poor? The evils of political despotism have now been replaced by the poison of economic monopoly.[30]

All anarchists concurred with Chu's view that this "poison" was the product of a bad social system where a few, by monopolizing wealth, managed to live off the "sweat and blood" of the many.[31] In other words, the political revolutions that had created democracies and republics had made things worse by giving capitalists access to power, thus increasing their ability to exploit laborers. Under these systems, everything served the interests of the rich. Even science was utilized, not for the benefit of humanity but in the interests of the powerful. Capitalists, whether they were good or bad as individuals, were motivated in their activities by the pursuit of profit. While machinery had made unlimited

27. Ibid.
28. See "Wuzhengfu shuo," installments in *XSJ*, nos. 40–47.
29. Wu, "Jiu shehui zhuyi," 2.
30. Min, "Shenlun minzu minquan shehui" (Discussion of national and democratic society), *XSJ*, no. 6 (27 July 1907): 4.
31. Min, "Bagong" (Strikes), *XSJ*, no. 92 (10 April 1909): 5–8.

production possible, people did not benefit from production, because capitalists used machines in their search for profit. When production increased to the point where they could not find consumers for their products, they shut down production, throwing laborers out of work and causing immense misery. In a statement reminiscent of Revolutionary Alliance views on capitalism, Chu Minyi observed that as long as such a system prevailed, the advance of the "industrial arts" (*gongyi*) only served to create poor people by decreasing the need for labor: "People do not realize that the more advanced the industrial arts, the richer are the rich and the poorer the poor."[32] Those who advocated social revolution, Chu noted, were those who understood the failure of the capitalist system. He himself advocated "a political revolution" against rulers (literally "a revolution for political rights," *quanli geming*), and "an economic revolution" against capitalists (literally, "a revolution for livelihood," *shengji geming*).[33] While such a program sounded similar to that of the Revolutionary Alliance, its premises were quite different: Revolutionary Alliance writers saw a republican political revolution as a means of carrying out the social revolution; anarchists believed that a republican revolution would only increase the power of the bourgeoisie, the class they had in mind, though they did not use the term.

Anarchists acquired these ideas, as did Sun Yat-sen, from observations on the persistence of inequality in European society.[34] They also believed, with Sun, that inequality was much more serious in the West than it was in China.[35] But, unlike Sun, they did not think that such problems could be resolved or prevented through government action. Commenting on a letter from a "friend" who thought that constitutional government could take measures to forestall the emergence of inequality in China, an editorial in the *New Era* observed that it was only prejudice for government that sustained "faith in the ability of government to secure peace, and the refusal to see that government itself obstructed the advance of humanitarianism, that it was the source itself of all evils."[36] Although anarchists discussed economic issues, politics and the state were the focal point of their opposition to political revolution. Their mistrust of political revolution was grounded in their belief that political institutions in society only

32. Min, "Gongren" (Workers), *XSJ*, no. 79 (26 December 1908): 4.
33. Min, "Bagong," 8.
34. Min, "Gongren," 4.
35. Min, "Puji geming," *XSJ*, no. 18 (19 October 1907): 2.
36. Ibid., *XSJ*, no. 17, 4.

represented the interests of the minority that commanded wealth and power. Like the European anarchists, whose philosophy they accepted in toto, Chinese anarchists were opposed to all kinds of government, no matter how different in form or substance of the relationship between state and society. Their opposition to capitalism was itself encompassed within their opposition to the state, for it was the state, with its laws, armies, and police, they believed, that defended the interests of the power-ful in society.[37]

In the intellectual atmosphere that prevailed in China during the first decade of the century, these ideas were not likely to appeal to many. The issue of the day was the reorganization of political institutions to create a stronger state, one that could unify and defend the country; the revolution-aries added strident anti-Manchuism. It is not surprising that anarchist ideas drew considerable criticism, mainly from other revolutionaries; it is somewhat surprising, however, that the exchanges between anarchists and their opponents were carried out in a relatively mild tone, in contrast to later controversies among socialists. The acrimonious exchange between Wu Zhihui and Zhang Binglin in 1908 was the exception. Anarchists themselves saved their most vituperous rhetoric for the Manchu govern-ment and Liang Qichao's constitutionalists. In other cases, they responded to their critics with patience, explaining their position with laborious ef-fort, careful not to offend fellow revolutionaries.[38] The reasons for this effort are not complex. In spite of their radical departure from republican ideology, most of the anarchists remained members of the Revolutionary Alliance, tied to it through personal relationships. The disagreement was among "friends."

To some of the critics of the anarchists, their major weakness was their idealism, which blinded them to the realities of Chinese society, especially the backwardness of the people, who did not have the educational and moral qualifications required by anarchist principles. But the majority of critics focused on the implications of anarchism for China's national struggle, especially its possible consequences in undermining the anti-Manchu struggle and rendering China vulnerable to further aggression by other nations.

To the charge of idealism, anarchists responded that while they were idealists, they were not blind. The struggle for anarchism had to be immediate, they argued, but they did not expect to achieve their goals for

37. Ibid., 2–3.
38. Min, "Wuzhengfu shuo," *XSJ*, no. 31 (25 January 1908): 2.

a long time to come. They believed, however, that the struggle was worth the undertaking because anarchism was the world trend, a necessary end of human evolution that had the backing of scientific demonstration.[39] They also added, indignantly, that while the moral and educational level of the people in China might be low, it was no lower than that of the officials who governed them.

Most of the exchanges, however, revolved around the issue of nationalism. In these exchanges the Paris anarchists demonstrated their ability to be flexible about their ideals, a characteristic that would mark their careers. On the issue of anti-Manchuism they were firm. They believed that the emperor should be overthrown—not because he was Manchu, but because he was the emperor.[40] They were unwilling to condone the racism that was implicit in the anti-Manchu arguments of the republicans, and they spoke reprovingly of the "revanchism" of nationalists such as Wu Yue, who had attempted to assassinate a group of Manchu officials in 1905. Racism, they believed, only served to reinforce boundaries between different peoples, which obstructed evolution toward a better society. They were willing to support patriotism only if it did not lead to hatred or fear of other nations and races.[41]

They were more willing to go along with republican revolution. "Political revolution is the starting point; social revolution is the ultimate goal," Li Shizeng and Chu Minyi stated.[42] Republican revolution was to be supported, the Paris anarchists believed, because it would move Chinese society a step closer to socialism. While their patriotism no doubt was an element in their willingness to compromise with republicanism, they may also have derived their inspiration from their intellectual mentor, Élisée Reclus, who himself had been a supporter of republicanism in France. The Paris anarchists viewed the state historically and believed that republican government was more advanced than monarchy in its willingness to share power with the people, at least some of the people. There were some qualms about this view. Chu Minyi observed on one occasion that constitutional government, in giving citizens the illusion of sharing power with them, caused the transfer of loyalty from the family (as under despotism) to the state; this was the main reason for the greater strength and resilience of constitutional governments: the people, having an interest in

39. Zhen (Li Shizeng), "Bo Xin shiji congshu Geming" (A refutation of *Revolution* in the *New Era* compendium), *XSJ*, no. 5 (20 July 1907): 1–2. This was Li's response to a criticism of *Revolution*.
    40. Li and Chu, *Geming*, 1.
    41. Min, "Shenlun minzu minquan shehui," 4.
    42. Li and Chu, *Geming*, 1.

the state, were more willing to serve in its defense.[43] This argument was commonplace at the time among nationalists who wanted a stronger China. Though Chu did not draw any conclusions from this observation, the implication was obvious that constitutional government made the task of achieving anarchism more difficult; *New Era* anarchists opposed Manchu establishment of a constitution as a deceptive measure that aimed to achieve greater power for the Manchu throne, a feeling they shared with other revolutionaries.[44] Otherwise, they viewed constitutionalism as a step toward anarchism, not away from it. They explained on a number of occasions that they advocated socialism not as a substitute for republicanism, but because socialism included republicanism, insisting only that the revolution seek to go beyond republican government.[45] One of the Paris anarchists would become involved in politics after the establishment of the Republic in 1912; the others continued to make efforts to advance the cause of revolution through education and refused to participate formally in politics. Their informal activities would be another matter.

Anarchists also dismissed the argument that China needed nationalism because it suffered from foreign aggression, or that their revolution would render China vulnerable to further aggression. To the first, Li responded that foreign aggression did not change the problem of oppression qualitatively; it only made heavier the burden of revolutionaries who had to struggle against foreign oppression in addition to their struggle against the Chinese ruling class. To the second, they responded with their faith, characteristic of anarchist attitudes throughout, that since the revolution was to be universal in scope, other states would be too busy coping with pressure from their own populations to engage in aggression against China.[46] Besides, they pointed out, the people's militia, which would replace the regular army, would be more effective in defending China than a regular army, which only served the interests of those in power.

To see the anarchist idea of social revolution only in political and social terms would be to see only a part, and not the most fundamental part, the premise, of the anarchist argument. Ultimately, this idea of revolution was a moral one: it sought not just to transform institutions

43. Min, "Puji geming," *XSJ*, no. 23 (23 November 1907): 3–4. For Reclus's views, see Marie Fleming, *The Anarchist Way to Socialism: Élisée Reclus and Nineteenth Century European Anarchism* (London: Croom and Helm, 1979).
44. Ran, "Rui Fang" (Rui Fang), *XSJ*, no. 9 (17 August 1907): 3–4.
45. Min, "Shenlun minzu minquan shehui," 3.
46. Zhuhun/Zhen, "Laishu/fuda" (Letter and answer), *XSJ*, no. 6 (27 July 1907): 1.

but rather to transform human psychology, which to the anarchists was at once the point of departure for and the goal of revolution. Human psychology was bound up with the question of the role of interest in society which the anarchists, unlike Sun Yat-sen, saw not just as an economic but also as a moral question.

To the anarchists, the test of a true revolution was whether it was "public" in its orientation or, in a more literal rendering, whether it pursued "the public way" (*gongdao*). This was also the ultimate test of whether a revolution was a social revolution. As Li put it: "What we speak of as a revolution of the many and a revolution of the few refers to whether it is really public (*gong*) or private (*si*), not to the actual number of people involved at any one time."[47] These ideas were crucial to Chinese political thinking at the turn of the century and place the anarchists squarely in the context of contemporary thought. The terms *gong* and *si* had slightly different meanings in different contexts, but they were always juxtaposed as opposites. *Si* could mean selfishness, partiality, or particularity; *gong* denoted selflessness, impartiality, or universality. In all these usages, however, *si* implied favoring what was of interest to the self, while *gong* meant the ability to transcend self-interest and to realize or to express the good of the many. In the anarchist view, revolution was a process whereby particular interest was abolished to be replaced by public concerns in human minds, society, and politics. The basic goal of revolution was, therefore, moral; specifically, it was the creation of "public morality" (*gongde*).[48] Chinese anarchists believed, as do anarchists in general, that public-mindedness, an instinctive sociability, as it were, was innate in human beings; the task of revolution was not so much to create public morality out of nothing as to abolish the institutions that stood in the way of its realization. Chu Minyi pointed to morality as the distinctive characteristics of humankind and described as the goal of the education he proposed the achievement of true morality, which implied the abolition of all distinctions between self and others.[49] The ultimate goal of revolution was to achieve unity on a universal scale, a unity that was not simply social but also ethical and spiritual.

Partiality, in the anarchist view, was the root cause of all the problems of contemporary society. To quote Chu again: "Contemporary society is a self-seeking and self-interested society (*zisi zilizhi shehui*). A self-seeking

47. Zhen, "Tanxue" (On learning), *XSJ*, nos. 7 and 21 (3 August and 9 November 1907); no. 7:1.
48. Ran, "Wuzhengfu zhuyi yi jiaoyu wei geming shuo," 10.
49. Min, "Wuzhengfu shuo," *XSJ*, no. 38 (14 March 1908): 2.

society is not a true society, a self-interested society is not a fair (*gongping*) society."[50] The separation of self from others was not just a social problem; it was contrary to the very "organic structure" (*jitizhi jiegou*) of natural existence.[51] Anarchism, they believed, promised to do away with this separation and, with it, considerations of interest as a determinant of human behavior:

> Anarchism means no national or racial boundaries. Even more important, it means no distinction between self and others, no notion of benefiting the self and harming others. When this has been achieved, true freedom, true equality, true fraternity will appear. That is why anarchism accords with public-mindedness and truth.[52]

On these same grounds anarchists rejected competition as a determinant of existence, insisting that mutual aid was the source of human evolution.

This opposition to partial interest on the grounds of its basic immorality was not only the ethical basis for anarchist opposition to politics and capitalism, it was also the basis for anarchist disagreements with fellow revolutionaries. Racism (*zhongzu zhuyi*) and nationalism (*guojia zhuyi*) were, according to the anarchists, just such expressions of partiality. Anarchists opposed enmity to the Manchus as Manchus, who ought to be opposed because they selfishly held on to political power. Nationalism was bad because it fostered unjustified hostility to the people of other nations.[53] Selfishness declined, they believed, as the scope of human loyalties expanded. Thus: "The advance from the selfishness of the individual to racism and patriotism, the advance from racism and patriotism to socialism represent the progress of universal principle (*gongli*) and conscience (*liangxin*)."[54] Not until all boundaries had been abolished could humanity achieve "universal principle." This, the anarchists argued, ought to be the guiding goal of the Chinese revolution.

For these reasons the Paris anarchists rejected China's heritage in uncompromising language. That certain elements of Chinese tradition fostered private over public morality had been argued by others, most articulately by the constitutional monarchist Liang Qichao. With Liang, however, this criticism of China's heritage led, not to a call for a wholesale attack on tradition, but rather to a plea for the gradual nurturing of habits of public life in order to create a "new citizenry." Anarchists,

50. Ibid., *XSJ*, no. 35 (22 February 1908): 3.
51. Ibid., *XSJ*, no. 41 (4 April 1908): 2.
52. Ibid., *XSJ*, no. 33 (8 February 1908): 4.
53. Min, "Shenlun minzu minquan shehui," 4.
54. "Yu yourenshu lun Xin shiji," 1 (n. 14 above).

sensitive to the role ideology played in perpetuating authority, called for
a revolution that would eradicate the authoritarian ideological legacy of
the past, as well as that of the institutions that sustained it. One, citing
Engels for inspiration, suggested that China's "national essence" (which
conservatives propagated) should be consigned to the museum because
it was contrary to civilized life.[55] The Paris anarchists concentrated their
attacks on Confucianism and the ideology of familism as the twin pillars
of authority in Chinese society. While they were not the only ones at
this time to criticize Confucianism or the family, they did so more
systematically and vociferously than others, and they certainly stood out
among their contemporaries for presenting these issues as *the* primary
issues of change in China. In both respects, they anticipated issues that
would rise to the forefront of Chinese thinking during the New Culture
Movement a decade later. In this sense, they were China's first cultural
revolutionaries.

The first issue of *New Era* included a short piece on Confucius, which
debunked him as a thinker of the age of barbarism whose only virtue had
been to be a little more knowledgeable than his ignorant contemporaries.[56] Paris anarchists saw in Confucian teachings the source of the superstitions in Chinese society that had oppressed women and youth and
served as an instrument of power, a counterpart in China to religion in
other societies.[57] Superstition, they believed, was the basis for authority,
but it was even more difficult to overthrow than authority itself, especially where religion and politics were not clearly distinguished. In China
a "Confucius revolution" was the prerequisite to achieving all other goals
of revolution.[58]

The attack on Confucianism was accompanied by an attack on kinship
and pseudokinship relations that for centuries had been cornerstones of
Chinese social thinking. "Family revolution, revolution against the sages,
revolution in the Three Bonds and the Five Constants would help advance
the cause of humanitarianism."[59] Paris anarchists viewed the family as the
major source of selfishness in society: though people were born into society

55. Fan, "Guocuizhi chufen" (Disposal of national essence), *XSJ*, no. 44 (25 April
1908): 1.
56. "Cizhi wei Zhongguo shengren" (This is China's sage), *XSJ*, no. 1 (22 June
1907): 3.
57. See the two articles by Zhen, "Nujie geming" (Revolution of women) and "Nannu
geming" (Men-women revolution) in *XSJ*, nos. 5, 7, 8. This is no. 8 (10 August 1907): 1.
58. Jue Sheng, "BaiKong zhengyan" (Soliciting the overthrow of Confucius), *XSJ*, no.
52 (20 June 1908): 4.
59. Zhen, "Sangang geming" (Three bonds revolution), *XSJ*, no. 11 (31 August
1907): 2.

(that is, the public realm), the family privatized their existence and converted what was public into what was private. Chu Minyi described the family as the basis of all inequality: "Today's society is a class society. It is like a high tower in appearance. Marriage is its foundation. Property, family, national and racial boundaries are all levels of the tower, with government at the top."[60] This is a common anarchist view, but within the context of Chinese political thought, which had long viewed the family as a paradigm for politics, it had a special significance. The Three Bonds (that bound ruler and minister, father and son, husband and wife) were to the anarchists the superstitions that perpetuated the power of the family, which was based not on principle but on authority. Family power was bolstered by the practise of ancestor worship, which was contrary to "truth," secured the despotism of tradition, was economically wasteful (in using up good land for graves), and bound the living to the dead. Anarchists advocated a "thought revolution" to eliminate these superstitions, and an "economic revolution" to eradicate the power of the family by making individuals economically independent.[61]

These premises of anarchist thinking reveal why education held such an important place on the anarchist agenda and why anarchists should have believed revolution and education to be the two sides of the same coin, the one "negative," the other "positive."[62] Revolution was to clear away material obstacles to the liberation of human potential, but it was education that would nurture the morality that anarchist ideals demanded. "There is no morality other than learning," proclaimed the title of an article in the New Era.[63] This was a commonly held anarchist view: that the morality of a people was proportionate to their learning. Education would change human psychology, and this would lead to changes in behavior and morality. The relationship between education and revolution was conceived dialectically, with the advance of one inducing the advance of the other in the endless evolution of humanity.

This emphasis on education as revolution brought out an important feature of the anarchist idea of social revolution: that there was no distinction between the process and the goals of revolution, between means and ends. Revolution was necessary to make anarchist education possible; without such education revolution could not be attained. While anarchists on occasion ventured to offer their views on when the revolution

60. Min, "Wuzhengfu shuo," XSJ, no. 38:4.
61. Zhen, "Sangang geming," 1, 2.
62. Min, "Wuzhengfu lun," XSJ, no. 40 (28 March 1908): 2.
63. "Lun zhishi yiwai wu daode," XSJ, no. 79 (26 December 1908).

might occur, these predictions were superfluous because revolution was ultimately a continuing process with no foreseeable end. Perhaps most revealing in this regard was the distortion of the etymology of the term *revolution* by Li and Chu in their important essay entitled "Revolution" (*Geming*). Using the foreign original, "revolution," the authors explained that the word was composed of "re" and "evolution," in other words, re-evolution, which they then explained in Chinese to mean "ever new" (*gengxin*). We cannot be certain whether the distortion was intentional or the result of misunderstanding; circumstantial evidence points to the former. There was at least one essay published in the *New Era* that traced the word *revolution* correctly to its root, "to revolve."[64] The underlying intention of the representation of "revolution" as "re-evolution," moreover, was to portray revolution and evolution as different aspects, or phases, of the process of human progress, which was also important in Reclus's thinking on revolution.[65] Whatever the reasons, this etymological interpretation corresponded to the anarchists' view of revolution as a process without end. In the words of Li Shizeng:

> Progress is advance without stopping, transformation without end. There is no affair or thing that does not progress. This is the nature of evolution. That which does not progress or is tardy owes it to sickness in human beings and injury in other things. That which does away with sickness and injury is none other than revolution. Revolution is nothing but cleansing away obstacles to progress.[66]

THE TOKYO ANARCHISTS

The Tokyo anarchists agreed with the basic premises of the Paris anarchists: the social scope of revolution, its moral basis, its universalistic goals, and the importance of education as a means of achieving anarchism. There was also considerable interchange between their two journals. The *New Era* contained reports on the activities of the Tokyo anarchists, and *Natural Justice* frequently reprinted foreign works that had first been published in the *New Era*. Nevertheless, the two groups were separated by a wide ideological gap, both in their understanding of anarchism and in the conclusions they drew from it concerning contemporary problems. The disagreement rose to the surface on at least one occasion when the *New Era* criticized Liu Shipei's understanding of anarchism.

64. Min, "Puji geming," *XSJ*, no. 17 (12 October 1907): 4.
65. Fleming, *The Anarchist Way*, 77.
66. Zhen, "Jinhua yu geming" (Evolution and revolution), *XSJ*, no. 20 (2 November 1907): 1.

Liu Shipei had made his fame as a classical scholar before he turned to anarchism, and he was a prominent leader of conservatives who propagated the idea of "national essence," of which the Paris anarchists were critical. Liu's commitment to China's cultural heritage was to shape his anarchism. In light of this, it is possible that the more radical aspects of the anarchism that *Natural Justice* propagated was the work of He Zhen, his wife, with whom he published the journal.

The general objectives of *Natural Justice* were stated in its first few issues: "To destroy existing society and institute human equality is the general objective. Aside from women's revolution, it advocates racial, political, and economic revolution. Hence the name, *Natural Justice.*" With issue number eight in October 1907, this statement was revised to read: "To destroy national and racial boundaries to institute internationalism; resist all authority; overthrow all existing forms of government; institute communism; institute absolute equality of men and women."

While these goals were close to those of the *New Era*, especially in their later formulation, the two groups of anarchists differed significantly in their anarchism as well as in the sources of inspiration for their ideals. Native sources, viewed with contempt by the Paris anarchists, held a prominent place in the pages of *Natural Justice*. This reflected an important difference in the way they perceived the relationship between anarchism and native ideas and ideology.

The Tokyo anarchists, too, rejected those aspects of premodern Chinese ideology that condoned hierarchy between classes and sexes. On the issue of political ideology, however, they believed that premodern Chinese thought came closer to upholding anarchist social ideals than its counterparts elsewhere. In a speech to the first meeting of the Society for the Study of Socialism, Liu stated that though the Chinese political system had been despotic in appearance, the power of the government had been remote from the lives of the people, who thus had considerable freedom from politics. Furthermore, he argued, advocacy by the major ideologies of China, Confucianism and Daoism, of laissez-faire government had helped curtail government intervention in society. As a result, he concluded, China was more likely than other societies to achieve anarchism; he implied, in fact, that if only Chinese could be purged of their habits of obedience, anarchism could be achieved in China in the very near future.[67] The fifth issue of *Natural Justice* carried

67. See the report "Shehui zhuyi jiangxihui diyici kaihui jishi" (Record of the first meeting of the society for the study of socialism), *XSJ*, nos. 22, 25, 26. This is no. 22 (16 November 1907): 4.

a picture of Laozi as the father of anarchism in China. In his utopian scheme Liu acknowledged his debt to Xu Xing, an agrarian utopianist of the third century B.C., who had advocated a rural life as the ideal life and promoted the virtues of manual labor by all without distinction, including the emperor. Liu noted that whereas he himself advocated cooperation, Xu had promoted self-sufficiency, but otherwise he saw no essential difference between Xu's ideas and his own.[68]

Among Western anarchists, Liu found in Tolstoy confirmation of the ideals that he had first discovered in native sources.[69] Like Tolstoy, he idealized rural life and manual labor and opposed a commercialized economy. He believed that Chinese society had begun to degenerate with the emergence of the money economy at the beginning of the Christian era. The money economy had led to the strengthening of despotism; the commercial economy had led to the impoverishment of many, prompting government efforts under Wang Mang to establish control over land. Liu almost certainly had the contemporary Revolutionary Alliance advocacy of "the equalization of land rights" in mind when he described this development as one that enhanced despotic government. His suspicion of commercial economy also underlay his hostility to recent changes in Chinese society. He emphasized the destruction of the rural economy under pressure from Western commerce, and the ensuing crisis this had created for the peasantry. He also expressed a strong dislike for the urbanization that had set in with recent economic changes. Shanghai, the symbol of China's modern economy, represented to Liu a moral sink where men degenerated into thieves, and women, into prostitutes.[70]

Liu, in other words, perceived anarchism only as a modern version of a rural utopianism that had long existed in China. This accorded with his view of socialism in general. He traced socialism from Plato to the modern world without assigning any peculiar distinction to modern socialism.[71]

In light of Liu's approach to anarchism, it is not surprising that he drew conclusions different from those of *New Era* anarchists concerning the path China should follow in pursuit of the good society. Unlike the

68. Shenshu (Liu Shipei), "Renlei junli shuo" (On the equal ability of human beings), *Tianyi bao* (Natural justice, hereafter *TYB*), no. 3 (10 July 1907): 24–36, 34–35. The pagination here is that of the Daian reprint of this journal.

69. Shenshu, "Dushu zaji" (Random notes on books read), *TYB,* nos. 11–12 (30 November 1907): 416–17. These were notes on a book by Tolstoy, *Rendao zhuyi* (Humanitarianism).

70. Shenshu, "XiHan shehui zhuyixue fada kao" (Examination of the development of the study of socialism in the Western Han), *TYB,* no. 5 (10 August 1907): 91–97.

71. Shenshu, "Ouzhou shehui zhuyi yu wuzhengfu zhuyi tongkao" (Examination of anarchism and socialism in Europe), *TYB,* no. 6 (1 September 1907): 145–48.

New Era anarchists, who perceived republican government as a progressive development, Liu argued that if China could not achieve anarchism immediately, it would be better off under the old regime than under the "new politics" (*xin zheng*): "Reform is inferior to preserving the old, constitution is inferior to monarchy." He offered three reasons for his position: the old educational system was superior to the new, which favored the rich; the proposed parliamentary system would enhance the power of the elite and, therefore, contribute to inequality; the increased power of capital would result in the concentration of wealth and deprive the people of the self-sufficiency they had hitherto enjoyed. Liu bolstered his argument with statistics on poverty in various countries, which, he believed, showed that development increased inequality in society.[72]

Tokyo anarchists placed a great deal more emphasis on the plight of the people in China than did the Paris anarchists. *New Era* discussions of anarchism carried an aura of abstract intellectualism. In its three years of publication, the journal published only two articles wholly devoted to the question of labor, and even those were of an abstract theoretical nature—in spite of the fact that these years were a high point in syndicalist activity in France. *Natural Justice,* in contrast, paid considerable attention to the condition of women and the peasantry in China.

He Zhen was probably responsible for the attention the journal devoted to the issue of women's oppression. The Tokyo anarchists derived their inspiration on this issue from Engels's *The Origin of the Family, Private Property and the State,* which, in presenting the oppression of women as a consequence of the emergence of the patriarchal family with the rise of urban civilization, may have struck a resonant cord with their antiurban bias. He Zhen was deeply critical not only of the oppression of women under the old society but also of what modern urban society and factory labor did to women.[73]

While both groups of anarchists were equally critical of women's oppression, the Tokyo anarchists' stance on the question of rural society was distinctive and, from the perspective of Chinese socialist thought, significant. The *Hengbao* in 1908 published anonymously a number of articles on the peasant question.[74] By this time Liu Shipei had returned to China,

72. Shenshu, "Lun xinzheng wei bingminzhi gen" (New politics is the root of the people's sickness), *TYB*, nos. 8–10 (combined issue) (30 October 1907): 193–203.

73. Peter Zarrow, *Anarchism in Chinese Political Culture* (New York: Columbia University Press, 1990), chap. 6.

74. "Wuzhengfu geming yu nongmin geming" (Anarchist and peasant revolutions) and "Lun nongye yu gongye lianhezhi kexing yu Zhongguo" (A system combining agriculture and industry can be applied in China). Reprints in *Wuzhengfu zhuyi sixiang ziliao xuan*

and these anonymous articles may have been the work of another prominent figure among the Tokyo anarchists, Zhang Ji. As far as I know, these
were among the earliest serious discussions in Chinese socialism of the role
of the peasantry in the revolution and of the meaning of revolution for the
peasantry. One article, lauding the peasants' tendency toward communitarian living and anarchism, called for a "peasants' revolution" (*nongmin
geming*). Others discussed economic cooperation among the peasantry.
Perhaps the most interesting was an article, inspired by Kropotkin, that
advocated the combination of agriculture and industry in the rural economy. There is no need to belabor the significance of this idea, which has
been an important feature of Chinese socialist thinking from Mao Zedong
to Deng Xiaoping. Whether later Communists were familiar with these
publications is impossible to say. Li Dazhao's first writings in the early
1910s, which showed an antiurban bias that led Maurice Meisner to describe Li as a populist, sounded like some of Liu Shipei's writings on the
question of commerical urban society. The works of Kropotkin that inspired these ideas in the *Hengbao*, chief among them *The Conquest of
Bread*, had first been translated into Chinese in the *New Era*. By the time of
the May Fourth Movement these works were popular readings among
Chinese radicals and provided the inspiration for the communitarian ideals and the communal experiments that proliferated at the time. Although
we cannot be certain about the influence of these ideas of the Tokyo
anarchists on later socialist thinking, they were the first to enunciate the
ideas, and there is evidence to suggest that their ideas may have become in
later years a component of Chinese socialists' thinking on the future relationship between agriculture and industry and on the relationship of urban
to rural society.

    The sensitivity on these questions may have been a consequence of the
Tokyo anarchists' proximity to China, which gave them access to the
burgeoning popular resistance movements on the eve of the 1911 Revolution. I think, however, that there were other, intellectual, reasons for the
journal's attention to these problems. He Zhen's presence was possibly the
most important factor in the journal's attention to problems of women.
Liu's idealization of rural life was responsible for the attention he devoted
to the peasantry, in whom he discovered the modal personality for anarchist society. Liu's description of utopian society offers an instructive con-

---

(Selection of materials on anarchist thought), ed. Ge Maochun et al., 2 vols. (Beijing: Beijing
daxue chubanshe, 1984), 1:158–66.

trast to the one drawn up by Wu Zhihui a few years later in *New Youth* (*Xin Qingnian*).[75] The most conspicuous feature of Wu's utopia was its fascination with mechanical innovations, which in the future would even obviate the need for walking, since conveyor belts would connect homes and workplaces. Liu's utopia described an essentially rural society and is striking for its preoccupation with the disposal of labor; basic to his utopia was universal manual labor as a guarantee to an egalitarian existence. All anarchists believed in the virtues of manual labor. In later years, the Paris anarchists would establish a work-study program in France, which stressed the combination of manual and mental labor as the key to the material and moral transformation of Chinese society. In these early years, however, it was Liu who stated most trenchantly a belief that combining manual and mental labor would eliminate social inequality and create an ideal anarchist personality. Liu's antimodernism was largely responsible both for the close attention he paid to the concrete problems of rural life in China and for his idealization of attitudes associated with rural existence.

That it was not the modernist anarchists in Paris but the antimodernist Liu Shipei and his associates in Tokyo who were the first to introduce labor as an integral component of anarchist revolution is worth emphasizing because it may explain an ambivalence toward the question of labor in education in later years, when modernists as well as antimodernists adopted it as a means of changing China.[76] The function of labor in education as a principle of an ideal social organization, as seen by the antimodernist anarchists in Tokyo, was to culminate in Mao's Marxism during the Cultural Revolution. (It is ironic that an ideal born of antimodernism may have given the impetus to one of the most radical efforts to reorganize Chinese society.) The idea of labor in education as a practical means to educate and civilize Chinese, implicit in the attitudes of Paris anarchists, found its way into the thinking of liberals and conservatives alike and has been revived in recent years by the post-Mao regime.

It is not clear what sources inspired Liu Shipei to include labor as a component of an anarchist revolution.[77] Although Chinese intellectuals

75. For further discussion, see Wolfgang Bauer, *China and the Search for Happiness*, trans. Michael Shaw (New York: Seabury, 1976), 352–53.

76. Antimodernism here implies neither conservatism nor opposition to change, but rather a questioning of the basic social, economic, and cultural premises of modernist ideology embedded in assumptions that all technological and social change is good because progressive—what we might describe as a fetishism of modernity.

77. Liu's utopia is reminiscent of the utopia of Cai Yuanpei discussed in chapter 3. Note that Cai stressed that everyone should work in some professional capacity (as he would in later years as well) rather than equalization through equal labor. It is also possible that Karl

in Tokyo were familiar with fragments of Marx's works, where they may
have encountered references to the need to abolish the division of mental
and manual labor as a condition of Communist society, it is more likely
that Tolstoy's "laborism" and Xu Xing's native agrarian utopianism
directly inspired Liu, legitimized by the urgings of Tolstoy himself. (Xu
Xing's utopianism would be forgotten in later years, whereas, by the time
of the May Fourth Movement, Tolstoy's "laborism" or "pan-laborism,"
fanlaodong zhuyi, was popular with Chinese intellectuals).[78] By 1908
these sources were combined with Kropotkin's *Conquest of Bread* and
Fields, Factories and Workshops of Tomorrow to yield a plan for social
organization that prefigured in many of its essentials the Maoist plan for
China as it took shape in the late fifties.

Liu first presented the idea in his plan for a future society, "On Equalizing Human Labor" (*Renlei junli shuo*), published in 1907 in *Natural
Justice*. The utopia described an agrarian society in which everyone labored equally. Labor was intended to abolish inequality, as well as to
guarantee everyone an independent existence as the condition of equality.
Children would be raised in public residence halls, supervised by older
people, who would also teach them. At age six they would begin to learn
the new universal language. Starting at age ten, they would spend half the
day in study, the other half in manufacturing labor. The practical skills
they acquired in education would also help them produce for their own
livelihood. Between the ages of twenty and fifty, everyone would engage in
productive and social service activities, with jobs allocated according to
age. At fifty they would enter residence halls to tend to the raising of
children. For all his antimodernism, Liu did not object to the use of la-
borsaving devices. Technological advance would guarantee that no one
would have to work for more than two hours a day to guarantee a subsistence for himself or herself as well as for the society at large, which would

---

Marx and Friedrich Engels contributed to Liu's ideas. *Tianyi bao* in nos. 16–19 (combined
issue) published parts of the *Communist Manifesto*, including the ten-point program for the
achievement of socialism. Points 9 and 10 refer to the practise of labor and the combination
of industry and agriculture under socialism.

78. See the translation by a Qu Fei of "I Duerside da Riben baozhi xinwenshe shu"
(Tolstoy's letter to Japanese periodical and newspaper association), *TYB*, no. 5 (10 August
1907): 99–102, where Tolstoy praised East Asian agrarian society, warned against the
fetishism of modernity, and pointed to European (as well as Japanese) societies as examples
of the baneful effects of modernization, which he believed would soon bring these societies
down. Judging by its content, this letter was not significantly different from a letter Tolstoy
sent about the same time to Gu Hongming, entitled "Letter to a Chinese." For a discussion,
see Derk Bodde, *Tolstoy and China* (Princeton: Princeton University Press, 1950), 47–58.

be reorganized now around small districts of one thousand people each. The rest of the time would be spend in leisure and learning activities.[79]

While there is no apparent relationship between this ideal of an agrarian social organization and the 1908 *Balance* pieces inspired by Kropotkin, the basic message was the same. The latter argued that industrialization should take place away from urban centers because otherwise it would lead to a separation of agriculture and industry, with negative consequences for both—and for society as a whole. These essays taken together point to the conceptualization of society that underlay Tokyo anarchists' anarchism: an agrarian society that integrated industrial and agricultural production, that was therefore directed at production for need, to which the equal practise of labor by all was central. Tokyo anarchists' antimodernism was opposed, not to the products of modern science and technology, but only to the social organization created by modernization; within a social context organized according to human scale and needs, the products of modernity could be made to serve human needs, instead of dehumanizing life, as they seemed to be doing in the contemporary West and Japan, as well as in the emerging modern urban centers in China.

The same orientation, finally, sensitized Liu to the problem of imperialism in China. He was, to my knowledge, the first Chinese intellectual to see in socialism a means to liberate China from Western oppression. An essay in *Natural Justice* was remarkable for anticipating views that would become prevalent in China after the Chinese had been exposed to Lenin's analysis of imperialism. In the essay he argued that the emergence of concepts of socialism and universalism (*datong zhuyi*) promised the liberation of Asian peoples from the imperialism of the "white race" and the Japanese. This task required, he believed, the mobilization of the people (he even cited the Sanyuan li incident of the first Opium War as an example of the people's ability to resist foreigners), cooperation with other oppressed peoples of Asia, and the various "people's parties" (*mindang*) in advanced countries. Most interesting was Liu's observance that revolution would not succeed in advanced societies until Asia had been liberated, because the exploitation of the Asian peoples strengthened governments and the ruling classes in the West.[80]

Liu's views on anarchism were anathema to the Paris anarchists, with their commitment to science, industrial society, and progress. While in

79. For further discussion, see Zarrow, "Chinese Anarchists," 138–40.
80. Shenshu, "Yazhou xianshi lun" (The contemporary trend in Asia), *TYB*, nos. 11–12 (combined issue): 345–68.

general they were supportive of the Tokyo anarchists, they criticized Liu for his equation of modern anarchism with native utopianism. First, they responded, Liu had no conception of progress, which lay at the basis of modern anarchism. It was wrong, therefore, to compare what modern anarchists wished to achieve with the aspirations of primitive people, or to equate anarchism with erratic efforts to achieve a more egalitarian distribution of property, as in the "well-field" system of ancient China. Second, they criticized Liu for his suggestion that Chinese society had been characterized in the past by political laissez-faire, which did not fit the facts. China had been ruled for centuries by a political despotism; what Liu claimed added up to, at the very least, an assertion that there was no difference between a society with government and one without it. The superstitious faith of Chinese society in hierarchy, which accounted for the prevalence of "habits of obedience," was itself a product of oppression. Finally, they found humorous Liu's claim that China might be closer to anarchism than other societies. What was required, they suggested, was not talk about levels of anarchy, but effort, awareness, and scientific knowledge.[81]

These disagreements were not over abstract issues but entailed different attitudes toward the modern West, as well as toward the problems of changing China. The Paris anarchists were Francophiles who found much of value in the modern West but little to be proud of in China's past. They valued science to the point of scientism, made industrialism into a utopia (as Bauer has observed of Wu), and with all their debunking of capitalism, were fascinated with the civilization that capitalism had created.[82]

Liu had the nativist's suspicion of the West. While he admired certain Western values, he believed that the Chinese heritage contained the equivalents of those same values, and more. He found much of value in Chinese civilization (though not necessarily in Confucianism) and was to devote his life to the preservation of its "essence."[83] Although he was unmistakably an antimodernist, his very antimodernism sensitized him to issues that would assume enormous significance in later years in Chinese radicalism. Such was the case with his sensitivity to the question of imperialism, to which the Paris anarchists, with their unabashed cosmopolitanism, were completely oblivious. His case parallels the qualms about West-

81. See the response to the report on the meeting of the Society for the Study of Socialism, in *XSJ*, no. 24 (30 November 1907): 4.

82. Bauer, *China and the Search for Happiness*, 350–55. For an elaborate discussion of Wu Zhihui's "scientism," see Daniel Kwok, *Scientism in Chinese Thought, 1900–1950* (New Haven: Yale University Press, 1965).

83. Bernal, "Liu Shih-p'ei and National Essence."

ern powers of a "conservative" of the same period, Liang Qichao, who argued that Revolutionary Alliance socialism would weaken China vis-à-vis the West by undermining China's economic development, an idea that Revolutionary Alliance socialists derided. In the early years of this century, it was still the more "conservatively" inclined Chinese who saw Western intrusion as a major problem of Chinese society. Only in the twenties would Chinese socialists merge their social revolutionary demands with anti-imperialism. Liu was one of the first to do so. He was also the first, to my knowledge, to show concern for the consequences for China of urbanization and to turn to rural China in a search for moral and material answers, a search in which major Chinese socialists such as Li Dazhao and Mao Zedong would join in later years. Finally, his insistence on the need to combine manual and mental labor as a means of transforming the Chinese personality would assume immense importance among other anarchists during the New Culture Movement (though his contribution was not acknowledged) and retain its importance all the way to Mao's Cultural Revolution.

VISION AND REVOLUTION

Prior to the Revolution of 1911, anarchism was one of the two main currents in Chinese thinking on social revolution, which had been stimulated by the introduction to China of socialist ideas at the turn of the century. The Revolutionary Alliance had incorporated "social revolution" in its political program in 1905 as a means of preventing in China's economic development the social ills that had accompanied the rise of capitalism in Europe. Revolutionary Alliance socialism conceived of socialism as "social policy," the use of political intervention by the state to curtail inequality and, therefore, control social conflict.

Anarchism introduced a new theme into Chinese social revolutionary thinking: social revolution as cultural revolution. In contrast to Revolutionary Alliance socialists, whose attention was focused on the state, the anarchists, in their rejection of the state, turned to society as the proper realm of revolution. Key to their idea of social revolution was the transformation of the individual, since it was a basic premise of anarchism that a society could be only as good as the individuals who constituted it. Anarchists viewed inherited social institutions as institutional manifestations of the principle of authority, which distorted the individual psyche and prevented the free play of the instinctive sociability of human beings, the only basis for a good society. The abolition of existing institutions, therefore, must be accompanied in the creation of a good society by a cultural transformation (both intellectual and ethical) of the individual to restore to humanity, as it were, its pristine sociability. The strongly cultural connotations of the anarchist idea of social revolution were responsible, I think, for the immense popularity of anarchism in China a decade later, during the New Culture Movement, when the anarchist conception of change diffused widely in Chinese thinking.

Anarchist themes continued to bear an intriguing resemblance to issues in premodern Chinese politics. The preoccupation with the moral basis of politics, the concern with nourishing public over private interests, the assumption that in education lay the means to moral transformation—all point to a possible affinity between anarchism and the native ideological legacy of Chinese anarchists. That native political vocabulary infused the language of anarchism would seem to lend support to such an interpretation.

This interpretation can be sustained only if we ignore the new self-image that the Chinese anarchists held and, even more important, the content of the anarchist advocacy of social revolution, an entirely new concept in Chinese politics. The very existence of two camps of anarchists, one upholding native traditions, the other opposing them, militates against any simplistic view of anarchists as prisoners of a cultural or a political unconscious. Associations of anarchism for the Paris and Tokyo anarchists were determined not by an unconscious activity of inherited beliefs and dispositions, but by conscious choices made in response to problems that were products of the material and ideological conditions of early-twentieth-century Chinese society, in particular the problems of revolution and the relationship to contemporary world civilization, and a host of more specific questions to which these problems had given rise.

Anarchist writing was indeed infused with the vocabulary of Confucianism, Daoism, and Buddhism. Earlier, Revolutionary Alliance writers had on occasion resorted to the social vocabulary of premodern Chinese society in explaining their own socialist notions of class. Anarchists used native vocabulary, utopian or otherwise, with much greater frequency. This practise of using a native vocabulary no doubt made for considerable confusion concerning the relationship of anarchism to native social and moral ideals, but it would be improper to conclude from the confounding of the vocabulary that the ideas themselves were confounded by the anarchists. Kenneth Chen has explained that when Buddhism was first introduced to China, Buddhists used the vocabulary of Daoism to render Buddhist concepts intelligible to the Chinese, who had no native equivalents for those concepts. This practise, described as "matching terms" (*geyi*), may help explain the Chinese use of a native vocabulary to express anarchist ideals in the early twentieth century.[84] It does not follow that anarchist ideas lost their revolutionary identity in the process, just as Buddhism did not lose its identity much earlier for being expressed through a Daoist vocabulary. There was confusion, to be sure; a somewhat mysterious and vague association with Buddhist ideals would characterize a great deal of Chinese anarchist thinking in the twentieth century. But ultimately, as is evident in the revolutionary impact of anarchism on Chinese thinking, the association was to transform the meaning of the native vocabulary that was used initially to express anarchist ideas.

The anarchist ideas of morality and revolution illustrate the need to go beyond the vocabulary to its content in order to appreciate this problem fully. Paris anarchists took morality to be the end of revolution. True morality, they believed, could be achieved only with learning—not just any learning, least of all the kind of learning that Confucians had prized, but scientific learning. Li Shizeng dismissed as "particular" (*si*) learning all learning that could not stand the test of modern science.[85] Science, whose conclusions were independent of national or cultural orientations, represented to him the only "universal" (*gong*) and therefore true learning. He excluded from the realm of scientific learning politics and law, "false morality," and religion, including within it only, in addition to the natural sciences, sociology and anthropology.[86] Anarchist scientism clearly distinguished the anarchist perceptions of the fundamentals of learning and, therefore, of morality, from those of their Confucian predecessors, for whom true learning had been all that the anarchists sought to abolish.

With regard to anarchist utopianism, which resonated with certain themes in native utopian traditions, it is clear that anarchists held an activist idea of revolution that distinguished their goals from the eremitic escapism of the Daoists, to whom they were sometimes compared. Responding to a correspondent who compared anarchist ideals to the idea of "nonaction" (*wuwei*), an ideal of politics that infused most Chinese schools of political thought, Li Shizeng observed: "Anarchism advocates radical activism. It is the diametrical opposition of quietist nonaction. Anarchism does not only advocate that imperial power does not reach the

84. For a discussion of this practise, see Kenneth Chen, *Buddhism in China: A Historical Survey* (Princeton: Princeton University Press, 1964).
85. Zhen, "Tanxue," *XSJ*, no. 7:2.
86. Ibid., *XSJ*, no. 21:4.

self, it also seeks to make sure that it does not reach anyone else."[87] Embedded in this statement is a distinction between traditional political escapism and modern revolutionary politics: the one seeking to establish a space apart from the existing political order, the other seeking to take over and to transform political space in its totality. That China had its Bodhisattvas who sought to save humanity and that modern anarchism has had its escapist eremitists does not change the fundamental differences in the conceptualization of political space between anarchism and native Chinese political traditions; it only points to the need for circumspection in drawing parallels between ideas that are inherently open to wide ranges of interpretation and draw their meaning not from abstractions but from their concrete historical context.

Anarchism expressed a utopian universalism and a humanitarian vision that was in many ways far removed from the immediate concerns of contemporary Chinese society. But it was not irrelevant. For the first two decades of this century, anarchist ideas played a central role in ideological debate. During the period 1907–1910 anarchism provided a perspective for the critique of ideologies of reform and revolution. The Paris anarchists, in their futurism, were critical of the limitations in the ideology of nationalist revolutionaries, who rested their hopes on the state. Liu Shipei, with his antimodernist anarchism, was able to see that the "new policies" of the Qing government were not the harbingers of political openness and social welfare that many thought them to be. I think we can say that their contemporaries, intrigued by these questions, took the anarchists more seriously than historians have taken them.

Anarchists were utopian, to be sure, but their very utopianism accounts for their ability to express concerns among Chinese intellectuals that were no less real for being politically irrelevant, at least in an immediate sense. Anarchist utopianism was itself the expression of a universalistic urge in Chinese thinking that gained in meaning as the Chinese conception of China was particularized with the emergence of nationalism. Against a world torn apart by national interest and conflict, anarchism held up the possibility of a humane civilization in which China could participate. This utopianism on occasion took a comical form: a "Mr. Humanity" (*Rendao shi*) from England, in an open letter to the Chinese ambassador in England, charged that the latter, in tampering with student mail, broke "the law of humanity," and exposed "to the civilized

87. Zhen, "Da Chee shi" (Response to Mr. Chee), *XSJ*, no. 3 (6 July 1907): 2.

world that Chinaman are [sic] savages."[88] There was nothing comical, however, about the many anarchists who over the years risked government wrath for their pursuit of "humanity," which authorities deemed to be subversive of public morality and order.

Utopianism is a relative concept. If we take them seriously enough, ideas such as democracy and freedom, which we bandy about as a matter of course, are as utopian as anything to which the anarchists aspired; indeed, anarchism appears utopian because anarchists have shown a tendency to take these ideas seriously. Those who criticized the anarchists for being too "idealistic" were not always aware that the Republic or the socialism that they advocated were quite "utopian" when viewed from the perspective of those conservatives who had an even more pessimistic view than they had of the Chinese ability for self-government. Utopia has been a force in history because one person's utopia has been another's reality.

The Chinese anarchists were idealists but they were not "blind," as the Paris anarchists said of themselves. Though anarchists promoted anarchism as a total revolutionary philosophy, they projected their vision far into the future and were prepared to compromise their ideals to meet immediate needs. Indeed, anarchists would make a very real contribution in the new ideals they introduced into education, which they believed was the only reliable means to achieve anarchist society. Anarchists' ideals could even become "functional" to the ends of political power, as they did when anarchists in the twenties held up their ideal of unity and universality against Communists who, in promoting class struggle, seemed to be bent on prolonging social divisions. Aside from personal relations, this was an important element in the Guomindang flirtation with anarchists in the 1920s.

Anarchists were not the only utopians in early-twentieth-century China, which, as a period of political and ideological transformation, provided fertile grounds for utopian thinking. Kang Youwei the reformer had produced the first utopian work of this period; although Kang's *Datong shu* was not yet published when anarchism emerged in Chinese thought, Kang's utopian thinking may have influenced at least one of the anarchists, Wu Zhihui, who apparently visited with Kang before leaving for Europe. Nevertheless, anarchist utopianism differed from that of Kang Youwei. Kang's utopia was a utopia of the future, which reflected in content his thinking on the present but did not shape his present con-

88. *XSJ*, no. 28 (4 January 1908): 2.

cerns. Anarchist utopianism was a revolutionary utopianism because it was an immanent utopianism, which presupposed that the present provided the point of departure for the path to utopia. It derived its inspiration, at least for the Paris anarchists, from the "scientism" of Kropotkin, which, however rationalist and ahistorical it may be, portrayed anarchism not as a future dream but as a necessity of human evolution. While Kang Youwei was satisfied (if not entirely happy) to live with the present world of nations and families, of competition and conflict, anarchist utopianism by its very nature called forth immediate criticism of the contemporary world and of efforts to change it. As James Pusey has argued, the anarchist (especially Kropotkinite) challenge to Darwinian assumptions—which set "mutual aid" against competition—was a major source of attraction to the anarchists.[89]

Anarchism may have made its most important contribution to Chinese social revolutionary thought in the revolutionary utopianism it promoted. China has been a revolutionary society in the twentieth century, not just because of the revolutionization of its society and politics, which nourished the revolutionary faith, but also because of a faith in revolution as an ultimate value, a means to a better world. Laski has observed that Marxism blended utopia and revolution to turn the process of revolution itself into a utopia.[90] This, I think, applies more to anarchism than to Marxism. In China anarchists were the first to articulate a faith in revolution as an endless process of change; this idea not only was important in revolutionary thinking in general but left its imprint on some currents in Marxist thinking as well. A notion of revolution as utopia was implicit in the 1903 statement by Zou Rong in a classic of Chinese revolutionary thought, The Revolutionary Army: "Ah, revolution, revolution! If you have it you will survive, but if you don't you will die. Don't retrogress; don't be neutral; don't hesitate; now is the time." Whether Zou's statement was inspired in any way by the anarchist ideas that were already finding their way into China is difficult to say; social Darwinism was much in evidence in his essay. But the idea was one that the Paris anarchists echoed, now clearly inspired by "mutual aid," but expressed in the vocabulary of Buddhism: "Revolution! Revolution!! Revolution!!! Since the beginning of the world, there has not been a year, a month, a day, an hour, a minute, a second, without revolution. Revolution moves forward without rest, tireless in its intrepidity. It is the key to the progress of the

89. James Pusey, China and Charles Darwin (Cambridge: Harvard University Press, 1983), 370–433.
90. Melvin Lasky, Utopia and Revolution (Chicago: University of Chicago Press, 1976).

myriad worlds (*daqian shijie*)."[91] Revolution was to society as the propeller to the ship, constantly moving it forward under the guidance of universal principle, as the propeller moved the ship forward in accordance with the compass. Revolution was not simply a solution to practical problems, it was the destiny of humanity.

91. Min, "Wuzhengfu shuo," *XSJ*, no. 34 (15 February 1908): 3.

CHAPTER FOUR

Anarchists against Socialists in Early Republican China

Anarchism germinated in Chinese thought in the radical culture of Chinese students studying abroad. Like other currents in Chinese radicalism, it was a product of Chinese intellectuals' confrontation with other societies that already showed the strains of modernity and struggled with alternatives to the dominant capitalist ideology of development. Chinese students' experiences abroad had a liberating effect on their thinking; the same experiences made them wary of what they found.

It was not until after the Revolution of 1911 that anarchism appeared within China. The literature that anarchists produced abroad found its way into the mainland before 1911, and the already visible movement of Chinese intellectuals between China and the outside world had introduced anarchism to intellectuals at home; but it was in the period of relative political freedom that followed the republican Revolution of 1911 that anarchist activity took form on Chinese soil. Over the next decade anarchism would become an integral part of the thinking of radical intellectuals and help nourish a radical culture that burst forth in full bloom with the May Fourth Movement in 1919.

Paris anarchists played a significant part in the unfolding of anarchism in the early Republic. Shortly after the revolution, they returned home to establish several societies in China. These societies, however, were ephemeral; their contribution lay more importantly in the educational programs that took Chinese intellectuals to France in increasing numbers and culminated late in the decade in the "diligent-work frugal-study" program (*qingong jianxue*), which was to play a crucial part in the radicalization of Chinese youth. These activities also served as a conduit between Europe and China, feeding into Chinese anarchism developments in anarchism in Europe.

Within China, the most important development was the appearance of anarchism in Guangzhou, which was also to have a long-term influence on the development of anarchism. Although radical in their consequences, the activities of the Paris anarchists were moderate (took the form, in fact, of cooperation with government authorities in China and France). Under the leadership of the charismatic leader Liu Sifu (Shifu, 1884–1915), the Guangzhou anarchists promoted a radical anarchism that would be responsible for important new developments in anarchist activity and would foreshadow the direction Chinese radicalism would take in the 1920s, in which the Guangzhou anarchists were to play a direct and significant part.

Most important among these developments was the establishment in the late 1910s of an alliance between intellectuals and the workers, a movement spearheaded by anarchists. Both groups of anarchists would play an important part in nurturing an awareness among intellectuals of the importance of labor and in providing social spaces within which intellectuals came into contact with laborers. But there was also a divergence between them that went back to the early Republic. The Paris anarchists, on the one hand, increasingly focused their attention on education and rendered anarchism into an abstract social philosophy—so abstract, in fact, that it did not prevent them from engaging in highly "unanarchist" activities and would culminate in the 1920s in their association with the Right wing in the Guomindang. Guangzhou anarchists, on the other hand, while they were also concerned with problems of culture and education, were conspicuous for their revolutionary purism and played an important part in nourishing a social radicalism that would on occasion bring the two groups into opposition.

The Guangzhou anarchists also played an important part at this time in consolidating an anarchist identity by drawing a clear line between anarchism and other socialisms, which also found their way into Chinese radicalism in the early Republic. The questions they raised concerning socialism foreshadowed the themes that in the 1920s would form the basis for anarchist criticism of Marxist communism.

The focus in this chapter is on the anarchism of Shifu and his followers and on the debates between anarchists and socialists, which were also the first debates in China *within* socialism. In the next chapter we will return to the activities of the Paris anarchists.

ANARCHIST CURRENTS IN THE EARLY REPUBLIC

The arguments, and the literature that informed them, of the anarchists in Tokyo and Paris indicate that by the eve of the republican Revolution in 1911, Chinese radicals had a sufficient grasp of anarchist theory to determine what was and was not anarchism. Indeed, anarchist writings in the early Republic no longer associated anarchism with nihilism; and although anarchists never repudiated assassination as a method of anarchist revolution, in practise conversion to anarchism was accompanied by a renunciation of assassination activity, as in the case of Shifu. More fundamentally, these writings now portrayed anarchism as primarily a social philosophy, a current within socialism that had arisen in response to the problems created by the emergence of industrial society in the West. And anarchist activity took the form of social activity to transform society at its very base. This new orientation was accompanied, as we have seen with the Paris anarchists, by a disassociation of anarchism from anarchistic currents within premodern Chinese thought. At the same time, it presented anarchists with a new problem: how to distinguish anarchism from other currents in socialism, which was especially urgent because the several socialist groups that emerged in the early Republic overlapped in their ideas of social revolution. This was the central issue of debate between Shifu and the socialists in 1913–14. Anarchism was already a problem within socialism.

Nevertheless, within this social phraseology, anarchism retained the intense moralism of its origins, though anarchist morality possibly assumed a new visage: it was no longer just an assertion of moral authenticity against the deprivations of politics but, especially in the eyes of the Francophile Paris anarchists, a socially important means of civilizing the Chinese population. Traces of the initial reception of anarchism were also visible in the continued association of anarchist morality with Buddhism (and, to a lesser extent, with Daoism); conspicuous among the anarchists of the early Republic was the Buddhist monk Taixu, and Buddhist associations infused, at least initially, the anarchism of Shifu and his followers.

Before the republican Revolution in 1911 there was at least one instance of a Chinese intellectual who sought to put into practise the anarchist convictions he had acquired abroad. This was Jing Meijiu, later the editor of the prestigious *Guofeng ribao* (National customs daily), whose supplement, *Xuehai* (Sea of learning), was to be a major source of anarchist ideas in the 1920s.[1] Jing had been a participant in the activities of the Society for the Study of Socialism while a student in Tokyo and had been deeply impressed with the Japanese anarchist Kotoku Shusui's lectures at the meetings of the Society, which converted him to anarchism. After his return to China, he actively sought to spread anarchism in Taiyuan, Shanxi, his native province.

In a lecture on socialism at Shanxi University in Taiyuan in 1912, Jing traced the origins of socialism to the French Revolution and French socialists of the first half of the nineteenth century, placing particular emphasis on Saint-Simon as the "most famous" of socialists. He clearly viewed socialism as a response to capitalist exploitation of the people, which had intensified with the industrial revolution. While in his account Marx held a place of secondary importance to Ferdinand Lassalle, he observed that Marx's analysis of "surplus value" in *Capital* had "moved the hearts of a whole generation." He presented anarchism as the most "extreme" of all socialisms. In his opinion, none of the socialisms surpassed anarchism in "seriousness of the search for world peace and social happiness, loftiness of ideals and purity of doctrine."[2] He observed further that there was some affinity between this extreme socialism and utopian counter-traditions in Chinese philosophy. Anarchism was most relevant at that time, he averred, because government had failed to resolve the social problems of industrial society.

Jing's account of socialism clearly bore traces of the anarchism of the Tokyo anarchists. He recalled that while listening to the lectures of the Society for the Study of Socialism, he was inspired to plan a short book that would "synthesize anarchism and the theories of Laozi." He was most moved, however, by the Tokyo anarchists' advocacy of abolishing the distinction between mental and manual labor, which he believed had become worse in the contemporary world. He was apparently also impressed by their emphasis on the equality of men and women. In 1911–12 Jing initiated what may have been the first experiment in China to combine labor and learning, focusing on women. He undertook in Taiyuan to establish a factory for women, intended to bring them economic independence. He also recruited contemporary feminists to teach the women workers in the factory. In his plan for the distribution of the factory's income, the largest portion was to go to labor, followed by

1. Jing Meijiu, "Zuian" (Account of crimes), in *Xinhai geming ziliao leipian* (Materials on the 1911 Revolution) (Beijing: Zhongguo shehui kexue chubanshe, 1981), 54–160.
2. Ibid., 140, 143.

"talent" (*caili*) and capital. This, according to Jing, indicated the respect socialists accorded to labor.[3]

What became of this experiment is not clear. Jing felt that with the success of the republican Revolution and the decline of anarchism in Japan anarchism lost some of its appeal among Chinese radicals. He himself was elected to the new republican parliament (along with another anarchist associated with the Tokyo anarchists, Zhang Ji, which would draw the ire of Shifu). But as late as the 1920s his publications were a source of the agrarian anarchism that had emanated from Tokyo before 1911.

In 1912 Paris anarchists also brought their activities home. While they would shift their attention almost immediately to education, a society they established in early 1912 yields insights into the basically moralistic thrust of their conception of anarchism—and of education. (It would also serve to promote their anarchism, albeit in disguised form, as a similar society was revived in Beijing University a few years later.) This was the Promote Virtue Society (*Jinde hui*), whose informal leadership included Li Shizeng, Wu Zhihui, Zhang Ji, as well as the Revolutionary Alliance (and later Guomindang) leader Wang Jingwei. The society had a complex structure of rules that also determined membership, which consisted of five types, in increasing order of rigorousness:

> The lowest category of membership called for a person not to visit prostitutes and not to gamble; in successively more demanding levels of membership, it was stipulated that the person should not take concubines, not serve as an official or a member of an assembly, and not smoke, drink, or eat meat.

A similar but simpler society was established at about the same time by an associate of the Paris anarchists, Cai Yuanpei (who would also become the first minister of education under the new Republic), the Six No's Society (*Liubu hui*). Also aimed at behavioral improvement, the society forbade its members to visit prostitutes, gamble, take concubines, eat meat, drink liquor, or smoke.[4]

It is important to stress, especially in light of later activities of the Paris anarchists, that these societies revealed their understanding of anarchism in practise that was characterized by a willingness to compromise the principles they professed. In spite of the prohibition against the participation of higher-level members in politics, one of the founders of the Promote Virtue Society, Zhang Ji, would shortly become a member of parlia-

---

3. Ibid., 74 and 144–45.
4. For a discussion, see Robert Scalapino and George T. Yu, *The Chinese Anarchist Movement* (Berkeley: Center for Chinese Studies, 1961), 37, 38.

ment; when Shifu criticized him for this, Wu Zhihui quickly came to his defense. The very complexity of the rules for membership may be seen as a function of their ideological "flexibility," to enable the recruiting of members of differing levels of commitment. Both societies, moreover, revealed an ethical orientation that perceived anarchism primarily as a means of transforming behavior. While they professed opposition to politics, and an intention to overthrow the state, Paris anarchists proved quite willing to function within the context of the state so long as they could pursue this cause of ethical transformation. This willingness would come to the fore in the 1920s, when they carried out their anarchist activities under the Guomindang umbrella, in service of a party rule that in theory they repudiated.

Not so with the other two groups that were to play the most important part in propagating anarchism in the early Republic, whose ideological purism was to sustain a distinctive anarchist identity well into the 1920s: the Guangzhou anarchists who gathered around Shifu after 1912, and the "pure" socialists led by the "revolutionary monk" Taixu. The more important of these in the long run were the Guangzhou anarchists, whose publications and organizational activities would play a crucial part in the flourishing of anarchism later in the decade. The "pure" socialists, however, also played some part in the early Republic in spreading anarchism and would contribute to the numbers of anarchists (and to anarchist organizational activity) in the May Fourth period.

Shifu and the Guangzhou anarchists would occupy center stage in anarchist activities in the early Republic, and they will be discussed at length later. We will consider here the "pure" socialists and the Chinese Socialist party (*Zhongguo shehui zhuyi dang*) of Jiang Kanghu, of which they were an offshoot, in order to elucidate the complex relationship between socialism and anarchism in these early years. The establishment of the Chinese Socialist party preceded the organization of Shifu's group and may have contributed to it, both because it helped create a space in Chinese politics for the dissemination of socialist ideas and because its eclectic socialism served as a source of anarchist ideas, which became evident when the "pure" socialists broke with the party in October or November 1912, countering the state socialism of Jiang with an anarchist socialism of their own. The confusion over anarchism created by the socialism of the Chinese Socialist party and the Social party established by the "pure" socialists was to be a major cause of controversy between Shifu and both groups of socialists in 1913–14.

Jiang Kanghu (1883–1945) had gained prominence early on for his advocacy of progressive causes, in particular in the areas of equality for women and of education. In the early 1900s, he did educational work under Yuan Shikai, promoted women's schools, and taught at the Imperial University at Beijing (later Beijing University). He was exposed to socialism in 1907–1910, when he went abroad to study, first in Japan and then in Europe. While he was in Europe he came to know the Paris anarchists and contributed two articles to the *New Era*. There is considerable evidence in his later writings that he learned at least some of his socialism from this publication. Nevertheless, when he began to promote socialism, it was more along social policy lines, even though his policies differed from the similar socialism that Sun Yat-sen and the Revolutionary Alliance advocated.

Jiang returned to China from Europe in late 1910, still a relative unknown. What brought him national prominence was a lecture he gave on July 1, 1911, in Hangzhou, probably the first public lecture on socialism ever to be given in China. Entitled "Socialism and Women's Education," the lecture was more radical in its statements on women and the family than in what it said on socialism. It seemed radical enough to the governor of Zhejiang province, who thought it as dangerous as "flood waters and wild beasts" and petitioned the throne to punish Jiang. Jiang was able to escape punishment through the intercession of his highly placed acquaintances. But the incident brought him national fame. The same month he organized the Socialist Research Society (*Shehui zhuyi yanjiu hui*), which became the core for the Chinese Socialist party, China's first socialist organization, established in November 1911, barely a month after the uprising that was to bring down the monarchy by the end of the year. The Chinese Socialist party announced an eight-point program: support the Republic; abolish racial boundaries; reform the law and respect the individual; destroy the system of inheritance; organize public organs to spread equal education; promote productive industries and stimulate laborers; abolish all taxes but the land tax; limit military spending and encourage competition other than the military (to provide an outlet for the human urge to compete). Until it was proscribed in 1913, the Chinese Socialist party propagated socialist ideas in China through lectures and publications.[5] At its height, it claimed 200 branches

5. Jiang Kanghu, *Hongshui ji* (Flood waters collection, hereafter *HSJ*), 53–55. For information on Jiang's activities, see his *Jinshi sanda zhuyi yu Zhongguo* (*Three great modern ideologies and China*) (Nanfang daxue, 1924), 37–54. In addition to teaching at the University of California at Berkeley, Jiang also worked at the Library of Congress during his years in the United States.

and 400,000 members. These figures may be too high, but Bernal has confirmed a large membership for the party in East China. What these members knew about socialism is another matter.[6] Jiang himself remarked that most were quite ignorant of socialism, and judging by his own knowledge, there is little reason to doubt his word. The party was diffuse, more a study group than a political party, and its members included anarchists as well as social democrats, which accounted for the split in late 1912.

Taixu and the radical Buddhist monks associated with him, who were from the beginning inclined to anarchism, may have joined Jiang's party initially because of uncertainty concerning its program. Taixu had been ordained as a monk in 1904, but was quickly radicalized by the emerging revolutionary movement and began to participate in the activities of the Revolutionary Alliance. A prominent representative of what Holmes Welch has described as the "Buddhist revival" in the early twentieth century, his exposure to secular radical literature had convinced him that Buddhism "had to be made relevant to contemporary secular circumstances." His reading of anarchist works in 1910–11 led him to an anarchist socialism and into the Chinese Socialist party.[7]

When Taixu and his associates broke with the Chinese Socialist party in late 1912, the reason they gave was the insufficiency of state socialism to achieve socialist goals (they also distinguished state socialism from anarchism as "narrow" and "broad" socialism).[8] The Social party (*Shehui dang*) that they established (to be distinguished from Jiang's Chinese Socialist party) took as its basic principle "the fundamentalness to the pursuit of human happiness of the transformation of social organization." As the party program put it, the Social party broke with the Chinese Socialist party because "socialists recognized no national boundaries while the Chinese Socialist party did, socialists opposed government while the Chinese Socialist party did not." According to the program, the Social party would seek to (1) abolish "class" divisions created by differences in wealth (hence communism), by distinctions between high and low (hence respect for the individual), by distinctions on the basis of intelligence (hence educational

6. Martin Bernal, "Chinese Socialism before 1913," in *Modern China's Search for a Political Form*, ed. J. Gray (London: Oxford University Press, 1969).

7. For Taixu and the Buddhist revival, see Holmes Welch, *The Buddhist Revival in China* (Cambridge: Harvard University Press, 1968).

8. Fen Xia (Shajin), "Xiayi shehui zhuyi yu guangyi shehui zhuyi" (Narrow and broad socialism), *Shehui shijie* (The world of society), no. 1 (15 April 1912). Reprinted in *Wuzhengfu zhuyi sixiang ziliao xuan* (Selection of materials on anarchist thought, hereafter WZFZYSX), ed. Ge Maochun et al., 2 vols. (Beijing: Beijing daxue chubanshe, 1984), 1:223–44.

equality); (2) eliminate all divisions among people on the basis of state, family, and religion (which Taixu and others identified with ancestor worship and the lineage system).[9] This, they believed, was a "pure" socialism, which they identified explicitly with anarchism. As one writer pointed out, anarchism was not restricted to opposition to government, as was suggested by the Chinese term *wuzhengfu* (literally, no government), but meant the abolition of all "naked power" (or, "tyrannical authority," *qiangquan*), which was counterposed to "universal principle" (*gongli*).[10] The Buddhist elements in the Social party's anarchism were evident above all in the insistence on abolishing all distinctions. Hua Lin, in a contribution to the party's journal, *Liangxin* (Conscience), advocated "noboundaryism" (*wushijie zhuyi*), which meant that the abolition of distinctions must be extended beyond humankind to all living creatures, hence that they "should study not just world language (Esperanto) but animal languages as well to create a single language."[11]

These discussions of socialism and anarchism in the Chinese Socialist party's journal, *Humanity* (*Rendao*), and the various journals published by the Social party, such as the *World of Society* (*Shehui shijie*) and *Conscience*, gave both anarchism and socialism in general a greater visibility in the politics of the early Republic than we have suspected in the past. In the long run, they help explain why interest in socialism might have flourished in the May Fourth period. In an immediate sense, they were to provoke the first efforts among Chinese radicals to come to terms with the complexities of socialism.

SHIFU AND GUANGZHOU ANARCHISM

Shifu was anything but typical among Chinese anarchists. Widely respected for his seriousness of purpose and deeply committed to practising what he preached, after his death in 1915 he was to acquire the image of a paradigmatic anarchist. By the 1920s his ideas had achieved the status of ideology: *Shifu zhuyi*, or Shifu'ism. Wu Zhihui observed on one occasion that if all Chinese anarchists were like Shifu, anarchism could be

9. "Shehui dang yuanqi ji yuezhang" (The original covenant of the Socialist party), *Liangxin* (Conscience), no. 1 (20 July 1913). In Ge Maochun et al., *WZFZYSX* 1:249–50. For an elaboration of the program, see "Shehui dang gangmu shuoming shu" (Letter clarifying the program and goals of the Socialist party), in ibid., 251–53.
10. Jiashen, "Wuzhengfuzhi yanjiu" (Examination of anarchy). *Liangxin*, no. 1 (20 July 1913). In *WZFZYSX* 1:253–54.
11. "Wushijie zhuyi," *Liangxin*, no. 2 (August 1913). In *WZFZYSX*, 265–66.

realized in five hundred years (instead of the three thousand that he expected).[12]

Nevertheless, Shifu's career illustrates the path that led radicals of his generation to anarchism.[13] He was born in 1884 and was radicalized while in Japan in 1904–1906. He joined the newly established Revolutionary Alliance and for the next two years engaged in assassination activities. An accidental explosion in 1907 cost him one of his hands and landed him in jail for the next two years. If the jail experience had a significant effect on him, it is not evident in his writings. Upon his release, he joined the China Assassination Corps (*Zhina ansha tuan*), which was to play an important part in South China in the events leading up to the revolution in 1911. While the spirit of self-sacrifice was still important in motivating those who engaged in assassination as a political tactic, Krebs has observed that the corps represented a transformation of style from individual acts of heroism toward group activity with greater coordination and discipline.[14]

Shifu was probably familiar with the anarchist ideas of Chinese radicals in the early 1900s, but there is little evidence that anarchism had any influence on his thinking beyond what was commonly understood by it in this period. His writings in jail showed a preoccupation with the moral basis of politics but owed their inspiration to contemporary debates on Chinese "national essence" rather than to anarchism.[15]

After his release from jail Shifu began to read the literature on socialism and anarchism that had begun to emanate from Tokyo and Paris; Zheng Peigang recalls that at this time Shifu recommended that Zheng read the material on socialism published in the *People's Journal* (*Minbao*) of the Revolutionary Alliance, the *New Era,* and *Natural Justice,* as well as various collections on anarchism compiled by the Paris anarchists.[16] This may also be the time when he became interested in Buddhism (he had come to know Taixu during his activities in the Assassination Corps,

12. See his contribution to the special issue on Shifu of *Minzhong* (People's tocsin) 2, no. 3 (March 1927).

13. Most of this information on Shifu is derived from the excellent study of Shifu and early Chinese anarchism by Edward S. Krebs, "Liu Ssu-fu and Chinese Anarchism, 1905–1915" (Ph.D. diss., University of Washington, 1977).

14. Ibid., 188.

15. Ibid., 117–24.

16. Zheng Peigang, "Wuzhengfu zhuyi zai Zhongguo ruogan shishi" (Some facts on anarchism in China), in *Guangzhou wenshi ziliao* (Historical and literary materials on Guangzhou), no. 1 (1963): 175. Zheng was from the same county as Shifu; his older brother Zheng Bian had been a close associate of Shifu's from the beginning. Zheng Paigang's account of his radicalization is quite revealing (ibid.).

though it is difficult to say if this had anything to do with his interest in Buddhism).

The conversion came during a trip to Shanghai and the Yangzi region in 1912 that Shifu (along with several associates) took with the possible intention of assassinating China's new strongman, Yuan Shikai. Conversion seems an appropriate term because Shifu's adoption of anarchism took place in religious surroundings (in a small Buddhist monastery near West Lake in Hangzhou), had all the characteristics of a religious ritual (including a name change to Shifu, literally meaning teacher, from his given name of Liu Sifu), and was accompanied by a conscious renunciation of the activities that had brought him to anarchism (assassination).[17]

The Conscience Society (*Xinshe*) that issued from the meeting in Hangzhou was similar to the societies Paris anarchists had organized earlier in the year, which had taken as their main focus the ethical improvement of their members. The twelve points in its covenant enjoined its members not to eat meat, drink liquor, smoke tobacco, use servants, ride in sedan chairs or rickshas, get married, use family names, serve as officials, serve in assemblies, join political parties, serve in the military, and follow religion.[18]

It was not until after their return to Guangzhou that Shifu's group acquired a clearly anarchist identity. The Conscience Society remained the "spiritual" (Krebs's words) framework for the group. In Guangzhou, Shifu and his followers launched the Cock-crow Society (*Huiming xueshe*) to propagate anarchism. In 1913 the group also started a journal of its own, the *Cock-crow Record,* which after its second issue was changed to *Minsheng* (People's voice, from *Pingminzhi sheng,* literally, "Voice of the Common People"). Anarchism in Guangzhou was on its way.[19]

When the Cock-crow Society came into existence, its membership consisted entirely of members of Shifu's family (four sisters and two brothers) and a number of close friends with whom he had been involved in radical activities over the previous years. Members of the society shared a common household, and to all appearances, Shifu had the status of a patriarch, though a democratic and benevolent one, who

17. Krebs, "Liu Ssu-fu," 244–46. Krebs's discussion of the Buddhist influence on Shifu and the Conscience Society is perceptive. While some aspects of Buddhism were blended into the practises of the group, Shifu clearly distinguished anarchism as a "rational" and "scientific" belief system from Buddhism, as well as from other Chinese traditions. See 252–57.

18. Ibid., 246, for the list.

19. Ibid., 264–69, for this society.

inspired members of his household by the example of his commitment to anarchism.[20]

There were probably other anarchists in Guangzhou. Once it had come into existence, however, Shifu's group served as the center of anarchist activity, which within the next two years attracted within its compass young anarchists who in later years would emerge as prominent leaders in the anarchist movement in China—a tribute to Shifu's seriousness of purpose.[21] Primary among the group's activities was the cultivation of a communal life among its members. Shifu's household operated as a commune, though it would appear that kitchen duties were assigned to his sisters. The group also planned for a short while to acquire land outside of Guangzhou to establish an agrarian commune (datong village), though this came to nought.[22]

Three of the group's public activities were particularly important because of their contribution to the spread of anarchism in China. First were publication activities. The group's journal, People's Voice, was to be the longest-lived of anarchist journals in China (from 1913 to 1922, irregularly after Shifu's death in 1915) and an important source of anarchist theory and activity. Shifu's group also played a crucial part in disseminating across the country the anarchist literature that had been made available in New Era and Natural Justice. Selections from the journals were compiled and published as books (in editions of five thousand copies). Thanks to these efforts, by the time of the May Fourth Movement there was more literature on anarchism (and original writings of European anarchists) available in China than for any other current in European radicalism. Shifu's own writings were distributed by his followers and would help shape a whole generation's understanding of anarchism.[23]

Second was the teaching of Esperanto. Shifu did not initiate the teaching of Esperanto, but he placed a great deal of emphasis on it as part of an internationalist program. Guangzhou anarchists, who learned Esperanto

20. Ibid., 266–67. Also see Mo Jipeng, "A Memoir of Shih Fu," unpublished ms., 52–58. I am grateful to Ed Krebs for sharing this ms. with me.
21. The list of those who came to be involved with Shifu's group reads like a who's who of Chinese anarchism in the 1920s: in addition to his brother, Liu Shixin, these included Huang Lingshuang, Huang Zunsheng, Liang Bingxian, Ou Shengbai, Yuan Zhenying, and Zheng Peigang.
22. Mo Jipeng, "Memoir," 66–71. Mo's account suggests that the inspiration came from Chinese utopias, as well as from European "utopian socialists."
23. See Zheng Peigang, "Some Facts on Anarchism," 175, and Krebs, "Liu Ssu-fu," 269–77 for the group's publication activities.

in the school he conducted in Guangzhou, would play an important part in spreading it to other parts of China in later years.[24]

Most important may have been the initiation of labor organization in South China, which would make anarchists the organizers of the first modern labor unions in China. While anarchists had earlier written of the need to bring together radical intellectuals and laborers, it was Shifu's group that first undertook such activity, propagated syndicalism in China, and, until the mid-twenties when they began to lose ground to the Communist party, provided leadership in the labor movement. Members of Shifu's group (prominent among them his brother, Liu Shixin) were responsible by the end of the decade for organizing nearly forty labor unions in Guangzhou, for the first celebration of Labor Day in China in 1918, and for the publication of the first journal (in Shanghai) devoted to labor, *Labor Magazine* (*Laodong zazhi*). Shifu apparently initiated labor organization as soon as he had established Cock-crow Society; according to one report, in 1913 he established a *Jueran julobu* (Resolution [?] Club), which served as the center for labor organizing. The initial effort had the greatest success, not with workers in the modern industrial sector, but among "masons, shoemakers, barbers, and restaurant employees."[25] This would also be the case in later years.

In late 1913, in the midst of a resurgence of political oppression, Shifu's group was forced to leave Guangzhou. After a brief sojourn in Macao, the group moved in 1914 to Shanghai. Shortly before his death from tuberculosis in March 1915, Shifu launched in Shanghai the Society of Anarcho-Communist Comrades (*Wuzhengfu gongchan zhuyi tongzhi hui*). A counterpart to the society and bearing the same name was established at about the same time in Guangzhou, led by Shifu's brother, Liu Shixin. These societies would serve after Shifu's death as the point of departure for anarchist organization during the May Fourth Movement.

Shifu was an anarchist-communist, a self-acknowledged disciple of Kropotkin. His ideas on anarchism differed little from those of the *New*

24. Krebs, "Liu Ssu-fu," 279–85. See also Wang Yan, "Wuzhengfu zhuyi yu shijieyu" (Anarchism and Esperanto), in *Guangzhou wenshi ziliao*, no. 1 (1962): 40–47.

25. Huang Yibo, "Wuzhengfu zhuyizhe zai Guangzhou gao gonghui huodong huiyi" (Recollection of anarchist labor union activities in Guangzhou), in *Guangzhou wenshi ziliao*, no. 1 (1962): 1–17; Liu Shixin, "Guanyu wuzhengfu zhuyi huodongde diandi huiyi" (Remembering bits and pieces of anarchist activity), in Ge Maochun et al., WZFZYSX 2:926–29. The reference to the early activities was from an official British report. See Daniel Y. K. Kwan, "Deng Zhongxia and the Shenggang General Strike, 1925–1926" (Ph.D. diss., University of London, 1985), 43. I am grateful to Dr. Kwan for sharing his dissertation with me.

Era anarchists. He derived much of his knowledge of anarchism, and the arguments he used in its defense, from the earlier anarchists.

Shifu, too, called for a social revolution in China. There was little ambiguity in his concept of social revolution. Unlike Jiang, but like the earlier anarchists, he used *social* in contradistinction to *political*. He believed that the social realm of life had little, if anything, to do with the political; he would not even entertain the idea of politics as an appendage to society. Politics, he seemed to believe, was extraneous to society, a force imposed upon society from the outside. Accordingly, he opposed all participation in politics. *New Era* anarchists, too, had opposed political participation and argued that true revolutionary action must be social action.[26] Unlike the latter, however, Shifu's seriousness allowed no compromise; his criticism of Zhang Ji even brought him into conflict with Wu Zhihui, one of the doyens of anarchism in China. In the early Republic, Shifu came to represent opposition to political action and the defense of a social revolution that not only was distinguished from political revolution but sought to abolish politics. "Political revolution is the revolution of heroes, the revolution of a minority," he observed; "social revolution is the revolution of the common people (*pingmin*), a revolution of the great masses."[27]

Shifu did display some hesitation over the timing of revolution, however. He remarked on one occasion that the revolution could be achieved immediately; but most of the time, his statements on the timing of revolution suggested that it would be some time before a successful anarchist revolution could be launched. At the present, he believed, only a small vanguard was aware of the necessity and the principles of revolution; most of the people lacked the knowledge that would make them good anarchists. He recommended, for instance, that workers establish syndicates at once, but he believed that the immediate tasks the syndicates ought to undertake were education of the workers and the achievement of moderate economic ends such as higher wages and shorter working hours. The fundamental task of overthrowing capitalist society and establishing an anarchist one must await the diffusion of knowledge of anarchism.[28]

The immediate task of anarchists was, therefore, to spread the word.

26. Qian Ye (Wu Zhihui), *Jiu shehui zhuyi yizheng gemingzhi yilun* (Clarifying the meaning of revolution through socialism) (Paris: Xin shiji congshu, 1906).

27. Shifu (Liu Sifu), *Shifu wencun* (Writings of Shifu, hereafter *SFWC*) (Guangzhou: Gexin shuju, 1927), 131–38, 170.

28. *SFWC*, 6, 170, 5, 81–83.

This was reflected in Shifu's program for revolutionary action. As he said repeatedly in his writings, he regarded propaganda as the first method. Through newspapers, books and pamphlets, lectures and schools, he said, the teachings of anarchism must be taken to the common people:

> [It] is essential that a majority of the people be steeped in the brilliance of our doctrines, the perfection of our theories, and the excellence of our future organization, and that labor is humankind's natural duty and mutual aid its inherent virtue.[29]

Shifu then named secondary methods—resistance and disturbances—that could hasten the diffusion of propaganda. The former could take the form of resistance to taxation and military service; it also could include strikes by workers and general strikes. "Disturbances" included assassination and other forms of political violence. Once the propaganda reached saturation point, "the great revolution of the common people" (*pingmin da geming*) could take place. In this revolution the masses would overthrow the government and the capitalists and make a fresh start in building a new society.[30] The form this society would take, moreover, must be reflected in the organization for revolution, the main reason to delay the revolution until the people were ready.

Government and the capitalist system were the twin objects of revolution; Shifu described sometimes one, sometimes the other, as the greatest enemy of the people, but to him both were equally important. To those who objected that China did not have any big capitalists, he responded that small capitalists, too, were capitalist. In the "Proclamation of the Society of Anarcho-Communist Comrades" of July 1914 and "The Goals and Methods of the Anarcho-Communist Party" published later in the same month, he summarized both the objects and the goals of the revolution. The proclamation stated: "We advocate wiping out the capitalist system to rebuild [society] as a communist society; and, moreover, not using government to oversee it. Put simply, we advocate absolute freedom in economic and political life."[31] The proclamation went on to describe the capitalist system as the greatest enemy of the people and the source of all evil in society. All of the resources of production—land, capital, and machinery—were concentrated in the hands of a few landlords and capitalists, the people were industrial slaves, and all the benefits went to the privileged minority. The anarchists pledged death to this

29. *SFWC*, 48.
30. *SFWC*, 48.
31. *SFWC*, 53.

great evil, eradication of the right to private property, and the return of all the means of production to society. Basing their own action on the principle "from each according to his ability, to each according to his need," the Society declared its intention to organize a free communist society, without distinction between male and female, with every person contributing as much as possible. The laborers could draw upon the fruits of their labor for their own needs without any limitations. Although the government claimed to maintain order for the people under the present system, the proclamation observed, in reality it transgressed against people's freedom. Thus government, too, must be eliminated so that people could enjoy their right to a free life and exercise their ability to govern themselves. The proclamation then described the differences between present society and the society envisioned by the anarchists:

> As "anarchism" takes opposition to authority as its essential principle, our party will completely eradicate and sweep away all the evil systems of present society which have an authoritarian nature, and, operating with the true spirit of freedom, equality, and fraternal love, we will reach our ideal society— without landlords, capitalists, leaders, officials, representatives, or heads of families; without armies, prisons, policemen, courts, or law; without religion and without the marriage system. At that time there will be in society only freedom, the great principle of mutual aid, and the prosperous happiness of labor.[32]

"The Goals and Methods" stated these ideas in a programmatic list that briefly called for (1) public ownership of the means of production and all the products thereof; (2) abolition of classes; (3) abolition of government and all institutions, such as laws, police, and the military, associated with government; (4) spontaneous, democratic public associations to coordinate production and distribution; (5) abolition of marriage, and the public rearing of children; (6) free public education for all; (7) labor for all mature adults (twenties to forties), after which they would retire to public retirement homes; (8) labor to be restricted to two–four hours a day and to be combined with intellectual-esthetic pursuits; (9) abolition of all religion and dogma to give free play to the morality of mutual aid; (10) an international language with the goal of abolishing all national boundaries.[33]

There was not much in this program that was original with Shifu. Some of the ideas came from Kropotkin's writings, especially the *Conquest of Bread* (which had been translated in the *New Era*), others from

32. *SFWC*, 54.
33. *SFWC*, 45–47.

writings by other anarchists. Some of the same ideas (on labor, education, family) had been incorporated a few years earlier in a description of utopia by Liu Shipei in *Natural Justice* (see chapter 3).

This was, in a sense, true of all of Shifu's ideas, which were distinguished not by their originality but by his passion in propagating them. His basic premise was one that he shared with all anarchists, Chinese or foreign: that human beings had a natural morality, which was undermined by institutions that fostered immorality. Shifu believed that all human beings were naturally endowed with conscience (*liangxin*) and were inclined by nature to mutual aid and love, as well as labor. Authoritarian institutions blunted such innate inclinations, and the institutions of property drove humans to selfishness, with the result that the pursuit of private ends overshadowed, even obliterated, the pursuit of public goals. This was the source of all conflict and exploitation in society. If these institutions were overthrown, the natural morality of people would reassert itself, and humankind would be able to shed its beastly heritage and enter the realm of humanity, where the moral and the rational would be one and the same, where all the distinctions between self and society would disappear, and where the individual would discover freedom in spontaneous association with others.[34]

This basic premise of the natural goodness of people was not new in Chinese thought, and it is evident that some Chinese were drawn to anarchism because of an affinity they perceived between anarchism and ideals long embedded in Chinese thought, whether Confucian, Daoist, or Buddhist. Liu Shipei thought that Chinese had an advantage over others in achieving anarchism because of their Confucian and Daoist heritage, which favored restricted government.[35] A series of articles in the *New Era* described the statement on utopia in the ancient Chinese work *Li Yun* (Evolution of rites) as a depiction of anarchist society, even if the author read into that statement a great deal that was not justified by the original.[36]

Shifu shared these idiosyncrasies of Chinese anarchism. There is evidence of Buddhist influence on his thought. His Conscience Society was established in an atmosphere permeated by Buddhism, and the Covenant of the Society sounded more Buddhist than anarchist. Yet such analogies

34. *SFWC*, 1–12.
35. Liu Shipei, speech at the first meeting of the Society for the Study of Socialism. Reported in *Xin shiji* (*XSJ*), no. 22 (16 November 1907).
36. "Liyun datong shiyi" (Explanation of great unity in the *Evolution of Rites*), *XSJ*, no. 38 (14 March 1908): 2.

must not be taken too far. If some Chinese were drawn to anarchism because of its affinity with elements in native thought, others criticized such interpretations as perversions of anarchism. Shifu was one of the latter. When he defended the possibility of the selflessness of human beings, it was not on the basis of native ideas but on Kropotkinite "science."[37] Like the *New Era* anarchists before him, he found nothing but corruption and selfishness in the ideology and institutions of the Chinese tradition. He rejected vehemently any suggestion that anarchism could be compared to anarchistic philosophies of the past, such as Daoism. Daoism, he believed, was negative; what he advocated was positive.[38] Shifu meant that whereas Daoists may have rejected government in the name of an eremitic existence, he sought to transform existing society and to revolutionize human life as a whole. Shifu rejected politics, not to escape it but to abolish it. His social revolution was informed by a social theory that had nothing in common with traditional political reasoning. And in making such analogies we must remember that most of the Chinese who shared with Shifu the same tradition were frightened by what he advocated: a revolution of the people that promised to overthrow existing society in its totality.

ANARCHISM AGAINST SOCIALISM

The purity of Shifu's vision of revolution made it inevitable that he would not tolerate any distortion of socialist ideals. Indeed, in 1914 he launched a series of attacks in the *People's Voice* on other socialists. Jiang Kanghu was his main target, but he included in his polemics Sun Yat-sen and the pure socialists (the splinter group of anarchist inclination from Jiang's socialist party). By this time, Sun and Jiang were both out of the country. Those who engaged Shifu in discussion were mostly the pure socialists and one or two of Jiang's followers. Jiang himself sent at least one response from the United States (where he was a professor in the Oriental Languages Department at the University of California in Berkeley), the nature of which may be gleaned from the extensive quotations in the essay Shifu wrote to refute it. To appreciate the issues involved in this first debate among Chinese socialists, a brief summary of Jiang Kanghu's ideas on socialism, which provoked the debate, is necessary.

Jiang's socialism often seemed contradictory and confusing, partially

37. Krebs, "Liu Ssu-fu," 252–57.
38. *SFWC*, 18.

because of the lack of a systematic exposition of his views: he explained his socialism for the most part in public lectures, and his emphases varied with his audiences. As Shifu was to point out, however, Jiang also suffered from considerable confusion over the goals and means of socialism. Even when he presented his ideas more systematically in the 1920s, a good bit of the confusion remained. Nevertheless, his views were not without an inner logic, and most of his contradictions are traceable to his eclectic view of socialism.

Like other socialists, Jiang saw social revolution as the essence of socialism. The Chinese Socialist party declared: "People's armies have arisen. They undertake racial revolution, speak of political revolution. But politics is the expression of society. Therefore, social revolution is the basis of all affairs."[39] In a piece he published in San Francisco in 1914, after he had left China, he sounded an even more radical note:

> The faith of the people is gone in republicanism. Their belief that it was the Manchus only who were oppressive is shattered. There remains but one thing. *The social revolution.* That and that only can bring relief to the toiling millions of China. Their only hope lies in this: the taking over of the entire mechanism of production and operation of it by the workers for the workers—the Socialist or Industrial Republic. (Italics in original)[40]

This was not all rhetoric. Jiang, of course, did not advocate political violence. In the declaration of the Socialist Research Society, he described socialism as "an ideology of peace and happiness, not a radical or dangerous one; a constructive, not a destructive, ideology," and blamed the occurrence of violence in socialist history upon the persecution to which socialists were continually subjected. He also described the socialism of this society as "nonextremist."[41]

While revolutionary politics was not integral to Jiang's idea of social revolution, he did envision the revolutionization of society over the long term. In this respect, his advocacy of social revolution was not different from that of Sun Yat-sen and the Revolutionary Alliance, which was intended to forestall, not to initiate, violence in society. Like Revolutionary Alliance socialists, moreover, Jiang believed that China did not yet suffer from the deep social divisions and exploitation that characterized Western society, and could, therefore, avoid violence and achieve socialism with greater ease than Western societies. On another occasion he

39. *HSJ*, 53–54.
40. Jiang Kanghu, *China and the Social Revolution* (San Francisco: Chinese Socialist Club, 1914), 23.
41. *HSJ*, 26, 27.

observed that most socialists, including social democrats, thought violence was necessary to achieve socialism, but he remained noncommittal,
describing the issue as academic.[42]

Indeed, Jiang believed, much as Sun and Revolutionary Alliance socialists did, that socialism, rather than presenting a threat to the republican
order, would fulfill the promise of republican government. Western societies had fallen short of the ideals of equality and democracy, he believed,
because they had failed to institute socialism, and democracy could not
be realized without socialism.[43] For the same reason, he argued, socialism
needed republicanism, for otherwise the collectivization of property
would lead to despotism.[44] Specifically, for China, he argued that because
of the persistence of habits left from despotism of the state and the family,
and because of the existence of internal and external oppression, it was
necessary to bolster republican institutions with socialist policies. In his
defense of the Chinese Socialist party before the government, he argued
that socialism served the cause of the state and the development of the
economy, including commerce, industry, and taxation. In other words,
his socialism was meant to further not just the cause of justice but the
cause of the nation as well. He presented similar arguments to Shanghai
merchants to induce them to support his party. Above all, Jiang bolstered
his arguments with the observation that socialism represented a new tide
in world politics and that China could not afford to close its doors to this
thought and isolate itself from the world.[45]

Jiang's socialism consisted of a vague humanitarianism that sought to
guarantee, not equality so much as equality of opportunity by clearing
away institutional and ideological obstacles to equality inherited from the
past. Indeed, when he did define socialism, he defined it vaguely as "humanitarianism" or as "the pursuit of common welfare and happiness for
humankind." "Socialism," he explained, "is the ideology of great unity
(*datong*), not of differentiation. [It] does not heed racial, national, or
religious boundaries. [All is] for the public good, not the self; [all are]
treated with equal benevolence. [All will enjoy] absolute equality, absolute freedom, absolute love."[46] Jiang's vision of the good society may

42. *HSJ*, 18 and 40.
43. *HSJ*, 41.
44. *HSJ*, 97. This point had been made earlier by Hu Hanmin in his defense of socialism
in the Revolutionary Alliance. See Min Yi, "Gao feinan minsheng zhuyizhe" (Response to
attacks on the principle of people's livelihood), *Minbao* (People's journal), no. 12 (6 March
1907): 102.
45. *HSJ*, 43–44; 76–77.
46. *HSJ*, 82, 15, 26.

have been inspired by his readings in the *New Era*, for it did have anarchist overtones. He observed in one of his essays that humanity was "naturally" evolving toward a "world socialism" when there would be no state, race, family, or religion, and the only distinctions between people would be those of learning and profession. In such a society there would be no need for customs duties or military expenditure. Old views of politics, law, livelihood, and old customs would be transformed until no obstacles divided the individual from the world. Such a world would be governed without action. Jiang concluded that this was the world dreamed of by the anarchists, the world of the "great unity" of Confucius, the Heaven of the Christians, and the Paradise of the Buddhists.[47] As this last statement suggests, Jiang also viewed socialism as merely the latest manifestation of a longing for good society that was a common heritage of humankind, with an especially long history in China.

All this, however, lay in the future. "Pure" or "strict" socialism, which he identified with communism, was not on the agenda for the present; he therefore preferred to advocate a "broad" socialism that was not inconsistent with contemporary political organization. One of his reasons for advocating broad rather than strict socialism was the rather academic reason that until knowledge of socialism acquired greater depth, it was impossible to say which type was the most desirable; insisting on one type or another would only create sectarianism.[48] Jiang did not believe that the workers in China were yet mature enough to create socialism; and since socialism required the participation of workers, at the present it was best to propagate, rather than try to institute, socialism.

Jiang was aware of the eclecticism of his position when he discussed his own socialism. Of all the currents in socialist thought, he believed himself to be closest to social democracy, which he viewed as being akin to communism, a transitional stage on the way to the ideal society. But even this does not adequately convey his efforts to reconcile different kinds of socialism. In a letter he wrote to the government in December 1912 to protest the proscription of the "Pure" Social party, he undertook a survey of socialism and divided it into the socialism of philosophers, scientists, political scientists, ecclesiastics, educationalists, laborers, the state, anarchist-communists, individualists, Esperanto, and the single-tax. He then went on to describe his own views:

47. *HSJ*, 41.
48. *HSJ*, 4.

What I hope for, what I advocate, is derived from the thought of philosophers, based on science, adopts the spirit of the ecclesiastics and the attitude of educationalists, and grasps the affairs of laborers. It holds on, on the one hand, to radical republicanism, and, on the other hand, to a progressive collectivist system [which he had earlier equated with communism]. [It seeks to] eliminate taxes and the military, and stresses education and industry. [It] takes the individual to be the nucleus of society and the world its realm. [It seeks to realize] self-governance for the individual and great unity for the world. This kind of hope, this kind of advocacy, could be called individual socialism; it could also be called world socialism.[49]

Given this eclecticism, Jiang's formal statements about the goals of his socialism tell us little about the main thrust of the ideas he propagated. His immediate programs for the achievement of socialism, however, are a great deal more revealing. Jiang viewed three policies as fundamental to his socialist program: public education, freedom of occupation, and independence of wealth, or the abolition of inheritance. The two he talked about the most, the first and the third, were incorporated into the program of the Chinese Socialist party.

Public education was the cornerstone of Jiang's socialist program. He perceived inequality in education as the source of all inequality in society: "Economic inequality arises from inequality in ability; inequality in ability arises from inequality in education." In China, education was unequal because it was private, family education; in countries where public education had been instituted, inequality of wealth made for unequal access to education, with the result that the rich monopolized education and sustained economic inequality. Jiang believed that inequality in ability arose not from natural differences but from inequality in access to education. He advocated that every individual be given free education by public organs from birth to maturity. If this could be done, then each individual would gain independence of livelihood and serve himself or herself as well as society. In a few generations the inequalities inherited from family background would disappear, and all would be able to seek livelihood in equality. The only remaining inequalities would be in the professions and learning, not of class and wealth. Jiang's emphasis on education accorded with his belief that social change must start with change in the individual.[50]

Occupational freedom would have a similar effect. If each individual sought an occupation in accordance with his or her talents, the virtuous

49. *HSJ*, 97.
50. *HSJ*, 63, 28–29, 9.

would seek to advance and the degenerate would not dare to remain idle. Rights and obligations would be harmonized. And since each would exert himself or herself to the utmost, both society and the individual would benefit.

Finally, Jiang viewed inheritance as the "greatest crime in the world," "the source of all inequality," and advocated what he called "independence of property" (*caichan duli*). Inheritance not only perpetuated inequality, it had a demoralizing effect on the individual. What a person inherited did not represent his or her labor. Such wealth not only was unjustifiable, it also nurtured a parasitic dependence on the family. In Jiang's solution all wealth acquired during the lifetime of an individual would revert to the public coffers at the individual's death so that each generation would have to make a living for itself. This way, the inequality that attended every individual at birth would be eliminated, and greater independence would be stimulated.[51]

All three items of Jiang's socialist program were informed by his ultimate commitment to the individual as the source and the end of socialism. Jiang even distinguished himself from other socialists by his emphasis on the individual:

> From beginning to end, I have taken the individual to be the [basic] unit of the world. This is my difference from socialists in general who take society as their only premise. If society is taken as the sole premise, the result is to disdain the individual: trampled upon [in this way], the individual loses worth as the unit [of the world], which, in turn, obliterates the spirit of independence and initiative. [This] reduces the individual to the [level of the] scales of fish and dragons, or the cog in a machine.

Jiang described his individualism as the "new individualism" (*xin geren zhuyi*). The new individualism, unlike the old individualisms that consisted of self-seeking or the search for individual sovereignty, simultaneously stressed the independence and the interdependence of individuals.[52] Jiang believed in the possibility of achieving this new individualism more on utilitarian than on ethical grounds. He argued that all people by nature sought to maximize their security and happiness (*anle*). Since ideas on how to achieve this end differed, the search for happiness of each interfered with the search for happiness of others, so that none felt secure in his or her happiness. Therefore, they had to learn that to benefit the self, one had to benefit others: "Benefiting the self is the goal of all people; benefiting others is the means to achieving that goal." To achieve the new individual-

51. *HSJ*, 106, 30, 29, 31.
52. *HSJ*, 31.

ism, Jiang argued, all obstacles that stood between the individual and the world ought to be abolished, in particular religion, the state, and the family.[53]

His new individualism, Jiang believed, rendered his socialism superior to others. He was opposed to the egalitarianism of communism, which he otherwise admired, on two grounds. First, the ideal of "from each according to his ability, to each according to his need" left no way to deal with those who did not contribute according to their ability but simply took advantage of the system. Jiang thought this consequence to be very likely, given human inclinations. Second, Jiang was a social Darwinist in outlook and saw competition as the key to progress. If absolute equality prevailed, he believed, society would stagnate.[54] He had expressed this view as early as 1909 in his defense of free enterprise in his *New Era* article, and he would hold it throughout his career.[55] On these two grounds, he was reluctant to abolish property (as long as it was acquired by individual effort) or unequal remuneration for different kinds and levels of labor. As long as people had incentive, he believed, they would strive to better their lot, and the whole society would benefit. What he sought in socialism, as was noted above, was independence and equality of opportunity, not egalitarianism.

Jiang's socialism contained much that was unorthodox, even unsocialist, but his arguments were not without a logic of their own. The problems of his socialism are best appreciated in terms of his earlier preoccupations with the family and women's liberation. Jiang was involved in the problems of women's education long before he became a socialist. In his earliest available essays, the problems that preoccupied him were the oppression of women and the means to abolish it. He blamed the family structure for the inferior role women held in society and, long before the idea was to become prevalent during the New Culture Movement, described the family as the source of all evils in society.[56] The family suppressed the individuality of women and, by denying them education, made them dependent on males. The cure, he believed, was to educate women and provide them with professions that they might gain independence and compete with males on an equal basis. When he turned to advocating socialism, Jiang generalized these problems of women and

53. *HSJ*, 35, 36.
54. *HSJ*, 28.
55. Xu Ancheng (pseud. Jiang Kanghu), "Ziyou yingye guanjian" (Views on private enterprise), *XSJ*, no. 97 (15 May 1909).
56. *HSJ*, 3.

the family to the whole of humankind. This connection between his socialism and his perceptions of the problems of women might explain why August Bebel's *Women and Socialism* was a favorite book of his, as Bernal has pointed out, and why the first lecture he ever gave on socialism was essentially a lecture on women's problems. It also explains the peculiarities of his socialist program: his emphasis on the new individualism, on inheritance, on the need to seek independent livelihood—ideas he had articulated first in his discussions on women's problems. Jiang's socialism, one is tempted to observe, was more antifamily than anticapitalist in its program.[57]

At issue in Shifu's polemics against the socialists was the nature of socialism. In spite of the pedantic nature of the discussion, which often presented the problem at hand as a problem of scholarship, the polemics were motivated mainly by a struggle over the intellectual leadership of the socialist movement in China. It is clear from many of Shifu's statements that he was irked by the claims of Sun and Jiang to the leadership of socialism in China, and even more by the willingness of many to take them at their word.[58]

Nevertheless, the polemics raised issues of substance that were to divide anarchists and other socialists in ensuing years. The starting point of the discussion was the question whether Sun and Jiang were really socialists. This inevitably led to the question of what constituted socialism, and to answer this Shifu (and to a lesser extent Jiang) turned to analysis of the terminology and history of socialism. Shifu obviously desired to vindicate his views, but in the process he did much to clear away the terminological confusion that had plagued Chinese socialism for a decade. Most of his criticisms, moreover, were quite justified if not unbiased.

What brought Sun into Shifu's polemics was a lecture Sun had given in 1912 to a gathering of the Chinese Socialist party. In his lecture Sun reiterated his commitment to socialism and elaborated on the socialist program he had advocated since Revolutionary Alliance days: the utilization of Henry George's single-tax policy to equalize landownership, and the control of monopolies. He also embarked on a prolonged dis-

---

57. Bernal, "Chinese Socialism before 1913."
58. *SFWC*, 32, 191. The major articles Shifu wrote were "Sun Yixian Jiang Kanghu zhi shehui zhuyi" (The socialism of Sun Zhongshan and Jiang Kanghu), *Minsheng* (People's voice, *MS*), no. 6 (18 April 1914); "Lun Shehui dang" (The Socialist party), *MS*, no. 9 (9 May 1914); "Da Jiang Kanghu" (Answer to Jiang Kanghu), *MS*, no. 8 (2 May 1914); "Bo Jiang Kanghu" (Refutation of Jiang Kanghu), *MS*, no. 15 (21 June 1914), written in response to Jiang's "A Critique of a Critique of Socialism," which he had written in the United States; "Jiang Kanghu zhi wuzhengfu zhuyi" (The anarchism of Jiang Kanghu), *MS*, no. 17 (14 July 1914). The discussion here is based on reprints in *SFWC*.

course on socialism, where he acknowledged Marx as the father of socialism but insisted that Marx's ideas be complemented with George's because George had made equally important contributions to socialism. Sun also described communism as the highest ideal of all socialism, but expressed doubt that people were morally prepared for the realization of that ideal.[59]

Shifu attacked Sun and Jiang in the same article. His arguments against the two varied with the different policies they proposed, but basically he levied the same charges against both. First, he said that neither Sun nor Jiang advocated social revolution, that both advocated social policy. They were not even socialists, since they did not propose to abolish private property, the sine qua non of all socialism. Jiang's inheritance scheme and Sun's single-tax policy were both characteristic of state socialism, which was quite different from socialism (as Jiang himself had stated in one of his writings). Second, he charged them with ignorance of socialism. Neither of them was clear about the differences between capitalism and socialism, and they easily blended the two. They were not even aware of the differences among socialists, as was evident in Sun's equation of Marx and George and in Jiang's many statements confounding anarchism, communism, social democracy, and state socialism. Socialists were one in advocating the abolition of private property, Shifu pointed out, but there was a basic difference among socialists over how this goal was to be achieved. Socialists (including Marxists) argued for collectivism, that is, control of property by public organs—namely, the state. Only anarchists advocated communism, which signified direct control of property by the people themselves. Jiang, in Shifu's opinion, displayed utter ignorance of this fact in his contradictory statements about communism. Shifu also criticized Jiang for his belief in the necessity of competition, which ran counter to the spirit that underlay socialism.[60]

Shifu's criticism of the pure socialists was in a different vein. The pure socialists had broken with Jiang's party because of their anarchist inclinations, and indeed their program revealed their anarchist premises. Shifu was not entirely happy with this program, which displayed nativistic and nationalistic tendencies, but his basic criticism was of their retention of the word "socialist" in their party name. If they were anarchists, he stated, they should call themselves anarchists and not socialists.[61]

The controversy that followed revolved around the question of what

59. *Sun Yixian shehui zhuyi tan* (Sun Yat-sen's discussion of socialism) (n.p., 1912).
60. *SFWC*, 21–32.
61. *SFWC*, 34–36.

constituted socialism, and the relationship of socialism to anarchism. To refute his opponents, Shifu drew upon his considerable knowledge of the history of socialism to clarify questions on the evolution of terminology. The details were often tedious and pedantic, but his major points were, briefly, these: (1) socialism and anarchism represented two different currents from the beginning. Jiang was wrong in his assertion that until Bakunin's split with Marx in 1871, anarchism had been indistinct from socialism. Though Shifu was willing to acknowledge Marx's contributions to socialism, he rejected Jiang's suggestion that Marx was the "pope" of socialism. He himself viewed Marx as a state socialist who had derived most of his collectivist ideas from Saint-Simon;[62] (2) anarchism was more scientific than Marxism. Marx was a scientific socialist, but Kropotkin had given socialism a firmer scientific basis;[63] (3) anarchism was broader in compass than socialism. "Socialism pertained to the economy, anarchism to politics." But while all anarchists were of necessity also socialists, socialists were not anarchists, because they were not opposed to government; anarchism, therefore, contained socialism.[64] Shifu rejected the suggestion that since the concept of society included everything within it, socialism represented the broader concept. Society, he argued, did not cover politics, which was extraneous to it; it was not correct to say, therefore, that socialism could include anarchism.[65]

In rejecting terms such as "extreme socialism," "pure socialism," "nongoverning" (*wuzhi*) that had been used variously to describe anarchism, Shifu was able to clarify a number of terminological and conceptual questions pertaining to anarchism and point out its autonomous content. Not least important was his clarification of the meaning of the common Chinese term for anarchism, *wuzhengfu zhuyi* (literally, no-governmentalism), which many apparently took literally as only the rejection of government, nothing more. Shifu, citing the original foreign terminology, pointed out that the misunderstanding was a matter of translation, and that anarchism included opposition to all authority, not just government. Moreover, he explained, this was only the negative aspect of anarchism. On the positive side, anarchists sought to reorganize society and establish a totally new kind of society.[66]

His contribution to the discussion, however, went beyond matters of

62. *SFWC*, 232–51.
63. *SFWC*, 218.
64. *SFWC*, 15–16.
65. *SFWC*, 211–13.
66. *SFWC*, 147–48.

terminology. Shifu was quite justified in his critique of the confusion over socialism in the thinking of Sun and Jiang. His own terminological purity was rather vacuous; anarchists in the West did not disassociate themselves from the term *socialism,* and Kropotkin himself used *anarchism* and *socialism* interchangeably in his writings. In the case of Sun and Jiang, however, the confusion was basically conceptual. Both men confounded not only different currents in socialism but socialism and capitalism as well. Their ideas on socialism echoed the views of late-nineteenth-century social reformers who used socialist policies to preserve and improve, not to overthrow, the existing capitalist system. Sun, as Shifu pointed out, never quite understood capitalism, and while he was opposed to monopoly capital, he never rejected capitalism as such. That this was an accurate diagnosis is evident in the essay by Hu Hanmin published a number of years earlier in the *People's Journal* to explain Sun's policies. If Hu's explanation reflected Sun's views, and there is little reason to think it did not, Sun himself advocated equality of opportunity, not an egalitarian socialism.[67]

The same was true of Jiang's socialism, as we have already noted. Shifu observed in one of his essays that Jiang peddled the ideas of Saint-Simon in China.[68] While Jiang's own writings did not acknowledge any intellectual debt to Saint-Simon, there are intriguing resemblances between Jiang's and Saint-Simon's ideas, especially in Jiang's emphasis on the abolition of inheritance, his view that learning should be the only basis for inequality, his stress on professional education, and his insistence on the creation of an "industrial republic" to replace the existing one.[69] Jiang's insistence that inherited inequality should be abolished and everyone be given an equal start in life through education was quite reminiscent of Saint-Simon, who rejected hereditary inequality but not that inequality which was a product of differences in personal effort and learning. Whether Jiang owed his ideas to Saint-Simon or not, it is clear that his socialism did condone inequality. In later years, Jiang would change the details of his program but never this basic premise; if anything, he became more sympathetic to capitalists even as he continued to advocate socialism.[70]

Shifu's own views, too, contained serious flaws, not the least of which

67. Min Yi, "Gao feinan minsheng zhuyizhe," 102.
68. *SFWC,* 17.
69. See G. D. H. Cole, *A History of Socialist Thought* (New York: Macmillan, 1953), 1:40–50.
70. See Jiang Kanghu, *Jiang Kanghu yanjiang lu* (Speeches of Jiang Kanghu), 2 vols. (Shanghai: Nanfang daxue, 1923).

was the consistency he imposed upon socialism and anarchism. There is no question that he had a better grasp of the history of socialism in Europe than his adversaries had; nevertheless, his was a history of socialism seen through anarchist eyes. He reduced all socialists to a uniform field of collectivism, a term he equated with state socialism, in contradistinction to communism, which he identified with anarchism. He saw Marxism in terms of its contemporary manifestations, which represented various modes of accommodation of the capitalist state, and completely ignored the revolutionary vision that had informed Marx's own writings, a vision that did not differ significantly from the anarchist one. Moreover, Shifu was himself selective in his use of history. While he pointed to their emphasis on the abolition of inheritance as proof that both Marx and Jiang were state socialists, he ignored the fact that it was Bakunin's insistence on the abolition of inheritance (which Marx had opposed as a petit-bourgeois measure) that had divided the Basle Congress of the First International in 1869. It is possible, of course, that Shifu was unaware of this conflict, but he did display knowledge of other intricate aspects of the conflicts within the International, and it would be surprising if he did not have access to this rather conspicuous fact.[71]

Like Kropotkin himself, Shifu ignored the fact that anarchists owed much of their social theory (the analysis of classes and capitalism) to Marxism.[72] The anarchist contribution to socialist theory lay in their insistence on the need to recognize the autonomous power of the state, which Marx had encompassed (at least on the surface) within the structure of social interests. But there was little in anarchist social theory that went beyond Marx's formulations. By ignoring this, Shifu was able, unjustifiably, to claim the whole territory of socialism for anarchism.

Finally, Shifu missed the point about socialism in his insistence that socialism pertained only to the economy and that politics existed independently of society (which contradicted his own belief that politics served class interest). He came closer to the truth with anarchists who, while they have not ignored the problem of social relations, have been most conspicuous for their preoccupation with authority, especially political authority.[73] But the distinguishing feature of socialist theory lies in its integration of various aspects of existence into a unified analysis so that it is impossible to explain one aspect in isolation. However socialists may have differed other-

71. *SFWC*, 24. For Bakunin's views, see *Bakunin on Anarchy*, ed. Sam Dolgoff (New York: Knopf, 1972).
72. Martin Miller, *Kropotkin* (Chicago: University of Chicago Press, 1976), chap. 12.
73. Paul Avrich, *The Russian Anarchists* (New York: Norton, 1978), 83–84.

wise, they did not separate economic, social, and political problems: the goal of economic change was also to effect changes in social and political relations. Shifu denied any significant role to politics, of course, but this premise of the integratedness of economic, social, and political relations was implicit in the theory that he himself upheld. His efforts to restrict the scope of socialism, therefore, are best understood in terms of his urge to prove the superiority of anarchism by endowing it with an all-encompassing scope that covered what socialism purportedly did not.

If anarchism has a broader scope than socialism, Marxist or otherwise, it is in the loyalty to the vision of humanity that all socialists have shared without being equally persistent in their loyalty. And if Shifu had an edge over his adversaries in these polemics, it was due, not merely to his superior knowledge, but, equally important, to his visionary consistency. Jiang and Sun did indeed make statements about socialism that were indefensible in terms of vision or theory; but they did show some sensitivity to the realities around them. Shifu ignored almost totally the conditions within which he propagated his ideas. Like other anarchists, his views on revolution were ahistorical, based on certain universal premises about human beings and their relationship to society and politics. On the rare occasions when he did refer to China's specific conditions, he conceded (without saying so) that Chinese were not yet ready for the revolution he advocated. In fact, he, like other anarchists, faced a dilemma that he was unwilling to acknowledge: that the revolution that would usher in anarchist society must await the education of people to prepare them for anarchism, but that such education was impossible as long as bad society persisted. His anarchism provided a vision but no way of achieving it.

CONCLUSION

Anarchist-socialist differences reflected a basic difference in the conceptualization of the role of self-interest in society. On the one hand, anarchists rejected the naturalness of interest and viewed it as the fabrication of a social structure warped by power and exploitation. They believed that interest could be abolished if society were reconstituted in accordance with the natural cooperative inclinations of humanity. Socialists such as Sun and Jiang, on the other hand, held a different view of interest, each for his own reason. Jiang, taking the pursuit of self-interest as a natural endowment of humanity, denied the possibility of abolishing it. Sun, while he rejected this premise, nevertheless thought that the pursuit of self-interest had accounted for the immense development of the West under capitalism and believed that, if kept within bounds, it would also contribute to China's development.

The attitudes of Sun and Jiang toward politics were functions of these premises concerning interest. Anarchists, who saw in politics one of the basic sources for the undermining of natural morality, viewed the abolition of politics and the abolition of "selfishness" as part of the same process. Both Sun and Jiang saw in politics a means—the only means—to control private interest and bring it into the service of society, rather than of a privileged minority.

Socialists and anarchists were one in their belief that China required more than a political revolution, that society itself would have to undergo important changes if their goals were to be realized. But they held different views about how this was to be achieved. Anarchists advocated a "spontaneous" revolution that would abolish all existing institutions. Both Jiang and Sun, however, advocated a revolution whose goal was to curtail precisely that eventuality. Jiang was muddy on this issue at the time, though he would state it more explicitly at a later time. Sun was very clear all along that his policies were "hygienic," designed to forestall the sharpening of class conflict to the point where only a social upheaval could resolve it. Both sought to harmonize conflicting interests in society through the intermediacy of politics.

These two modes of approach to social change and revolution represented the two basic messages socialism conveyed to Chinese revolutionaries in the years before 1919: a vision of total revolutionary transformation, and a political theory that showed the way to reorganize interest in order to achieve greater equality and minimize conflict. Regardless of the peculiarly Chinese coating these messages assumed in China, they reflected the two major currents in European socialism at the turn of the century. Sun and Jiang advocated diffuse socialisms that did not even reject basic institutions or ideas of capitalism, and they could point for support to trends in European socialism, which increasingly had come to accommodate capitalism and strove to use the power of the state to regulate interest in society. As socialism lost its revolutionary vision, anarchists remained the only ones to retain their faithfulness to the original goals of socialist revolution.

Anarchists were unable, however, to convert their vision into revolutionary reality. This was especially a problem for the Chinese anarchists, who did not even have a constituency for the social revolution they proposed. In the end, they too had to fall back upon the argument that the people were not yet ready for anarchism.

This would change in the 1920s when Chinese society experienced large-scale mass mobilization. The revolutionization of Chinese society (accompanied by a general loss of faith in politics) increased receptivity to the anarchist argument. And anarchists proved to be better prepared than most in responding to such spontaneous mobilization. Many of Shifu's disciples resurfaced at this time to provide leadership to the anarchist movement.

This time, however, anarchists were to find a more serious competitor on the Left. After the establishment of the Communist party in 1921, anarchists had to compete with the Communists over the leadership of mass movements, and though they initially had an advantage over the Communists both in the student and in the labor movement, by 1921–22 they had already begun to lose ground to the latter. The Communists believed in social revolution as fervently as did the anarchists, but to them social revolution meant the basis for a new kind of politics, not a substitute for it. Anarchists, philosophically suspicious of political organization, were not able to coordinate their activities sufficiently to compete with the Communists for any length of time. The Communists shared their vision (which deprived the anarchists of their major propaganda appeal) and had the edge over them in organization as well as in consciousness of the realities of power.

CHAPTER FIVE

Radical Culture and Cultural Revolution

Anarchism in the May Fourth Movement

In the early afternoon of May 4, 1919, three thousand students from three Beijing universities gathered at Beijing's Tiananmen Square to demonstrate against the Versailles Peace Conference decision in favor of Japan on the Shandong Question. The students had originally intended to continue their demonstration in the foreign legation quarters in Beijing, but finding their way blocked by the legation police, they proceeded instead to the house of Cao Rulin, a Foreign Ministry official who had drawn the ire of the patriotic students for his pro-Japanese sentiments. The students were stymied momentarily by the police who had cordoned off the house, and by the imposing wooden gates that shut them off. Suddenly, a fourth-year Beijing Higher Normal College student from Hunan, Kuang Husheng, rushed to the house, smashed the thick wooden shutters of the gate window, climbed in, and flung open the gates to let in the rest of the students. He then set the torch to the house with the matches with which he had come prepared. Kuang was an anarchist.[1]

1. Kuang Husheng, "Wusi yundong jishi" (Record of the May Fourth movement), in *Wusi aiguo yundong* (The May Fourth patriotic movement), 2 vols. (Beijing: Shehui kexue yanjiu yuan, 1979), 1:498; and "Annaqi zhuyi zai Zhongguode zhuanpan huodong duanpian" (A brief discussion of the propagation and activities of anarchism in China), in *Wenshi ziliao xuanji* (Selections from literary and historical source materials) (Beijing: Wenshi ziliao chubanshe, 1983), 90:121. Kuang had participated in revolutionary activities in Hunan before he enrolled in Beijing Higher Normal College (present-day Normal University). He later became a teacher in Hunan First Normal in Changsha (a source of many radicals at this time, including Mao). In the mid-1920s he ran an experimental school in Shanghai (see below, chap. 8). He was apparently adept at martial arts. He and his comrades participated in the events of May 4, 1919, apparently all prepared to die. See Kuang, 494.

It was appropriate that this dramatic event, which set off the chain of events that was to become the May Fourth Movement, was carried out by an anarchist. Kuang's action dramatized the anarchist influence on Chinese intellectuals of the May Fourth period. Anarchism was soon to become anachronistic in China. The May Fourth Movement presaged a rising tide of patriotism, which would gradually render anarchism marginal in Chinese radical thinking. But the years immediately before and after the May Fourth Movement represented the apogee in the hold of anarchism upon the Chinese radical imagination. The May Fourth Movement was truly a revolutionary moment in modern Chinese history. It kindled the radical imagination and seemed to give substance to the utopian hopes of a whole generation. Kuang himself recollected that during the march to Cao's house "individuals lost their identity in the mass, everyone sang together, everyone marched together."[2] His sentiments stand as a metaphor for the revolutionary hopes the movement evoked among the young students. Anarchism expressed these hopes.

If "social change was at the heart of what progressive May Fourth publications advocated and discussed" by 1919, the language of anarchism was the tongue in which this advocacy found its expression.[3] By the eve of the May Fourth Movement, anarchists' vocabulary had already become integral to the language of radicalism in China. This is not to say that Chinese intellectuals wholesale became anarchists. In an immediate sense, anarchism benefited from the turn the Chinese revolutionary movement took in about 1919; it moved into the center of mainstream radical thinking, it spread beyond a few centers to become a national phenomenon, and there was a virtual explosion in the numbers of anarchists as anarchist groups and publications proliferated throughout the country.[4] More important in the long run, however, anarchist ideas entered the language even of those who could not be described as anarchists in any strict sense of the word. Anarchism became central to revolutionary discourse.

2. Kuang, "Wusi yundong jishi," 494.
3. *Wusi shiqi qikan jieshao* (Introduction to the periodicals of the May Fourth period), 3 vols. (Beijing: Sanlian shudian, 1979), vol. 1, pt. 1, 321.
4. Between 1919 and 1928, ninety-two anarchist societies were established in various parts of China, many of them publishing their own journals. Although these societies did not survive long enough to be significant, their numbers and geographical spread indicate the popularity of anarchism. The numbers peaked in 1922–23. See the listing in *Wuzhengfu zhuyi sixiang ziliao xuan* (Selection of Materials on Anarchist Thought [*WZFZYSX*]), ed. Ge Maochun et al., 2 vols. (Beijing: Beijing daxue chubanshe, 1983), 2:1059–87, and *Wusi shiqide shetuan* (Societies of the May Fourth period), 4 vols. (Beijing: Sanlian shudian, 1979), 4:325–51.

The popularity of anarchism at this time had much to do with the reorientation of Chinese radical thinking with the so-called New Culture Movement after 1915, which brought to the fore intellectual concerns—and a radical mood—that resonated with the themes anarchists had raised over the previous decade. Ironically, the October Revolution in Russia in 1917 initially helped stimulate in China an interest, not in Bolshevism or Marxism, but in anarchism. Anarchists were not passive beneficiaries of this reorientation, however. As the only group of "organized" social radicals in China, they actively promoted anarchism, injected an anarchist strain into New Culture thinking, and engaged in organizational activities that helped shape the form radical activism took in the May Fourth period.

CONTEMPORARY WITNESSES

In early 1920 the U.S. Department of State instructed its consular officials in China to report on "Bolshevist" activities. Over the next year, a stream of reports on "Communistic Activities" flowed into the files of the State Department. American consuls in China went combing the country in search of "Bolshevists," mobilizing the help of their British colleagues on occasion, and, where possible, prevailing upon Chinese officials to put a stop to "Bolshevist" activities. Although they did not uncover as much activity as they might have wished, in one or two places they did discover an alarming level of "Bolshevist" activity. By far the largest number of dispatches issued from the American consulate in Amoy, which discovered that "Bolshevist . . . doctrines" had "made a considerable impression" in, surprisingly, the Zhangzhou region of Fujian province. An April 10, 1920, dispatch from the Amoy consulate on the subject "Bolshevist Propaganda" is quoted at length for its revelations:

> I have the honor to report that Bolshevist propaganda is carried on in the city of Changchow, inland from Amoy, the seat of the military government of General Chen Chiung Ming [Chen Jiongming] commanding the Southern forces.
>
> I am informed that teachers in the Chinese government schools at Changchow have been spreading the Bolshevist doctrine, and occasionally breaking out and waving the red flag. At a recent athletic meeting, held on a large scale, at Changchow, pamphlets in Chinese advocating anarchical communism were circulated. I enclose a rough translation in English of one such pamphlet, which was handed personally by General Chen Chiung Ming to a foreign visitor to Changchow who was present at the athletic meet. General Chen Chiung Ming is reported to have made an address at a tiffin to officials and foreigners, held on the athletic grounds, and to have himself advocated some

of the socialistic doctrines set out in the pamphlet. Turning to the foreign missionaries present, he is reported to have said that the Savior himself was a socialist, and what is a socialist but a Bolshevik.[5]

An April 24 dispatch forwarded to the embassy in Beijing included additional translations of Bolshevist pamphlets, as well as a proclamation issued by the magistrate of Amoy. The latter read:

> The propagation of Anarchism and Bolshevism is contrary to the public peace and morals, destroying virtue and the Five Human Relationships (parents and children; husband and wife; brother and sister [sic]; sovereign and subject; friends).
>
> Hereafter anyone may arrest persons engaged in distributing this printed matter and send them to the court or hand them over to the police, to be severely punished.[6]

The confounding of anarchism and Bolshevism in these reports, whatever it may say about the political education of American diplomats, was nevertheless typical of the confusion that prevailed at this time over the relationship of these radical ideologies. But not everyone was confused. In a "service report" he filed to the State Department in December 1920, John Dewey observed, with reference to the case of a student who had been arrested two months earlier in Beijing for spreading "Bolshevist" literature, that he investigated and found that "it was truly anarchistic, advocating the abolition of government and the family, but no Bolshevist." Though there might be a few Bolsheviks around the country, Dewey continued, they had "nothing to do with the general tone and temper of radical thought in the country."[7] Had American consular officials in Amoy investigated the "Bolshevist literature" they discovered in Zhangzhou with the same perspicacity, they might have reached a similar conclusion: this literature was clearly anarchist, produced and distributed by followers of Shifu, who had accompanied Chen Jiongming to Fujian in 1918.

Dewey was to be proven wrong concerning the prospects of Bolshevism in China. But his assessment of the situation in 1919–20 was accurate. In the eyes of contemporaries, anarchism was by far the most important current in Chinese radical thinking of the time.

In June 1919, Chen Duxiu wrote in the *Meizhou pinglun* (Weekly

5. American Consulate, Amoy, "Bolshevist Propaganda in the Amoy Consular District" (Dispatch no. 306), 10 April 1920, in *Records of the Department of State Relating to Internal Affairs of China, 1910–1929* (Washington, D.C.: The National Archives, 1960), Roll 71.

6. Ibid. (Dispatch no. 313), 24 April 1920.

7. John Dewey, "Bolshevism in China," Service Report (2 December 1920), in ibid.

critic) that toward the end of the Qing dynasty, officials accused everyone who was politically suspect of being a member of the *Tongmeng hui* (Revolutionary Alliance). Since the Revolution of 1911 they had all learned to praise the Revolutionary Alliance. Now, he complained, everyone who was politically undesirable was called an anarchist, despite the fact that there were actually few anarchists in China.[8]

Chen's comment suggests that it was government stereotyping of radicals, rather than the popularity of anarchism, that created the impression of widespread anarchist activity in China. This had some truth to it. An accurate estimate of the number of anarchists in China at that time may never be possible; it is unlikely, however, that there were ever more than a few hundred active and committed anarchists at any one time. Anarchist associations were loosely organized, short-lived, and diffuse in membership. Anarchist efforts to organize a coherent federation foundered before the unwillingness of anarchists to submit to organization discipline.

Nevertheless, Chinese officials made a strenuous effort to suppress anarchist activity, which itself was a major reason for the fluidity of anarchist associations. Government agents infiltrated anarchist organizations, anarchist publications were often suppressed as soon as they had come into being, and anarchists had to keep on the move to escape government detection and arrest.[9] This constant motion, necessitated by government suppression, was ironically a possible reason for government fears of a widespread anarchist conspiracy.

The Chinese government during this period identified "extremism" (*guoji zhuyi*) with anarchism, and in its constant efforts to track down extremists, gave publicity to the anarchist cause. The internal documents of the Beijing government reveal that authorities were genuinely concerned about the effects on the population—students, workers, and especially soldiers—of the "seditious" literature that kept popping up in post offices across the country. Concerning an appeal to soldiers, written by a Baoding anarchist named Li Desheng, an official wrote in May 1919 that if this kind of "crazy talk" was permitted to spread, it would "disturb order and destroy the peace, which would not only threaten the existence of the state but extinguish humanity; it was a spark that

8. Chen Duxiu, "Tongmeng hui yu wuzhengfu dang" (The Revolutionary Alliance and anarchists) in *Duxiu wencun* (Collection of works by Chen Duxiu), 2 vols. (Shanghai, 1922), 2:44.

9. See the reports by police agents in *Zhongguo wuzhengfu zhuyi he Zhongguo shehuidang* (Chinese anarchism and the Chinese Socialist party), ed. the No. 2 Historical Archives (Nanjing: Jiangsu renmin chuban she, 1981), passim.

would, if not extinguished, start a prairie fire." In late June 1919, Cao Kun, then military governor of Zhili province, predicted similar results if anarchist advocacy of revolution against kinship relations (*sangang wuchang*), for economic equality, labor organization, and "freedom to achieve humanitarianism" were allowed to spread among students who were just beginning to quiet down from the activities of the May Fourth mobilization. Another report from 1920 observed that extremists who advocated "social anarcho-communism" (*shehui wuzhengfu gongchan zhuyi*), while not comparable to bandits, were more dangerous to the state than bandits.[10]

Nevertheless, if the strength of anarchism at this time was more an impression created by governmental persecution than a reality, as Chen suggested, it was an impression that was shared widely. In a 1919 essay, "More Talk of Problems, Less Talk of Isms," Hu Shi pointed to the anarchists (in addition to Marxists) as examples of ideological thinking.[11] Chen himself implicitly conceded the appeals of anarchism when he condemned the "nihilistic tendencies" of Chinese intellectuals for nourishing anarchist thinking. By 1919 Chen was an implacable foe of anarchism; his statement reflected the frustration he felt with the popularity of anarchism among Chinese intellectuals. Two years later, he was to respond to a suggestion that the various organs of the Communist party be moved from Shanghai to Guangzhou with the observation: "Anarchists are all over this place, spreading slanderous rumors about us. How can we move to Guangzhou?"[12] As late as 1922, the Soviet government in Moscow invited an anarchist group to visit the Soviet Union with the hope of converting them to the Bolshevik cause.[13]

Anarchists may have been weak, but they were still the most numerous among proponents of radical social revolution, they were still better organized than others in the early twenties, and there was more systematic anarchist literature available to Chinese intellectuals than was true of any other ideology of Western origin. Although anarchists proved in the long run to be unable to organize themselves into a coherent movement, they had a large number of organizations scattered all over China in the early

---

10. Ibid., 19, 31, 75.
11. Hu Shi, "Duo yanjiu xie wenti, shaotan xie 'zhuyi' " (More discussion of problems, less discussion of "isms"), *Meizhou pinglun* (Weekly critic) (20 July 1919).
12. Bao Huiseng, "Wo suozhidaode Chen Duxiu" (The Chen Duxiu that I knew), in *Chen Duxiu pinglun xuanpian* (Selected essays on Chen Duxiu), 2 vols. (Henan renmin chubanshe, 1982), 2:296.
13. *Zhongguo wuzhengfu zhuyi he Zhongguo shehuidang,* 77–79. Also see Liang Bingxian, *Jiefang bielu* (An alternative record of liberation) (n.d., n.p.), 33.

twenties, and, at least in the major urban centers, anarchist mobility provided these organizations with some measure of loose organization. In the immediate years after the May Fourth Movement, there were anarchist societies in Beijing, Shanghai, Nanjing, Tianjin, Guangzhou, Zhangzhou in Fujian, Hankou, Chengdu, and Changsha, with more than one society in some cases. Overseas, there were Chinese anarchist societies in France, Singapore, the Philippines, San Francisco, and Vancouver.[14] These societies published their own newsletters and periodicals to spread anarchist ideas. They also served as cores for mass mobilization when the political situation allowed (or instigated) such mobilization.

The anarchist presence in the May Fourth period was even more evident in the spread of anarchist literature in the Chinese press and of anarchist publications themselves. During the two years 1922 and 1923, more than seventy anarchist publications appeared inside and outside China.[15] To be sure, like the societies that published them, these publications were short-lived; many did not last beyond one issue; all that remains of them today are announcements of publication in other anarchist journals. These publications also had limited circulation and quite possibly did not reach beyond the locality in which they were published. Still, they provide evidence for the widespread popularity anarchism enjoyed at this time. There were anarchist publications of long duration and national scope: *Minzhong,* published 1922–1927, first in Guangzhou and then in Shanghai; *Xuehui,* supplement to the *Guofeng ribao* in Beijing; *Gongyu,* published in Paris; and *Chunlei* (followed by *Jingzhe*), in Guangzhou. These periodicals, on the one hand, propagated anarchist ideas; on the other hand, they concentrated increasingly after 1921 on criticism of communism and the Soviet Union. Through these publications, Chinese had access to the most recent developments in world anarchism.

Perhaps more important for present purposes, by 1919 there was more anarchist literature available to Chinese than any other socialist literature. A survey of anarchist writings from this period shows that, through the accumulated efforts of anarchists over the previous decade, an interested Chinese reader could have gained a more comprehensive understanding of anarchism through Chinese language materials than was possible for any other Western social and political philosophy. A May 1918 list in the anarchist journal *Ziyou lu* (Records of freedom) included works by

14. *Wusi shiqide shetuan* 4:152–351 refers to these places.
15. Ibid., 325–51, for list of anarchist journals during this period.

Kropotkin, Bakunin, Goldman, and Tolstoy. A March 1919 list in *Jinhua* (Evolution) cited additional works by Kropotkin, plus works by Grave, Reclus, and Louis Blanc.[16] The rejuvenated *People's Voice* in 1922 published a list of works that had been published by that society between 1912 and 1920: the list included works by Kropotkin, Tolstoy, and Malatesta, among others, some of them published in editions of up to 5,000 copies.[17] Chinese could also see what their favorite anarchists had looked like, through the 50,000 postcards of Western anarchists (and of anarchist colonies such as the Colonie d'Aiglemont in France) the society had published in 1913. All this was, of course, in addition to the writings by Chinese anarchists themselves.

By 1919 anarchist works and writings appeared regularly in the mainstream press. Articles on Tolstoy's "pan-laborism" appeared not only in anarchist periodicals but in the radical and liberal press in general, including influential publications such as the *Eastern Miscellany* (*Dongfang zazhi*), where even conservative authors found it a directly relevant idea. Even more widespread was the interest in the anarchist idea of "mutual aid" and its progenitor, Kropotkin, who in 1919 may have been the most revered European radical in Chinese eyes. His "Appeal to Youth" was to be responsible for converting (or at least turning) numbers of young radicals to anarchism.[18] Works such as *Mutual Aid, The Conquest of Bread,* and *Fields, Factories and Workshops,* as well as his autobiography, were readily available and found their way into periodicals with a broad readership; one Sichuan anarchist recalled that these were among the most popular readings of the day in 1919.[19] In March 1919, the *Light of Learning* (*Xuedeng,* supplement to *Current Affairs, Shishi xinbao,* in Shanghai associated with the antirevolutionary Research Clique) began to serialize Li Shizeng's translation of *Mutual Aid.* Later in the year the *Weekend Review* (*Xingqi pinglun*) in Shanghai serialized *The State,* the only lengthy foreign work to appear in that journal. Articles on Kropotkin, or translations of

16. Ibid., 166, 190.

17. *Minsheng* (*People's voice*), no. 30 (15 March 1921).

18. See Xia Yan, "Dang wusi langchao zhongdao Zhejiang shihou" (Encounter with Zhejiang in the midst of the May Fourth tide), in *Wusi yundong huiyi lu* (Reminiscences of the May Fourth Movement), 3 vols. (Beijing: Zhongguo shehui kexue chubanshe, 1979), 2:732. Also see Jiang Jun, "Lu Jianbo xiansheng zaoniande wuzhengfu zhuyi xuanchuan huodong jishi" (Record of Mr. Lu Jianbo's anarchist activities in his youth), in WZFZYSX 2:1011.

19. Fan Puqi, "Sanshi nian qiande 'Annaqi zhuyi xuehui' " (The Anarchist Study Society of thirty years ago), in *Zhongjian* (*The middle*) 1, no. 8 (4 November 1948): 24. This brief memoir also contains some interesting information on the use of the theater by young radicals in Sichuan to spread anarchism.

his works, were staples of the reading public. Bakunin's *God and the State* was another popular anarchist work of the time.

The proliferation of anarchists during the May Fourth Movement, and the diffusion of anarchist ideas, may be taken as prima facie evidence that the New Culture Movement provided fertile ground for the efflorescence of anarchism in China. Indeed, the intellectual and social mobilization of the late 1910s, which was to become the New Culture Movement, might well have seemed to the anarchists the fulfillment of their wishes for the direction of the revolutionary movement in China. For the previous decade, anarchists had been the most persistent, and the most systematic, exponents of the ideas on social change that rose to the forefront of radical thinking after 1915. As these ideas gained currency, anarchists and the social philosophy of anarchism moved from the periphery to the center of Chinese thought—not just metaphorically, in thought, but also geographically, from Guangzhou and places abroad to Beijing.

THE NEW CULTURE MOVEMENT AND ANARCHISM

The New Culture Movement, the first unambiguous manifestation of the demand for "cultural revolution" in the Chinese revolutionary movement, got under way in 1915 and blended in 1919 with the May Fourth Movement, which spread the message of "new culture" broadly beyond the small group of intellectuals (mainly in Beijing) to which it had been restricted initially. Its ideological premises and demands are well known and do not require extensive elaboration. Here I shall only highlight its most outstanding concerns.[20]

According to historiographical convention, the movement was initiated by the prominent intellectual Chen Duxiu (later a dean at Beijing University and the first secretary-general of the Communist party) when he founded the *New Youth (Xin qingnian)* magazine in late 1915 and began to advocate a new culture for China. Over the next few years, Chen was able to recruit some of China's most prominent intellectual and literary figures, and the demand for a new culture came to encompass all aspects of intellectual life, from new ideas to new writing to a new ethical basis for Chinese society. In 1917, when Cai Yuanpei was appointed chancellor of Beijing University, the movement acquired an institutional basis in China's premiere educational institution. The atmosphere created by the cultural movement contributed to the eruption of student protest

20. The most comprehensive account is Chow Tse-tsung, *The May Fourth Movement: Intellectual Revolution in Modern China* (Stanford: Stanford University Press, 1967).

in Beijing in May 1919 against foreign claims on Chinese territory. Though primarily patriotic in its orientation, the May Fourth Movement in turn created conditions for the further spread of the demand for a new culture, which by mid-1919 had become national in scope. The merging of the two movements in 1919 represented a major turning point in the history of the Chinese revolution and has retained a paradigmatic significance since then.

The movement originated, most immediately, in the accumulation of patriotic sentiment against foreign (especially Japanese) encroachment on China. More important from the long-term perspective of the Chinese revolution is what it reveals about the ideological and social conditions of revolution. The turn to culture was a response to the failure of the political institutions created by the republican Revolution of 1911, which not only created a disgust of politics, but turned intellectuals away from the pursuit of political solutions to search for answers to China's political problems at the more "fundamental" level of culture and mentality. It would be erroneous to assume that this represented a shift from public to private concerns. Indeed, advocates of a new culture had come to view politics as being in the realm of "selfishness," "corruption," and the pursuit of private interest, and believed that a genuine public consciousness could be created in China only outside of politics, a position reminiscent of the first generation of radicals but now reinforced by the experience of a political revolution.

This intellectual reorientation in turn drew its significance from the coming of age of a new generation of Chinese intellectuals. The New Culture Movement was not simply an intellectual movement, it was also a movement of new intellectuals who were intensely concerned with public and patriotic issues, but also sought to assert their presence in public affairs. It is possible to speak of the emergence in the late 1910s of an "intelligentsia" in China who no longer conceived of themselves as political servants but rather discovered an identity in opposition to politics. The new national institutions (and, to a lesser extent, professions) provided them with a social basis of their own; and the realm of culture articulated their orientation as a social group to problems of society. Their initially cultural radicalism was to be transformed by the May Fourth Movement, which brought them out of their universities into the streets. The encounter with the rest of the population would add a social dimension to their cultural concerns and transform the cultural radicalism of the New Culture Movement into the social radicalism of the twenties.

The ideology of the New Culture Movement is best viewed at a number of levels. At the most formal level was its call for "science" and "democracy," historically regarded as the movement's foremost characteristic. Leaders of the movement viewed the cultivation of habits of scientific thinking and democracy as the most fundamental elements in the creation of a new culture—and a new generation of Chinese. This was to lead to an unprecedented affirmation of modern Euro-American culture and to a total repudiation of the hegemonic native tradition, Confucianism, which now represented all that was backward and superstitious against the "enlightenment" of modernity. The attack on the past included an attack on its textual and social underpinnings. A new culture demanded a new language; New Culture leaders called for a new literature, as well as for the replacement of "classical" writing by a "colloquial" style, to overthrow the hegemony not just of the old texts but of the old elite, which derived its power from command over the texts. Socially, the attack on the past was carried over to an attack on the institutions through which the past lived on, chiefly the family, now seen as the vehicle for the transmission of Confucian social values. The overthrow of the family was crucial to the liberation of youth from the past and, therefore, to the creation of a new generation of Chinese. The affirmation of modernity was to lead to an "iconoclastic" (in Lin Yu-sheng's term) repudiation of the past, which was total because the New Culture Movement ultimately challenged the very values that held the old society together.[21]

In its very preoccupation with culture, the New Culture Movement (like the May Fourth Movement in general) was itself a cultural phenomenon; in other words, the advocates of new culture, and their youthful audience, not only advocated a new culture, they tried to live it. In its concern with culture, the movement focused on education as the primary means for changing China; while formal education was central to its conception of education, it was not a limiting boundary. In bringing education closer to everyday life, the movement (intentionally or not) pushed education out of formal institutions. The result was the creation out of a movement of ideas a radical culture that sought the immediate fulfillment of those ideas in social practise. A by-product of this culture was a profound idealism (both in the sense of a belief in the fundamentalness of ideas and in the sense of the immediate possibility of realizing

21. Lin Yu-sheng, *The Crisis of Chinese Consciousness* (Madison: University of Wisconsin Press, 1979).

their promise). As the *Manifesto of New Youth* (magazine) put it in late 1919:

> Our ideal new era and new society are to be honest, progressive, positive, free, equal, creative, beautiful, kind, peaceful, full of universal love and mutual assistance, and pleasant labor; in short, happiness for the whole society. We hope that the hypocritical, the conservative, the negative, the bound, class-divided, conventional, ugly, vicious, warring, restless, idle, pessimistic elements, happiness for the few—all these phenomena will gradually diminish and disappear.[22]

Participants in the New Culture Movement viewed it as a Chinese "Renaissance." In later years, the movement—in its emphases on "science" and "democracy"—would be compared to the European Enlightenment, which still holds an important place in representations of the movement. Liberal historians have stressed the movement's liberalism; Communist historians on the whole have agreed with this assessment, adding as a social dimension the bursting forth of a bourgeois revolution in China.[23] I think we cannot identify the New Culture Movement with any one ideology, if by *ideology* we understand an articulate conception of the world with an exclusive structure of social and political action. The New Culture Movement was not informed by an ideology that, having captured the consciousness of a generation, stood guard, as it were, at the gates of that consciousness to determine the flow of ideas. The New Culture Movement *was* a movement of ideas, a consciousness in the making with a history of its own. Anarchism was one of these ideas. Anarchist ideas were readily available to anyone who sought them; during these years more people sought them than ever before or after in Chinese thought. Anarchists proliferated, and anarchism spread in Chinese thought as the movement gained momentum.

The efflorescence of anarchism during the May Fourth period is not inconsistent with the representation of the May Fourth Movement (in its New Culture phase) as an Enlightenment. Anarchism in Europe had deep roots, April Carter has argued, in the political philosophy and outlook of the eighteenth-century Enlightenment; it is possible to view an anarchism such as Kropotkin's as an uncompromising reaffirmation of the Enlightenment promise when others, including liberals, had already given up on

22. Quoted in Chow, *May Fourth Movement,* 174–75.
23. Vera Schwarcz, *The May Fourth Enlightenment Movement* (Berkeley and Los Angeles: University of California Press, 1985). For an example of the latter, see He Ganzhi, *Jindai Zhongguo qimeng yundong shi* (The modern Chinese enlightenment movement) (Shanghai, 1947).

the possibility of its realization.[24] Any such analogy, however, is of necessity imperfect and may conceal more than it reveals. The popularity of anarchism was bound up primarily with concrete problems that emerged as the Chinese revolution unfolded following the republican Revolution of 1911, problems to which anarchism seemed to offer solutions consistent with the prevailing mood of Chinese radicals. One Chinese historian has written:

> Under the conditions of several thousands of years of feudal despotism, especially with the decline of government with constant warlord disaster and repeated by ineffective efforts at governmental reform, it was easy for the people at large to become disgusted with politics. On the other hand, the Chinese intelligentsia was mostly of petit-bourgeois origin; it had a personality that was subjective, superficial, evanescent, and impatient. When they began to demand revolution, what best suited their taste was not scientific socialism but empty and high-blown utopias, and anarchism which flaunted existing customs.[25]

It is questionable that when members of the Chinese intelligentsia turned to "scientific socialism" after 1920, they became any the less petit-bourgeois, but the statement tells us something about the mood that prevailed during the immediate May Fourth period.

In his 1936 interview with Edgar Snow, Mao Zedong reminisced: "At this time [1918–19] my mind was a curious mixture of ideas of liberalism, democratic reformism and utopian socialism. I had somewhat vague passions about 'nineteenth century democracy,' Utopianism and old-fashioned liberalism, and I was definitely anti-militarist and anti-imperialist."[26] Chow Tse-tsung has observed of this statement that "this 'curious mixture of ideas' was not a particular state of mind belonging to a particular young student at the time. It actually represented the main current of thought of the active and restless youth in the middle of the May Fourth Movement."[27] Chinese youth responded with enthusiasm to the flood of New Learning that inundated the intellectual world after 1915. A generation that sought liberation in ideas absorbed as the proverbial sponge every idea that promised liberation, without much regard for its ideological origin or its social and political implications. The mood that prevailed at the time was not reflective discrimination but a euphorious revolutionary eclecticism that could imagine a basic unity in diverse ideas so long as

24. April Carter, *The Political Philosophy of Anarchism* (New York: Harper Torchbooks, 1971).
25. *Wusi shiqi qikan jieshao* 1, pt. 2:188–89.
26. Edgar Snow, *Red Star Over China* (New York: Grove Press, 1961), 147–48.
27. Chow, *May Fourth Movement*, 75.

these appeared progressive, democratic, and scientific. Under the circumstances, the ideas anarchists contributed to the New Culture Movement were not easily distinguishable as anarchist ideas, especially since the anarchists did not claim them explicitly for anarchism. But the open-endedness of anarchist ideas proved to be an advantage in the diffusion of anarchism among Chinese youth. The "utopianism" to which Mao referred was at the time largely a product of the diffusion of anarchist ideals among Chinese intellectuals. Anarchism had no monopoly over the ideas that were to become commonplaces in Chinese thinking of the May Fourth period; but anarchists had been the most consistent promoters of those ideas in the years that preceded the New Culture Movement, and now, on the left wing of New Culture thinking, they stood ready to benefit from the diffusion within the Chinese intellectual scene of ideas of which they were the most enthusiastic proponents.

Anarchist inspiration probably played some part in the thinking of New Culture leaders who were not otherwise anarchists. Liberals such as Hu Shi disliked anarchism for obvious reasons. But others were more open to anarchist ideas. More than one biographer has suggested that Chen Duxiu, who was to turn against anarchism after 1919, was aware of anarchist ideas before 1911 and was possibly sympathetic to them.[28] There is no concrete evidence for this suggestion, even it if seems plausible. In the early part of the New Culture Movement, Chen worked closely with anarchists in Beijing University and, as editor of *Xin Qingnian*, seemed to be more than willing to publish anarchist contributions. An important statement he made in 1917, where he urged a shift of attention from politics to culture, was inspired by a speech given by the anarchist Li Shizeng; the intellectual authorities he called upon to support his position were all anarchists, Wu Zhihui and Zhang Ji, in addition to Li.[29] In 1918 he contributed an article to the anarchist periodical *Labor* (*Laodong*).[30] Li Dazhao, who disapproved of anarchists because of their advocacy of terror, was attracted in 1913 to the socialism of Jiang Kanghu, which had overlapped anarchism. In the May Fourth period, even after he became a Marxist, he was a foremost proponent of "mutual aid."[31] Yi Baisha, brother of the more

28. For a recent example, see Lee Feigon, *Chen Duxiu: Founder of the Chinese Communist Party* (Princeton: Princeton University Press, 1983).
29. "Jiu sixiang yu guoti wenti" (Old thinking and the question of national formation), *Xin qingnian* (*New youth*) 3, no. 3 (1 May 1917).
30. "Rensheng zhenyi" (The real meaning of life), *Laodong* 1, no. 1 (20 March 1918). This was a reprint of an article originally published in *Xin qingnian* in February 1918.
31. Maurice Meisner, *Li Ta-chao and the Origins of Chinese Marxism* (Cambridge: Harvard University Press, 1967), 14–133. Also see Nohara Shiro, "Anarchism in the May Fourth Movement," tr. in *Libero International*, nos. 1–4 (January 1975–April 1976).

famous Yi Peiji (later the head of the anarchist-inspired Labor University in Shanghai), and prolific critic of Confucianism in *New Youth* magazine, was, according to Chow Tse-tsung, an anarchist.[32] So were Qian Xuantong, prominent philologist and historian, and Zhou Zuoren (brother of Lu Xun and important literary figure in his own right, who would play an important part in the mass New Village Movement in 1919).[33]

The interest in anarchism was partially a product of the coincidence between the issues raised by the anarchists and the issues that became the focal points of intellectual concern during the New Culture Movement. Charlotte Furth once observed that with the exception of the advocacy of science, there was no New Culture idea that had not been taken up by Chinese intellectuals in earlier years.[34] One might argue, on the basis of anarchist literature before 1915, that all the ideas of the New Culture Movement, including science, had been anticipated by the anarchists a decade before the movement. Anarchists, moreover, had raised these ideas more systematically than had any others on the Chinese scene. It would seem "natural," therefore, that anarchism should have received the attention it did during the New Culture Movement. Anarchists, obviously, were not mere observers of the New Culture Movement, they participated. They not only "influenced" the intellectual orientation of the movement, they provided its vocabulary.

Anarchists had consistently advocated the cause of "science" against tradition, religion, and superstition. They had been the first in China to call for a revolution against Confucianism. Their insistence on individual liberation, especially the liberation of women, had led them to a repudiation of the family and of the Confucian values (the Three Bonds and the Five Constants) that informed the Chinese family. They had called for an ethical revolution that would transform individuals; and while they had seen in education a key to such transformation, they had viewed education not as formal education but as education in the transformation of quotidian life. Most relevant, however, may be the logic of the anarchist argument. Anarchists had repudiated politics, not only in the name of freedom, but also because they viewed politics as inimical to a genuine public consciousness and an organic social existence. Their advocacy of

32. Chow, *May Fourth Movement*, 301.
33. Liang Bingxian, *Jiefang bielu*, 7, for Qian Xuantong. See text below for Zhou Zuoren.
34. Charlotte Furth, "May Fourth in History," in *Reflections on the May Fourth Movement*, ed. Benjamin I. Schwartz (Cambridge: Harvard University Press, 1972).

social revolution, which set the social against the political, had focused on cultural revolution as a primary means to social change, not as a substitute for changing social institutions and relationships but as an indispensable moment in social transformation, with which a new generation could articulate concerns that were emerging into its consciousness. Anarchism as social philosophy lost its remoteness as social problems in China awakened youth to problems to which the anarchists had pointed a decade earlier.

We are accustomed to thinking of the New Culture Movement in terms of its intellectual leaders and the abstract ideas they injected into the Chinese intellectual scene. While these ideas were significant "moments" in the unfolding consciousness of the movement, their significance lay not in their abstract power but in their relevance to the practical problems of a whole new generation of Chinese intellectuals.

To appreciate the appeal of anarchism in New Culture thinking, or of any of the currents of thought that went into the making of the New Culture Movement, it is necessary to view the movement not simply as an intellectual movement or as a revolution in the reified realm of ideas, but as a movement of real living people who sought in ideas solutions to concrete practical problems. The turn to culture as the arena for significant change was itself provoked by the failure of the republican experiment in China and by the political degeneration that followed. As Chen Duxiu put it in 1917 (referring to a recent speech by Li Shizeng, which had argued for the priority of ethical change):

> If we desire to consolidate the Republic today, we must first wash clean the anti-republican thinking that infuses the minds of our countrymen, for the ethical basis that underlies the state organization and the social system of a Republic is the diametrical opposite of the ethical basis that underlies the state organization and social system of monarchical despotism: one is founded upon the spirit of equality; the other on a distinction between classes of high and low. The two cannot be reconciled.[35]

What China needed, Chen concluded, was reeducation in republican ethics and literacy. Even the literary revolution, an important undertaking of New Culture leaders, was tied to this practical question: the reform of writing was not an end in itself (at least not to everyone) but rather a means to purge the hegemony of old ideas and make new ideas accessible to larger numbers of people.

The corruption of Chinese politics at this time gave to the message of a

35. Chen, "Jiu sixiang yu guoti wenti."

revolution in ideas a practical urgency it had not had earlier. Even more significant in this respect, I think, were the social implications of cultural revolution. If it was revulsion over existing politics that turned Chinese intellectuals to the realm of culture, the cultural revolution they sought to achieve was not simply a revolution in ideas but a revolution in the ethical basis of society that would transform not only the state but social organization as well. The message of cultural revolution was most powerful where it promised to transform existing social institutions, chiefly the family, because it licensed a struggle against the authority of the old where it impinged directly upon everyday life. Chinese youth was no doubt dissatisfied with the old-fashioned rulership over China, but it was the promise of the overthrow of authority in everyday life that drove it to the New Culture Movement and provided the movement with the social substance for its historical significance. Ultimately, the motive force of the movement was to be provided by the new generation of young intellectuals who came of age in the late 1910s, whose idealism only exacerbated the alienation they felt from a social system they had ceased, unlike their predecessors, to take for granted. Perhaps the most important contribution of the older generation of intellectuals who initiated the movement was to give Chinese youth the confidence to create a social space where it could breathe freely, and a vocabulary for its yearnings. As one *New Youth* reader phrased it:

> This Spring I read your magazine for the first time. As if woken by a blow on the head, I suddenly realized the value of youth. We should emulate the West, and abolish the old and welcome the new. I am like somebody who is sick, and who must breathe in fresh air and exhale the old. Although at present I am not what you might describe as a new youth, I am sure that I can sweep from my mind all the old thoughts of the past. The credit for all this goes to the save-the-youth work you have been doing.[36]

The struggle against the authority of the old was not some struggle between the old and the new in the realm of abstract ideas; it was a real-life struggle in a society where the culture that intellectuals rebelled against was very much alive in the social structures of power and authority. The icons that New Culture youth sought to destroy were icons that watched over their everyday existence. The intellectual radicalism of New Culture leaders found its fulfillment in the social radicalism of a generation to whom the burden of the past was not an idea but a lived experience. This youth was to take over the leadership of the movement rapidly,

36. Quoted in Ma King-cheuk, "A Study of Hsin Ch'ing-nien (New Youth) Magazine, 1915–1926" (Ph.D. diss., London University, 1974), 67.

and when it did, it escalated the radicalism of the movement beyond the expectations of some of its original leaders, who discovered that they no longer controlled the events they had set in motion. When the New Culture Movement is viewed from this perspective, the increasingly ineffective efforts of those participants who took it as a movement of ideas pure and simple, and tried to keep it that way, appear not as the essence of the movement but as an ideological position within it, that held forth the intellectualism of the movement to keep in check the social radicalism their ideas had unleashed.

The call for cultural revolution, though it obviously glorified the new and denigrated the old, did not necessarily reject all that was old, but focused on those aspects of the Chinese tradition that legitimized institutions that reproduced "social relations of domination and subordination,"[37] especially where it related to youth and women. Wu Yu, the uncompromising critic of Confucianism, attacked Confucianism not because it was "old" (he did not extend the same attack to Daoism and Legalism but used them rather to criticize Confucianism), but because it upheld the Chinese family system. His remark that "the effect of the idea of filial piety has been to turn China into a big factory for the manufacturing of obedient subjects," is revealing of the material, because social, understanding of culture that infused the call for cultural revolution in these years.[38] It was not abstract issues of cultural or ideas, but the call for the struggle against the hegemony of the old over the young, of men over women, of the rich over the poor, of state over society, in short, against authority, that in these years fashioned a social movement out of ideas.

The New Culture idea of culture, as it had emerged by the May Fourth period, was a social idea of culture: cultural revolution, in other words, required the revolutionization of basic social institutions. There was a conjuncture between the social logic of this idea of cultural revolution and the cultural logic of the anarchist idea of social revolution. Indeed, the distinction between culture and society lost its meaning in either idea of revolution that conceived of society as the institutional embodiment of a culture of authority, and of culture as the architectonic expression of social structures of domination and oppression. In their search for cultural liberation, New Culture youth sought out social spaces where they could live in freedom. More than any other group participating in the

37. The phrase is from Raymond Williams, *Literature and Revolution* (Oxford: Oxford University Press, 1977).
38. Quoted in Chow, *May Fourth Movement*, 304.

New Culture Movement, anarchists offered to youth such spaces. Anarchists promised that their idea of New Culture was to change not ideas but life at its most basic, everyday level. The work-study institutions they promoted, perhaps even the syndicates, represented spaces in which youth could find a new life. As Wang Guangqi was to observe in 1920, work-study groups were not simply utilitarian institutions, but havens from the families youth sought to escape, where they could live in freedom and equality.[39]

The social plight of Chinese youth, as well as its hopes and the promise of the New Culture Movement, has been captured most cogently in the autobiographical novel *Family* by the prominent Chinese anarchist writer Bajin, who came of age at this time (and became an anarchist, adopting the name Bajin, made up of the first syllable of Bakunin's name and the last syllable of Kropotkin's).[40] Anarchist and New Culture concerns resonated not just at the level of ideas, but at the very social basis of the ideas and in their underlying logic.

This is not to claim the New Culture Movement for anarchism, nor to reduce the anarchist advocacy of social revolution to New Culture concerns. There were many points of divergence between the general concerns of the New Culture and May Fourth movements and anarchism; not the least important of these were the patriotic frustrations and aspirations that would shortly redirect the course of the New Culture Movement. Anarchism, while integral to New Culture thinking, occupied a place in its broad spectrum somewhere on the left. Indeed, anarchist participation in the movement was to bring to it concerns that turned its preoccupation with culture in the direction of social change. Anarchists were not passive beneficiaries of the movement; through their activities, they contributed both to the radical activity of the movement and to its ideological orientation. Ironically, anarchists, for all their incapacity for organization, would make the most important contribution by providing organizational principles to the radical experiments with new forms of social life the movement produced.

Anarchists were also to benefit from the October Revolution in Russia, of which they were the first Chinese interpreters. Thanks mainly to their interpretations, the prevailing impression in China initially was that the Bolshevik revolution was not a Marxist but an anarchist revolution. Given its prestige in China, the revolution in 1918–1919 was to stimulate consid-

39. *Wusi shiqide shetuan*, 370, 443.
40. Olga Lang, *Pa Chin and His Writings: Chinese Youth Between the Two Revolutions* (Cambridge: Harvard University Press, 1967), 7.

erable interest in anarchism among radicals, including those radicals who shortly would turn to the establishment of a Communist party in China. In the immediate May Fourth period, communism in China was still for the most part identified with anarcho-communism, which, Chinese Communist historians have complained, delayed, in the confusion it created, the acceptance of Marxism by Chinese radicals.

ANARCHIST ACTIVITY AFTER 1915

As of 1915, there were two identifiable and related groups of anarchists in China: the Paris anarchists, and the Guangzhou anarchists of the Anarchist Federation (in Shanghai and Guangzhou), which Shifu had established before his death. By the time of the New Culture Movement, Li Shizeng and Wu Zhihui were among China's most prominent intellectuals; of the same generation as the initiators of the movement, such as Chen Duxiu, they were well placed through personal connections to influence cultural life. Guangzhou anarchists were younger and more local in orientation. They were also more puritanical in their loyalty to anarchist principles. Although not so influential as the Paris anarchists, they were more active at the local level and more involved with social organization. Many of them were students and schoolteachers and provided much of the anarchist social activism during the New Culture Movement. After 1919 they would emerge as intellectual leaders in the anarchist movement as well. While on the whole they followed the lead of the older anarchists, there was also some tension between the two groups over anarchist purity in personal life, as well as the nature of anarchist activity, a tension no doubt exaggerated by regional loyalties.

The Paris anarchists were to make the most visible contributions to the New Culture Movement. This was due not so much to their ideas as to their activities in the realm of education. The work-study program they initiated after 1911 became in these years a training group for anarchists and an effective means for the propagation of anarchist ideas. Indeed, some of the ideas generated by this program were to last beyond the anarchists and have a lasting effect on revolutionary thought in China.

After the 1911 Revolution, Wu Zhihui and Li Shizeng, the two leaders of the Chinese anarchists in Paris, had returned to China to work within the context of the new republican regime. In 1912 they established the World Society (*Shijie she,* named after the society the anarchists established in Paris in 1906) to promote education, especially education abroad, which they thought would resolve basic social problems, including class division. As the declaration of the Association put it, "Far-sighted men regard the fact that higher education is not yet universal as the reason why classes are born. They grieve about this and [think that] the way of remedying the situation is to make education equal [for all]."[41]

Out of this goal was born the New Society Movement (*xin shehui yundong*), which sought to increase people's happiness by "advancing their morality." The anarchists of the World Association, who were also Francophiles, believed that France, with its libertarian and revolutionary tradition, offered the most attractive environment for Chinese students who wanted a modern education. With this goal in mind, in 1912 they established the Society for Frugal Study in France (*Liufa jianxuehui*). Frugality, the anarchists believed, would not only serve the practical goals of the movement, but also help build moral character.[42]

The Society for Frugal Study sent a number of students to France (and Britain) before World War I, but this activity declined with the onset of the war. During the war few Chinese students went to France for study. Anarchist activity in France, however, had a boost from another source: Chinese labor. During the war, about 200,000 Chinese laborers were imported to help with labor shortage created by the war. Some of these laborers worked as coolies in French armies, others in French factories. After the war many would stay on in France as workers.

In 1914 anarchists had established the new Society for Diligent-work and Frugal-study, whose major aim was to educate Chinese workers in France. Before 1911 the anarchists had employed Chinese labor in their printing plant and in the bean curd factory they had established to support their activities. Their educational activities with these workers provided the model for the educational activity they would undertake later.

Anarchists played a crucial role in the importation of Chinese workers into France during the war. In 1916 they established the Sino-French Educational Association in cooperation with French business and academic leaders. The major activity of the Association was to recruit Chinese workers for France. In their school for the workers they devoted their efforts to the improvement of workers' behavior and morality.

41. Quoted in Paul G. Clifford, "The Intellectual Development of Wu Zhihui: A Reflection of Society and Politics in Late Qing and Republican China" (Ph.D. diss., London University, 1978), 325.

42. For information on these activities, see Clifford, "Wu Zhihui," and Paul Bailey, "The Chinese Work-Study Movement in France," *China Quarterly*, no. 115 (September 1988), 441–61. Chinese scholars have made available extensive materials on this movement recently. See Qinghua daxue Zhonggong dangshi jiaoyan zu, *Fufa Qingong Jianxue yundong shiliao* (Historical materials on the diligent-work frugal-study movement in France), 3 vols. (Beijing: Beijing chubanshe, 1979).

These workers were also given a rudimentary education in general subjects as well as in labor organization. Anarchists served as lecturers in the school; Cai Yuanpei was prominent among them.[43]

After the war the Society for Diligent-work and Frugal-study turned once again to students. Applying to students their experiences in educating laborers, the Society arranged for students to find work in France in order to finance their studies. By 1919 there were about ten schools in China to prepare students for study in France. By 1920 there were in France more than a thousand students in the program of the Society for Diligent-work and Frugal-study.

The work-study program was to have an important effect on radical politics in China. Not all of the Chinese students who went to France under anarchist auspices became anarchists. Among the program's "graduates" were those who would become leaders of the Communist party as well as of the patriotic Chinese Youth party. Nevertheless, its immediate effect was the publicizing of the anarchist cause in China. Even those among its graduates who rejected anarchism went through an anarchist phase and were initiated into radicalism through anarchism.

Equally important were the ideological ramifications of the anarchist programs. The extended contact with Chinese workers in France expanded consciousness of labor and the laborer, first among anarchists, and then among other groups in China. The work-study program meant different things to different people. To some it was merely a practical means for providing Chinese with a Western education. It also produced ideals that would have an important influence on New Culture thinking and the generation of New Culture youth.

The anarchists connected with Shifu, or initiated into anarchism by the activities of his group, played a less visible but equally important role in spreading anarchist ideas in China at this time. Shifu's death at an early age in 1915 had left this group without a clear leadership in these years. Nevertheless, Guangzhou anarchists were to fan out from their base in the South to major metropolitan centers, spreading the anarchist message and organizing anarchist groups that were to serve as lodes for anarchist activity.

In Guangzhou itself the most significant anarchist activity revolved around labor organization. Before 1915 the anarchists had displayed inter-

---

43. These speeches were printed in *Huagong zazhi* (began publication in January 1917), ostensibly the journal of Chinese laborers in France. Cai's speeches were published as part of *Cai Jiemin xiansheng yanxing lu* (Record of Mr. Cai Jiemin's speeches) (Beijing: Beijing daxue chubanshe, 1920).

est in syndicalism and labor education; their ideas, according to Ming Chan, had influence on labor even in these years.[44] Xie Yingbo, the influential labor leader in Guangzhou, had been associated with Shifu in the China Assassination Corps before 1911 and was himself a syndicalist; this connection possibly facilitated anarchist entry into the labor movement. Anarchists participated in the first celebration of May Day in China in 1918. In the same year they helped organize a Guangzhou Teahouse Labor Union, which drew a membership of 11,000 workers from among trade guilds and teahouse employees.[45] In the next year barbers in the area were organized under anarchist influence. Through Xie Yingbo, anarchists were also influential in the Mechanics' Union. These unions have been described as the first modern labor unions in China. Shifu's brother, Liu Shixin, played a leading part in these activities.[46]

Anarchists were also engaged in the propagation of anarchist ideas, usually under the guise of Esperanto schools. By 1915 (after the Shifu group had been forced out of Guangzhou and moved to Shanghai), there was an anarchist school in Shanghai in addition to the one in Guangzhou. According to one source, by 1914 there were Esperanto schools in Tianjin, Fuzhou, Shanghai, Beijing, Chengdu, among others.[47] It is not likely that all these schools were established by anarchists, let alone anarchists of Shifu's group. Nevertheless, there was an intimate relationship in these years between Esperanto and anarchism; and Esperanto textbooks, such as the one edited by Ou Shengbai in Guangzhou, served to spread anarchist writings in some security from the authorities.[48]

Some of the Guangzhou anarchists followed Chen Jiongming to Fujian in 1918 where, under his protection, they propagated Shifu's anarchism. As in the case of Xie Yingbo, the labor leader, Chen's connection to the anarchists was a personal one; he, too, had been associated with Shifu in the China Assassination Corps and after 1911 extended his protection to Shifu and his followers. The protection, however, went beyond purely personal considerations. Chen himself, ironi-

44. Ming K. Chan, "Labor and Empire: The Chinese Labor Movement in the Canton Delta, 1895–1927" (Ph.D. diss., Stanford University, 1975), 42.

45. Ibid. The Mutual Aid Society Xie organized in 1920, according to Ming Chan, claimed "a membership of more than 100,000 workers from over 100 affiliated unions" by 1922 (50).

46. Liu Shixin, "Guanyu wuzhengfu zhuyi huodongde diandi huiyi" (Remembering bits and pieces of anarchist activity). WZFZYSX 2:926–39.

47. Wang Yan, "Wuzhengfu zhuyi yu shijieyu" (Anarchism and Esperanto), in Guangzhou wenshi ziliao (Historical and literary materials on Guangzhou), no. 1 (1962): 45.

48. Ibid., 41. This "Esperanto Reader," according to Wang, was used widely nationwide.

cally for a militarist, had some sympathy for anarchism; according to Winston Hsieh, at this time he was also responsible for financing the Sino-French University in Lyons.[49] One anarchist recalled that under his leadership Zhangzhou in these years became a "model" city. Anarchists operated freely under his protection and even published a newspaper.

Both lines of anarchist activity, the work-study program in France and the activities of Shifu's followers in China, illustrate the ambivalent relationship of anarchists to the authorities whose overthrow they advocated. This relationship reflected a persistent tendency among Chinese anarchists to instrumentalize anarchism in the service of goals that contradicted their own professed aims. The Paris anarchists hobnobbed openly with both the political and the economic elite in China and abroad; the Sino-French Educational Association was a semiofficial organization. Shifu's followers, much more clearly anarchist in their identity at this time, accepted protection from the authorities when they could.

This acceptance was partially due to a genuine need for protection. Discussions of radical activity in China at this time rarely stress the adverse political circumstances under which radicals operated. Wu Zhihui's name was among those listed by the Shanghai police as dangerous "Bolshevists" in China. Chinese authorities, central or local, were ever ready to suppress "extreme radical" activities. American consuls were able to get the local authorities to intervene against the anarchists in Fujian, in spite of Chen's protection. Radical literature was often smuggled between false covers to avoid detection, as is illustrated by the example of an anarchist manifesto published in Baodingfu, which authorities discovered within the covers of a Chinese bible.[50]

Anarchist association with authority was also a consequence of the persistence of personal relationships that often contradicted the verbal commitments of the anarchists. It also gave anarchists false hopes about the possibility of reliance on authorities that appeared favorable to their cause. Anarchists were to discover this, much to their regret, in 1928, when their flirtation with the Guomindang under Chiang Kai-shek was to result in a tragic betrayal of their cause by Chiang—and by the doyens of anarchism

49. Winston Hsieh, "The Ideas and Ideals of a Warlord: Ch'en Chiung-ming," Harvard Papers on China, 16:214. For further information on Chen and the anarchists in Fujian, see Liang Bingxian, Jiefang bielu, 10–12, 15–18.

50. "Remarkable Discovery at Paotingfu—Chinese Communist Manifesto—Circulated in Gospel of St. Luke," Peking and Tientsin Times, 22 March 1922. Anarchists were quite creative; they even smuggled materials in loaves of bread. See Zheng Peigang, "Wuzhengfu zhuyi zai Zhongguode ruogan shishi" (Some facts on anarchism in China), Guangzhou wenshi ziliao, no. 1 (1963): 195. References to these anarchists appeared frequently in the student paper at Beida, Beijing daxue rikan (Beijing University daily), beginning in 1917.

in China, who obviously placed their personal relationships and official influence above their "long-term" ideological commitments.

With the appointment of Cai Yuanpei as the chancellor of Beijing University, anarchist activity, like the New Culture Movement in general, gained a new momentum. The appointment of Cai was particularly meaningful for the anarchists, because Cai had long been involved with the Paris anarchists (most recently in the work-study program in Paris), and was himself a philosophical anarchist (see chapter 2 above).

After 1917 Beida was to emerge as a center of anarchist activity in China. No one has suggested that Cai tried actively to propagate anarchist ideas at Beida, but his reforms at the university created an atmosphere in which anarchists could flourish, and he was responsible, albeit indirectly and in somewhat reified form, for publicizing ideas that had originated with the anarchists. His reforms attracted to the university anarchists who had been his close intellectual associates over the previous decade, such as Li Shizeng (who taught moral philosophy as well as biology) and Wu Zhihui (an academic adviser). Of the Guangzhou anarchists Huang Lingshuang and Yuan Zhenying were professors at the university, Ou Shengbai and others enrolled as students. According to Xu Deheng, anarchists constituted one of the three major groups in the university faculty, in addition to the New Youth group and the conservatives.[51]

Cai's own activities could at least have been construed by the anarchists as favorable to their cause. One of the important components of his educational philosophy was the fostering of a group spirit and habits of mutual aid. To this end he encouraged students to establish groups that ranged all the way from discussion groups to cooperatives. Soon after he became chancellor he sponsored the establishment of the Promote Virtue Society (*Jinde hui*).[52] This society, which derived its name from the anarchist society of 1912, adopted for its guidelines the principles of another: Shifu's Conscience Society (*Xinshe*). The declaration of the society referred specifically to the *Jinde hui* of the early Republic which, it said, had been founded by socialists such as Cai, Wu, and Li, to deal with the questions of how to achieve communism and abolish marriage.[53] The society was able to recruit about a thousand members by the May Fourth period.

51. Xu Deheng, "Wusi yundong zai Beijing" (The May Fourth Movement in Beijing), in *Wusi yundong huiyi lu* (Beijing: Zhongguo shehui kexue chubanshe, 1979) 1:212.
52. Liang Zhu, *Cai Yuanpei yu Beijing daxue* (Cai Yuanpei and Beijing University) (Ningxia renmin chubanshe, 1983), 158–65.
53. "Beijing daxue zhi Jinde hui" (The Promote Virtue Society of Beijing University), *Beijing daxue rikan* (Beijing Student daily), 19 January 1918.

The teaching of Esperanto was another area of anarchist activity. The anarchist Sun Guozhang (later associated with the radical *Fendou* [Struggle] magazine, which advocated a nihilistic anarchism) was in charge of the teaching of Esperanto; according to a notice in the student daily of the university in December 1917, his Esperanto class had attracted fifty-three students, although it is hard to tell whether these students were all from Beida.[54] In the same month, the paper started to serialize an article by Ou Shengbai on Zamenhof, the inventor of Esperanto.

There is also considerable evidence that anarchists formed a powerful group within student activities in the university. In February 1918 Sun Guozhang became the editor of the student daily, which then began to publish articles in Esperanto (Chen Duxiu was a faculty adviser).[55] In 1920 Zhu Qianzhi, later to gain fame as a proponent of nihilist anarchism, became editor of the student weekly. Under his editorship the weekly published debates on anarchism and labor; two of its issues carried the pictures of Kropotkin and Bakunin on the cover.[56] There is also indirect evidence of anarchist power in the university. In 1918 students at the university organized a society to protest Japanese activities against China. The students wanted to call the society the Patriotic Society (*Aiguo hui*), but, according to Xu Deheng, changed the name to Save-the-Nation Society (*Jiuguo hui*) under pressure from the anarchists.[57]

If anarchists were active in the various organizations in the university that were not explicitly anarchist, they also had their own organizations. In 1917 students and faculty organized the Truth Society (*Shishe*) to promote anarchist goals. Its members were Huang Lingshuang, Hua Lin, Ou Shengbai, and Yuan Zhenying, all leaders of the anarchist movement in the 1920s. In 1919 this society was replaced by Evolution Society (*Jinhua she*), which brought Beida anarchists together with anarchists from other parts of China. Other Beida anarchists, led by Zhu Qianzhi, established in 1923 the Struggle Society (*Fendou she*) to propagate their own version of anarchism.[58]

Anarchist activity was reflected in anarchist publication. Anarchists

54. *Beijing daxue rikan*, 13 December 1917.

55. Ibid., 8 February 1918. With the February 16 issue the paper added an Esperanto headline.

56. *Beijing daxue xuesheng zhoukan* (Beijing University student weekly), nos. 12, 16. It was also here that Huang Lingshuang and Zhu Qianzhi had earlier debated anarchism. No. 12 framed Kropotkin's portrait with the slogans "Free organization, free association, mutual aid, mutual support."

57. Xu Deheng, "May Fourth Movement in Beijing," 212.

58. *Wusi shiqi qikan jieshao* 3, pt. 1:215. For Chen, see Zheng Peigang, "Some Facts on Anarchism," 186.

had participated in the New Culture Movement from the beginning through their contributions to *New Youth*. The names of Wu Zhihui, (Huang) Ling Shuang, (Yuan) Zhen Ying, Hua Lin, (Liang) Bingxian appeared frequently in the journal before 1919. Their contributions to *New Youth*, however, lacked a clear identity.[59] These contributions ranged from discussions of Nietzsche's philosophy to translations of Tolstoy and Emma Goldman. They were almost wholly in support of that journal's advocacy of individual liberation from social institutions. While they performed an important function in acquainting *New Youth* readers with the names of famous anarchists and their views on the individual, marriage, and the family, they did not impart any clear picture of anarchism as a comprehensive social and political philosophy with an identity of its own.

More important as sources for anarchism were a number of journals published by the anarchists, or guided by them. In August 1916, Chinese in France started to publish the *LuOu zazhi*. Ostensibly the organ of the Sino-French Educational Association, the journal publicized the views of the anarchists who dominated that organization. Its editor was Chu Minyi of the *New Era* anarchists. Among the most prolific contributors were Cai Yuanpei, Li Shizeng, Wang Jingwei, and Wang Shijie. This was followed in January 1917 by *Huagong Zazhi* (Chinese laborers' journal), a journal addressed to Chinese workers in France. The journal published pieces to educate the workers and rid them of their undesirable habits; its mottoes were "diligence, frugality, and study." Lectures by Li Shizeng and Cai Yuanpei in the workers' school took up most of the journal's space devoted to discussions.

In July 1917 Truth Society at Beida began to publish *Ziyou lu* (Records of freedom). According to Huang Lingshuang, Truth Society was one of the three "legs" of the "tripod" of anarchism in China, the others being *Xinshe* (Conscience Society) in Guangzhou and the *Qunshe* (Masses Society) in Nanjing. *Records of Freedom* was devoted "to the search for anarchist organization in politics and advocacy of the true principle of communism in economics."[60] Its contributors included prominent members of a rising generation of anarchists. Aside from Huang Lingshuang, these were Hua Lin, Ou Shengbai, and Yuan Zhenying.

---

59. The one exception was the translation into Chinese of an essay (published simultaneously in Chinese and English), "Xie yu tie" (Blood and iron) from the English anarchist periodical *Freedom*. This essay, translated by a Ru Fei, openly advocated socialism and social revolution from an anarchist perspective. *Xin qingnian* 1, no. 4 (15 December 1915).

60. *Wusi shiqide shetuan* 4:164.

Other anarchist periodicals appeared in 1918: *Renqun* (Masses) published by the Masses Society in Nanjing, and the *Pingshe zazhi* (Peace Society journal) published by Peace Society in Shandong. These journals were short-lived because of internal difficulties and harassment by authorities. In January 1919 four anarchist societies (People's Voice in Guangzhou, Masses in Nanjing, Peace Society in Shandong, and Truth Society in Beijing) merged to establish a new society, *Jinhua she* (Evolution Society), and started publication of a new journal, *Jinhua zazhi* (Evolution magazine) in Nanjing. The journal barely made it past the May Fourth Movement, when it was closed down by the authorities.[61]

The participants in these activities give us a clue to the rapid spread and proliferation of anarchist groups outside major urban centers during the May Fourth Movement. According to Liu Shixin, the Masses Society in Nanjing drew its membership from former members of the Socialist party (the "Pure" socialists of Taixu's group).[62] Members of the Socialist parties of the early republican period, with their anarchist inclinations, may have provided a pool of potential members. It will be recalled that Jiang Kanghu himself had returned to China at this time, and was engaged once again in organizing activities among which was a "three/two society" (no government, no family, no religion: from each according to his ability, to each according to his need). If not anarchist, strictly speaking, it is plausible nevertheless that these groups in the provinces did play a part in the propagation of anarchism.

The most novel anarchist publications in the period before the May Fourth Movement were two journals devoted to labor, *Mirror to Labor* (*Laodong baojian*) and *Labor* (*Laodong*), both published in 1918. Of these two, by far the more important was *Labor*, China's first journal devoted specifically to the promotion of the cause of laborers (and to carry "labor" in its title). *Mirror to Labor* raised labor issues mainly in passing in its discussions of general issues of anarchism, which were continuous with discussions in *People's Voice* earlier. *Labor*, edited by Liang Bingxian, addressed questions of labor directly. The journal discussed the conflict between labor and capital and advocated social revolution to resolve it. Among its "firsts" were discussions of the significance of May Day and of labor activities in China. It was also the first journal in China to discuss the

---

61. See the order of the Ministry of Communications concerning the banning of *Jinhua* and other anarchist publications, in *Zhongguo wuzhengfu zhuyi he Zhongguo shehuidang*, 19.
62. Liu Shixin, "Anarchist Activity," 932.

176   Radical Culture and Cultural Revolution

implications of the October Revolution in some depth, which unexpectedly would benefit the cause of spreading anarchism.

THE OCTOBER REVOLUTION AND ANARCHISM

There is some evidence that Chinese radicals initially viewed the October Revolution in Russia not as a Marxist but as an anarchist revolution—or at least a revolution that was consistent with anarchist goals. One Chinese historian has written of radicals in Guangzhou:

> At the time [i.e., before the May Fourth Movement in 1919], quite a few people thought that the victory of the October Revolution in Russia was the victory of anarcho-communism. Radicals who were dissatisfied with the situation in China and wanted a revolution began, therefore, to believe in anarchism.[63]

Lest this be viewed as an idiosyncrasy of Guangzhou, where anarchism had strong roots, we may note that Shao Lizi, prominent Guomindang member and a participant in the early activities of the Communist party, recalled the same tendency in Shanghai.[64] According to Maurice Meisner, following the October Revolution the name of Kropotkin began to appear with greater frequency in the writings of Li Dazhao, later China's "first Marxist." Indeed, Li's own writings on the October Revolution in late 1918 were infused with the language of anarchism.[65]

Much of this confounding of the October Revolution with anarchism was a consequence of worldwide confusion over the Revolution in 1918. Prominent anarchists, including Emma Goldman and Kropotkin himself, believed early on that the Revolution, if not anarchist, at least had the potential for developing into an anarchist social revolution. In China the confusion was compounded with the association of the idea of "social revolution" with anarchism. Until the 1920s anarchists were the only ones in China consistently to advocate a social revolution from below. The October Revolution, which quickly came to be hailed by radicals worldwide as the first genuine social revolution in history, plausibly appeared to Chinese radicals as an anarchist revolution. That opponents of the Revolu-

63. Zhu Zhengjia, ed., *Zhonggong dangshi yanjiu lunwen xuan* (Selected essays on the history of the Community party of China), 3 vols. (Changsha: Hunan renmin chubanshe, 1983), 1:161.
64. Shao Lizi, "Dang chengli qianhoude yixie qingkuang" (Certain circumstances surrounding the establishment of the party), in *Yida qianhou* (The period of the first congress), 2 vols. (Beijing: Renmin chubanshe, 1980), 2:70.
65. Arif Dirlik, *The Origins of Chinese Communism* (New York: Oxford University Press, 1989), chap. 3.

tion vulgarly labeled it "anarchist" may have confirmed the impression. Anarchists themselves, even anarchists in the Soviet Union, such as Emma Goldman and Alexander Berkman, would not renounce the association of anarchism with the Bolshevik Revolution until 1922, even if they had grown suspicious of it by early 1919. This was also when Chinese anarchists abandoned hopes in an anarchist-Bolshevik cooperation in the cause of social revolution.

Anarchists in China in 1918 actively contributed to this association of anarchism with the October Revolution. The two discussions of the October Revolution published in the second issue of *Labor* in April 1918 are among the most detailed reports on the meaning and ideology of the Revolution to be published in China in 1918. (This was also the issue to celebrate May Day for the first time). These reports may have shaped the views of Chinese radicals on the Revolution well into 1918 and, in their identification of anarchism with a revolution that carried considerable prestige in radical eyes, helped add to the prestige—and the propagation—of anarchism as well. An article by one Yi Cun, entitled "The Political Strategy of the Extremists in Russia" ("Iguo guojipai shixingzhi zhenglue"), described the Revolution in terms of its internal and external policies. Quoting Trotsky, the author described the Revolution as "a revolution in the broad sense" (*guangyidi geming*), meaning that the Revolution was not restricted to politics but extended to the economic realm as well, and also that it was not merely national but global in its aspirations, as was shown by efforts to export the Revolution. As the author put it, "The revolution accomplished by the Russians is a world revolution, it is a social transformation (*gaige*)."[66] It was a revolution, he observed, that bureaucrats and the wealthy feared but which laborers and the poor welcomed. There is little question of the sympathies of the author, who referred to the revolutionaries as "brothers" (*xiongdi*) and "compatriots" (*tongbao*).

A similar tone pervaded the second article, "A Brief Account of Lenin, the Leader of the Russian Social Revolution" ("Iguo shehui gemingzhi xianfeng Lining shilue"), which described Lenin as "the most enthusiastic proponent of universalism (*datong zhuyi*)" in the world. As in the first article, this discussion, too, stressed as the goals of the Revolution the immediate termination of the war and the redistribution of property to relieve the poor. It described the revolution in "our neighbor Russia" as a

66. Yi Cun, "Iguo guojipai shixingde zhenglue" (The political strategy of the extremists in Russia), *Laodong*, no. 1 (20 March 1918): 9.

"social revolution to make equal the rich and the poor." More significantly, the author stated that "while people fear these two words, social revolution, it is nothing but a natural tendency of the world."[67] A similar statement was repeated in an essay in the third issue of the journal, "An Analysis of Lenin, the Reality of the Russian Revolution" ("Liningzhi jiepei, Iguo gemingzhi zhenxiang"). Anticipating Li Dazhao by two months, the author stated: "The French Revolution gave birth to the civilization of the nineteenth century; the Russian Revolution represents the tendencies of the twentieth century."[68]

In ensuing issues (the last one was no. 5 in July 1918), *Labor* published other discussions of the Russian Revolution, including one on the various socialist groups in Russia and their publication organs, an article on the consequences of peasant liberation, and brief biographies of Trotsky and Breshkovskaya. I have not seen these issues and am unable, therefore, to analyze their content. Suffice it to say here that these discussions were interspersed with the many articles the journal published on labor and anarchism. Prominent among its causes was Tolstoy's "laborism" (*laodong zhuyi*), which Li Dazhao would hail a few months later as a basic feature of the Revolution.

On the basis of the articles in the earlier issues, it is possible to state that *Labor* portrayed the October Revolution as a revolution in perfect harmony with anarchist aspirations. An article in the first issue, which was devoted to the discussion of labor's struggles against the war in Europe, described the ideology of the October Revolution as "anarcho-communism" (*wuzhengfu gongchan*), first, and freedom, equality, and universal love, second. The same piece described the goals of the Revolution as the establishment of anarchy, the abolition of private property and religion, and the termination of the war.[69] The articles in the following issue of the journal, which I have already discussed, echoed these views in their depiction of Bolshevik policies as efforts to get rid of laws, and of Lenin as a thoroughgoing internationalist "who had no conception of national boundaries." The article in number three cited above would seem to have corrected these views by pointing to the fact that the Bolsheviks traced their lineage to Marx, who had been at odds with anarchists. But the general impression to be gained from the journal, especially considering its

---

67. *Laodong*, no. 2 (12 April 1918).
68. Quoted in *Wusi siqi qikan jieshao* 2, pt. 1:170.
69. Laoren, "Ouzhan yu laodongzhe" (The European war and laborers), *Laodong*, no. 1:17.

overall anarchist context, was that the Russian Revolution did not deviate significantly from anarchist notions of social revolution.

By early 1919 some anarchists would turn against the October Revolution and Bolshevism; others continued to view it favorably and even to regard it as basically anarchist. As late as 1920 the area of Fujian under Chen Jiongming, a hotbed of anarchist activity, was known as "the Soviet Russia of Southern Fujian," and anarchists there (led by Liang Bingxian who now edited the anarchist journal in Fujian) served as a major source of information on the Soviet Union and the progress of the revolution. They were high on the list of people to contact of the Comintern agent Gregory Voitinsky when he arrived in China in March 1920 to organize communism. When the *New Youth* magazine became an organ of the incipient Communist party in September 1920 and added a new section on the Soviet Union, Chen Duxiu asked the anarchist Yuan Zhenying to edit it.

THE DIALECTICS OF REVOLUTION: SOCIAL REVOLUTION AND ETHICAL TRANSFORMATION

By the late 1910s anarchism in China had assumed a more complex visage. In addition to the social anarchists, there were anarchists for whom anarchism represented an extreme individualism of the kind that had been advocated by Max Stirner (Zhu Qianzhi), or pointed the way to the fulfillment of an esthetic conception of life (Zhou Zuoren and Hua Lin). Chinese anarchists also discovered "new" foreign anarchists, notably Emma Goldman, whose writings on love and the family (and later on the Soviet Union) acquired enormous popularity during the New Culture Movement; Goldman would make a profound impression on one anarchist in particular, Bajin, who would come to view her as his spiritual "mother" and form a lifelong devotion to her.

The increasing variety of anarchisms, and the proliferation of anarchist groups in the aftermath of the May Fourth Movement, makes it nearly impossible to summarize the thinking of Chinese anarchists at this time. Much of this remains to be uncovered. I will restrict the discussion here to the social anarchists and focus on those ideas that were to make a lasting impression on May Fourth radicalism—and the revolutionary discourse in China.

Anarchists spread their ideas in these years not only in anarchist journals, but through contributions to publications of general interest, as well as the circulation of pamphlets (among which Shifu's writings were very prominent), which through clandestine means found their way into even provincial localities. No less important as "texts" on anarchism were anarchist activities, which were particularly important in the emergence of a radical culture among May Fourth youth.

Among the ideologies that went into the making of the New Culture Movement, anarchism emerged early on as the ideology of the radical Left, which sought to steer the cultural revolution in the direction of a social revolution, saw in the cultural transformation of Chinese society a means of moving China toward socialism, and desired, at least in theory, to expand the cultural revolution beyond intellectuals to encompass the "common people" (*pingmin*).[70] Studies of the New Culture Movement, including studies by Communist scholars, leave the impression that socialism was not a significant component of the movement until after 1919 when, under the influence of the Russian Revolution, Chinese intellectuals began to show interest in it. This is misleading, and valid only if we deny the socialism of the anarchists. It is true that the word *socialist* does not appear very often in New Culture literature before 1919. Chinese anarchists themselves did not advertise their anarchism in their contributions to mainstream journals such as *New Youth* or the *Renaissance;* the word *anarchism* appears rarely in anarchist contributions to these journals, and then in the description of the political philosophy of authors such as Tolstoy and Emma Goldman, whose works the anarchists translated into Chinese. What distinguished anarchist writings in these years was not their claim to socialism, but their advocacy of a social revolution, the hallmark of socialist ideologies in China since 1905. During the New Culture Movement, anarchists were to emerge as the champions in Chinese thought of a social revolution that went beyond changes in culture or politics, and though their ideas may not be readily identifiable as constituting a socialist program, they were responsible for introducing into New Culture discourse not just socialist ideas and a socialist vocabulary, but a socialist vision as well. This not only prepared the ground for the efflorescence of socialism following the May Fourth Movement, but also helps explain why anarchism should have enjoyed the greatest popu-

70. Authorities were particularly concerned about this aspect of anarchist advocacy, which made anarchists seem the most dangerous group among Chinese radicals. At a time of economic crisis and depression, they believed, anarchist efforts to radicalize workers and students posed a grave threat to the state. See *Zhongguo wuzhengfu zhuyi he Zhongguo shehuidang,* 34, 74. The American charges d'affaires in Beijing, Charles deTenney, echoed these fears in an April 26, 1920, dispatch to the State Department: "It must be understood that there is a large class of landless and penniless Chinese to whom the prospects of looting are an attraction and who may be influenced by the propaganda."

larity among competing social revolutionary ideologies in the early May Fourth period.

Anarchist ideas and activity in the May Fourth period followed along the lines established by earlier anarchists. Basic to them was the anarchist commitment to social revolution through education, whose ultimate goal was the ethical transformation of individuals to discover the "natural" anarchist inclinations that were a universal human endowment. Two aspects of this endowment became particularly prominent in discussions of anarchism in the May Fourth period, with lasting implications for revolutionary discourse: "mutual aid" and the combination of labor and learning in the creation of a new generation of youth. By 1919 these two ideas had become fundamental to the experiments in the reorganization of social life (a communal movement, so to speak) that expressed more eloquently than words the radical culture that anarchists had helped fashion.

A brief summary of the premises concerning the role of education that had earlier informed the anarchist idea of social revolution may be useful here, for these same premises shaped the ideology of May Fourth anarchists. Anarchists believed that a revolutionary society could be only as good as the revolutionary process that produced it. In the earliest phase of anarchism in China, anarchists such as Zhang Ji had believed that "the ends justified the means." Anarchists continued to express a similar orientation in later years. Anarchist writing and programs well into the twenties often displayed a penchant for violence: "propaganda by the deed" was a regular feature of anarchist programs; and in 1925 the Manifesto of Hunan anarchists declared bravely that "one bomb is better than a thousand books."[71]

Determination of the extent to which anarchists practised the kind of violence they preached must await a different kind of research. The evidence is that the majority of anarchists (and the most influential) placed peaceful propaganda and education ahead of violence, which was consistent with the conception of revolution that underlay most anarchist writing: that violence and oppression perpetrated in the name of revolution would create a violent and oppressive society that betrayed the promise of revolution. Indeed, the distinctive feature of the anarchist program of social revolution was that revolution, in order to produce a genuinely revolutionary society, must in the very process of revolution create the

71. "Hunan qu wuzhengfu zhuyizhe tongmeng xuanyan" (Manifesto of Hunan anarchists), Hudson Collection, Package 6, part 2.

institutions of the future. Basic to this program was a conception of revolution as a process rather than as a discrete historical undertaking. Anarchists by the May Fourth period refused to distinguish ends and means, the goals of revolution from the means employed to achieve those goals. Revolution must in its progress create the institutions that contained, in embryo, the society of the future. These institutions would in turn secure the further progress of revolution by providing social spaces for the transformation of individuals and their social consciousness. To the anarchists this revolutionary dialectic ruled out the utilization of any means that contradicted the ultimate goals of the revolution, since bad means would further distort the social nature of individuals and lead them away from, not toward, the cherished goal of revolution. This, we shall see, was the point of departure for anarchist critiques of Bolshevism in the twenties.

New Era anarchists a decade earlier had established the place of education in revolution: education was but the positive aspect of revolution, as violence was its negative aspect. The negative purpose of revolution was to clear away the institutional and material obstacles to the liberation of the human potential; but it was education, its positive aspect, that nurtured the morality demanded by the anarchist ideal and made possible the creation of the embryonic anarchist institutions that marked the progress of social revolution.

The anarchist revolutionary idea resolved itself ultimately into a dialectic between the individual and social institutions: the diffusion of anarchist morality among individuals would lead to the substitution of embryonic anarchist social institutions for authoritarian institutions, which would, in turn, further promote the progress of anarchist morality—until, eventually, anarchism came to encompass all aspects of life for all of humanity. Education, in other words, was revolution; revolution, education.

Anarchists viewed learning, especially scientific learning, as an important component of the education they proposed. "There is no morality other than learning," Wu Zhihui had proclaimed in the *New Era*. The Truth Society in Beida adopted as its basic guideline the slogan of "advancing morality and cultivating knowledge."[72] The Declaration of Progress Society in 1919 stated, quoting Thomas Huxley: "If the present advance of learning cannot fundamentally alter the decadent condition in which the great majority of humankind lives, then I can say only one thing: let us quickly call upon that merciful comet to wipe out this globe,

72. *Wusi shiqide shetuan* 4:162.

and us with it."[73] Anarchists commonly held that the morality of a people was proportionate to their learning. The progress in learning, in other words, was in itself a progress toward the kind of society they envisaged. As in earlier years, this underlay their call for the universalization of education, which they believed was the prerequisite to human progress.

The stress on education is a reminder of the basically reformist and evolutionary approach to revolution that characterized Chinese anarchism; in the Declaration of Evolution (*Jinhua*) Society in 1919, Huang Lingshuang reiterated Li Shizeng's explanation in *New Era* of "revolution" as "re-evolution," as a means of securing the inevitable advance of society.[74] Nevertheless, anarchists assigned a deeply radical function to education. The goal of education (as of revolution) was to eliminate "authority" (*qiangquan*), and thereby enable individuals to discover their true selves. Anarchists saw in authority the fundamental cause for the distortion of the natural goodness of people and believed that, once authority had been eliminated, the basic goodness of humanity would reassert itself in the formation of an anarchist society. Authority was diffused throughout present society, embodied in its various institutions. In the words of Huang Lingshuang, "What we mean by authority is not merely the militarism of Germany and Austria, or the 'supermanism' of Nietzsche, but the politics, religion, law and capitalism of present society which obstruct the realization of freedom and happiness by humanity as a whole." Huang neglected to spell out one institution of authority whose repudiation by the anarchists would add enormously to their appeal during the May Fourth period: the family. Anarchists had believed all along that the family was the embodiment of authority in everyday life; it was also, as the manifesto of Hunan anarchists put it, "an instrument for the production of selfishness."[75]

With the abolition of authority, the instinctive goodness (and sociability) would assert itself, and the tendency to selfishness, plunder, and oppression of individuals under present-day society would be eradicated. As a manifesto that issued from Zhangzhou (most probably one of Shifu's essays) put it, "the principle of anarchical communism" was "a truth hidden in every individual's mind."[76] Moral transformation, or

73. *Wusi shiqi qikan jieshao* 3, pt. 2:494–95.
74. *Wusi shiqide shetuan* 4:162.
75. "Hunan qu wuzhengfu zhuyizhe tongmeng xuanyan."
76. This manifesto, which was widely circulated, was, judging by its contents, Shifu's "Wuzhengfu qianshuo" (Anarchism explained simply), in *Shifu wencun* (Collected works of Shifu) (n.p.: Gexin shuju, 1927).

rather moral restitution, of the individual was key to the anarchist view of an education that would result in social revolution.

This morality was ultimately a social morality. Anarchists desired to abolish institutions that embodied authority, institutions that divided people from one another and obstructed the creation of an organic society that derived its cohesiveness not from coercion but from the "natural" tendency of humankind to voluntary association. The anarchist conviction in the possibility of realizing such a society was grounded in a vision of humanity that was at once natural, esthetic, and rational. "Anarchism is the means to (achieving) beauty, Communism is the way to (achieving) goodness," Huang Lingshuang wrote in his prefatory essay to *Records of Freedom* in 1917. At the heart of this vision was a conviction in the instinctive goodness of human beings. A letter in the same issue of the journal stated: "The morality of anarchism is equality, universal love (*boai*) and freedom; there is not one among these that is not in accord with the spontaneous growth of human natural endowments."[77]

"The principle of anarchical communism . . . is a truth hidden in every individual's mind," the Zhangzhou manifesto had declared, and explained that this truth ("anarchical morality") was "nothing but labor and cooperation, both of which are natural gifts to human beings and are not derived from the outside." (Cooperation presumably was *huzhu*, "mutual aid," in the original.) By 1918 the creation of institutional spaces that would permit the practise of "mutual aid" and the combination of labor and learning appeared as the most prominent aspects of the anarchist conception of the process of social revolution, and for all the reformism implicit in the insistence on education as the means to revolution, these goals were quite radical in their cultural implications. Mutual aid was to the anarchists the cornerstone of anarchist morality, as it had been to Kropotkin. In his "Anarchist Morality," Kropotkin had written:

> The ant, the bird, the marmot, the savage have read neither Kant nor the fathers of the church nor even Moses. And yet all have the same idea of good and evil. And if you reflect for a moment on what lies at the bottom of this idea, you will see directly that what is considered as *good* among ants, marmots, and Christians or atheist moralists is that which is *useful* for the preservation of the race; and that which is considered *evil* is that which is *hurtful* for race preservation. (Italics in original)

77. *Wusi shiqide shetuan* 4:164, 167.

Kropotkin viewed solidarity, therefore, as "a natural law of far greater importance than that struggle for existence," and concluded that the "law of mutual aid," not competition, was "the law of progress."[78]

Chinese anarchists, following Kropotkin, took this natural tendency to mutual aid as the essential content of human goodness (liangxin). They endowed this tendency with the status of a universal scientific principle (gongli) and set it against Darwinian notions of conflict, which, they believed, encouraged "men to eat men." Hua Lin argued that nineteenth-century science had proven that man was a "social animal."[79] Cai Yuanpei lectured to Chinese workers in Paris that division of labor and social interdependence were fundamental characteristics of human society.[80] Mutual aid was rational, not only because it was natural to humankind (and the rational operation of the cosmos), but because it had the blessings, the anarchists believed, of modern science.

If mutual aid was one instinctive endowment of humanity, labor was the other. "Anarchist morality," Shifu wrote in 1914, was "nothing but 'mutual aid' and 'labor': the two are instinctive to humanity." He went on to explain that "labor is humankind's natural duty and mutual aid its inherent virtue."[81] In the anarchist conception labor was not simply utilitarian, a necessity for the sustenance of life, but was a moral imperative of human existence. What made labor unpleasant was its coercive nature; with the liberation of humankind, labor would realize its true nature as a fundamental human endowment.

The stress on mutual aid as an instinctive endowment of humanity was present in Chinese anarchism from its origins in Paris before 1911, spread through the writings and translations of Li Shizeng, who himself had been trained as a biologist, and was responsible for introducing to China Kropotkin's ideas on mutual aid as the motive force of progress in nature and society alike. Labor received scant attention in Chinese anarchist writings before 1911. In the hundred some issues of New Era published before 1911, only two articles dealt with labor, and those in the most general terms. Labor as a necessity of anarchist society had received greater attention from Liu Shipei, the leading light of the Tokyo anarchists, who had incorporated into his anarchist utopia the performance of

78. Peter Kropotkin, "Anarchist Morality," in Kropotkin's Revolutionary Pamphlets (London: Benjamin Blom, 1968), 91, 95.
79. "Shishe ziyou lu" (Records of Freedom of Truth Society), Wusi shiqi qikan jieshao 3, pt. 1:216–17.
80. Cai Jiemin xiansheng yanxing lu, 339–41.
81. Shifu wencun, 49–50.

manual labor by each individual. The anarchist federation of Shifu in 1915 had also stressed the importance of universal labor.

The increasing attention Chinese anarchists devoted to labor in the late 1910s was possibly a consequence of their intensifying relationship with laborers, both in China, in the syndicalist activities of the Guangzhou anarchists, and in Paris, where anarchists were involved in the education of the laborers they had imported into France. There was also a subtle but significant change in these years in attitudes toward labor. Even in the "Declaration of Anarcho-Communist Comrades," cited in chapter 4, Shifu displayed an ambiguity on the question of labor. He presented labor as an instinctive human endowment, but went on to explain that labor would become more pleasant in the future with help from technology. By the time of the New Culture Movement, however, anarchists presented labor, not as a necessary evil, but as a manifestation of the essential beauty of anarchist morality and human instinct. This was possibly due to greater familiarity with those writings of Kropotkin that extolled the virtues of labor, *The Conquest of Bread* and *Fields, Factories and Workshops,* both widely read in China in the late 1910s. All that is possible to say with certainty, however, is that the stress on labor as one of the two natural endowments of humanity, and a moral imperative that was an expression of the natural goodness and beauty of the human spirit, appeared more and more frequently in anarchist writings as the anarchist involvement with labor gained in momentum in the years after 1915. By 1919 mutual aid and labor appeared to many as cornerstones of anarchist philosophy and the means to achieve the good society of the anarchist vision.

The anarchist argument for universal labor sheds light on anarchists' approach to the question of class and class conflict. Anarchists called for the abolition of class oppression, or the authority exerted by one class over another, which they viewed as another manifestation of the selfishness created by a social order based on the principle of authority. The anarchist position on the question of class, however, was problematic. While their analysis of class oppression overlapped with Marxist explanations of this problem, they differed from Marxists (at least mainstream Marxists of the day) in the causes to which they attributed class oppression and, therefore, in the solutions they offered. Anarchists took account of the economic basis of class oppression and placed the abolition of private property and production for profit high on their agenda of social revolution. Shifu, who was more radical than the Paris anarchists in this respect, pointed to capitalism as one of the twin evils of contemporary society, the other being the state. Nevertheless, anarchists in general exhibited a more moralistic appreciation of class oppression than the materialist Marxist understanding of class division and conflict in terms of the process of production. While anarchist analyses often referred to the bourgeoisie and the proletariat, their descriptions of classes, more often than not, juxtaposed the rich against the poor, those who did not labor against those who did, and mental against manual labor. This was consistent with the anarchist view that, ultimately, power and authority, and the selfishness they generated, were the cause rather than the effect of economic inequality.

Beneath their radical class rhetoric, anarchists rejected class conflict as a means of resolving class oppression. This was to be articulated fully after the May Fourth Movement in the course of anarchist critiques of communism, but it was already expressed in anarchist writings in the 1910s. Anarchists believed that class conflict was just another expression of selfishness in society and, instead of resolving social questions, merely perpetuated them in another guise. Anarchism offered a means to resolving this problem peacefully. As Wu Zhihui stated in *Laodong* in 1918: "So the *Labor* magazine wishes to make clear the principles of class war and to research methods of pacifying it, so that along with the laboring people of the whole world, we can resolve this problem and seek a correct life."[82] Classes, the anarchists believed, could be abolished only with the abolition of authority as the architectonic principles of society.[83]

To summarize, then, anarchists perceived two interrelated functions in education. First was the accumulation of learning necessary to purge individuals of their "superstitions," which encompassed all the ideological convictions that undergirded authoritarian society. More important, education must create those spaces where, free from the authority of existing institutions, individuals would be able to realize their natural propensity to social existence. Especially important in this regard were institutions that promoted mutual aid and the free exercise of labor. The one prepared the ground for the other in a dialectical interplay between consciousness and social institutions, which the anarchists viewed as the essential content of the social revolution they espoused.

Anarchist activity during the New Culture Movement was a direct expression of this idea of social revolution. Anarchist writings in these years promoted these ideas; but much more eloquent in conveying anar-

82. "Laodongzhe yan" (Laborers speak), no. 1, 2.
83. "Hunan qu wuzhengfu zhuyizhe tongmeng xuanyan."

chist philosophy, and much more effective in the propagation of anarchist ideas were the efforts of anarchists to translate their vision into the
beginnings of an anarchist reality in the womb of contemporary society.
Anarchist social activity not only provides us with an ideological text in
which the utopian vision of the anarchists assumes concrete form, it also
enabled the anarchists themselves to articulate the practical constitution
of their vision of humanity.

These activities ranged from the diligent-work frugal-study program
in France to the syndicalist activities of the anarchists in China, from the
Jinde hui at Beida to the New Village Movement (*xincun yundong*), of
which Zhou Zuoren was the major proponent, but especially the work-
study movement, which, around the May Fourth Movement, assumed
the proportions of a "thought tide" in the Chinese student world. While
these activities differed widely in scope and constituency, they had one
purpose in common: to provide youth with an institutional environment
in which to cultivate habits of mutual aid and labor. For some anarchists they also represented small organizations that were the starting
point of anarchist reorganization of society as a large association of
small-scale organizations.

Of these activities, the syndicalist movement and the work-study movement in France were most significant. The anarchist syndicalist movement represented the emergence of the modern labor movement in China.
Anarchists spearheaded the labor movement in Guangzhou and Hunan
and possibly in Shanghai. With the exception of Guangzhou, these anarchist origins would be short-lived; anarchists began to lose ground to the
Communists almost immediately after the establishment of the Communist party in 1921.[84] Nevertheless, anarchists showed a consciousness of
Chinese labor before any other radical groups and contributed to the
diffusion of this consciousness during the New Culture Movement.

Moreover, the tactics the anarchists employed in the organization of
labor were to become common tactics of labor organization in China:
establishment of workers' schools and clubs to educate labor in the process of organization. These tactics were partially a consequence of anarchist belief that Chinese labor was too backward culturally to permit
immediate labor organization. As late as 1918, Wu Zhihui wrote in
Labor that the establishment of a labor party (*gongdang*) in China must

---

84. Ming Chan. Also see *Shifu wencun*, 36. This accorded with the anarchist belief that
worker organizations must be outside of politics. See 83–84.

await the education of the working class.[85] Anarchists believed that if labor organization was to be effective, and in accordance with anarchist principles, laborers had to do their own organizing. The education of laborers must accompany any efforts at labor organization in order to enable laborers to take charge of their own organizations.

These tactics also reflected, however, the deep-seated anarchist belief in social revolution as a process of education. To the anarchists, syndicates were not merely organs for representing labor interests but new social institutions in which to promote anarchist morality. When the time arrived for the final social revolution, these institutions would serve as the units of anarchist social organization.[86] This goal was possibly more important to some anarchists than the promotion of labor interests, which may have been a reason that anarchists found themselves unable to compete with the Communists in the twenties.

Whatever the reasons may be for the success or failure of anarchist syndicalist activities, it was important that these activities brought Chinese labor and students together for the first time. It is difficult to say what effect this may have had on the consciousness of Chinese laborers: it certainly left its imprint on the consciousness of students. The encounter would ultimately result in the explosive mixture that burst forth in the 1920s in urban social revolution.

More immediately significant was the work-study movement in France, of which the anarchists were the architects and which was basically a product of anarchists' experiences in educating the laborers they had imported to work in their *dofu* factory before 1911, and then the large numbers of Chinese laborers who, through their agency, had gone to work in French factories during the war. These experiences had inspired in them the idea of laboring intellectuals that was the basis of the work-study program. Indeed, it was in such journals as the *Journal of Chinese Students in Europe* (*LuOu zazhi*), which began in 1916, and *Chinese Laborers' Journal* (*Huagong zazhi*), which began in 1917, both in Paris, that anarchists first started propagating the idea of combining labor and study.[87]

The reasoning underlying the work-study movement was quite practical. As in the case of the laborers whose education the anarchists had

85. "Lun gongdang buxing youyu gongxue busheng" (Absence of a workers' party stems from the stagnation of work-study), *Laodong*, no. 1:3. On the educational tasks of syndicates, see *Shifu wencun*, 81–83.
86. Ibid. See also p. 56 for the necessity of revolutionary organizations to anticipate future society.
87. *Wusi shiqi qikan jieshao* 3, pt. 1:193–203.

conducted as spare-time education in night schools, students who went to France on the program would work part of the time to finance their education, and would also study part-time. To many in China, including participants in the program, the appeal of the work-study program lay in its practical aspects: it provided the means to acquiring an education that might otherwise have been financially difficult or impossible. To some, such as Hu Shi and Wang Jingwei (who was himself involved in the program and was, for a while, editor of *Luou zazhi*), this practical aspect was the most important aspect of the program. Hu Shi saw in it a parallel to the part-time work part-time study programs he had encountered in the United States; but he objected to the more idealistic aspects of the program as obstacles to its success.[88] Many of the Chinese students who participated in the program seem not to have shared the idealistic zeal of its sponsors, who often complained that students cared little about labor and were concerned mainly with "making it" by acquiring an education.[89]

To the anarchists who had initiated the program, the idea of combining labor with learning had a much more ambitious significance. Hua Lin remarked that if China was to change, the change would be accomplished by those who participated in work-study.[90] An article in *Labor* stated: "With work and study combined, workers will become scholars, scholars will become workers, to create a new society that will realize the goal of 'from each according to his ability, to each according to his need.' "[91] Possibly the most eloquent advocate of work-study was Cai Yuanpei, who saw in this combination the solution not only to "the problem of youth acquiring an education, but to the weightiest problems of China and the world."[92]

As the work-study movement gained momentum there was a noticeable change in anarchist writings toward the glorification of labor. *Laodong* magazine in 1918 adopted as its guidelines "reverence for labor and the promotion of 'laborism' (*laodong zhuyi*)."[93] Labor was to be valued beyond its contribution to production. Ethically, labor was "the

88. Hu Shi, "Gongdu huzhutuan wenti" (The problem of labor-learning mutal-aid groups), *Xin Qingnian* 7, no. 5 (1 April 1920): 2.
89. Huang Liqun, *Liufa qingong jianxue jianshi* (Brief history of the diligent-work frugal-study program in France) (Beijing: Jiaoyu kexue chuban she, 1982), 41.
90. Hua Lin, "Gongxue zhuyi ji fangfa" (Labor-learning'ism and its method), *Luou zhoukan*, no. 45 (12 September 1920): 1.
91. "Gongdu zhuyi jinxing zhi xiwang" (Hopes in labor-learning'ism), *Laodong*, no. 4, quoted in *Wusi shiqi qikan jieshao* 2, pt. 1:178.
92. Cai, "Gongxue huzhutuan di da xiwang" in *Cai Yuanpei yanxing lu* (Record of Cai Yuanpei's speeches) (Shanghai, 1932), 555.
93. "Laodongzhe yan," *Laodong* 1, no. 1 (20 March 1918): 2.

greatest obligation of human life," and "the source of civilization." Morally, labor was "the means to avoid moral degeneration and help moral growth, it was a means to forging spiritual willpower." Work, the guidelines stated, "helped not only the individual but society as a whole." "Laborism" was to become a common term of New Culture vocabulary during the May Fourth period, comparable in its popularity to "mutual aid."

ANARCHISM AND CULTURAL RADICALISM IN THE MAY FOURTH PERIOD

By late 1918 anarchist writing and activity had brought anarchist ideas of social revolution through education into the language of the New Culture Movement. Two leaders of the movement were particularly important in publicizing these ideas. One was Cai Yuanpei, the chancellor of Beijing University, who himself had long been an associate of the Paris anarchists and participated in their activities in Paris. Starting at this time and for the rest of the decade, Cai would be one of the foremost advocates of combining labor with learning in education. In the late twenties he was to play a leading part in the founding of the anarchist-inspired Labor University in Shanghai.

The other was Wang Guangqi who, though not of equal prominence, had a strong influence on Chinese youth as head of the Young China Association (*Shaonian Zhongguo xuehui*), possibly the most important student organization of the immediate May Fourth period, which included in its membership some of the most important figures in the founding of the Communist party in 1920–21 (including Li Dazhao, Mao Zedong, Yun Daiying, and Deng Zhongxia), as well as young radicals who would later found the Chinese Youth party (*Zhongguo qingnian dang*). Under the leadership of Wang, who showed an unmistakable inclination to anarchism in 1919, the Young China Association would emerge in 1919 as the foremost exponent of reorganizing China from the bottom up through the agency of "small groups" (*xiao zuzhi*), an idea that figured prominently in socialist thinking in 1919. Wang himself became a major promoter of the communal experiments in 1919 that went under the name New Life Movement (*Xin shenghuo yundong*) that displayed a clear anarchist inspiration and orientation.

The anarchist advocacy of labor caught the popular imagination in a phrase used by Cai Yuanpei in a speech late in 1918. Cai proclaimed:

The world of the future is the world of labor! The labor we speak of is not the labor of metal workers, of carpenters, and so forth. The undertaking of all those who use their own labor power to benefit others is labor regardless of whether it is mental or manual. Farmers do the labor of cultivating, merchants do the labor of transporting, writers and inventors do educational labor. We are all laborers. We must all recognize the value of labor. Labor is sacred (*laodong shensheng*).[94]

Labor to the anarchists was the great equalizer. Anarchists differed from Marxists in their class analysis in the emphasis they placed on those who labored and those who did not. The economic problems of contemporary society, they believed, arose largely from the exploitation of laborers by a parasitic class. The major distinction, as Cai's statement implies, was not between the proletariat and the bourgeoisie, but between those who labored and those who did not. The distinction had a special relevance in China, where Confucian tradition had for two thousand years drawn a distinction between mental and manual labor as the justification for distinguishing the governors and the governed. The combination of manual and mental labor was, to the anarchists, a means of overcoming economic exploitation in society. Cai's views on this question are relevant to an understanding of anarchist views on labor and its significance for achieving social equality:

In our ideal society, all people will live according to the principle "from each according to his ability, to each according to his need." "According to his ability" points to labor; whether it is manual or mental, all is labor that contributes to the existence of humankind and the advance of culture. Needs are of two kinds: physical needs such as clothing, food, and shelter, and spiritual needs such as learning. Now there are some people who do not do any work, or do work that is not real work. Those who do real work cannot but work bitterly and work long hours. Aside from them, the rest use special privileges to take and waste in huge quantities what humankind needs. Consequently, the real workers do not get enough of what they need. Perhaps they get some of what they need physically, but they are totally deprived of what they need spiritually. Is this not a great obstacle to the advance of culture? If we want to eradicate this obstacle, we must first realize a life where labor and learning proceed together.[95]

94. "Laogong shensheng," 27 November 1918. Originally published in *Beijing daxue rikan*. In *Zhongguo xiandai shi ziliao xuanpian* (Materials on modern Chinese history), 3 vols. (Heilongjiang renmin chubanshe, 1981), 1:30–31.

95. "Guowai qingong jianxuehui yu guonei gongxue huzhutuan" (Diligent-work frugal-study abroad and labor-learning mutual-aid groups at home), *Cai Yuanpei yanxing lu*, 58–59.

This, the anarchists believed, would be a revolution from below and would avoid all the bloodshed of a violent upheaval, which must follow if the human condition is not ameliorated.

The work-study program in France, and the ideas it generated, served as the inspiration for communal experiments around the idea of work-study that assumed the proportions of a "tide" in 1919–20. These experiments went by different names. The most famous was the Labor-Learning Mutual-Aid Group (*Gongdu huzhu tuan*), established in Beijing at the end of 1919 and sponsored by Wang Guangqi, who himself had participated in the work-study program in France and who went through an anarchist phase at that time. Almost equally famous was the Work-Study Association (*Gongxue hui*), established on May 3, 1919, by students at Beijing Higher Normal College. The following day a member of this group, Kuang Husheng, was to lead the attack on Cao Rulin's house. Also part of this "tide" was the New Village Movement, in which Zhou Zuoren played a leading part. These experiments in turn inspired similar experiments in other major urban centers, such as Tianjin, Shanghai, Wuchan, Nanjing, and Guangzhou.

Although these work-study groups were not identical, they shared certain characteristics that point to their anarchist inspiration. Mutual aid and labor were essential to their functioning. Work-study groups were supposed to finance the educational activities of their members through income from group enterprises or individual labor. In either case, the income of the group would be pooled as the basis for a communal (*gongtong*) life. Division of labor within the group was to be organized to enhance interdependence among the members. The guiding principle in most cases was "from each according to his ability, to each according to his need."[96]

The New Village Movement is interesting because of its peculiarities. Unlike the other work-study groups, the major goal of "new villages" as conceived by Zhou Zuoren was not study, but the promotion of labor (except for those with special talents). What makes the New Village idea most interesting, however, was an agrarian impulse that lay at its origins: "new villages" were conceived as agrarian communes that would carry the anarchist message into the countryside. The New Village Movement of the May Fourth period was inspired by a similar movement in Japan, in particular the movement initiated by Mushakoji Saneatsu, which itself

96. See the regulating principles of some of these organizations in *Wusi shiqide shetuan* 2:360–528, passim.

had taken its inspiration from Tolstoy and Kropotkin. Nevertheless, before the May Fourth period, both the socialists of Jiang Kanghu and the anarchists of Shifu had experimented with "new villages" of their own. The New Village Movement was not comparable in its influence to the work-study experiments, but it did have some influence in Beijing where, in a number of schools students organized their own "new villages" and engaged in some agricultural cultivation to meet their own subsistence needs.[97]

All these experiments were quick failures. The Beijing Labor-Learning Mutual-Aid Group lasted only about four months before it foundered upon the economic difficulties it encountered. This was to be the common fate of all May Fourth communal experiments. In a situation that made economic enterprise and employment difficult, the groups rapidly fell victim to financial difficulties. Some were to conclude, as Dai Jitao did, that the work-study groups did not offer a solution to problems that went deep into the economic structure of the society in which they had hoped to achieve their utopian aspirations.[98]

As long as they lasted, however, the work-study groups seemed to offer a glimpse of Chinese intellectuals of the good society. One author, writing in *Liberation and Reform* (*Jiefang yu gaizao*), saw in labor-learning the beginning of a new era in human history: " 'The principle of labor-learning' (*gongdu zhuyi*) is a new stage in the evolution of human life, [it] is a beautiful product nurtured by the new thought tide of the twentieth century, and the foundation for the new society of the future."[99] Wang Guangqi, the sponsor of the Labor-Learning Mutual-Aid Group in Beijing, was even more ecstatic about the possibilities offered by work-study:

> Labor-learning mutual-aid groups are the embryo of a new society, the first step to the fulfillment of our ideas.... If the labor-learning mutual-aid groups succeed, the ideal of "from each according to his ability, to each according to his need" will be gradually realized. The present labor-learning mutual-aid movement may well be described as a peaceful economic revolution.[100]

97. An "extensive" discussion of Zhou's New Village Movement is available in Ding Shouhe, *Cong wusi qimeng yundong dao Makesi zhuyi de chuanpo* (From the May Fourth enlightenment movement to the propagation of Marxism) (Beijing: Renmin chubanshe, 1978), 215–19. For a comparison of the principles of new villages with *gongxue* organizations, see *Wusi shiqi qikan jieshao* 2, pt. 1:299–300.

98. Jitao, "Gongdu huzhutuan yu zibenjiade shengchanzhi" (Labor-learning groups and capitalism), *Xin qingnian* 7, no. 5 (1 April 1920):5–12.

99. "Ping 'gongdu zhuyi' " (Labor-learning'ism), *Jiefang yu gaizao* 2, no. 3 (1 February 1920): 3.

100. Wang Guangqi, "Gongdu huzhutuan" (Labor-learning mutual aid groups), *Shaonian Zhongguo* 1, no. 7 (15 January 1920). Reprinted in *Wusi shiqide shetuan* 2:379.

Neither, however, equalled in ecstasy the contributor to *Gongxue* (Work-study) magazine of the Work-study Association, who saw in labor and learning the two tracks of "the railroad to Heaven."[101]

In terms of the long-term significance of anarchist ideas in revolutionary discourse, most important may have been the initial attraction to anarchism at this time of the radical activists who would later emerge as the leaders of the Communist party. Li Dazhao's attraction to anarchism in the aftermath of the October Revolution was replicated by other founders of the Communist party who, with the possible exception of Chen Duxiu, all went through an anarchist phase before turning to Marxism in 1920–21. According to Liang Bingxian, both Mao Zedong and Qu Qiubai were correspondents with the People's Voice Society.[102] Yun Daiying acknowledged in his diaries that he was an anarchist in the late 1910s; Zheng Peigang recalls that he was also a contributor to *Labor* in 1918.[103] In 1917 Yun established a Mutual Aid Society (*Huzhu she*) in Wuhan. Many other later Communist leaders were participants in the work-study program in France, among them Zhou Enlai and Deng Xiaoping and lesser-known names such as Xu Teli who would later play important parts in the Communist educational establishment.

The Communist party, when it was established in 1920–21, was founded on student associations that arose during the radical movement and culture of the early May Fourth period.[104] As with other societies of the time, anarchist principles played an important part in their organization in providing guiding principles of social life; "mutual aid" and the practice of labor to sustain the societies appeared in this context not as remote ideals but as functional principles in the organization of new styles of collective living. Before they were recruited into the incipient Communist party organization in 1920, these societies in their ideological orientation were inclined to anarchism rather than to Marxism, as their members have acknowledged in their recollections.

It was also through anarchist inspiration that many of the later Communists were introduced into social activism. Mao Zedong became involved in labor activity in Hunan through his association with anarchist

101. *Wusi shiqi qikan jieshao* 2, pt. 1:297.
102. *Jiefang bielu*, 6.
103. Zheng Peigang, "Some Facts on Anarchism," 185. Also see Yun Daiying, "Huiyi wusi qianhou jianli shetuande huodong" (Recollections of organizational activities around the May Fourth period), in *Wusi yundong huiyi lu (xupian)*, 31.
104. For an extensive discussion of the formation of Communist groups and the role anarchism played in them, see Arif Dirlik, *The Origins of Chinese Communism* (New York: Oxford University Press, 1989), chap. 8.

labor leaders, as did Deng Zhongxia and Zhang Guotao in Beijing, who were among the foremost labor organizers of the Communist party in the 1920s. The work-study program in France, which brought students and laborers together, produced some of the most effective labor leaders in the Communist movement.

Anarchists, who were among the first radicals to turn to agrarian organization, may have provided the inspiration for the first Communist agrarian organizers. Peng Pai, the most prominent Communist agrarian organizer of the twenties, was inclined to anarchism when he made his first forays into the countryside. So was Shen Xuanlu, Zhejiang radical and coeditor with Dai Jitao of the Guomindang Marxist publication, *Xingqi pinglun* (The weekend critic). Shen, a Guomindang member and a member of the Zhejiang provincial assembly, had a background as a landlord but found inspiration in Tolstoy. His activities in Zhejiang would lead to one of the first major rural movements to emerge out of May Fourth radicalism.[105]

This anarchist phase in the radicalization of later Communist leaders made for considerable confusion between Marxism and anarchism in 1919–20. It may also have imprinted on their minds memories of radical practises that, as practises of everyday radical culture, may have been more lasting in their implications than formal intellectual commitments.

105. For Peng Pai, see Robert Marks, *Rural Revolution in South China* (Madison: University of Wisconsin Press, 1984). For Shen Xuanlu's activities, see *Weiqian nongmin yundong* (The peasant movement in Weiqian) (Beijing: Zhonggong dangshi ziliao chubanshe, 1987).

CHAPTER SIX

The Anarchist Alternative in Chinese Socialism, 1921–1927

The appearance and rapid ascendancy of Marxian communism (or Bolshevism) in the 1920s has long overshadowed in historians' consciousness the role anarchism played in nourishing social revolutionary thinking and activity for the previous decade and a half, which contributed directly to the founding of the Communist party of China in 1921. Well past the establishment of communism, anarchism continued to serve as a fecund source of social revolutionary ideals that kept alive a radical alternative to Bolshevism. Anarchist thinking and activity during this period overlapped with the Communist party's conception of revolution, but also sharply differed with it on questions of strategy and the ultimate premises of revolution.

Communist party spokesmen (then and now) have charged that anarchism was a petit-bourgeois ideology that offered no viable strategy of revolution. By the late twenties, when the decline of anarchism as a contender in the revolution had become all too apparent, anarchists themselves were willing to concede some validity to this assessment. Anarchists' behavior showed a fickleness that belied their professions of commitment to the cause they espoused; even those, such as Ou Shengbai and Huang Lingshuang, who played leadership roles in the movement seemed to give priority to personal interest over a sustained commitment to the movement.[1] This may have been a general characteristic of radical activ-

---

1. According to a British report in Hong Kong, "forty" anarchist leaders left for France in 1922, considerably weakening the labor movement in Guangzhou. See Daniel Y. K. Kwan, "Deng Zhongxia and the Shenggang General Strike, 1925–1926" (Ph.D. diss.,

ism in the May Fourth period. Initially, the founders of the Communist party, too, seemed uncertain in their commitment to the cause; in their case, however, the necessary submission to organizational discipline gradually brought about some regularity in behavior. Anarchists, who continued to insist on the ultimate autonomy of the individual and re- sisted organizational discipline, had no comparable institutional frame of reference to give direction to their activity. In the absence of organiza- tional coherence, there were no checks on interpretive autonomy; and ideological activity, too, remained self-centered and fluid in its orienta- tion. The proliferation of anarchist groups in the aftermath of the May Fourth Movement, ironically, enhanced the impression of diffuseness and transiency. About the only thing that unified the anarchists was opposi- tion to other revolutionaries (especially the Communist party).

We must remember that the ineffectiveness of the anarchist approach to revolution was due in some measure to the anarchists' conscious self- limitation in the choice of revolutionary strategy, as a consequence of their efforts to remain true to the revolutionary ideals embedded in the anarchist vision. In terms of specific revolutionary tactics, and at the local level, anarchists were quite creative. They took the lead in China in devising tactics of popular mobilization that, although without conse- quence in their hands, would be put to effective use by the Communist party in its own quest for revolution. The contrast has much to tell us about the ingredients that made for revolutionary success in the circum- stances of Chinese society, and also about the price that revolutionary success was to exact in the attenuation of revolutionary ideals.

Anarchists demand our attention, not for who they were or what they accomplished, but because against a revolutionary strategy that presup- posed a necessary compromise of revolutionary goals in order to confront the demands of immediate political necessity, they reaffirmed a revolution- ary consciousness that provides an indispensable critical perspective from the Left on the unfolding of the Chinese revolution. Like anarchism world- wide (with one or two exceptions), anarchism in China went into a decline during the decade following the October Revolution in Russia and would

---

University of London, 1985), 45. Ou Shengbai and Huang Lingshuang left Guangzhou in 1923, the former for France, the latter for the United States. In 1922 Chen Duxiu published a letter from Huang stating that he had decided to follow Chen Duxiu into Bolshevism, which worried the anarchists. In 1923 Huang sent an open letter to anarchist journals reiterating his commitment to anarchism. See *Xin Qingnian* (New youth) (1 July 1922) for the letter to Chen. For Huang's confirmation of his anarchism, see "Lingshuang zhi mojun han" (A letter from Lingshuang), *Chunlei yuekan* (Spring thunder monthly), no. 1 (10 October 1923): 105.

disappear as a significant force in radical politics by the late twenties. The decline of anarchism was in historical hindsight not just the decline of anarchist influence, it also signaled the disappearance of a social revolutionary vision that had fashioned radical thinking for the previous two decades.

The significance of anarchism does not lie merely in the critical perspective it affords to historians and socialists. In the eyes of contemporaries, anarchism was a serious contender in the Chinese revolution, and, at least until the mid-twenties, there were more anarchists than Marxian communists in China. So long as Chinese radicalism retained the exuberant idealism that had characterized it at the turn of the decade, anarchism continued to impress radicals for the authenticity of its revolutionary vision. In the midst of the mass mobilization of the 1920s, the revolutionary movement in China appeared not as the work of revolutionaries (as it had earlier and would again after 1927) but as the outburst of a spontaneous popular revolutionary fervor that not only sought to break with the past but also promised seemingly limitless possibilities for the future. In this environment, anarchism exerted considerable appeal, and revolutionaries continued to imagine the real possibility of a China reorganized along the lines of anarchist social models.

ANARCHISTS AND MARXISTS: COLLABORATION AND SPLIT

Some anarchists expressed opposition to the Bolshevik government in Russia as early as spring 1919, and a major debate between Chen Duxiu and the anarchist Ou Shengbai in early 1921 would draw the boundary between anarchist and Marxist conceptions of revolution; but a definitive split between the two groups did not become apparent until 1922. Indeed, for nearly two years following the May Fourth Movement anarchists and Marxists collaborated in revolutionary activity, and there was considerable confusion over the relationship of anarchism to Marxism. The confusion had much to do with the context of radical activity in the immediate May Fourth period and with the circumstances of the founding of the Communist party.[2]

The May Fourth Movement in 1919 marked a shift in the attention of Chinese radicals toward an unprecedented concern with social change.

2. The discussion here draws on Dirlik, *The Origins of Chinese Communism* (New York: Oxford University Press, 1989), which may be consulted for further information and sources.

Cultural change, which had preoccupied radical intellectuals for the preceding three years, appeared by summer 1919 to be part of a broader
problem of social transformation. The October Revolution in Russia had
already stimulated a sharper awareness of the problem of social revolution before May 1919. The participation of Chinese laborers in the May
Fourth Movement from early June 1919 drew Chinese intellectuals' attention to the cleavages in Chinese society, which they took to be a consequence of an emerging capitalist economy, and brought the question of
social change to the forefront of radical consciousness. The result was an
increasing concern with class relations in Chinese society, and a turn to
socialism as a means of resolving the problems presented by class cleav-
age and conflict.

In the long run, this new concern would help the spread of Marxism
among radical intellectuals. The immediate result, however, was to provoke attention, not to Marxism per se, but to a variety of socialisms
that were at odds with Marxist premises of revolution, especially Marxism of the Bolshevik variety. We have noted that because of a prior
association of social revolution with anarchism, the immediate effect of
the Bolshevik revolution in China was to stimulate interest, not in Marxism but in anarchism. Now other varieties of socialism were added to
the radical repertoire. Social revolution had become a prominent issue
in Chinese radicalism, but there was considerable uncertainty over the
course it should take.

In the years 1918–1920, Chinese anarchists like anarchists elsewhere
were ambivalent toward Bolshevism. The initial anarchist response to the
October Revolution was one of enthusiasm, which not only created a
favorable impression toward the Revolution among radicals, but also
suggested to some that the Bolsheviks were guided by anarchist intentions. By early 1919, as news of the Bolshevik suppression of anarchists
reached the outside world, anarchist reports grew more somber. A piece
in the anarchist journal *Evolution* accused the Bolsheviks of "piratism,"
denying that the Bolsheviks were socialists, because to call them socialists
would be to admit that socialism permitted "people to eat one another."
Others in 1919 objected to the Bolshevik promotion of class struggle
because, they believed, it betrayed the humanitarian goals of revolution.
These criticisms were sporadic, however, and other anarchists were quick
to rush to the defense of Bolshevism. While Bolshevism fell short of the
ideals of social revolution, they argued, under contemporary circumstances it provided the only viable model of revolution; anarchists should
defend the Revolution and help move it along the path of a true social

revolution. Whatever qualms anarchists may have had concerning Bolshevism, these did not stop them from propagating favorable news of the Revolution or even responding positively to the first Comintern overtures in China.[3] Their differences were as much a function of internal differences over the conception of social revolution and of the foreign sources to which they had access as they were of the conflicting evidence issuing from the Soviet Union.

A similar ambivalence characterized the attitudes of other social radicals toward the Bolshevik Revolution, issues of class conflict, and Marxism—including those radicals who in 1920–21 would establish the Communist party. I must emphasize here that until November 1920 (when an embryonic Communist organization came into existence), it is not possible to speak of Marxists, or of a clearly defined Marxist political identity, in Chinese radicalism. A Marxist ideological identity was clearly established only after the founding of the Communist party; even then, uncertainties would persist.

When the Communist party was established in 1921, it was on the basis of Marxist study groups that had come into existence during the summer and fall of 1920, which in turn drew upon the study societies of the May Fourth period that had sprouted in major urban centers with the intellectual ferment of preceding years. As we have seen, these study societies were ideologically diffuse and were animated by vague ideals and organizing principles informed by anarchism. While the Bolshevik revolution had stimulated interest in Marxism among the intellectuals in these societies, in general intellectuals shared in the prevailing suspicion of the Bolshevik revolution in Russia and were committed to a peaceful social revolution through social reorganization from below. When some of them did convert to Marxism and assumed a Communist identity in late 1920, they did so as the result of a prolonged period of transformation that required them to break with their May Fourth legacy.[4]

The uncertainties of this period of transformation were the condition for anarchists' collaboration with the radicals who were to establish the Communist party. According to the anarchist Zheng Peigang, sometime during the summer of 1919 Huang Lingshuang collaborated with his colleagues at Beijing University, Chen Duxiu and Li Dazhao (the two founders of the Communist party in 1920), in establishing a Socialist Alliance (*Shehui zhuyizhe tongmeng*), which itself was possibly a product

3. Ibid., 31, 149.
4. Ibid., chap. 9.

of a clandestine meeting of East Asian radicals held in Shanghai under Comintern guidance.[5] Similar alliances were established elsewhere, though details are not available.

It is not clear whether there was a direct connection between these alliances and the Marxist study societies that came into existence in 1920, following the arrival in China of the Comintern organizer Gregory Voitinsky. These societies were to provide the immediate building blocks for Communist organization, but anarchists continued to participate in their organization and activities. In the Marxist study society in Beijing, anarchists may have outnumbered those who later became Marxists. The society in Guangzhou initially consisted exclusively of anarchists and two Soviet advisers. In other places, too, there was initial collaboration.

Anarchists, moreover, played an important part in these societies. Out of deference to its anarchist members, the Beijing society abstained from establishing organizational regulations. More important, both in Beijing and in Guangzhou, anarchists were responsible for publishing the labor journals that the study groups initiated. These journals promoted an attitude toward labor that was consistent with the syndicalist views of their anarchist editors, including the repudiation of the political involvement of laborers.[6]

While this collaboration was largely a product of the internal dynamics of Chinese radicalism, it was also encouraged by Comintern advisers in China, who were quick to recognize the importance of anarchism in Chinese radicalism and hoped to recruit anarchists to the Bolshevik cause. As late as spring 1922, well past the establishment of the Communist party, anarchists were invited to send delegates to the Congress of the Toilers of the East in Moscow.

Effective collaboration came to an end in November 1920, when an embryonic Communist organization came into existence with the reorganization of regional Marxist societies into a national organization. The Communist organization at this time announced a draft program (central

5. Zheng, "Wuzhengfu zhuyi zai Zhongguo ruogan shishi" (Some facts concerning anarchism in China), *Guangzhou wenshi ziliao* (Historical and literary materials on Guangzhou), no. 1 (April 1963): 191. For the meeting in Shanghai, in which Japanese and Korean radicals were present, see Thomas A. Stanley, *Osugi Sakae: Anarchist in Taisho Japan* (Cambridge: Harvard University Press, 1982), 132–35. According to Stanley, this meeting was held in October, with at least one session in Chen Duxiu's house; if so, then the socialist alliances would have been established before this meeting.

6. Dirlik, *Origins*, chap. 9. Also see the reprint of *Laodongzhe* (Laborers) of the Guangzhou anarchists, in whose publication Liu Shixin, Liang Bingxian, Ou Shengbai, and Huang Lingshuang all collaborated. (Guangzhou: Guangdong renmin chubanshe, 1984). The editor, Sha Dongxun, offers a useful summary of the circumstances of the journal's publication (125–35), as well as materials related to the journal.

to which was the establishment of a "dictatorship of the proletariat") and organizational rules intended to enforce a uniform discipline nationally. Anarchists, who were unwilling to condone dictatorship of any sort or a regulated organizational discipline, withdrew from the new organization.

The first polemics between anarchists and Communists accompanied this split. Communist historians in general present these polemics as a defense of Marxism against its opponents. There is no doubt some truth to this, although it is only a partial truth because it misses the crucial significance of the debate for the ideological unification of the Communist party itself. According to this view, anarchists had been on the attack against Bolshevism since 1919; at this time, Communists took up the cudgel in defense of their ideology. While it is true, as we have seen, that anarchists were critical of developments in the Soviet Union and were opposed to "the dictatorship of the proletariat," this interpretation ignores the fact that Communists cooperated with anarchists well into the fall of 1920 and that some anarchists, as in Beijing, had even been members of the Communist nuclei initially. Besides, when the attack was launched against the anarchists, it was in the internal party organ, the *Communist,* which suggests that the attack was initially directed not against anarchists in general but against anarchists in the party and, even more important, nonanarchist party members who were yet to shed the anarchist ideas with which they had been "tainted" since the May Fourth period. This suggests that the polemics against the anarchists, which sought to expose the deficiencies of anarchism, were intended primarily as a campaign for ideological purification within the party. The tone of the discussions confirms this interpretation.

Neither the split nor these polemics ended hopes for unity between the two groups of social revolutionaries. Anarchists were invited to and attended the Congress of the Toilers of the East in early 1922. Huang Lingshuang recalled in 1923 that upon his return from the Congress, Chen Duxiu (now the secretary-general of the Communist party), suggested further collaboration on the grounds that anarchists and Marxist-Communists shared similar goals.[7] In 1923 Ou Shengbai in turn extended a similar plea to Chen Duxiu.

Such hopes would never completely die out, and in later years some anarchists would join the Communist party. Nevertheless, it is possible to speak of a break in 1922 between the two movements. The Second Congress of the Communist party in July 1922 brought about a more tightly

7. Huang Lingshuang, Letter.

regulated organization than the first Congress had done in 1921, which further discouraged the anarchists from collaboration. It is possibly more important that with the Second Congress the Communist party initiated efforts toward an alliance with the Guomindang, which in the expansion of power it promised marginalized the need for recruiting anarchists to the Communist cause. Both sides may have given up on the possibility for further collaboration, which may account for the fact that, compared with the earlier debates, the polemics after 1922 assumed a much more virulent tone. The anarchists' turn against Bolshevism after 1922 was part of a worldwide anarchist abandonment of hope in Bolshevism as a possible means to a genuine social revolution.

ANARCHISM AND BOLSHEVISM:
THE PARTING OF THE WAYS

The Communist polemics against anarchism did not get under way until November 1920, in the newly established organ of the Communist party, the *Communist* (*Gongchandang*). Nevertheless, it was the founder of the party, Chen Duxiu, who in September fired the first salvo against the anarchists in his essay "On Politics," published in *New Youth* magazine (which had just been made the public organ of the Communist group in Shanghai).[8] Chen's article addressed anarchists as well as other socialist competitors. The discussion here is restricted to what he had to say about anarchism.

Chen's discussion addressed itself, on the one hand, to those who were opposed to the discussion of politics and, on the other hand, to those who advocated political discussion. In the first group he included scholars such as Hu Shi and Zhang Dongsun, merchants of the Shanghai chamber of commerce, and the anarchists. His main concern was with the anarchists. He believed that the opposition of the first two groups to politics was temporary and relative, based upon fear of warlords; anarchist opposition to politics was fundamental, absolute, and systematic, and called for careful consideration.

Anarchists' opposition to politics, Chen conceded, had considerable validity. Their criticism of the state and "naked force" (*qiangquan*) in politics was based on plausible evidence. The states of the past, he pointed out, citing Franz Oppenheimer, had indeed usurped people's

8. For further details, see Dirlik, *Origins*, 217–34. Chen's essay was entitled "Tan zhengzhi." Version used here is from *Duxiu wencun* (Collection of works by Chen Duxiu), 2 vols. (Shanghai, 1922), vol. 1.

rights by the use of political authority. The anarchist position was also supported by Bertrand Russell, who had argued in his *Principles of Social Reconstruction* that while the state was in theory the concentrated expression of popular sovereignty, in reality it constituted itself as a power outside of and above society.

Chen agreed with anarchist views on past and present states. Where he disagreed with them was in their extrapolation from past states to future states. Anarchists argued that no matter how the state and its laws were reformed, they would still be based on coercion; no fundamental change was possible, therefore, that did not reject absolutely the state and its laws. Against this position, Chen offered two sets of arguments, one "theoretical," the other "factual." Theoretically, he argued that "anyone who understands evolution theory" ought not to speak of fundamental or nonfundamental, since the denial of reason to the reality of the world deprived action of any ability to penetrate it. Moreover, he argued, indiscriminating opposition to "force" (*qiangquan*) was unscientific. Human beings used force daily in their efforts to conquer nature for human purposes; there was nothing wrong with the use of force that served human ends. "Whether or not force is evil depends on how it is utilized," he concluded, since "evil does not inhere in force itself."[9]

"Factually," Chen presented three arguments in favor of using force. First, human misery was a product of the oppression of the many by the minority bourgeoisie; since the latter would not relinquish its power voluntarily, there was no way to achieve significant change without violent class struggle against it. Second, the bourgeoisie was experienced in the manipulation of power; even after its overthrow, therefore, force would be necessary to control it. Finally, force would be necessary even to direct the people at large. Human nature had a bad as well as a good side. Whatever original human nature had been, laziness and selfishness had by now become second nature to human beings. This would not change overnight with revolution, but would require the use of coercion for some time to come. Chen's concluding message to the anarchists was that those who were opposed to the state and the laws of the working class might as well "be viewed as friends of the bourgeoisie."

Anarchists were quick to perceive the implication of Chen's argument. The following issue of *New Youth* published letters from two anarchists, Zheng Xianzong and Ke Qingshe, that criticized Chen for his views on laws and politics, but especially for his implicit defense of the dictatorship

9. *Duxiu wencun* 1:546, 556.

of the proletariat.[10] Zheng criticized Chen for his seeming defense of a perpetual existence for the state. The state, he argued, represented only one stage in human progress and should not, therefore, be viewed as eternal. He rejected the distinction Chen had drawn between the past and the present, arguing that the state of its very nature prevented human fraternity by dividing people. It may have been necessary in the past, but now it was no more than a relic.

Zheng further criticized Chen for his assertion that anarchists rejected violence. Only some anarchists inspired by Tolstoy rejected violence, he pointed out, otherwise most anarchists agreed that violence was necessary in order to achieve liberation. But the need for violence would disappear with the success of the revolution. Capitalism would have no hope of resurrection once private property had been eliminated. If further suppression became necessary, it should be only on a temporary, transitional basis. Zheng also challenged Chen's view that force would be necessary to overcome ingrained habits of laziness and selfishness. In his opinion, Chen confounded the evils of one historical period with the eternity of human nature. Besides, he observed, even if some people did not work, it would be very difficult to establish standards for the correct application of violence that did not violate the rights of others. Zheng, in other words, preferred to err on the side of freedom from coercion. The other respondent, Ke, agreed with Chen for the most part, adding only that there was no need to worry too much about the state, because with the abolition of property the state would disappear automatically.

What seemed to bother the two anarchists the most was Chen's suggestion that the state, the dictatorship of the proletariat, might be a permanent fixture for the future as it had been for the past. In his response to Zheng, Chen denied that he had assigned permanence to the state. The major difference between himself and his two critics lay in the time period they assigned to the transition to a stateless society. He believed that the state would have to exist for a fairly long time, since it would take a while to purge the legacy of the past. He did not share their optimism that once private property had been abolished, the evils of capitalism would disappear automatically. Private property had taken hold of people's "hearts," and it would take some time to rid them of their attachment to it. He disagreed with Zheng for his suggestion that states divided people; people were divided by many things, including their language and religion. Aboli-

10. For this exchange, see *Shehui zhuyi taolun ji* (Collection of discussions on socialism) (Shanghai: Xin qingnianshe, 1922), 30–31.

tion of the state would not eliminate these other divisions. In this, as in the question of acquired habits, the weight of the past had as much power as instinctive nature. It would take effort, laws, and coercion to purge people of the hold of the past on them. As for standards, he argued, equal sharing of responsibilities and the periodic shifting of unpleasant tasks provided sufficient means for resolving the distribution of labor.

To Chen, revolution was not a single act but a continuing process, since he was not sure how long it would take for "reason to conquer instinct." What ultimately distinguished him from his anarchist respondents was the greater sense of pessimism that pervaded his reply to his critics. The state and coercion would be necessary for the foreseeable future (which was the only future he was willing to speak of) because there was no reason to be overly optimistic about human nature. Neither was it meaningful to speak of "fundamental" transformations, since the task at hand required piecemeal resolution of problems inherited from the past. Revolution was not a single enormous effort followed by an eternity of ease; it was a task that required continuing, and arduous, work. The recognition of this, of the material constraints imposed by society and history on human action, was to Chen the characteristic that distinguished the scientific from the utopian socialist.

Chen's answer to Ke was brief, as Ke's letter had been brief. Many opposed proletarian dictatorship, he pointed out, because it was not democratic; how democratic was it for workers not to be free in the present society? This initial clash between Chen and his anarchist respondents was carried out in a courteous tone that would characterize Communist debates with the anarchists in 1920–21. The debate itself appeared to be a debate within the same camp of radicals who agreed on the purpose of revolution if not on the means to it.

Communists' attack on anarchism began in earnest with the publication of the *Communist* in November. The *Communist* critique of anarchism is interesting because it was clearly an internal party affair, intended to purge the influence of anarchism among party members. If there was an immediate cause for the discussion of anarchism that got under way almost with the first issue of the *Communist,* it was the tightening of party organization at this time, which was to result in the exodus of anarchists. Initially, moreover, the discussion was a one-sided affair. To repeat what has been stated above, some anarchists had been attacking Bolshevism since early 1919, but it would be erroneous to view these attacks as the provocation for the discussion in the *Communist.* Other anarchists had been members of the Communist groups since the summer of 1920, and in the initial period of party formation, Communists and anarchists cooperated all over China. Communist criticism of anarchism now is best viewed, therefore, as an effort to clarify issues of Bolshevik versus anarchist revolution, which was still a source of considerable confusion among members of the Communist groups, most of whom had been under the sway of anarchist ideas until recently. The discussion of anarchism in the *Communist,* moreover, was not addressed to any group or individual, but took the form of asserting the superiority of Bolshevism over anarchism in general. Unlike the simultaneous debate with the Guild socialists, whom Communist writers freely described as "the running dogs of capitalism," the tone the journal adopted in the polemics with anarchists was one of extreme friendliness, intended more to persuade the anarchists to abandon their "wrongful" ways than to discredit them. This tone of friendliness persisted even when the ideological differences broke out in public debate between Chen Duxiu and his former student Ou Shengbai in the spring of 1921. Communist-anarchist polemics would not assume a tone of acrimony until 1922, by which time the inevitability of the break between the two groups had become obvious. The issue raised by Ou Shengbai at this time would provide the basis for anarchist attacks on the Communists until the end of the decade, when anarchism would disappear from the Chinese scene as a significant ideological alternative.

The *Communist* was the first Bolshevik propaganda organ in China and the first publication to propagate systematically a revolutionary Marxist ideology. In its six issues published between November 1920 and July 1921, its readers (mostly party members) were exposed for the first time to Lenin's ideology of revolution, mainly through translations of foreign works on Lenin and the October Revolution. It was here that sections of *State and Revolution* were first translated into Chinese, and Chinese Marxists first became cognizant of Comintern discussions on world revolution. Most of the journal was devoted to reports on Bolshevik-inspired movements around the world, labor movements in various countries (including long reports on the International Workers of the World), and conditions of labor in China. The journal also published discussions on the problems of revolution in China that represent the first publications in China to treat seriously the relevance of Bolshevism to the Chinese revolution. These articles, most of them written by Li Da, Zhou Fohai, and Shi Cuntong, were to lay the ground for discussions of Bolshevism in later years. At the time, however, anarchism seemed to be the most important issue.

The introduction to the journal in its first issue enunciated the political line that it would propagate as an organ of the Communist party. The editorial affirmed the priority of economic change to all other change. It presented capitalism and socialism as the only alternatives in economic organization in the contemporary world. Capitalism had developed in Europe and was already in decline. Socialism, on the other hand, was still emerging; Russia, it declared, had become a "laboratory" for socialism. Communist parties around the world followed the Russian example, and so should China, where the evil effects of capitalism were already beginning to be felt. Chinese laborers, the editorial asserted, filled the world; those abroad were slaves to foreign capital, those in China slaved for foreign and Chinese capitalists alike. If they were to be saved from this slavery, the example of the Russian Revolution provided the only course of action. The editorial rejected unequivocally parliamentary means to change as a "lie" intended to deceive laborers. The only way for laborers to liberate themselves was to wrest power from capitalists through class struggle and establish their own power. The ultimate goal was the creation of a stateless society, which would follow a guarantee that the capitalist class had no hope for revival. It ended with a call upon the anarchists to join the Communist party. Anarchists, too, opposed private property and capitalism; hence they must participate in the struggle to transfer power to the working class. To do otherwise would be to serve the capitalists whom they desired to overthrow.[11]

The agenda laid out in this editorial set the course for articles that followed in the *Communist*. The basic issue was social revolution, in particular, differences between an anarchist and a Bolshevik (now identified with "communism") strategy of social revolution. The idea of social revolution propagated in the *Communist* represented the emergence in Chinese socialism of a new idea of social revolution that integrated politics and the social movement in a process of social revolution. The state corporatist solutions favored by some socialists (including Guomindang socialists, state socialists, and "Jiang Kanghu socialism") had eschewed class struggle in the name of an immediate political revolution, leaving the task of social transformation to the period after the socialist political revolution had been achieved. Anarchists and the "social corporatist" Guild socialists, on the other hand, had rejected politics in the name of a social movement that would gradually transform society and thereby abolish politics altogether

11. *Gongchandang*, no. 1 (7 November 1920): 1.

or create a new kind of politics, as the case might be. The Communist idea of revolution that now emerged in Chinese socialism represented an idea of social revolution that gave equal importance to politics and the social movement, conceiving of them in a dialectical relationship in a process of social revolution. While Communist writers in the *Communist* dismissed offhand the socialism of the other alternatives, they took much more seriously the anarchist idea of social revolution, with which they expressed a sense of kinship. Any differences were presented as differences within the same revolutionary camp, pertaining to the means rather than the ends of revolution.

The author who went farthest in reaffirming the essential unity of Marxism and anarchism was Shi Cuntong, who asserted in "How We Must Carry Out the Social Revolution" ("Women zemmayang gan shehui geming") that he believed in all the goals of anarchism ("free organization," "free association," and the principle of "from each according to his ability, to each according to his need") even though he was not an anarchist. Shi portrayed "communism" and anarchism as merely different stages in history, with the one serving as the means to the other: "As I see it, if one wants to realize anarchism, one must first institute communism; only when communism has been fully developed can there be anarchist communism."[12] Shi, however, was not the only one to identify the two. Li Da, who may have stood at the other end of the spectrum from Shi in his suspicion of the anarchists, nevertheless stated in his important essay, "The Anatomy of Anarchism" ("Wuzhengfu zhuyizhi jiepei"), that even if the anarchists were not comrades of the Communists, they were still friends, since they shared in the goal of overthrowing capitalism. The problem with anarchists was that they had no method for overthrowing capitalism and acted out of emotion rather than reason. It was revealing that Li noted not only the popularity of anarchism, but that the number of anarchists was still on the rise. He invited them to join Communist ranks to speed up the overthrow of capitalism and the establishment of socialism. Li agreed with Shi that Communists and anarchists desired to achieve the same kind of society; like Shi, he added that the achievement of that society (where the principle of "from each . . . to each" would prevail) must await the realization of "limitless" economic abundance, which must be its material precondition.[13]

Against the anarchists the Communists argued the greater realism and

12. *Gongchandang*, no. 5 (7 June 1921): 11, 17.
13. *Gongchandang*, no. 4 (7 May 1921): 14–15. Also see, "Shehui gemingde shangjue" (Considerations on social revolution), in no. 2 (7 December 1920): 5.

rationality of their method of social revolution. Their reasoning took three related directions: that communism was superior to anarchism in its plans for economic development, which was essential to revolution and was particularly important in backward China; in accepting organization, it offered a better means of carrying out the class struggle, which would have no direction without organization; and, finally, that communism was more realistic in accepting the necessity of politics.

In his "Considerations on the Social Revolution" ("Shehui gemingde shangjue"), Li Da offered the most comprehensive argument for the economic superiority of communism over anarchism. Revealing a clearly Marxist appreciation of the problem, Li stated that while anarchists were concerned mainly with the problem of distribution, Communists focused on production, which was essential to the creation of an economic basis for socialism. In advocating a "centralist" (*jizhong*) approach to production, communism promised a means to achieving this end. Anarchists, on the other hand, with the economic "dispersal" (*fensan*) they favored, offered no means to balance production against consumption or to increase the wealth of society. For a socialist society, economic development required central intervention. This should be especially obvious to anarchists who proposed a society that presupposed "limitless" abundance.[14]

Li argued further that communism was superior to anarchism not only in showing the way to increased production but in the realm of distribution as well. Distribution had two aspects, income and consumption. Anarchists desired to equalize the latter, Communists, the former. Anarchists desired to abolish money and to distribute goods according to need. While this might be possible in the future, it could not be instituted at present, when there were not enough goods to go around. Li did not say how income equalization would prove superior in this respect except to note that with the continued use of money, it would be possible to regulate production and consumption. What he had in mind, presumably, was the continued existence of a commodity economy where people would have a choice on how to spend their money.

Whatever problems may have been suggested by Li's own alternative, the difference was clearly between the immediate creation of a Communist society, which stressed freedom of production and consumption, and a society that postponed its Communist goals until productive abundance had become a reality. Until then, state direction and control of the econ-

14. Ibid.

omy would be necessary to increase production. Shi Cuntong, who believed that the appropriate material conditions were essential to the creation of any society, reaffirmed this position in arguing that machine production in both agriculture and industry was the precondition for a socialist economy. In Western capitalist societies, with their advanced production, the grounds were ready for the establishment of socialism. In China this must await the development of production. People who thought that socialism would be easier to achieve in China because of the underdevelopment of capitalism, Shi argued, were misguided because they overlooked the material conditions necessary to socialism.[15]

Economic backwardness also provided a major reason for Communist arguments in favor of continued existence of the state. Especially because China was economically backward, argued Shi, the task of development must devolve upon the state. But politics was also important for the success of the revolution, as Zhou Fohai argued in two articles published in May and June 1921, respectively, "Why We Advocate Communism?" ("Women weishemma zhuzhang gongchanzhuyi") and "Seizing Political Power" ("Douqu zhengquan"),[16] which brought Leninist arguments to bear against anarchist opposition to power (*qiangquan*) and the state. Recalling Chen Duxiu's statement in "On Politics" that politics did not leave alone even those who wanted to leave *it* alone, Zhou argued that without the use of power, there would be no way to achieve revolutionary success or, if it could be achieved, to defend revolution against a bourgeois resurgence. A dictatorship of laborers was necessary not just to keep the bourgeoisie down after the revolution, but also to transform society and purge it of its past legacy. This would take a long time. Anarchists were too optimistic, he pointed out, about the "good-heartedness" (*liangxin*) of people who, they believed, would abandon all their selfish habits once the revolution had taken place. Shi Cuntong added that the free, self-governing bodies that the anarchists advocated as the basis for Communist society would be crushed right away unless there was a power to defend them.[17] Ironically, these authors conceded that organized state power was all the more important in the creation of socialist society in backward China, where it was not even clear that the majority of the population favored revolution.[18]

15. *Gongchandang*, no. 5:16.
16. *Gongchandang*, no. 4:23–30, and no. 5:3–9.
17. "Douqu zhengquan," 5–7.
18. *Gongchandang*, no. 5:18–20.

Finally, Communists argued that while social conditions for revolution existed in China, organization was necessary for the conversion of class consciousness into a weapon of revolution. In his "Considerations on Social Revolution," Li Da argued that there were already classes in Chinese society: there had long been class division in agriculture; with industrial development, a class division had also emerged between the bourgeoisie and the proletariat. While the Chinese bourgeoisie was small in numbers, it was indistinguishable from the foreign bourgeoisie, and the proletariat suffered at the hands of both. There were many possibilities for the organization of the proletariat, ranging from economistic trade unions to politically motivated organization. The possibility of these alternatives indicated that while class consciousness was a social phenomenon, it did not necessarily lead to spontaneous unity of the class in class struggle. The only way to achieve such unity was through political organization of the class. It was necessary to unify workers, peasants, soldiers, and intellectuals whenever possible, and to engage in "direct action" against the ruling classes and their state. While "direct action" was a Sorelian idea (and the *Communist* did publish a piece by George Sorel on Lenin) that anarchists also shared, what Li had in mind was a Bolshevik-style "direct action," such as that which had led to Bolshevik success in 1917. The spontaneous, free association in which the anarchists believed offered no means, in the Communists' view, of unifying class consciousness into the political force necessary for revolutionary success.[19]

In the absence of debate, Communist writers did not feel it necessary to explain how the goals they professed to share with anarchists could be achieved through means that clearly stood at odds with those goals. A basic anarchist proposition throughout had been that means and ends were inseparable in the process of social revolution, that undesirable means would inevitably lead to undesirable ends, that freedom could not be achieved through dictatorship. The question of ends and means would be important in anarchist attacks on the Communists later in the decade. For the time being, they were irrelevant to the Communist advocacy of revolution in the *Communist,* which was concerned not with ultimate goals but with immediate revolutionary strategy, and whose primary goal was to purge within the Communist party any continuing qualms about a Bolshevik strategy of revolution. What Communist authors argued, with considerable justification and self-consciousness if not with wisdom, was that noble though the goals of anarchism were, anarchism offered no

19. "Shehui gemingde shangjue," *Gongchandang,* no. 2:8–9.

means of achieving them. Whether this required the rejection of anarchist considerations on method is a moot question, at least historically. The immediate concern in early 1921 was to draw with unambiguity a distinction between Bolshevism and anarchism. The criticism of anarchism in the *Communist* may have achieved this purpose; its inevitable concomitant, however, was to drive the Communists themselves into an ideological corner, which obviated the need for a critical appraisal of the revolutionary methods they advocated. Anarchism may have been impractical, as they claimed, but whether it was therefore irrelevant in the consideration of revolutionary strategy is another question. The refusal to entertain this question, which had been of central importance to Chinese radicals of the May Fourth period, was the most cogent indication of the rapidity with which Bolshevism had taken hold of the revolutionary imagination of the Communists.

When an anarchist response came in March 1921, it was not in response to arguments within the *Communist* (of which the anarchists were presumably unaware, since the *Communist* was semisecret as an internal organ of the Communist groups), but in response to Chen Duxiu's public criticism of anarchism. The first debate between Marxists and anarchists following the establishment of the Communist nuclei erupted in March 1921, when Ou Shengbai responded in *People's Voice* to statements on anarchism by Chen Duxiu in a lecture at Guangzhou in the Law and Political Science University ("The Critique of Socialism"). The exchange of letters to which this led (restricted to Guangzhou, as far as it is possible to tell), marked the first public debate between Communists and anarchists.

This debate, unlike the *Communist* polemics against anarchism, was carried out at a very abstract, hypothetical level. Neither Chen nor Ou enunciated the concrete implications of their debate until the end, when Chen finally stated outright what had been in their minds all along. Until then, they both danced around the issues with hypothetical examples to prove or disprove the viability of anarchism, with charges and countercharges of misrepresentation and mutual charges of inconsistency.

The issue that provoked and dominated the debate was whether anarchism was compatible with group life. Chen had stated in his lecture that while anarchism had much of value to say with regard to the individual conduct of life, it was irrelevant where social organization was concerned because the anarchist advocacy of "absolute freedom" (*juedui ziyou*) was incompatible with group existence.[20] In his open letter to Chen, Ou took exception to this statement. He criticized Chen for blurring important distinctions among anarchists. While some anarchists such as Stirner had advocated "absolute freedom" for the individual, they were the exception rather than the rule. Anarcho-communists (with whom he identified himself) did not object to group life, or even to the interference of the group in individual lives; what they rejected was the despotism of the group over the individual, of the kind that was implicit in the use of abstract laws to coerce individuals. What they advocated was voluntary association (*lianhe*) that recognized the right of the individual not to participate in the group's activities, and the substitution for abstract laws of a flexible "public will" (*gongyi*) that would determine the group's functioning but, unlike laws, would be subject to change. Anarchists objected to indiscriminating interference in individual life without regard to whether the individual was good or bad. They themselves believed in the necessity of interference with individuals whose activities impinged upon the rights of others or threatened group existence. Instead of coercion, however, anarchists believed in education to change people for the better. To prove his case that anarchism was compatible with group life, Ou cited examples of voluntary association in the contemporary world. His examples, curiously, did not serve his argument; they included examples not only of temporary association such as cooperation in fire fighting, but even of associations of capital established to build railroads in Europe. They were, at any rate, rather easy for Chen to dispose of.[21]

The rest of the debate was devoted to threshing out these issues. Chen conceded that there were indeed differences among anarchists on the issue of freedom, but he insisted that all anarchists suffered from a basic contradiction over this issue; indeed, he observed, anarchists such as Stirner were preferable because they at least recognized the contradiction, whereas anarcho-communists such as Kropotkin tried to cover it up under a guise of communism. Chen was not sympathetic to Ou's other arguments. The insistence on the freedom not to participate in group activity, he argued, would only make group life impossible and unpredictable; what would happen to production, for instance, if individuals suddenly decided not to participate? While voluntary association might be possible on a contingent basis, as Ou's examples indicated, Chen believed that it provided no basis

20. *Shehui zhuyi taolun ji,* 90.
21. This debate was originally conducted in the *Xin qingnian* and the anarchist periodical *Minsheng.* It was reprinted in *Shehui zhuyi taolun ji,* 97–154. Ou's response, 97–101.

for sustained social existence that inevitably demanded coercion and sacrifice of individual rights to the welfare of the group. (What is the need for anarchism, he inquired sarcastically, if capitalism already provided the grounds for free association?) As for public will, Chen felt that it was unreliable because it was subject to the vagaries of "mass psychology," which could lead to terror as easily as to association. Chen had considerable praise for laws as elements in human progress; international laws, he pointed out, had made possible for the first time in history the creation of a global society. Public will, on the other hand, smacked of primitive society, which had been based on the despotism of the tribe over the individual. He rejected the distinction Ou had drawn between laws and "contracts" between individuals, on the grounds that the one was undesirable because it was above society, while the other was desirable because it was based on individual consent; to Chen, contracts were just another form of law and would be meaningless without the backing of "abstract laws."[22]

These arguments became more elaborate as the debate progressed. Two differences, however, were evident throughout. Chen believed that individual rights must be sacrificed to the interests of the group; Ou did not. It followed also that Chen believed in the inevitability and functionality of coercion in social existence; Ou did not. Chen upheld the importance of laws in social existence, while Ou believed that laws prevented people from doing what they would do naturally, associate with one another freely, since he believed as firmly as did Chen that "social existence was the premise of individual freedom." Ou was hopeful that education would gradually correct antisocial behavior by purging people of their acquired habits. Chen thought the anarchist position was excessively optimistic about the goodness of human nature, and he was especially suspicious of the possibility of effective education for social ends within the context of a "bad" society. Perhaps nothing illustrates better how far Chen had traveled ideologically since the May Fourth period than his skepticism regarding the potential of education for social change, a belief in which he had done so much to instill in his students and followers (including Ou) as a leader of the New Culture Movement.

Ultimately, however, this debate over the relationship of the individual to the group was a debate over revolutionary strategy. In his last response to Ou, Chen finally drew out the practical implications of the debate when he drew a distinction between different kinds of coercion. He himself was opposed to coercion, he stated, where it deprived people of their

22. Ibid., 102–8. See 147 for the statement on Stirner and Kropotkin.

humanity. Such was the case with class oppression, where one class deprived another of its humanity, or with gender oppression where the humanity of women was sacrificed to the interests of men. But these standards did not apply where the interests of the individual coincided with the interests of the group. Where interest was not private interest but public interest, there was no need to speak of coercion, since any sacrifice of the individual represented a sacrifice for the welfare of the group of which the individual was an integral part, and this merely added up to sacrifice for one's own self. To Chen, the rights of labor unions under capitalism and communism illustrated this distinction. In capitalist society, labor unions had the right to strike in defense of their rights because that represented the self-interest of laborers against the self-interest of the capitalists. In Communist society there would be no need for the right of workers to strike, because all production would be for society, and its benefits would accrue to members of the society equally. For laborers to strike would be equivalent to striking against themselves.[23]

A double standard, perhaps, but it pointed to the dilemmas of both Communists and anarchists, who shared an organic conception of society where, once the evils of class division had been overthrown, any conflict between private and public interest would gradually disappear. As in the case of the *Communist* criticisms of anarchism, the difference between Chen and Ou concerned not the ends but the means of revolution. Ou believed that revolution could be achieved without coercion, through the agency of education; indeed, to introduce coercion into the process of revolution was to nip in the bud its promise of a good society. Chen Duxiu, having lost his faith in the power of education, thought that other means were necessary to bring about the seamless society whose individuals had long lost the ability to associate freely, if indeed they had ever had it. One demanded a consistency that transcended history; the other saw in consistency an obliviousness to history that would only perpetuate human oppression at the hands of the past.

The differences between Chen and Ou, as with Marxists and anarchists in general, were not simply political but philosophical as well. In his critique of anarchism in the *Communist*, Zhou Fohai had argued that anarchists were overly optimistic about human nature, which deeply flawed their conceptions of change. Not only did anarchist optimism lead to unduly optimistic expectations of human beings in the future, it also made it impossible to explain the emergence of social evils in history: if

23. Ibid., 149–51.

people were naturally good and sociable, there was no way to explain the historical emergence of social division and oppression.[24] Chen Duxiu brought similar arguments to bear against Ou Shengbai when he criticized Ou's claim that people would be good in anarchist society because it was in their nature to be good, that their very sense of shame would prevent them from doing evil.

Their skeptical view of human capability for good, the Communists believed, made their approach to change more realistic. This was true to some extent, but the differences were relative rather than absolute. While some anarchists in China held an unqualified optimism concerning the goodness of human nature, such optimism was not shared by anarchists such as Ou Shengbai. Ou was not against interference with individual human beings, he was against coercion. What distinguished him from Chen in his debate was his insistence that education could achieve all the improvement in human behavior that was necessary for the establishment of a good society; even where education proved helpless, denial of social participation to recalcitrant individuals would do the job. What he criticized about present-day society was its immediate resort to coercion and punishment in the name of abstract laws, which left no room for individual improvement. Ou was even willing, as Chen was to recognize in the end, to consider the necessity of a transitional period of Bolshevism to prepare society for anarchism.

Communists, on the other hand, rejected the goodness of human nature only in an immediate sense, as a sufficient precondition of social revolution. They, too, shared in the belief that ultimately socialism, in its anarchist expression, was a possibility: to deny that possibility would in fact have been tantamount to denying the vision in the name of which they legitimized their own revolutionary effort. They assigned priority, however, to the achievement of appropriate material conditions that they believed were necessary to the functioning of Communist society. Once that had been achieved, they believed, communism would become a possibility. The human personality that they deemed necessary to a Communist existence did not otherwise differ significantly from its anarchist counterpart.

The difference pointed nevertheless to a fundamental philosophical and epistemological problem that has long plagued anarchists and Marxists, in China and elsewhere: how to describe postrevolutionary society in the political language of bourgeois society. Richard Saltman has argued

24. "Women weishemma zhuzhang gongchan zhuyi," 26.

perceptively that this was a problem for Bakunin in his confrontation with Marx and accounts for most of the inconsistencies in his anarchism.[25] Marx himself was deeply aware of the problem when he wrote that "the beginner who has learnt a new language always translates it back into his mother tongue, but he has assimilated the spirit of the new language and can produce freely in it only when he moves in it without remembering the old and forgets in it his ancestral tongue."[26] The problem for both Marxists and anarchists in this debate was how to speak in a new language without losing touch with reality. This was ultimately what divided Chen and Ou, the Marxists and the anarchists in China. Chen observed somewhere along the line that anarchists accused him of being unable to appreciate anarchism because he looked to the future through the spectacles of the present. How are we to create the future, he retorted, if we do not start with present reality?[27] His observation captured the pathos of both Marxism and anarchism in this initial confrontation.

Perhaps because of their mutual appreciation of this problem, the debate between Chen and Ou, as with the prior criticism of anarchism in the *Communist*, retained a certain level of courteousness and mutual respect in spite of an occasional note of acrimony. In his concluding lines to the debate, Chen had nothing but praise for his former student. Even if Shengbai was an anarchist, he noted, he recognized the necessity of class struggle and revolutionary activity, and even of a transitional stage in the revolution. He was, moreover, a follower of Kropotkin and a sincere revolutionary youth, unlike some of the "low-quality" Chinese-style anarchists (Zhu Qianzhi?). "I only regret," he concluded, "that there are few like him among Chinese anarchists."[28]

This debate was conducted in a relatively friendly tone, partly because of the close personal relationship between the two men, but also because among the anarchists, Ou Shengbai came closest to accepting a Marxist analysis of society. It is also possible that anarchists held back their criticism of Bolshevism so long as further cooperation with the Communists remained a possibility. After 1922, when the break between the two groups became evident, anarchist criticisms would assume a much harsher tone.

25. Saltman, *Social and Political Thought of Michael Bakunin* (Westport, Conn., 1983), 5.
26. Karl Marx, *The Eighteenth Brumaire of Louis Bonaparte,* in Karl Marx and F. Engels, *Selected Works* (Moscow: Progress Publishers, 1973) 1:398.
27. *Shehui zhuyi taolun ji,* 139.
28. Ibid., 155.

ANARCHISM AGAINST BOLSHEVISM AND MARXISM

While internal developments in revolutionary politics would play an important part in shaping anarchist attitudes toward Bolshevism, their criticism of the Soviet Union and of Marxism was almost entirely derivative of foreign anarchists' writings on the subject. Indeed, the latter's disillusionment with the Soviet Union may have played a significant part in the increasingly intransigent repudiation of Bolshevism by the Chinese anarchists. With the conclusion of the crisis in the Soviet Union that had been caused by foreign aggression and internal insurrection, and the end of "war communism," which ushered in the New Economic Policy, it was no longer possible for anarchists to blame the shortcomings of Bolshevik socialism on external causes. Such was the case with Emma Goldman and Alexander Berkman, who left the Soviet Union in 1921 in final disillusionment. Their attacks on the Soviet Union thereafter left a deep impression upon Chinese anarchists; it may even be suggested that the writings in particular of Emma Goldman, which were broadly circulated in China, and her personal contacts with Chinese anarchists were responsible in large measure for shaping Chinese anarchists' attitudes toward the Soviet Union. Also important was the testimonial against the Bolshevik government of Russian anarchists. Mme Kropotkin's criticisms of the Bolsheviks provided an authoritative voice in Chinese criticisms of the Soviet Union (Kropotkin had died in early 1921, relieving the anarchists who had been concerned about his safety of the need for caution in their criticisms). Most important, however, were the writings of Varlaam Cherkezov, a Georgian anarchist who had long been a close associate of Kropotkin's.[29] Before his death in 1925, Cherkezov wrote extensively on Marxism, to which he traced the failings of the Bolsheviks. His writings were translated into Chinese and incorporated freely into Chinese criticisms of Marxism. If Goldman shaped anarchist views on the Soviet Union, Cherkezov provided a theoretical perspective that extended the critique of Bolshevism to a criticism of its roots in Marxist theory.

BOLSHEVISM AND THE DISTORTION OF REVOLUTION

The Chinese who led the way in the criticism of Bolshevism and Marxism after 1922 either had personal experience of the Soviet Union or were personally acquainted with foreign anarchists critical of Bolshevism: Huang

29. Paul Avrich, *The Russian Anarchists* (New York: Norton, 1978), 39–40.

Lingshuang, Qin Baopu, Bi Xiushao, and Bajin. Huang's experiences in the Congress of the Toilers of the East in early 1922, as well as his contacts with Russian anarchists (including a visit with Mme Kropotkin), convinced him of the "bankruptcy" of Bolshevism; he resolved even before his return to China that the Chinese public should be informed of the true visage of Bolshevism.[30] Bi Xiushao, who was in France from 1920 to 1925, not only was acquainted with prominent French anarchists such as Jean Grave, but met Mme Kropotkin when she was in Paris in 1923.[31] Qin Baopu played an especially important part in these criticisms. Qin had been a student in the Soviet Union between 1920 and 1923, sent there with the first contingent of Chinese students to study in the Soviet Union in preparation for the founding of the Communist party. While there, he had extensive contacts with both Goldman and Mme Kropotkin as well as with other Russian anarchists. Upon his return to China in 1923, he was responsible for introducing Goldman's writings to the Chinese public and wrote a number of articles (and a book-length account of the Soviet Union) critical of Bolshevism. He was also responsible for introducing Goldman to Bajin. Bajin, who entered into a correspondence with Goldman at this time, which would last until her death, emerged quickly in the mid-twenties as a prolific translator of foreign anarchist works into Chinese, including works by Goldman and Berkman. He was the author of a number of pieces sharply critical of Bolshevism.[32]

The anarchists were by no means the only ones to engage in polemics against Bolshevism; they are singled out here because of their strategic role in introducing to China the writings and the views of foreign anarchists. As was noted above, the agenda for Chinese anarchist criticisms of Bolshevism was set in 1920–21, in Ou Shengbai's polemics with Chen Duxiu. The major issues of debate had been the dictatorial organization of the nascent Communist party and the inclusion in its program of the "dictatorship of the proletariat" as an immediate goal. Ou, voicing the feelings of many anarchists, had argued, against this program, that a genuine social revolution could be achieved only through voluntary association, which would guarantee to the revolution the accomplishment of its goal of a free communist society. Key to his conception of revolution

30. Huang, "Letter," 110–11.
31. Bi, "Wo xinyang wuzhengfu zhuyi," WZFZYSX 2:1025–26.
32. Qin Baopu, "A Memoir of My Meeting Ms. Goldman in Russia in My Early Days" (original Chinese), Letter to Prof. Lu Zhe (1987?). I am grateful to Candace Falk, editor, "The Emma Goldman Papers," University of California at Berkeley, for sharing this letter, as well as other materials on Goldman's relationships with Chinese anarchists.

was a transformation of social consciousness in *the process* of revolution, which would obviate the need for coercion when the revolution finally came about. Ou believed, with other anarchists, that the goal of revolution was not to create a new class rule but to abolish classes altogether (which would also eliminate the need for the state and politics, since he believed, with Marxists, that the state was a product of class conflict); the "dictatorship of the proletariat" would merely reproduce the evils of old society.[33]

Anarchist criticism of Bolshevism after 1922 further developed these objections. Anarchists rejected the view of the Bolshevik revolution as a genuine social revolution and portrayed it instead as a political revolution that had merely brought a new group into the control of an old-fashioned state. Huang Lingshuang recalled Mme Kropotkin's telling him that Bolshevik socialism was not real socialism, because real socialism could not be built upon a centralized state power (this, she said, had been Kropotkin's view before his death).[34] The declaration against anarchist-Bolshevik cooperation of a Red Society (*Hongshe*) in 1923 stated that in order to achieve the goal of revolution, another revolution would be necessary to overthrow this new power structure, which merely increased the number of revolutions necessary to achieve socialism and would lead unnecessarily to further sacrifice and bloodshed: "If we are to rely on Bolshevism as a transitional stage in moving from present society to anarchist society, it means that we have to go through two revolutions, one to achieve Bolshevism and another to achieve anarchism. Is this not a great sacrifice?"[35]

The central anarchist objection to Bolshevism was over the issue of the "dictatorship of the proletariat." In the last installment of his polemics with Chen, Ou Shengbai had observed that what the revolution ought to abolish was not merely oppressors but oppression itself, since as long as oppression existed, it did not matter who did the oppressing.[36] Bajin described the "dictatorship of the proletariat" as mere "revanchism," which not only did not create a better world but opened the way to further conflict: if workers became the new dictators, others would seek

33. For a more detailed discussion of these polemics, see Dirlik, *Origins*, chap. 10.

34. Huang, "Letter," 110. Bi also heard this in person from Mme Kropotkin. "Wo xinyang wuzhengfu zhuyi," 1025.

35. "Fandui anbu xishou xuanyan" (Declaration opposing anarchist-Bolshevik cooperation), *Xuehui* (Sea of learning), no. 109 (5 February 1923). See reprint in *Wuzhengfu zhuyi sixiang ziliao xuan* (WZFZYSX), ed. Ge Maochun et al. (Beijing: Beijing daxue chubanshe, 1983) 2:665.

36. Ou, "Da Chen Duxiu junde yiwen" (Answering Mr. Chen Duxiu's doubts), *Xuehai*, (February 1923). See reprint in WZFZYSX 2:658.

to overthrow *them*. Besides, he argued, "dictatorship of the proletariat" was meaningless because "at the present the proletarian class constitutes the majority in society, and there has been no such thing historically as a majority oppressing a minority."[37] As early as 1921, an unattributed piece in *People's Voice* observed, rather cleverly, that if the proletariat, following the overthrow of the bourgeoisie, itself climbed the "political stage" as the ruler, it would no longer be the proletariat (literally, common people, *pingmin*).[38]

In his report on the Soviet Union, Huang had observed that the "dictatorship of the proletariat" was nothing but a mask for a dictatorship of intellectuals in the Communist party.[39] Sanbo (Bi Xiushao?) added in his polemics with Zhou Enlai in Paris that the "dictatorship" was nothing but the dictatorship of a single party and, within the party, of a few leaders; it ought to be called in reality a "dictatorship of the leaders of the Communist party."[40] As Lu Jianbo put it in an extensive discussion of the "dictatorship of the proletariat" published in *Light of Learning* in 1924: "Facts tell us: the inner lining of the dictatorship of the proletariat is the dictatorship of a single party—the Leninist party. The Soviets have already been captured by bureaucratic socialists." Anarchists found ample evidence of this dictatorship, not only in the suppression by the Bolsheviks of other revolutionaries (the anarchists in particular), but also in the readiness of the Soviet government to turn its guns on the people, as in the Kronstadt rebellion of 1920.[41]

Economic dictatorship, anarchists believed, exacerbated the political dictatorship of the state; in the failure of Bolshevik socialism, "political centralization" (*jiquan*) was the other side of the coin to "economic collectivism" (*jichan*). Chinese anarchists had since the mid-1910s drawn a distinction between "collectivism" and "communism" (*gongchan*). Anarchism was truly communist; Marxian communism was in essence collectivist. The failure of Bolshevik socialism, they now argued, rested not only in its repudiation of democracy for dictatorship, but in its eco-

37. Li Feigan (Bajin), "Zailun wuchan jieji zhuanzheng" (Another discussion of the dictatorship of the proletariat), *Xuedeng* (Light of learning), no. 17 (1925): 1.
38. "Wuzhengfu gongchanpai yu jichan paizhi qidian" (Differences between anarcho-communists and collectivists), *Minsheng* (People's voice), no. 30 (March 1921), in *WZFZYSX* 2:565–66.
39. Huang, "Letter," p. 113.
40. "Iguo gongchan zhuyi shibaizhi yuanyin jiqi buqiude fangfa" (The failure of Communism in Russia and the way to salvage it), *Gongyu* (After work), September 1922. See *WZFZYSX* 2:598.
41. Jianbo, "Lun wuchan jieji zhuanzheng" (On the dictatorship of the proletariat), *Xuedeng*, nos. 20–22 (1924). See no. 20:1. See also Li, "Zailun wuchan jieji."

nomic basis in state collectivism, which was merely "capitalism in a
different form,"[42] since all it accomplished was the replacement of ownership by individuals with ownership by the state. This new form of
ownership exacerbated the exploitation of the people, since the state
now had a monopoly over employment and could set its terms as it
pleased. The anarchist argument was summarized by Ou Shengbai in a
cogent statement:

> Marxian socialism advocates the centralization not only of political power but
> also of capital. The centralization of political power is dangerous enough in
> itself; add to that the placing of all sources of wealth in the hands of the
> government, and the so-called state socialism becomes merely state capitalism,
> with the state as the owner of the means of production and the workers as its
> laborers, who hand over the value produced by their labor. The bureaucrats
> are the masters, the workers their slaves. Even though they advocate a state of
> the dictatorship of workers, the rulers are bureaucrats who do not labor, while
> workers are the sole producers. Therefore, the suffering of workers under state
> socialism is no different from that under private capitalism. Besides, while the
> power of individual capitalists to exploit the worker is relatively limited, the
> state can back up its exploitation with military force; hence the wretchedness
> of the worker at the very least equals that under capitalism.[43]

Ironically, anarchists perceived in the relaxation of economic controls
with the New Economic Policy a confirmation of their view that Bolshevism was but a transmuted capitalism. Qin Baopu, who wrote extensively on this issue, found in the Bolshevik call on foreign capital to help
develop the Soviet Union evidence of collusion between Bolsheviks and
foreign capitalists against the interests of the people; the Bolsheviks, he
believed, were less concerned about the people and socialism than about
the economic development of the state.[44] The Communist alliance with
the Guomindang in China was to provide anarchists with additional
evidence of the essentially "capitalist" nature of Marxian socialism.

THE CRITIQUE OF MARXISM

The anarchist critique of Bolshevism, of its economic policies as well as
its stance on the question of classes, implicated Marxism in the failure of
Bolshevik socialism. Some continued to blame the failure of socialism in

---

42. Jianbo, "Lun wuchan jieji zhuanzheng"; Baopu, "Makesi zhuyi piping" (Critique of
Marxism), *Xuedeng*, no. 19 (1924).
43. Ou, "Da Chen Duxiu," 663; Sanbo, "Iguo gongchan zhuyi," *WZFZYSX* 2:599.
44. Baopu, "Xin jingji zhengce" (New economic policy), *Xuedeng* (January–February
1924), in *WZFZYSX* 2:854–59.

Russia on the backwardness of Russian society, which, as an agrarian society, did not fulfill the conditions upon which socialism could be built.[45] Increasingly, however, anarchists traced the failure of the revolution to its Marxist premises. Cherkezov's analyses of Marxism provided them with the theoretical weapons they needed. In spite of a measure of simplification, these writings presented an analysis of Marxism that was more sophisticated than any other available in China at the time, including to the Communists, whose understanding of Marxism was shaped almost exclusively by a Leninist interpretation.

As it appeared in Chinese anarchists' writings (which for the large part consisted of rephrases of or direct quotations from Cherkezov), Marxism suffered from a fatal ambivalence, which had entered the theory at its very origins. It shared with all socialism, including anarchism, a vision of the future in which society would be "managed by free associations of workers' and peasants' organizations" (*Gongnong zuzhide ziyou xieshe gongtong guanli*).[46] At the same time, however, the method the theory suggested for reaching this goal compromised its vision irredeemably, since all of the key concepts that Marx had utilized to formulate his theory—hence the theory itself—were derivative of the ideas of bourgeois economists and philosophers, which meant that his methods were shaped by the premises and prejudices of bourgeois society. Marxism, in other words, suffered from a fundamental contradiction between its socialist visionary goal and a method for attaining that goal that was thoroughly infected by bourgeois ideology. The method itself, moreover, contained a contradiction: between a tendency that was social democratic but reformist and a tendency that was revolutionary but Jacobinist (hence divorced from the people). Different though they were, neither method broke with bourgeois politics.

While these writings insisted that Marx had lacked originality as a social thinker, since he had received all of his theoretical insights from others, they nevertheless recognized in him considerable complexity, drawing a distinction between a young Marx and a mature Marx in terms of his attitude toward the state. In his earlier writings, including the *Communist*

---

45. Huang, "Letter," 112; Sanbo, "Iguo gongchan zhuyi," 596–97.

46. The following discussion is based on a long essay by Lu Zhi, "Makesi zhuyi piping" (Critique of Marxism), a combination restatement and translation of Cherkezov's work. Lu says in his postscript that the essay was first published in *Minzhong*. The version used here is from part 5 ("Makesi zhuyidi pochan" [Bankruptcy of Marxism]) of *Ziyou congshu* (Compendium on freedom), 151–228. This was a valuable collection of anarchist writings from the twenties (mostly translations) published in 1928 by the Equality Society (*Pingshe*) in San Francisco. The Compendium was first published in Shanghai by the Freedom Bookstore (*Ziyou shudian*) in 1927.

Manifesto, Marx had privileged the state as an agent of change and seen in the socialist capture of the state the key to bringing about socialism. The Paris Commune had constituted a turning point in Marx's thinking; it had inspired him to a new view of socialism as "a federation of free associations" (*ziyou zuzhide lianbang*). Thereafter, he had abandoned his former reliance on the state as the agent of socialism. Although in his *Critique of the Gotha Program* he had once again turned to the theme of the "dictatorship of the proletariat," it was not clear whether he meant a "dictatorship of the state," as some Marxists claimed, or a dictatorship of the people after the example of the Commune.

If there was a "villain" in the account, it was Engels. It was Engels who had elevated Marx to the status of a creative genius, therefore covering up Marx's intellectual debt to bourgeois scholars. It was Engels who had sought to synthesize the irreconcilable philosophical ideas of materialism and the dialectic into a "dialectical materialism," which he then presented as a science (which, Cherkezov argued, distorted Marx because it privileged the deductive method over the inductive method, which Marx had favored, and restored to Marxism the Hegelian metaphysics, which Marx had repudiated). Finally, Engels had been responsible for restoring to Marxism its pre-Paris Commune prejudice for the state by once again privileging the state as an agent of change. In the process, he had also taken revolution out of Marxism and made it into a strategy of peaceful change.

Engels, in other words, appeared as the immediate source of contemporary social democracy. Lenin had broken with Engelsian Marxism both in his insistence on violence and in his elevation of the idea of proletarian dictatorship. He, too, however, had departed from the post-Commune ideas of Marx. Rather, his approach to Marxism had revived the Jacobinist tradition, which reduced the real revolutionaries—workers and peasants—to mere appendages to the revolution. While the Bolsheviks sought to represent themselves as champions of the people by claiming the Soviets for their own, this had little basis in reality, for the Soviets had been anarchist in inspiration and origin. Lenin's socialism, Cherkezov concluded, was but a "modified state capitalism," concerned primarily with carrying out the task of economic development, which in advanced countries had been accomplished by the bourgeoisie.

This portrayal of Marxism was itself quite reductionist in some of its key conclusions; nevertheless, it raised questions concerning Marxism that retain their significance to this day and, in the context of China in the 1920s, was without parallel in sophistication. The questions it raised

concerning the relationship of Marxism to its bourgeois legacy, the role
Engels played in the formulation of Marxism after Marx, and especially
the meaning of the "dictatorship of the proletariat" in the post-
Commune writings of Marx were basic issues, which are debated to this
day. Cherkezov, moreover, backed up his arguments with an extensive
coverage of Marxist and non-Marxist literature that was very impressive
for its grasp of fine details in the history of Marxism.

The issues Cherkezov raised quickly assumed nearly formulaic status in
anarchist discussions of Marxism, as may be gleaned from an article by
Shen Zhongjiu published in *People's Tocsin* in early 1927.[47] Shen raised
six objections to Marxism: (1) Marx had copied his most basic ideas from
others: class struggle (Guizot, Considerant, Blanc, Proudhon); the concentration of capital (Considerant); surplus value (Sismondi, Blanqui); rate of
profit (Ricardo); historical materialism (Vico, Herder). (2) Marxism is
utopian, not scientific because science is based on the inductive method
whereas Marxism is metaphysical; hence its errors on such questions as the
concentration of capital, or its inability to account for the role consciousness plays in society because of its assumption of technological determin-
ism, which ignores that it is human consciousness that creates technology.
(3) Marxism advocates private property; the state takes over production
and remunerates individuals according to their contribution, which turns
everyone into a capitalist. (4) Marxism is reformist, not revolutionary.
(5) Marxism advocates dictatorship of the few. (6) Marxism stresses industry and ignores agriculture; hence it is irrelevant to China. The last item, to
be discussed further, was a particularly Chinese concern; the rest were
merely summaries of Cherkezov's argument (as Shen acknowledged in his
essay).

Two of the issues that Cherkezov raised were of particular importance in Chinese discussions of Marxism: the concentration of capital,
and class struggle. An essay of Cherkezov's on the former issue appeared in anarchist publications more than once, complemented by Chinese discussions on the subject. The essay argued, based on empirical
data, that Marx had been wrong in predicting a progressive concentration of capital and suggested to the contrary that the number of independent businesses had been on the rise since Marx's time. Anarchists were
impressed by Cherkezov's idea that Marx had copied this notion from
other economists. More important, however, may have been the implica-

47. Tianxin (Shen Zhongjiu), "Gao gongchandangde qingnian" (To Communist youth),
Minzhong (People's tocsin) 2, no. 3 (25 March 1927): 205–22.

tions of the question for the future of socialism. In *Imperialism: The Highest Stage of Capitalism* Lenin had perceived in the concentration of capital a process that would facilitate the establishment of socialism; the state needed only to take over from large corporations in order to convert an economy from capitalist to socialist. The proliferation of small enterprises would suggest, to the contrary, that state socialism could be established only by going against economic trends, which lent additional support to the anarchist critique of Bolshevism. Whether anarchists also perceived in this an argument in favor of anarchism is more difficult to say.[48]

The issue of class was more complex, if only anarchists were themselves divided over it. Some anarchists rejected it altogether because they viewed class struggle as another expression of selfishness in society, which, in the social divisions it promoted, contravened the humanitarian goals of anarchism; this view of class would provide Guomindang-related anarchists with an ideological weapon against the Communists in the late twenties. Others, while they were willing to recognize the importance of class, were nevertheless reluctant to attribute to it the centrality with which Marxists endowed it. An unattributed article in *People's Voice* in 1921 argued that there was little reason to view all history as the history of class struggle, as Marxists claimed, because classes were not always distinguishable from one another in their interests; and even if class struggle at times moved to the center of history, it was not always central, since other loyalties (such as national loyalty) took precedence over class loyalty. Most interesting was the "thought experiment" the author suggested:

> Suppose someone suggests another method of revolution on the basis of the three lines in the *Communist Manifesto:* (1) Women of the world, unite; (2) overthrow the present-day male political order; (3) [establish] a woman's dictatorship. Put simply, "male-female struggle, dictatorship of women." They also suggest that this is the method of social revolution, and the means to the transition to communism. Should our social revolutionary method be the former (Marx's) or the latter (women's)? Or should we let each follow its own way? Whatever the choice might be, we think that people have no wish to heed this kind of theory.[49]

48. Mao Yibo, "Makesizhi 'ziben jizhong' de miushuo" (The erroneousness of Marx's "concentration of capital"), *Xuedeng* (12 December 1925).

49. " 'Jieji zhanzheng' he 'pingmin zhuanzheng' guoshi yongyu shehui geming ma?" (Are "class war" and "dictatorship of the common people" of use in social revolution?), *Minsheng,* no. 13 (July 1921), in WZFZYSX 2:587–90. A good discussion of the difficulties of class analysis was offered by Bibo (Bi Xiushao), "Jieji douzheng" (Class struggle), *Geming zhoubao* (Revolution weekly), no. 18 (1927): 244–49.

It would be possible but erroneous to read this statement as derogatory of women; the struggle of women for liberation was after all a primary concern for anarchists and a probable reason for questioning an exclusive focus on the proletariat. Rather, the point was to challenge the Marxist assumption of a central thread to history in class struggle and the consequent centering of the struggle for liberation on the proletariat. The goal, in other words, was to further open up the possibilities available in the struggle for liberation by denying to history a center.

Even those anarchists who took class struggle for granted viewed it in terms slightly different than those of Marxism: not as a function of the production process but rather in terms of rich and poor, those who lived off the labor of others and those who labored, or even the educated versus the uneducated. For anarchist advocates of class struggle, the concept created a problem, moreover, because of the relationship that the Leninist argument established between class and the dictatorship of the proletariat; while they conceded that class struggle was a basic datum of history, they insisted that classes could not be allowed to exist after the revolution because this would mean the inevitable resurrection of the state. The revolution, in other words, must pursue a strategy that would abolish not only existing class oppression but the very existence of classes. Ou Shengbai, who may have been closest to the Communists on the issue of class, explained:

> I advocate class war because I believe that classes must be extinguished; if the ruled classes do not unite to overthrow the ruling class, the class system cannot be easily abolished. But I wish to use class war to abolish classes, not to overturn them as you [the Communists] do; most anarchists pursue the syndicalist movement and advocate class war. When I speak of the working class, it is the real working class; I do not mean, as you do, organize a political party and view it as the working class, make the working class into a tool of the political party, or make the party into a dictator over the working class. Although I have refrained from criticizing the system in Russia, there is much about it that is not satisfactory. Under the present capitalist system, capitalists are our mutual enemy, and instead of attacking one another, we must give one another support. But if you try to carry the Russian system to China in its entirety, I cannot go along with it.[50]

Anarchist objections to the dictatorship of the proletariat further illustrate the ways in which anarchists found communism to be wanting in its conception of the role of classes in revolution. Suffice it to say here that where this particular issue was concerned, Chinese anarchists had already

50. Ou, "Da Chen Duxiu," 662–63. Other prominent proponents of class struggle were Liang Bingxian and the Sichuan anarchists Lu Jianbo and Mao Yibo.

elaborated arguments that they now developed further in their criticisms of Marxism. The portrayal of Marxism by Cherkezov lent additional support to these arguments. Marx's views on class were lacking in authenticity, Cherkezov suggested, because they had been copied from others; they were "counterrevolutionary" because they were rooted in bourgeois conceptions of politics. Marx's only difference from his "teachers" Guizot and Lorenz von Stein, both defenders of private property and the bourgeoisie, had been that whereas they had justified the dictatorship of the bourgeoisie, he had argued for a dictatorship of the proletariat. Class struggle, which to the anarchists and syndicalists meant economic struggle for liberation, meant to Marxists a political struggle, which basically differed little from bourgeois conceptions.[51]

ANARCHISTS AND REVOLUTION IN CHINA

For all their brave talk about the bankruptcy of Bolshevism and Marxism, anarchists were well aware by the mid-twenties that they were inexorably losing ground to the Communists. The alliance with the Guomindang (formalized in early 1924) significantly increased Communist access to the mass movements. By the time of the second National Labor Congress in 1925, Communists had replaced anarchists in the leadership of the labor movement; their influence over labor would draw further force from the mass mobilization that followed the May Thirtieth Incident in 1925, as would their influence over youth and women's movements and, starting in 1925, over the growing agrarian movement.

Anarchists themselves had the option of bringing their movement under the Guomindang umbrella. The Guomindang had its own ideology in Sun Yat-sen's Three People's Principles, of course, but unlike the Communist party, it was loose organizationally and accommodated disparate political positions under its ideological umbrella. As Shen Zhongjiu would write in 1927, the Three People's Principles were quite flexible in their broadness and their emphases could change with changing circumstances.[52] Besides, the doyens of anarchism in China, such as Li Shizeng and Wu Zhihui, were important members of the Guomindang; they now pressured their younger followers to join the Guomindang to compete with Communists.

51. Lu, "Makesi zhuyi piping," 194–203.
52. "Fakan ci" (Opening statement), *Geming zhoubao*, no. 1 (July 1927): 13. Shen was the editor and, according to Bi Xiushao, wrote this statement. He had earlier opposed alliance with the Guomindang.

After the Guomindang suppression of communism in 1927, many anarchists would collaborate with the Guomindang under the slogan "Use the Three People's Principles as a means to achieve anarchism" (*yi sanmin zhuyi wei shouduan, yi wuzhengfu zhuyi wei mubiao;* literally, "Take the Three People's Principles as method, anarchism as goal").[53] In the early twenties, however, the more activist among the anarchists, especially those connected with the Guangzhou and Sichuan anarchists, were reluctant to enter such an alliance. While anarchists collaborated with Guomindang labor leaders in the syndicalist movement in Shanghai in 1924–25 (and possibly also in Guangzhou), because of their opposition to politics they remained wary of any alliance with a political party. In 1912 Shifu had criticized Zhang Ji and Wu Zhihui for their participation in the Guomindang. His heirs now directed similar criticism at Wu Zhihui and Li Shizeng for their political activities.

Radical anarchists were also opposed to the nationalist goals of the revolutionary movement led by the Guomindang-Communist alliance. At the height of the nationalist movement in China, anarchists continued to criticize nationalism and patriotism as "obstacles to the progress of humankind," rooted in "selfishness and self-aggrandizement." They bemoaned the growth of patriotic sentiment since the May Fourth Movement, for they believed that nationalism inevitably strengthened the government and built walls around people that separated them from one another.[54] When Jean Grave in a letter gently rebuked Chinese anarchists for their inflexibility on this issue, reminding them that he and Kropotkin had supported World War I as a necessary compromise, Bi Xiushao (who had known Grave in France) responded that while anarchists were opposed to imperialism because of its oppressiveness, they could not support a nationalist movement that glorified patriotism.[55]

Beyond these issues of principle, anarchists opposed the Guomindang as a bourgeois organization that was counterrevolutionary in nature. Indeed, anarchists perceived in the Communist alliance with the Guo-

53. "Fangwen Fan Tianjun xianshengde jilu" (Record of a visit with Mr. Fan Tianjun), *WZFZYSX* 2:1043.
54. Feigan (Bajin), "Aiguo zhuyi yu Zhongguoren dao xingfude lu" (Patriotism and the Chinese path to happiness), *Jingqun* (Warning to the masses), no. 1 (1 September 1921), in *WZFZYSX* 2:541–43; (Wei) Huilin, "Shehui geming yu guomin geming" (Social revolution and national revolution), *Minzhong* 2, no. 1 (January 1927): 11–21; Tianxin (Shen Zhongjiu), "Gao guojia zhuyizhe" (To nationalists), *Minzhong* 2, no. 2 (February 1927): 100–5.
55. "Zhen Tian yu Faguo wuzhengfu zhuyizhe Gelafude tongxin" (Zhen Tian's [Bi Xiushao's] correspondence with the French anarchist Grave), *Minzhong* 2, nos. 4–5 (May 1927), in *WZFZYSX* 2:729–34.

mindang confirmation of their belief that Bolshevism was essentially bourgeois in orientation. In a long essay criticizing Communist rationalizations for joining the Guomindang, Mao Yibo pointed out that the so-called revolutionary Guomindang spent much of its time suppressing real revolutionaries.[56]

Anarchist attitudes toward their competitors on the revolutionary scene were summarized in 1926 in a "Manifesto of the Hunan Anarchist Alliance" (*Hunanqu wuzhengfu zhuyizhe tongmeng xuanyan*):

> We must break down the errors of other doctrines so that the masses may be led on to the correct path. The evil doctrines of the contemporary world, such as imperialism, militarism, capitalism, need not be broken down by us; the masses already oppose them. As for the others, such as Marxism (i.e., Bolshevism and Leninism), integral nationalism (*guojia zhuyi*), Three People's Principles, etc., they have on the surface some truth to them, and there are those among the masses who blindly pursue them. A little examination will show, however, that they are no more than modified revanchism (*baofu zhuyi*), commandism (*shouling zhuyi*), and aggressionism (*qinlue zhuyi*). These doctrines not only cannot resolve humankind's problems, they are, on the contrary, themselves obstacles to revolution in the path of human progress.[57]

REVOLUTION AND ORGANIZATION

Anarchists continued to phrase their own revolutionary goals in broad humanitarian terms. The Declaration of the Anarchist Federation in 1923 described the goals of revolution as the elimination of all that was contrary to reason, and the creation of a society of "mutual labor, mutual aid, and mutual love" (*hulao, huzhu, huai*).[58] The Equality Society (*Junshe*) in Sichuan sought to bring about "a world organized around love, not killing; a world of mutual aid, not competition."[59] In 1927 the anarchist-Guomindang periodical *Revolution Weekly* (*Geming zhoubao*) depicted the goals of anarchism as the elimination of all that was old, irrational, and harmful and, therefore, unsuited to existence; and the creation of a social organization that was new, rational, and beneficial to human existence.[60] All anarchists agreed that the goal of an authentic revolution was to transform

56. Yibo (Mao Yibo), "Ping Chen Duxiu xianshengde jiangyan lu" (Critique of Mr. Chen Duxiu's collection of speeches), *Xuedeng*, no. 20 (November 1924).

57. Hudson Collection (The Hoover Institution), Package 6, part 2.

58. "Guangzhou zhenshe xuanyan" (The declaration of Guangzhou Reality Society), *Chunlei*, no. 1 (10 October 1923): 4.

59. "Junshe xuanyan" (Declaration of Equality Society), *Banyue*, no. 21 (1 January 1921), in WZFZYSX 2:535.

60. Bibo (Bi Xiushao), "Women shishei?" (Who are we?), *Geming zhoubao*, nos. 16–18 (1927). See no. 16:172.

social consciousness and life at its quotidian level, in order to create recep-tivity to such a conception of society; their own role was to "incite" the masses to action to achieve such a consciousness. Wu Zhihui estimated at one point that the anarchist revolution would take about "three thousand years" to achieve (though he added, a few years later, that if every anar-chist was a Shifu, it might take only "five hundred years").[61] It would also take many, many revolutions to achieve this goal.

Anarchists in the twenties, unlike those in earlier years, could no longer afford to be satisfied by vague statements of revolution. The Com-munist challenge was to compel anarchists to pay closer attention to concrete issues of revolution. While they were opposed to the Communist strategy of revolution, anarchists had to evolve a strategy of their own to prove their viability as an alternative to the Communists. This was the most important development in Chinese anarchism in the twenties. It was evident in the increasing attention devoted to three questions with which the Communists presented them: organization, revolutionary strategy, and the defense of revolution (an alternative, in other words, to the "dictatorship of the proletariat").

The need to organize, and to find a suitable means of organization, were major anarchist preoccupations. Anarchists insisted that they were not opposed to organization (as the Communists charged), that they opposed only the kind of organization that was inconsistent with the revolutionary society they sought to create—in other words, political organization that took as its aim not social revolution but the conquest of political power, which was hierarchical and coercive in its internal func-tioning.[62] Qin Baopu charged with "laziness" anarchists who believed that anarchism should not be organized, or that anarchist organization had no room for discipline, rules, and regulations. Organization was a necessity of revolution, he asserted; anarchist organization was distin-guished from others in that it must be based on "the will of the masses" (*qunzhong yizhi*). Like other anarchists, he believed that anarchist organi-zation must move from the bottom up. He proposed as the initial task of organization the founding of "small organizations" (*xiao zuzhi*) in locali-ties, productive units, and schools. These organizations would associate with others in their proximity in "local congresses" (*quhui*). Except over fundamental issues that required congress decision, the small organiza-

61. Zhihui (Wu Zhihui), "Jinian Shifu xiansheng" (Remembering Mr. Shifu), *Minzhong* 2, no. 3 (March 1927): 162.
62. Sanmu (Li Shaoling), "Wuzhengfu zhuyi yanjiu" (Examination of anarchism), *Chunlei*, no. 2 (10 December 1923): 3–4.

tions would be independent in carrying out day-to-day affairs, represented by their secretaries. In this manner, he believed, whole counties and provinces could be organized for action. While other anarchists at the time called for a national congress of anarchists, Qin believed that such a congress would be premature until after localities had been organized. With the country thus organized, once revolution broke out at the centers of political power, it would spread rapidly. What was most important for the time being was to organize the masses without the use of coercion—which alienated them, as the Bolshevik example showed—and to neutralize those others who were potentially opposed to revolution. He envisaged a violent revolution, for he believed that power holders were unlikely to relinquish their power voluntarily.[63]

While Qin's proposals represented mainstream anarchist thinking on the question of organization, others were willing to go still further. *People's Vanguard* magazine, more radical than most in its advocacy of class struggle and its opposition to the Guomindang, published an article by Mao Yibo that sounded much like the Bolshevik strategy the anarchists opposed. Although revolution was class struggle and must ultimately depend for its success on the consciousness of the masses, all revolutions historically had been the work of the few whose consciousness was in advance of the masses they represented; they, therefore, must play a strategic part in arousing the consciousness of others and in leading them in revolution.[64]

Under contemporary circumstances organization from the bottom up was possibly a hopeless dream (as the Communists believed) without a larger organizational umbrella to coordinate and to protect it; but the majority of anarchists refused to entertain any such project. In 1927 Shen Zhongjiu was still pleading with fellow anarchists to overcome their qualms about participating in a national congress.[65] As we have seen, anarchist efforts to federate local anarchist organizations were in the end fruitless because they shied away from any suggestion of centralization in the movement.

Anarchist suspicion of centralization accounts also for the direction

63. Baopu, "Wuzhengfudang geming fanglue" (Strategy of anarchist revolution), in *Ziyou congshu*, part 3 ("gemingzhi lu" [the path of revolution]), 359–60.

64. (Mao) Yibo, "Geming zhongzhi zhishi jieji yu wuchan jieji" (Intellectual and proletarian classes in the revolution), *Minfeng* (People's vanguard) 2, no. 1 (13 February 1927), in WZFZYSX 2:795–97. Mao, with the Sichuan anarchists Lu Jianbo, his spouse, Deng Tianyu, and Fan Tianjun from Guangzhou, was among the leaders of the Young Anarchist Federation, which represented the anarchist Left in the late twenties.

65. Xintian (Shen Zhongjiu), "Duiyu kai dahuide yijian" (Views on a national congress), *Ziyou ren* (Free people), no. 3 (May 1924), in WZFZYSX 2:758–61.

anarchist revolutionary activity would take. In their discussions of revolutionary strategy, anarchists took as their immediate goal the overthrow of the state and capitalism. In "How to Resolve the Problems of Present-day Chinese Politics," Ou Shengbai, who was held in high esteem by fellow anarchists for his attention to concrete revolutionary problems, discussed the sad state of Chinese politics over the preceding ten years and outlined a program of action:

> On the basis of these experiences, we deeply feel that the causes of popular misery are these: (1) Because of the present political system power is concentrated in a few hands with the result that the majority of the people do not have the opportunity for free participation. (2) Because of the capitalist system all means of production are concentrated in the hands of the capitalists with the result that the benefits that ought to accrue to laborers are usurped by capitalists.
>
> Therefore, if we wish to pursue the happiness of the people, we must seek to reform both the political and the economic system; the principle of reform is nothing but advancing from a situation of extreme absence of freedom to relative freedom. The important points are these: (1) abolish the system of warlord and bureaucratic control nationally and provincially to institute burghers' self-government in cities and to establish a national association of self-governing cities and villages; (2) abolish capitalism, return all means of production to public ownership by the producers, so that only the producers have the right to use and enjoy them.
>
> From the perspective of political theory, the narrower the scope of state power, the freer are the people; therefore, before the abolition of the state, those who pursue the happiness of the people should diminish the power of the state to a minimum. Economically, the products of labor should belong to the self or those with whom the self wishes to share; so that each exerts himself or herself to the utmost in the increase of production. Therefore, "burgher self-government" and the "socialization of production" are the paths to freedom and equality.[66]

While most anarchists agreed that economic and political power holders constituted the major targets of revolution, there was some disagreement over who was to be included among the forces that would carry out the revolution. Ou Shengbai, Qin Baopu, and syndicalists such as Shen Zhongjiu and Lu Jianbo conceived of revolution in class terms and looked to urban and rural laborers as the main force of revolution. Intellectuals were more problematic; while Baopu restricted revolution to the "masses," and included the "petit-bourgeoisie" among the forces that had to be "neutralized," Mao Yibo, as we have seen, privileged intellec-

---

66. Ou Shengbai, "Zhongguo muqiande zhengzhi wenti ruhe jiejue," *Minzhong* 1, no. 5 (10 July 1923), in *WZFZYSX* 2:635–36.

tuals with a vanguard role for their revolutionary consciousness. Anarchists also differed over their emphases on urban and rural laborers, although they did not necessarily view rural and urban revolution as mutually exclusive. Some, however, did believe that because China was an agrarian society, the proletariat had but a small role to play in the revolution; one such anarchist pointed to peasants, women, and soldiers as the groups on which anarchists should concentrate their attention.[67]

REVOLUTIONARY INSTITUTIONS OF ANARCHISM: LABOR SYNDICATES AND RURAL COMMUNES

Anarchists had long argued that a meaningful social revolution must in the very process of revolution create the institutions on which future social organization would be based. Two institutions were foremost in anarchist discussions of revolutionary strategy at this time and also provided the main objects of anarchist revolutionary activity: syndicates for organizing urban laborers, and communes for the organization of villages. Some anarchists also believed that the "people's militia" (mintuan) in the villages, an age-old institution in China, could be utilized fruitfully both in carrying out and in defending the revolution.

Chinese anarchists, starting with Shifu's federation in Shanghai in 1915, had stressed syndicates (gongtuan, to be distinguished from "labor unions," gonghui) as organizations that would serve not only as agents of revolution but as the cores for laborers of future social organization. The "Declaration of the Shanghai Branch of Anarcho-Communists" stated in 1924:

> The society of the future not only will stamp out bureaucrats, capitalists, and their appendages, but also put an end to distinctions between intellectuals, workers, peasants, and merchants. Everyone will labor for society and become laborers who will work both with their minds and their hands. In order to meet the needs of production for necessities or luxuries, to satisfy general or particular needs, these laborers will organize themselves in a variety of groups (tuanti). These groups will federate freely with other groups, and replace present-day political organization. In order for these freely organized groups to fulfill their promise, it is absolutely necessary to overthrow the present system. But these groups cannot be established overnight; if a basis for them is not instituted presently, when the revolution comes about and the old system is overthrown without a new one to replace it, all will be chaos. It is best for the workers of the whole world or the whole country to unite (tuanjie qilai), to declare war upon capitalists and the government through such methods as the

67. " 'Jieji zhanzheng' he 'pingmin zhuanzheng,' " 590.

general strike (*zongtongmeng bagong*), on the one hand, and, on the other hand, to establish a foundation for future society. It is because of this that many anarchists also advocate syndicalism.[68]

Shanghai was in the twenties the center of anarchist syndicalist activity. Anarchists had been the first to organize modern labor unions in China, first in Guangzhou and then in central China, in Hunan. Their influence in labor unions declined (though it did not disappear) in Guangzhou after the alliance with the Guomindang allowed the Communists to make inroads into labor organization in the South. In central China the bloody suppressions of labor organization in 1922–23, and once again the increase in Communist influence, drove Hunanese anarchists to Shanghai, where they quickly assumed an important role in the burgeoning syndicalist activity. The Federation of Shanghai Syndicates organized in 1924 held sway over forty to fifty labor organizations and roughly fifty thousand workers.[69] The federation (which the Communist labor organizer and historian Deng Zhongxia would describe as an organization of "vagabond unions") was *not* an anarchist organization; Guomindang labor leaders played an important part in it, and some of its member unions were less interested in the promotion of labor interests than in reconciling labor and capital—which was not necessarily inconsistent with the anarchist wish to bring about a revolution that transcended class interest. Anarchists possibly played an important part in day-to-day activity, however, and the ideological slogan of the federation, "Let us ask for bread only, and leave politics alone," reflected the orientation of the anarchists, who sought to spread among federation members the anarchist message: "Resolve economic problems, oppose all politics, engage in direct action, do not rely upon any party,"[70] as did the use of "syndicate" over "labor union" by the federation in describing itself.

Anarchists had also been the first among Chinese social revolutionaries to raise the question of a rural revolution. Shifu's followers had made the first attempt to establish an agrarian commune in the mid-1910s. Under anarchist inspiration, the idea of "going to the people" had gained currency in Chinese radicalism during the May Fourth Movement. The New Village Movement that flourished in 1919–20 referred not to the establish-

68. "Wuzhengfu gongchandang Shanghaibu xuanyan," *Ziyou ren*, no. 3 (May 1924), in *WZFZYSX* 2:753.
69. Kosugi Shuji, "Shanghai koodan rengookai to Shanghai no roodoo undoo" (The Federation of Shanghai Syndicates and the Shanghai labor movement), *Rekishigaku Kenkyu* (Historical studies), no. 392 (January 1973): 18–19.
70. For the federation, see Jean Chesneaux, *The Chinese Labor Movement, 1919–1927* (Stanford, 1968), 223–27, 252–59, as well as Kosugi.

ment of rural communes but rather to communes that made agricultural work part of their daily activity; it nevertheless helped spread a rural orientation among urban radicals. In the aftermath of the May Fourth Movement anarchists took the lead in carrying revolution to the countryside. It is also possible that Communists who distinguished themselves in agrarian activity in the early 1920s, such as Peng Pai in Guangdong, turned to agrarian activity initially under anarchist inspiration.

Anarchists in the twenties believed that agrarian activity should go beyond the establishment of "new villages," which were "escapist" in nature, and seek to revolutionize the existing village.[71] At least some among the anarchists took this to heart. Judging by the literature (which is sparse and sporadic), anarchists associated with Jing Meijiu in the North may have played a significant part in this regard. Jing, the editor of *National Customs Daily,* had been introduced to anarchism in 1907–8 while a student in Japan, and his anarchism carried the imprint of the Tokyo anarchists, who promoted an antimodernist anarchism that drew upon native ideals and Tolstoyan ideas and stressed a rural life in which mental and manual labor, agriculture and industry, would be combined. Jing himself had engaged in attempts to promote cooperative enterprises in his native Shanxi even before the 1911 Revolution.[72] The *Sea of Learning,* supplement to his *National Customs Daily,* often published articles on rural revolution. In June 1923 a draft program for an Alliance for an Agrarian Movement (*Nongcun yundong tongmeng*) appeared in the paper and stated as its goal "the use by tillers of their own power to acquire for themselves profit and happiness." The Alliance program was to advance the organization of tillers, establish a federation of such organizations, help the tillers acquire land, and promote self-government.[73]

The *Sea of Learning* was not alone in promoting an agrarian movement. Anarchist periodicals were rife with reports on attempts to establish communes or promote rural revolution across the face of China. An anarchist objection to Marxism was that Marxism, with its preoccupation with the proletariat, had a blind spot toward the peasantry and ignored 80 percent of the world's population. Communism was unsuitable in China, some anarchists believed, because China was still a largely

71. Daneng, "Xiangcun yundong tan" (On the agrarian movement), *Chunlei,* no. 2 (10 December 1923), 2.

72. Jing, "Zuian," in *Xinhai geming ziliao leipian,* 145, 147.

73. "Nongcun yundong tongmeng guiyue caoan," *Xuehui,* no. 236 (29 June 1923), in *WZFZYSX* 2:673–74.

agrarian society; some went so far as to criticize the Communists for their fetishism of development, which led them to overlook the virtues of agrarian society. They argued that anarchism was much more suitable in organizing a society where, owing to thousands of years of agrarian existence over which the state had little power, the population had evolved habits of self-government conducive to anarchism. Others added that revolution was easier in the village, both because of these habits and for tactical reasons; unlike the proletariat, which had to compel the bourgeoisie to turn over their property to workers, all peasants needed to do by way of struggle was to keep what they already had.[74] An anarchist society in Shaanxi in the North perceived in the self-governing village a model for anarchist reorganization of the world.[75]

Some anarchists argued that the village militia offered a particularly effective means for revolutionary reorganization of the village. As self-defense organizations for the rural population, they believed, the militia had played a revolutionary role throughout Chinese history, although most of the time the government had managed to bring them under control and turn them to counterrevolutionary purposes. The task was to render them independent and bring them around to opposition to the state. With the right training, not only the militia but even bandits could be brought around to the anarchist cause. Such training should include military training for both men and women, and education through films and public performances (plays and operas) as well as written materials on revolutionaries and revolution. Once this was accomplished, it was necessary to make sure that they were well provisioned and inclined toward union with other militia. The militia, thus re-formed, would play an important part not only in bringing about the revolution but also in defending it against counterrevolution. In the words of Li Shaoling:

> The last few years, I have constantly been thinking of a short-cut to revolution without much success. Education is the most reliable method but also very slow. The new village is very difficult under conditions of warlord rule; scattered uprisings sacrifice many lives without significant consequence. After much thought, I have decided that militia offer a relatively reliable *and* quick method. Just speaking of instances with which I am familiar, the cases of Hunan and Guangdong, in these two provinces the militia are strong; they often chase away government and warlord forces, or render them ineffective. While there are those in them who are no good, their revolutionary spirit in

74. Huang, "Letter," 118; Jianhun, "Bagong yu jugeng" (Strikes and seizing land), *Minzhong* 1, no. 5 (10 July 1923), in *WZFZYSX* 2:632–33.

75. "Shaanbei nongshe yundongde xuanyan" (Declaration of the village commune movement in northern Shaanxi), *Chunlei*, no. 1 (10 October 1923): 142.

opposing the government is inextinguishable.... I raise this issue with the hope that comrades will examine it with care.[76]

Some comrades apparently did. In the late twenties, Fan Tianjun participated in an anarchist-led militia in Fujian, which sought to establish a "base area" (after the Communist model). For a brief period its success was such that it even attracted the attention of Japanese anarchists who thought that Fujian might become the base for an East Asian anarchist revolution.[77]

SOCIAL AND CULTURAL REVOLUTION IN ANARCHIST ACTIVITY

Whether urban or rural, anarchist revolutionary activity followed a common pattern, one that reveals that in spite of a desire to meet the Communist challenge, it was an anarchist conception of revolution that shaped anarchists' revolutionary strategy. The point of departure *and* the end of this activity was the transformation of workers' and peasants' social consciousness, to stimulate a "self-awareness" (*zijue*) that would enable them to take charge of their own struggles against power. While anarchists did come to play leading roles in the organizations they established, they could claim with some fairness that, unlike their Communist counterparts, they did not seek to sway the masses through a political organization; rather, they wanted to help them organize in order to pursue their own interests (which is credible if only because this *was* the flaw in anarchist revolutionary strategy). The cornerstone of anarchist revolutionary activity was education, not education in the ordinary sense, which they rejected, but an education for revolution that made no distinction between formal education and propaganda, that took as its primary goal the transformation of quotidian life and consciousness. The tactics were simple: establish contact with laborers (proletarian or peasant); through the help of these contacts organize workers' clubs and part-time schools in which worker participation would be encouraged; gradually move on to the organization of a union as the confidence of laborers was secured. If these tactics do not sound very different from Communist tactics, it is because they were not very different, except in goals. Anarchists, however, had been using these tactics for nearly three

76. Sanmu (Li Shaoling), "Mintuan geming" (Revolution of people's militia), *Minzhong*, 1, no. 12 (July 1925), in *WZFZYSX* 2:709–10.
77. "Fangwen Fan Tianjun," 1040–41, 1045 (n.53 above).

years when Communists adopted them in their first overtures to labor in 1920.[78]

We have glimpses of these activities from two reports published in the Anarchist Federation journal, *Spring Thunder,* one on urban, the other on rural activities. The former was a report on anarchist activities in Shanghai published in early 1924. According to the report, anarchists of the Free People Society (led by Shen Zhongjiu, who cooperated closely with Hunanese anarchists in Shanghai) had been active in the establishment of the Federation of Shanghai Syndicates, as well as a complementary organization, Union of Young Laborers (*Laogong qingnianhui*). They published their own periodical, *Free People,* as well as two labor journals associated with these organizations, *Labor Ten-daily* (*Laodong xunkan*) and *Young Laborers Ten-daily* (*Laogong qingnian xunkan*). They conducted educational activity in factories with unions associated with the federation, spreading the message "resolve economic problems, oppose all politics, engage in direct action, do not rely upon any political party." In conjunction with these educational activities, they were planning for a labor university (*laodong daxue*).[79]

Anarchists would not achieve their dream of establishing a labor university until 1927 when, under the auspices of Guomindang anarchists, they were able to establish the National Labor University (*Guoli laodong daxue*), which for a brief period promised to fulfill their goal of training a new kind of labor leader, drawn from among the ranks of laborers, who would be at once a laborer and an intellectual, overcoming a distinction that had long divided society into "classes." The plans for such a university were laid as early as 1924. The statement of intention anarchists drew up at the time is revealing of their approach to labor and, therefore, of the ultimate intention underlying their revolutionary activities:

> What is laborer education? It is the kind of education to advance the self-awareness of laborers; it is the kind of education that will help laborers advance from the status of slave to that of human being (*ren*); it is the kind of education that will help laborers' abilities and show them how to pursue a labor movement. Simply put, laborers' education is the education of laborers to become human beings; it is an education in revolution because for laborers revolution and becoming human beings are inseparable. If they want to become human beings, to be independent and free, to sustain life, to satisfy their spiritual needs and not be exploited, controlled or oppressed, is there any way other than revolution?[80]

78. Liu Shixin, "Guanyu wuzhengfu zhuyi," 937, gives a brief account of these methods.
79. "Tongzhi xiaoxi," *Jingzhi,* no. 1 (1924).
80. Linyi, "Sinian qian Zhongguode laodong daxue" (The Chinese Labor University of four years ago), *Geming zhoubao,* nos. 29–30 (December 1927). See no. 29:286.

The report on agrarian activity (published December 1923) concerned an unnamed village in Guangdong where anarchists had been active for the previous two years. According to the author, Daneng (a pen name), the village school had played an axial role in these activities. Recalling the experiences in establishing a peasants' association, he related that they had started off with a night school where, in addition to teaching the villagers basic reading and arithmetic, they had told their pupils stories of world revolution and revolutionaries, which gradually made the villagers feel that revolution might bring about an improvement in their lives. On May Day they distributed pamphlets among the villagers, held a lantern parade, and concluded the festivities with a "revolutionary opera." Soon after, the villagers came to them with a request for organization.[81] Similarly, anarchists in northern Shaanxi combined general and revolutionary education to gradually mobilize villagers; in their case a general education to stimulate self-awareness combined with technical education to improve productive methods.[82]

Education remained for the anarchists the most "reliable" method of revolution. Nevertheless, the experience of failure in the face of oppression, and the challenge of the Communist advocacy of proletarian dictatorship, taught at least some of the anarchists that the creation of revolutionary institutions was not sufficient to make revolution, that they must also find ways to defend revolution against its enemies. This was a major reason in Li Shaoling's consideration of people's militia as an instrument of revolution. A similar idea was proposed in 1924 by the prominent Guangzhou anarchist Liang Bingxian, this time for urban areas. Liang argued that inasmuch as education was crucial to revolution, revolution entailed questions of power and would certainly end up in failure if it could not defend itself. He, therefore, proposed the establishment of "revolutionary corps" (*geming tuanti*) to supplement syndicates. Ultimately, the syndicates would provide the basis for social and economic reorganization, but in the period of transition the "revolutionary corps" would play a crucial role in overthrowing the power of the state and the bourgeoisie and defending the revolution against them. Liang's proposal emphasized urban areas but was not restricted to them. Revolution, he believed, could not be successful unless it encompassed rural areas.[83]

81. Daneng, "Xiangcun yundong tan," 4–5.
82. "Shaanbei nongshe yundongde xuanyan," 142.
83. (Liang) Bingxian, "Gemingde gongtuan" (Revolutionary syndicates), *Minzhong*, 1, no. 7 (10 March 1924), in WZFZYSX 2:701–4.

These schemes represented an anarchist answer to a transitional period in the revolution that for the Communists was encapsulated in "the dictatorship of the proletariat." Anarchists had earlier believed that once the revolution broke out, the "natural" inclination to anarchism in all human beings would quickly usher in anarchist society. That the revolution would involve power and require a period of armed preparation, warfare, and defense before achieving its social goals revealed a new soberness toward questions of revolution that anarchists owed to the Communist challenge.[84] They repudiated the dictatorship of the proletariat unconditionally, but they could not ignore the very real questions that it raised. Unlike their Communist opponents, who justified dictatorship by necessity but also learned quickly to celebrate it in endless affirmations of the indispensable vanguard role of the Communist party, anarchists remained disinclined to break with the commitment to popular initiative that informed their revolutionary vision. Their methods were at best reluctant compromises with the realities of power, but not compromise enough for any significant gains in the contest for revolutionary leadership.

IN RETROSPECT

"Heaven helps those who help themselves," an anarchist wrote in *People's Tocsin* in 1927, and went on to complain that for lack of an organization, anarchists were busy cultivating others' gardens instead of their own.[85] The reference was to anarchists' cooperation with the Guomindang. Such cooperation was not new, but when the Guomindang broke with the Communists in 1927, anarchists saw an opportunity to pursue their cause within the Guomindang. While some anarchists remained adamantly opposed to such cooperation (among them Ou Shengbai and the Sichuan anarchists Bajin and Lu Jianbo), others formerly opposed to it (such as Shen Zhongjiu) could not resist the temptation. The most visible manifestation of the cooperation was the Labor University and the journal *Revolution Weekly* associated with it, in which Shen Zhongjiu, Bi Xiushao, and Hunanese anarchists, as well as foreign anarchists such as Jacques Reclus (grand-nephew of Élisée Reclus who had first inspired Li Shizeng to anarchism in Paris) played important parts, under the sponsorship of the Guomindang anarchists Li Shizeng

84. See the stages of revolution Li Shaoling outlines in "Mintuan geming," 707–10.
85. Zheng Tie (Bi Xiushao), "Zhong women zijide yuandi" (Cultivating our own garden), *Minzhong*, 2, no. 2 (February 1927): 81–83.

and Wu Zhihui.[86] Other important anarchists, including Shifu's brother Liu Shixin, remained active in the labor movement in Guangzhou under Guomindang auspices.[87] Ironically, the anarchist rejection of politics seems to have made for some willingness to work with other political groups so long as anarchists were not compelled to abandon anarchism for another ideology.

For some the cooperation continued to the period of the war with Japan after 1937. Other anarchists would end up joining the Communist party. Through it all, the anarchists did make an effort to retain their identity as anarchists. The anarchists in Labor University turned to the criticism of Chiang Kai-shek and Wu Zhihui when in 1928 the Guomindang suppressed the mass movements they had hoped to lead. *Revolution Weekly* was shut down in 1929, and though the Labor University stayed open until 1932, by 1928 it had already lost the revolutionary mission it had initially assumed in anarchist eyes. Although anarchist plans for revolution may not have disappeared, they had evaporated.

These plans appear at first sight not as products of a serious pursuit of revolution but as the fanciful game-plans of young radicals playing at revolution (most of the anarchists were indeed quite young). I hope the evidence presented above will clear away such an impression. The anarchists may have been idealistic in their efforts to remain true to their vision, but they were deadly serious as revolutionaries. Their revolutionary activities overlapped those of the Communists; in their approaches to strategies of both urban and rural revolution, they were the first to utilize methods that would also become the methods of Communists and carry the latter to success when the political environment was hospitable. They were also willing to learn from the Communists and to risk some measure of compromise to meet the challenge of the Bolshevik strategy of revolution.

But they were unwilling to postpone their revolutionary aspirations indefinitely in order to achieve immediate success. This is not to suggest that anarchists were the only revolutionary purists on the scene or that they did not make serious errors. Their effort to discredit Marxism rather than to listen carefully to what Marxist theory had to say about society blinded them to concrete problems of revolution as much as the Communist disdain for anarchism blinded Communists to what *they* had to say about the relationship between revolutionary vision and practise. The vagueness of their social analysis deprived them (as the Communists

86. Bi, "Wo xinyang wuzhengfu zhuyi," WZFZYSX 2:1030–31.
87. Huang Yibo, "Wuzhengfu zhuyizhe zai Guangzhou," 5–14. See chap. 1, n. 13.

charged and they were willing to concede in the end) of a viable method of revolution.

The Communists themselves were vague on social analysis on occasion and believed in the possibility of alliances that transcended classes. But they had what the anarchists did not have: a political organization that ultimately stood as a point of reference for all revolutionary activity, coordinated and gave it direction, and was able, once it had realized the necessity, to protect such activity with power. Theory and vision, once they were embodied in the Communist party, acquired a concreteness and a purpose, which gave direction in Communist hands to the same methods of revolution that the anarchists had pursued. Anarchist revolutionary activities do indeed resemble purposeless revolutionary play in the absence of a comparable organization. Nevertheless, what endowed them with revolutionary seriousness was their realization that the organizational capture of revolution would irretrievably divert revolution from the intention that gave it meaning.

The opposition to organizational centralization per se does not reveal the full distinctiveness of the anarchist argument or its thoroughgoing radicalism. There is another, deeper aspect to the problem that brings into relief anarchist differences not just with Bolshevism but with Marxism, what we might call the "deep structure" of anarchism, which may in the long run be more significant than any specific contributions anarchism may have made to revolutionary strategy in China. I described this earlier as the denial of a center to revolution, which was an implicit determinant of anarchist revolutionary activity, not only in their rejection of an organizational center to revolution but also in their suspicion of any conceptualization of society that presupposed a center to society and history, be it the proletariat or even the very idea of class. Indeed, it may be suggested that the anarchist idea of freedom and democracy was inextricably linked with a desire to abolish a prevalent tendency to view society in terms of a "center." The editorial in the first issue of Spring Thunder, the journal of the Anarchist Federation, argued just such a case. The author, Wang Siweng (who was also the editor), based his case for anarchism on the assumption of the "naturalness" of division of labor and cooperation in society (fengong hezuode shehui shenghuo). What made this "natural" was that it was a reflection in society of the functioning of the cosmos as modern science understood it. Since the sixteenth century, when people still believed that human beings were the center of the universe, science had discovered that there was no power that was almighty and, therefore, the center of the universe. From the solar system to the minutest particles of life, from the solar system to all the solar systems in the universe, there was no single unit that controlled the universe or even the immediate space around it. Everything depended rather on relationships, which shaped the large as well as the small (the sun as much as the planets), made them equally independent and equally dependent on one another. Human organization must be egalitarian, because the organization of the cosmos was egalitarian (*yuzhoude zuzhi, gewei pingheng*). Likewise, human organization must strive to achieve freedom for all regardless of place, gender, class, or race because there was no such thing in the cosmos as one ruling entity.[88]

Wang did not acknowledge any debt to others in his essay, but textual similarities suggest that his discussion was mostly derivative of Kropotkin's "Anarchism: Its Philosophy and Ideal," where Kropotkin had initially made the case for "decentering" society and history so that humankind could reconstitute itself on the basis of freedom and equality, the preconditions for a social existence of mutual aid. Speaking of recent developments in astronomy, he wrote, cogently: "Thus the center, the origin of force, formerly transferred from the earth to the sun, now turns out to be scattered and disseminated." His survey of the modern sciences confirmed this fundamental finding of astronomy.[89]

It may be that in a world without center, politics, including revolutionary politics, has no point of departure. In this, however, anarchists saw not the threat of chaos but the possibility of a new beginning for humanity, this time on the basis of free and equal association. In this particular sense anarchists were also correct in arguing that Marxism shared much in common with the philosophies it rejected, because the pursuit of a center to replace the centers of old society would seem to be characteristic of all varieties of Marxism and of Marx's own location of a center to history in class struggle, which, as the anarchists pointed out, has led to a Marxist neglect of other struggles in history—and other possibilities of liberation.

In 1921 participants in the May Day parade in Guangzhou arrived at a crossroads where they were greeted by two portraits hanging on opposite sides of the street, one of Marx, the other of Kropotkin.[90] This may have been the last occasion for such an encounter. In ensuing years, Marx and

88. Si (Wang Siweng), "Hewei er xinyang wuzhengfu gongchan zhuyi" (What are anarcho-communist beliefs), *Chunlei*, no. 1 (10 October 1923): 5–19. Those arguments also distinguished the anarchists from antipolitical social conservatives, on the one hand, and individual-oriented libertarians, on the other hand.

89. Peter Kropotkin, *Revolutionary Pamphlets*, ed. Roger N. Baldwin (New York, 1968), 117.

90. Zheng, "Wuzhengfu zhuyi," 199.

Kropotkin inexorably moved farther and farther apart in the thinking of Chinese radicals. Anarchists were to lose by their rejection of Marx. Communists would win the revolution, but the repudiation of anarchism once the Communist party had been established would also exact a price from their revolutionary vision, if in less visible ways.

CHAPTER SEVEN

The Revolution
That Never Was

Anarchism in the Guomindang

Anarchists made an attempt in 1927 to acquire a voice in the Guomindang, perhaps even to shape its future. Their goal was not to take over the Guomindang politically, as some opponents charged, since they rejected politics, but rather to use the possibilities the party offered to channel the Chinese revolution in a direction consistent with anarchist goals. In hindsight, the attempt was futile, a last desperate, and somewhat opportunistic, act in anarchists' efforts to recapture the revolutionary ground they had lost over the previous three years to successful Communist inroads among the masses. Following this attempt, anarchism for all practical purposes would disappear as a significant force in Chinese radicalism. In the attempt, no less than in the suppression it invited, was inscribed the complex legacy of the history of anarchism in China.

In historical hindsight, the anarchist hope to remake the Guomindang in an anarchist image at the very moment that the party had turned against the social revolutionary movement in China appears, if not as an instance of a supreme revolutionary opportunism, then at best as another illustration of the seemingly limitless capacity of anarchists for self-delusion. This was not necessarily what a contemporary perspective yielded, however. The Guomindang, always incoherent as a political organization, was in 1927 in great disarray. True, the Northern Expedition it had launched in 1926 was in full swing and would once again reunify the country by 1928, the party was already in the process of establishing itself as the new national government, and it had just averted an internal threat by bloodily terminating its three-year-old united front with the Communist party, which had sought to direct the revolutionary movement toward Communist goals. While the suppression of Communists had compromised the Guomindang as a revolutionary force, it had not yet erased the popular image, or the self-image, of the party as the foremost force in the national revolution. Sympathy for the Communists in 1927 was by no means universal, and the full extent of the Guomindang counterrevolution would not become apparent until after the conclusion of the Northern Expedition in 1928 and the establishment of the new national government. But at its very moment of victory, the ideological future of the party seemed more uncertain than ever. It was deeply divided into factions, ranging from Marxists to hidebound reactionaries, each one of which sought to direct the party's future in accordance with its own interests and ideological proclivities. The future seemed to be up for grabs. Anarchists were one of the groups that attempted to grab it.

The key figures in the attempt to turn the Guomindang on an anarchist course were Li Shizeng and Wu Zhihui. After the party "reorganization" of 1924, they held formally "unofficial" but actually powerful positions as members of the Central Supervisory Committee, a watchdog committee intended to keep an eye on party affairs. Also on the committee were Zhang Ji and Zhang Jingjiang, two fellow anarchists from before 1911; the latter had financed anarchist activities in France before 1911, and had a close relationship with Chiang Kai-shek himself. From this position Li and Wu had criticized the Guomindang alliance with the Communist party since the reorganization of 1924 (which had allowed Communists into the Guomindang), and in 1927 were leaders in the move to purge not just the Communists but also the Marxists on the Guomindang Left. During the same period, they had been pressuring younger anarchist activists to join the Guomindang, and this bore fruit in 1927 when, in the aftermath of the first Guomindang purge of Communists in Shanghai in April, they were able to persuade several anarchists who had gained prominence in the labor movement in Shanghai to cooperate in the establishment of a Labor University (*Laodong daxue*), which would be the center, and the most important product, of anarchist activity in the Guomindang. So important was the part they played in the Guomindang in 1927–28 that the Guomindang Left perceived in their activities the threat of an anarchist takeover of the party.[1] In his survey of political

1. See, for example, Xiao Shuyu, "Womende guomin geming yu Wu Zhihui xianshengde quanmin geming" (Our national revolution and Mr. Wu Zhihui's revolution of all the people), in *Quanmin geming yu guomin geming* (Revolution of all the people and the national revolution), ed. Tao Qiqing (Shanghai: Guangming shuju, 1929), 17. For an anarchist's acknowledgment of such charges, see Ping, "Sici huiyide jieguo" (The results of the fourth plenary session), *Geming* (Revolution), no. 56 (September 1928): 189–92.

groupings published in 1930, Sima Xiandao was to point to anarchists as one of the important political groups in China.[2]

It was precisely this relationship to the Guomindang, however, that also divided the loyalties of the foremost leaders of Chinese anarchism and doomed the undertaking they initiated and, with it, the anarchists who followed them. In the mid-twenties few anarchists looked with favor upon the political involvements of Li and Wu in the Guomindang. Indeed, if opposition to the Communists united the anarchists in the twenties and increasingly shaped their attitudes toward the revolutionary movement, the question of their relationship to the Guomindang was to be highly divisive. In 1927, when some of them followed Li and Wu into the Guomindang, they had by no means abandoned their qualms about the Guomindang, or come to share the latter's view of the relationship between anarchism and the Guomindang, which quickly appeared in the different meanings they assigned to anarchist activity within the party. The divisions, and the threat anarchist activism presented to the Guomindang, would result quickly in the suppression of anarchism in which the Guomindang anarchists were to play an active if reluctant role. Anarchist activists of the younger generation who had hoped in 1927 to use the Guomindang to achieve anarchist goals discovered quickly that without a power base of their own, and deprived of the protection of Guomindang anarchists, their survival was contingent upon their willingness to serve as instruments in the party's attenuation of revolution. Their criticism of the Guomindang for its suppression of revolution, and manipulation of anarchist activities, met with quick reprisals. Li and Wu would continue to play central roles in the Guomindang in later years, but the Guomindang suppression of anarchism in the party, which was complete by 1929, was to deal anarchists a blow from which they would not recover.

ANARCHISTS AND THE GUOMINDANG

When the anarchists acquired an audible voice within the Guomindang in 1927, what was remarkable was the timing, not that they had acquired such a voice. Anarchist activity in 1927–1929 was the culmination of two decades of involvement in the Guomindang. Wu Zhihui, Li Shizeng, and others who led the way in 1927 were not only China's first anar-

2. Sima Xiandao, *Beifa houzhi gepai sichao* (Currents of thought after the Northern Expedition) (Beiping, 1930), chap. 3.

chists, they had been early members of the Guomindang. While on occasion they had been critical of the revolutionary methods of Sun Yat-sen, they had remained Guomindang members and by the twenties were widely regarded as party "elders." Their positions in the Central Supervisory Committee were indicative of the respect they commanded.

This long history of involvement with the Guomindang did not make any the less controversial the roles that Li and Wu (and other "Paris anarchists") played in the Guomindang as members of that committee. In a letter he wrote to Zhang Puquan (Zhang Ji) shortly after they had assumed their new positions, the prominent anarchist Hua Lin stated unequivocally that "the moment Li and Wu entered their relationship with the Guomindang, they as good as stopped being anarchists."[3] The relationship would be a divisive issue among the anarchists for the next three years and would splinter the anarchist movement after 1927.[4]

The fundamental issue was politics. The Paris anarchists, like all anarchists, viewed the overthrow of the state as a primary goal of the anarchist revolution, and had from their earliest days foresworn political involvement, not only because politics could have but one goal—access to state power—but also because they believed that politics, as the expression of partial interest in society, perpetuated social division and was, therefore, inimical to the anarchist goal of abolishing all social interest and division. The various informal societies they had established in China in the early days of the Republic all had made the renunciation of politics a condition of membership.

The political involvement of the Paris anarchists, in other words, contradicted their own professions of opposition to politics. The contradiction had been easier to ignore before 1911; the Revolutionary Alliance had been, as the name suggested, an alliance of revolutionaries against the monarchy, and anarchist membership did not signify much beyond participation in an antimonarchic movement. This contradiction was to become increasingly problematic thereafter. The Guomindang was a political party bent on acquiring political power, and involvement with it implied a tacit affirmation of politics. It will be recalled that when a

3. Letter appended to Wu Zhihui's response. See Wu, "Zhi Hua Lin shu" (Letter to Hua Lin), in *Wu Zhihui quanji* (Collected works of Wu Zhihui) (Shanghai: Qunzhong tushu gongsi, 1927), vol. 3, sec. 7, 24–35.
4. According to Bi Xiushao, when he began to cooperate with the Guomindang, Bajin cut off relations with him. See Bi, "Wo xinyang wuzhengfu zhuyide qianqian houhou" (Account of my anarchist beliefs), in *Wuzhengfu zhuyi sixiang ziliao xuan* (Selections on anarchist thought [WZFZYSX]), ed. Ge Maochun et al., 2 vols. (Bejing: Beijing University Press, 1984) 2:1022–38.

member of the group, Zhang Ji, had assumed a political position in the aftermath of the 1911 Revolution, he had drawn the ire of the Guangzhou anarchist Shifu, who had engaged Wu Zhihui in a debate concerning the propriety of anarchist involvement in politics. In ensuing years, the Paris anarchists had also served as intermediaries between the Chinese and French governments, first in the importation of Chinese laborers to Europe during the war and, following that, in the establishment of the work-study program. The roles they assumed in the Guomindang after 1924 merely confirmed for other anarchists their long-standing willingness to compromise anarchist principles, a sign, at best, of questionable commitment to anarchism, at worst, of political opportunism. The frontispiece to a special commemorative issue on Shifu of the important anarchist journal *People's Tocsin* (*Minzhong*) in early 1927 stated pointedly that "in China at the present, there is no one worthy of our respect other than Shifu."[5] Whether it was so intended or not, the statement had uncomplimentary implications for the anarchist elders from whom Shifu had learned his anarchism (Wu Zhihui was a contributor to the issue).

Among the Paris anarchists, Wu Zhihui seemed to be the one most prepared to defend anarchist involvement with the Guomindang and, in the 1920s, to urge fellow anarchists to do the same.[6] In his response to anarchist critics of such involvement, Wu gave two reasons why anarchists should support the Guomindang effort. First, anarchists and the Guomindang (as well as other revolutionaries, including the Communists) shared a common enemy, the warlords, whose overthrow was in the best interests of all revolutionaries. To soothe the anxieties of anarchists who were suspicious of Guomindang motives (prominent anarchists such as Mao Yibo believed that the Guomindang shared some of the counterrevolutionary characteristics of militarists and had more than its share of opportunistic politicians whose sole goal was to "become rich through office," *shengguan facai*),[7] Wu argued that the Guomindang in the 1920s was a new Guomindang, committed to revolution. Pointing to Kropotkin's support for the war effort during World War I, Wu argued that anarchists had always supported progressive causes, even when the cause was not their own. If the Guomindang at a later time lost its

5. Editorial, *Minzhong* (People's tocsin) 2, no. 3 (March 1925).
6. Wu Zhihui hinted in his letter to Hua Lin that Li Shizeng had earlier been critical of the political involvement of his fellow anarchists. See "Zhi Hua Lin shu," 32.
7. Yibo, "Ping Chen Duxiu xianshengde jiangyanlu" (Critique of Mr. Chen Duxiu's collection of speeches), *Xuedeng* (Light of learning), no. 20 (November 1924).

progressive character, there would be time enough for anarchists to oppose it.

This argument was similar to the one that had earlier justified Paris anarchists' membership in the Revolutionary Alliance; then, too, the anarchists had opposed the nationalist goals of the Alliance, but supported its struggle on the grounds of a prior need to overthrow the Manchu monarchy. Underlying this justification was a broader conception of the progress of revolution in history, which Wu now adduced as a second reason for anarchist support of the Guomindang. Paris anarchists had represented revolution as a long process with a number of progressive stages; the transition from monarchy to a republic was one such stage and must, therefore, be supported by anarchists without their losing sight of the anarchist goals of revolution toward which they must propel the revolution at all times.[8] Wu Zhihui still believed that anarchist revolution would take a very long time (at this time he estimated 3,000 years)[9] and urged his younger colleagues to forego revolutionary purity and support the Guomindang revolutionary effort, which, as a progressive step in the march of revolution, would bring anarchism one step closer to realization.

Wu's argument did not prove to be sufficiently plausible to most fellow anarchists, at least not in 1924. A lengthy rebuttal by the Zhejiang anarcho-syndicalist Shen Zhongjiu, published in July 1924 in the Shanghai anarchist journal Free People (Ziyou ren), offered counterarguments that typified anarchist opposition to participation in the Guomindang in the mid-twenties. What makes Shen's piece particularly interesting is not only that he was an articulate spokesman in these years against anarchist involvement in the Guomindang, but also that he would play an important part in anarchist activity in the party in 1927.[10]

Shen was impressed neither by the "common enemy" argument nor by Wu's assurances that the Guomindang was a "new" Guomindang committed to the cause of revolution rather than to usurping power for itself. The common-enemy argument was fallacious, he believed, because it could be used to justify alliance with anyone, including other warlords who shared the Guomindang's enemies. Besides, he pointed out, anarchists were not knights-errant of the type to be found in Chinese literature, ready to help whoever required their services; they had their own principles and were

8. Li Shizeng and Chu Minyi, Geming (Revolution) (Paris: Xin shiji congshu, 1907).
9. Richard Tze-yang Wang, "Wu Chih-hui: An Intellectual and Political Biography" (Ph.D. diss., University of Virginia, 1976), 233.
10. Xin Ai (Shen Zhongjiu), "Wuzhengfu zhuyizhe keyi jiaru Guomindang ma?" (Can anarchists join the Guomindang?), Ziyou ren (Free people), no. 5 (July 1924), in WZFZYSX 2:771–89.

concerned, not just with making revolution, but with what followed the revolution. Anarchists sought to overthrow not only warlords and imperialism but also the state and capitalism. For them to help the Guomindang establish a new state power would be to help erect a more powerful obstacle to anarchism than presently existed. Besides, Wu overlooked that the Guomindang had its own ideology in Sun's Three People's Principles and required loyalty to them as the price of admission into the party. The Three Principles were incompatible with anarchism; anarchists could not swear loyalty to them without ceasing to be anarchists. Therefore, "for anarchists to enter the Guomindang would simply be suicide because anarchists have even less reason for joining the Guomindang than the Communists." Contrary to Wu, Shen perceived in the example of Kropotkin's cooperating with other revolutionary parties a lesson for anarchists to avoid repeating a similar mistake: Kropotkin had in the end been betrayed by the very revolutionaries he had supported.[11]

Similarly, Shen rejected Wu's argument that the revolution progressed in necessary stages from democracy to the dictatorship of laborers to anarchism. This reasoning was a consequence, he believed, of a fallacious analogy between nature and society, which resulted in a deterministic view of revolution. Revolution ultimately depended on "humankind's striving to reach upwards and its capability to organize" (*renjiande xiangshang xin he zuzhi li*). It might be slow or rapid according to the power of the desire for progress or the ability to organize, but it was not bound by natural law. Indeed, Wu ignored that the stages he presented as natural in the progress of revolution were also mutually contradictory. Shen presented the problem in a terse formula: "Democracy—has government, has private property. Dictatorship of laborers—has government, has private property. Anarchism—no government, no private property." To go through these stages to reach anarchism, he concluded, was no different than going south in order to get north.[12]

Shen's rebuttal barely concealed his disdain for what he took to be the opportunism of anarchists who cooperated with the Guomindang. Even if the Guomindang were to be taken seriously as a revolutionary party, which he obviously doubted, its goals were contrary to anarchist principles and did not allow for cooperation. Judging by the anarchist press in the 1920s, most anarchists shared Shen's views. They were opposed to a limited revolution that took as its objectives the elimination of warlord

11. Ibid., 787.
12. Ibid., 786.

and imperialist control of China (which were the stated goals of the united front presented by the Guomindang and the Communist party). While these were goals they could share, they disapproved of the limitation of the revolution by the nationalistic motivations that informed it; at the height of the nationalistic upsurge that swept China in the mid-twenties, anarchists continued to oppose nationalism, not only because it could only issue in the establishment of a stronger state than before, but also because nationalism only served to "build walls around people" and further separate them from one another. They supported anti-imperialism but believed that the answer to abolishing imperialism was not nationalism but the abolition of capitalism.[13] So adamant were the anarchists in their opposition to a nationalist revolution that they even came under criticism from Jean Grave, who gently rebuked them in a letter by reminding them that during World War I he and Kropotkin had supported nationalism when it was clearly in a good cause.[14]

Such pressures did not go entirely unheeded. Some anarchists who were opposed earlier to collaboration with the Guomindang were by 1926–27 urging their colleagues to view the Guomindang as a "friendly party" (youdang) and join in the revolutionary effort to overthrow the power of the "old" parties.[15] By April 1927 Shen Zhongjiu himself and others associated with him were ready for collaboration.

Not all anarchists would come around to viewing the Guomindang as a "friendly party"; as far as it is possible to tell, influential Guangzhou anarchists, such as Liang Bingxian and Ou Shengbai, and Sichuan anarchists, such as Li Feigan (Bajin) and Lu Jianbo, continued to oppose collaboration. But a sufficient number collaborated to give Li Shizeng and Wu Zhihui the following they needed to make anarchism a serious presence in the Guomindang, especially in Shanghai. These included, in addition to Shen Zhongjiu, radical Hunanese anarchists who had been based in Shanghai since 1923, and Bi Xiushao, another Zhejiang anarchist who had gained visibility in anarchist activities in France. Most of those who collaborated with the Guomindang in 1927 had been involved in the syndicalist movement in Shanghai since 1924. Other anarchists involved in the labor movement in Guangzhou, most prominent among

13. (Wei) Huilin, "Shehui geming yu guomin geming" (Social revolution and national revolution), Minzhong 2, no. 1 (January 1927): 11–21.
14. For this exchange, see "Zhen Tian yu Faguo wuzhengfu zhuyizhe Gelafude tongxin" (Zhen Tian [Bi Xiushao]'s correspondence with the French anarchist Grave), Minzhong 2, nos. 4–5 (May 1927), in WZFZYSX 2:729–34.
15. Junyi (Wu Kegang), contribution to symposium, "Wuzhengfu zhuyi yu shiji wenti" (Anarchism and the question of practise), in WZFZYSX 2:826–49, p. 848.

them Liu Shixin, would also collaborate with the Guomindang after 1927.[16]

It may not be coincidental that anarchists involved in the labor movement would play a conspicuous part in the collaboration with the Guomindang. There are not ready-made explanations for the turnabout in anarchist activists' attitudes from opposition to collaboration with the Guomindang. One can point, however, to a conjuncture of circumstances brought about by changes in the revolutionary situation in China that inclined anarchists to collaboration, if not necessarily to the assumption of a Guomindang identity.

First was an intensifying sense of their irrelevance to the gathering momentum of the revolutionary movement, which was evident in the receding of anarchist influence not only among labor but also among educated youth who were increasingly drawn to the national struggle led by the Guomindang and the Communist party. The mid-1920s (especially following the May Thirtieth Incident in Shanghai) witnessed a virtual explosion in the influence of the Communist party, which would ultimately bring down the united front but which for the time being was most impressive for the gains the Communists had made at the expense of the anarchists, in whose eyes they were not just the foremost competitors on the social revolutionary Left but, because of their Bolshevik orientation, the foremost enemies of an anarchist revolution. The surge in mass mobilization, especially the labor movement, provided the Communist party with an opportunity for expanding its constituency; the alliance with the Guomindang formalized in 1924 facilitated the Communists' ability to convert this opportunity to actuality. Between 1925 and 1927 Communist party membership would increase from about one thousand to about fifty thousand. Almost half the membership, moreover, consisted of urban laborers, a higher percentage than the party would ever again command throughout its history.

The expansion of Communist power meant the decline of anarchist hopes for achieving leadership of the social revolutionary movement in China, which was particularly distressing to anarchists involved in the labor movement. The popularity of anarchism had peaked in 1922–23, when anarchists could still claim that there were "several thousand" anarchists in China, not a particularly large number but significantly higher than what the Communist party could claim at the time. Anar-

16. Liu Shixin, "Guanyu wuzhengfu zhuyi huodongde diandi huiyi" (Remembering bits and pieces of anarchist activity), in WZFZYSX 2:926–39.

chists, moreover, had initiated the modern labor movement in China and, as late as 1922, exerted significant influence among laborers both in the south, in Guangzhou, and in Hunan in central China. Driven from Hunan by warlord repression in 1922–23, Hunanese anarchists (along with anarchists from Zhejiang and Sichuan) had emerged as key figures in the Federation of Shanghai Syndicates (*Shanghai gongtuan lianhe hui*) that was established in 1924 (where they cooperated, at least at the ground level, with Guomindang-related labor leaders). It was also becoming increasingly evident that everywhere, including the anarchist stronghold in Guangzhou, anarchist influence over labor was on the decline, partly because the united front with the Guomindang gave the Communists much-needed prestige as national revolutionaries as well as the authority provided by the Guomindang in places like Guangzhou, and partly because of an inherent weakness of the anarchists in their inability to organize, which meant that however successful at the local level, they were unable to coordinate labor activities nationally. In 1922, when the first National Labor Congress had convened in Guangzhou, anarchist influence had frustrated Communist organizers' efforts to politicize the labor movement. By 1925, when the Second National Labor Congress convened in Shanghai, Communists had clearly established their supremacy in their leadership of labor.[17]

Judging by anarchist "appeals" to youth in 1926–27, the loss of anarchist influence was not restricted to labor but extended to the idealistic youth who in the early May Fourth period had been attracted to the anarchist message in large numbers. The delusion of youth who fell into the trap of nationalism was a constant theme in these appeals, as was the problem of how to recover anarchist leadership of youth, and other social movements.[18]

At the height of the social revolutionary movement in China, of which they had been the first and the foremost advocates, anarchists watched with a sense of despair their irrelevance to the actualities of social revolution. By late 1926 they were openly self-critical about their inability to organize, which, they believed, curtailed anarchist ability to influence the course of the revolutionary movement. Ultimately, however, they traced their increasing irrelevance to a "revolutionary purism," which accounted for the anarchist refusal to engage in concrete revolutionary activity so long as the revolution did not correspond to anarchist desires.

17. Ibid.
18. See, for example, Xin Tian (Shen Zhongjiu), "Gao Gongchandangde qingnian" (To Communist youth), *Minzhong* 2, no. 3 (March 1927): 205–22.

This was the thrust of a discussion prominent Chinese anarchists
undertook in late 1926 and 1927 concerning anarchist relationship to
the revolutionary movement, the results of which were published in
1927 under the heading of "Anarchism and the Question of Practice"
(*Wuzhengfu zhuyi yu shiji wenti*). The discussion as published included
only three essays, by Feigan (Bajin), Huilin (Wei Huilin), and Jun Yi
(Wu Kegang), whereas, according to Lu Jianbo, other anarchists had
participated in it originally, including himself.[19] The basic issue was
whether anarchists should continue to engage in an "academic" propagation of anarchist ideals, divorced from the masses and the concrete
conditions of revolution, or participate in the revolution to guide it
toward anarchist goals. The latter inevitably raised the questions of how
to participate and, by implication, of anarchist relationship to the
Guomindang, which, judging by the conclusions of the various essays,
was foremost in the minds of the participants in the discussion.

There was agreement over the first issue, but not over the second. All
agreed that the concern for revolutionary purity not only made anarchists
irrelevant to the revolutionary movement, but in some ways led to the
betrayal of anarchists' ideals in the priority it gave to revolutionary abstractions over a genuine concern for the people. The error, they suggested, rested in a confusion of the revolutionary movement with the
parties that led it. The revolutionary movement then in progress was not
a revolution of the Guomindang or of the Communist party, but a genuine revolution of the people. It was the obligation of anarchists to participate in the popular revolution, succor the people, and guide them toward
anarchism. As Bajin put it:

> China has already entered a revolutionary period. The revolutionary move-
> ment at the present is not a movement of the Guomindang but a revolutionary
> movement of the masses. Tens of thousands of workers are on strike, countless
> youth are on the battleground ready to risk their lives at the hands of the white
> terror or end up in jail. I am completely opposed to those who say that they are
> mere blind followers of a few leaders, that they just desire to achieve wealth
> through office, that they are running dogs of the new warlords, that they are
> disciples of the Three People's Principles, or that they merely wish to establish
> a bourgeois government. The Northern Expedition of the national armies is
> one thing, the Chinese revolutionary movement is still another thing. The
> struggle for liberation of a semicolonial nation may not be the goal of anar-
> chism, but anarchists cannot oppose it, they can only strive to make it go

19. Jiang Jun, "Lu Jianbo xiansheng zaoniande wuzhengfu zhuyi xuanquan huodong
jishi" (An account of Mr. Lu Jianbo's anarchist activities in his youth), in *WZFZYSX*
2:1009–22.

further. Similarly, we may not oppose the anti-imperialist movement just because capitalism has not yet been abolished. I hate the Soviet Union, but I hate
the imperialist powers even more; I hate the Guomindang, but I hate the
northern warlords even more—because the Soviet Union is nowhere near as
bad as the imperialist powers, nor is the Guomindang "birds of a feather" with
the northern warlords. If we can offer the masses something better, so much
the better; but to stick one's hands up one's sleeves and engage in opposition
from the sidelines, while perfectly all right for bourgeois scholars, is no less
than a crime for revolutionaries. It is all right for an individualist to say, "If it
is not complete, it is better not to have it," but a revolutionary cannot say any
such thing because that is not what the masses demand. . . . If we do not have
much influence in the present movement, it is our own fault. Right-wing
nationalists and the Research Clique must take great pleasure in watching us
stand on the sidelines and abuse the revolutionary movement as just a political
struggle or a war between warlords, or make the Guomindang into "birds of a
feather" with Zhang Zuolin.[20]

Bajin himself was opposed to collaboration, although some of his
remarks might have suggested at least a contingent approval of the Guomindang. Other anarchists were more willing to participate in the Guomindang struggle so long as they retained an anarchist identity and could
push the Guomindang toward the maximization of revolutionary goals.
Wu Kegang, who in 1924 had opposed Wu Zhihui's urgings for anarchists to join the Guomindang, had in the meantime assumed a more
positive attitude toward collaboration. He concluded his contribution to
the discussion with the words:

In my opinion, however bad the Guomindang may be, there are many in it
whose goal is not to achieve wealth through office but to carry out the revolution. Moreover, the struggle they are involved in now to overthrow foreign
aggression and the northern warlords is something that anarchists themselves
desire and should be doing. When it succeeds the Guomindang will still be far
from anarchism, but it is the height of ignorance about revolution to suggest
that the common people will be worse off than they are now.[21]

Wu by then was one of the advocates of the need for anarchists to view
the Guomindang as a "friendly party."
Judging by the collaboration that was to follow shortly after these
lines were published, it is possible to suggest that by early 1927 many if
not all anarchists shared some of these sentiments. We should note two
other conditions that had to be fulfilled before collaboration became a
reality. First, Li Shizeng and Wu Zhihui had to reassure anarchist activ-

20. "Wuzhengfu zhuyi yu shiji wenti," 833–34.
21. Ibid., 848.

ists that in collaborating with the Guomindang they need not abandon
their anarchism to influence the future of the party. This is at best a guess,
but one for which there is some circumstantial evidence. According to Bi
Xiushao, who was to play an instrumental role in bringing about the
collaboration and afterwards in anarchist activity in the Guomindang,
the meeting in April 1927 that initiated the collaboration was preceded
by more than half a year of meetings with important Guomindang anarchists, including Zhang Ji, Wu Zhihui, and finally Li Shizeng, who in
1927–28 would become the "godfather" of anarchist activity in the
party. What went on in these meetings Bi does not say (except in the case
of Zhang Ji, who bitterly complained about his popular image as a reactionary), but by the fall of 1926 the anarchists in the Central Supervisory
Committee were already engaged in efforts to terminate the alliance with
the Communists, and they probably at least held out to anarchist activists
the promise of future leadership in the labor movement; labor, we shall
see, was the first item on the agenda of the collaboration after April 1927.
Furthermore, the collaboration was accompanied by a change in the
public stance of the Guomindang anarchists themselves. While Li and Wu
(and Zhang Ji) had made no secret of their anarchism over the years, their
advocacy of anarchism as an option for the Guomindang was quite novel,
especially their open advocacy that the sacrosanct Three People's Principles could be interpreted from an anarchist perspective. We have no way
of knowing if they conveyed their intention to openly promote anarchism
in the party to Bi and others in order to draw them into the Guomindang,
but by May 1927 they were already doing so. Finally, there is little
question that anarchists who joined the Guomindang in 1927 behaved
with a surprising independence, making no effort to conceal that their
goal was to bring anarchism into the Guomindang. Even as they entered
the collaboration in April 1927, they continued to criticize the nationalist
goals of the Guomindang revolution, and they were uncompromising in
their advocacy of the cause of urban and rural laborers. Indeed, reading
through their protests in 1928 against the Guomindang suppression of
mass movements (and subsequently of anarchist activity within the
party), it is hard not to detect a sense that they felt betrayed not just by
the Guomindang but by the anarchists who had brought them into the
collaboration.

The second condition was the Guomindang suppression of communism. It may be no coincidence that the meeting in Shanghai at which
anarchists drew up their plans for activity within the Guomindang followed shortly on the heels of Chiang Kai-shek's suppression of commu-

nism, followed by a massacre not only of Communists but of Shanghai laborers as well. This, of course, was to taint from the beginning the willingness of the anarchists to collaborate with the Guomindang, for in their hatred for the Communists, they were willing to close their eyes to the victimization of the very laborers whose case they hoped to pursue in the Guomindang. It was this promise above all that drew them into the Guomindang, and the suppression of communism provided them with their opportunity.

Why they should have felt that they themselves would be immune to a similar suppression is difficult to say. Possibly it was assurances from Li and Wu that reassured them; or it may have been their belief that since they intended to help the laborers organize themselves rather than to use labor to their own political ends, as they believed the Communists had done, they could avoid a similar fate. Shen Zhongjiu's prophecy that collaboration with the Guomindang would prove "suicidal" for anarchists would come true within the year. But in the excitement of the possibility offered by the Guomindang of once again capturing leadership of the mass movements, Shen himself was willing to overlook his qualms of three years earlier.

The plans for the collaboration were drawn at a meeting in Shanghai in April in which the participants were Li Shizeng, Wu Zhihui, Bi Xiushao, Kuang Husheng, and Lu Wenhan.[22] The cornerstone of anarchist activity was to be a Labor University to train a new kind of labor leader and a new kind of intellectual, which would transform not only the Guomindang but ultimately the whole nation. Along with Labor University, anarchists would publish a new periodical, *Revolution* (or *Revolution Weekly, Geming zhoubao*), in which they would propagate anarchist ideas in a form appropriate to the cooperation with the Guomindang. Li and Wu would attend to the official aspects of the cooperation (Li also agreed to finance the whole undertaking initially); the younger activists would tend to the operation of the new university, as well as to the publication of the journal. The guiding principle of the cooperation was to be, according to another anarchist active in Shanghai at the time, "to use the Three People's Principles as a means to achieve anarchism" (literally, "take the Three People's Principles as means, anarchism as goal," *yi sanmin zhuyi wei shouduan, yi wuzhengfu zhuyi wei mubiao*).[23]

22. Bi Xiushao, "Wo xinyang wuzhengfu zhuyi," 1029–31.
23. "Fangwen Fan Tianjun xianshengde jilu" (Record of a visit with Mr. Fan Tianjun), in *WZFZYSX* 2:1043.

NATIONAL LABOR UNIVERSITY

The institutional center of anarchist activity in the Guomindang (as well as its most significant product) was the Labor University (*Laodong daxue*) established in Shanghai in the fall of 1927. Modeled after a socialist university for laborers that had been founded in 1902 in Charleroi, Belgium, Labor University owed its inspiration and conception to anarchist ideas of education (it was a direct outgrowth of anarchist educational experiments in Shanghai and, earlier, of the labor-learning program in Europe). Its goals were encompassed in the slogan "Turn schools into fields and factories, fields and factories into schools" (*xuexiao nongchang gongchanhua, nongchang gongchan xuexiaohua*).[24] Its basic goal was to realize a long-standing anarchist dream: to combine labor and learning in education to create a new kind of individual, a laboring intellectual, or an intellectual laborer. This, the anarchists believed, would abolish a fundamental distinction between social classes, achieve a peaceful social revolution, and launch Chinese society toward an anarchist future. Labor University was the first step in the revolutionization of Chinese education, and the key to a genuine social revolution. Its immediate goal was to train labor leaders of a new kind who could show labor the way to take charge of its own future. It is possible that anarchists conceived of it as a crucial step in the federalist reorganization of China.

Preparations for the new university began in the summer of 1927, led by a committee headed by no less than Cai Yuanpei, the foremost figure in Chinese education and chair of the newly established University Council (*Daxue yuan*) that the Guomindang intended to supervise the restructuring of the higher-education system. Cai, who commanded immense prestige for his reform of Beijing University a decade earlier, was himself

24. For the quotation, see Lu Han, "Zhongguo qingong jianxue chuyide taolun" (Discussion of a humble opinion on China's diligent-work frugal-study), *Geming*, 98–99 (June 1929): 272. Historians have usually misread the nature of Labor University. William Duiker views it as an outcome of Cai Yuanpei's "liberalism" (see *Ts'ai Yuan-p'ei: Educator of Modern China*, 89). Historians tend to co-opt anarchism for liberalism because they confound liberalness and liberalism. Yeh Wen-hsing describes Labor University as a "tame" experiment ("The Alienated Academy: Higher Education in Republican China," Ph.D. diss., University of California, 1984). The only work I know that captures the radical anarchist intentions of Labor University (and the only study devoted to its examination) is Chen Mingqiu (Ming K. Chan), " 'Zhishi yu laodong jiehe' zhi jiaoyu shiyan" (An educational experiment "to combine learning and labor"), in *Zhongguo yu Xianggang gongyun zongheng* (Dimensions of the Chinese and Hong Kong labor movement), ed. Ming K. Chan (Hong Kong, 1986), 61–77. For further discussion of the ideological underpinnings of Labor University, see chapter 3 in Ming K. Chan and Arif Dirlik, *Schools into Fields and Factories: Anarchism, the Guomindang, and the Labor University in Shanghai, 1927–1932* (Durham, N.C.: Duke University Press, 1991).

a philosophical anarchist who had long been involved in anarchist educational activities in Europe, who was a foremost advocate of combining labor and learning in education, and who was active after 1926 in the anti-Communist activities of the Central Supervisory Committee in cooperation with fellow Guomindang "elders" and anarchists Li Shizeng, Wu Zhihui, and Zhang Jingjiang.

The rapidity with which the planning committee completed its task testifies to the power and influence of the Guomindang anarchists. Yi Peiji, prominent Hunanese educator (and another associate of the group) and past principal of Hunan First Normal, was appointed president of the new university. A physical plant was purchased in Shanghai suburbs as the site for the university. Government support was secured to finance both the purchase and the improvement of the physical plant and other operating expenses. Basic to the conception of the university was the recruitment of students of laborer and peasant background, who could ill afford an education, to put an end to the monopolizing of education by the wealthier classes. To this end, it was decided that all students would be "public" (gongfei) students. The government would pay for their education as well.[25] The university would comprise three colleges: an Industrial Labor College (Laogong xueyuan), an Agricultural Labor College (Laonong xueyuan), and a Social Sciences College (Shehui kexue xueyuan). The choice of the third area reflected the anarchist belief that social science and social revolution were inseparable.[26] The plan also included "training" (xunlian) and "normal" (shifan) components in the university with an eye to the training of labor leaders. Eventually, elementary and middle schools were to be added to create a comprehensive educational institution.

Labor University was formally established in September 1927 and opened its doors to instruction in October with the Industrial Labor College, headed by the Zhejiang anarcho-syndicalist Shen Zhongjiu. Preparations for the Agricultural Labor College were completed the following month with the purchase of additional land, and by November that too was in operation with its own campus. Still another campus (on the site of the former Shanghai University) was established in the spring of 1928 for the Social Sciences College. By mid-1928 the other components of the

25. Ming K. Chan, " 'Zhishi yu laodong,' " 71–73, for the organization of Labor University.
26. Gong Ming, "Geming yu shehuixue" (Revolution and sociology), Geming, no. 33 (March 1928). Government regulations required a minimum of three colleges for an institution of higher education to qualify as a university.

university were in place and it was in full operation. As of mid-1928, the Industrial and Agricultural colleges had a total of 289 students (about half the number planned for). Two thousand laborers worked for the university in its agricultural and industrial undertakings, and the school already had a library with more than forty thousand volumes of Chinese and foreign works.

Considering the relatively small size of the student body, the investment in the university in its initial phase was highly impressive both in terms of financial resources and in terms of the educational-political attention it drew. The expenditures per student were even higher than in China's premier educational institutions, Beijing and Qinghua universities.[27] Even more impressive was the educational personnel involved. The committee of overseers included, in addition to the president, Yi Peiji, the four Guomindang anarchist elders, Li Shizeng, Wu Zhihui, Cai Yuanpei, and Zhang Jingjiang (in 1930 Yi was replaced as president by China's former ambassador to Belgium, Wang Jingqi). The professors at the university included some of the most prominent figures in contemporary natural and social sciences (although many of them were part-time), and the list of speakers in 1927–1929 reads like a who's who of Chinese education and politics, ranging from Dai Jitao and Shao Yuanchong of the Guomindang Right to the dean of Chinese literature, Lu Xun, on the Left.[28] What it meant to Chinese educators was spelled out by Cai Yuanpei in a speech he gave at the university in 1930 (by which time, ironically, the university had already under government pressure departed from its original mission), entitled "The Meaning of Labor University and the Responsibilities of Labor University Students" (*Laodong daxuede yisi he Laodong xueshengde zeren*). Having outlined the meaning of labor in education and society at large, Cai went on to say:

> Since China began to adopt the educational systems of foreign countries, there has been many a special school of agriculture or industry, or industrial and agricultural departments in universities. Such schools were originally intended to combine learning with practise; but once in China, their nature changed. Those who attended them wanted just to read books without any practise, and quickly became learned gentlemen. The children of peasants who went to school returned home to look down on their parents; the same with workers. Hence a proposal was made to establish a labor university. Although Labor University has much in common with industrial schools, we can say that it is revolutionary because its emphasis is on practise; what goes on in the classroom is merely

27. Ming K. Chan, " 'Zhishi yu laodong,' " 74.
28. See the essays compiled in *Laodong luncong* (Laodong essays) (Shanghai: Laodong daxue, 1929).

supplementary to this primary goal . . . students are not restricted to workers and peasants because even those who come from moneyed backgrounds are welcome if they are willing to labor. . . . The premise of Labor University is that students must do practical work, that labor is the only work. . . . In the future when labor universities are founded all over the country, they will need the students here to manage them; if students here have not labored, how will they undertake such responsibility? We must strive to labor now so that there is a foundation for the future. . . . There is another consideration. The students at Labor University enjoy special privileges of which many on the outside are envious. They say that the privileges of Labor University students are comparable to those of the nobility during the Qing dynasty. We can answer that we produce, that the school wants us to labor, so we labor, and having fulfilled our obligations enjoy the privileges; that is the answer. If on the other hand we just read books and do no practical labor, we will be no different from old-style agricultural and industrial schools, which is not right. The responsibility of Labor University students is to work; this is true not just for students in the Industrial and Agricultural Labor Colleges, but also for students in the Social Sciences College, who must strive to resolve the social problems of the world; that is the problem of the distribution of production. Our ideal is that the world in the future will consist only of peasants and workers. The problem of the peasant and the worker is *the* social problem. We have a Social Sciences College so that we can train individuals who have a practical understanding of the difficulties of workers and peasants, who can go among the workers and peasant masses to be one with them, and solve their problems. . . . In conclusion, labor is the point of departure and the foundation for Labor University; all must labor regardless of college or specialization.[29]

The anarchists who were involved in the day-to-day operation of Labor University shared the feelings expressed in this speech. Bi Xiushao, who was a key figure in the inception of Labor University and held a leading position under Shen Zhongjiu in the Industrial Labor College, criticized contemporary Chinese education (at least three decades ahead of Mao Zedong) for its continued emphasis on "reading dead books" (*du sishu*) and advocated instead a "living education" (or an "education in life," *shenghuode jiaoyu*); key to a "living education" was the practise of labor.[30] Bi recalled in later years that Shen in particular was anxious to set a good example to the students and required the staff to work longer and harder than others at less pay.[31]

It is impossible to estimate the number of anarchists involved in teaching and other work at the university. At least initially, they played a signifi-

29. For the complete speech, see Ming K. Chan, " 'Zhishi yu laodong,' " 67–71; this sec. 69–70.

30. Bi Bo (Bi Xiushao), "Laodong daxuede mudi yu shiming" (The goal and mission of Labor University), *Geming,* no. 9 (August 1927): 264–68.

31. Bi Xiushao, "Wo xinyang wuzhengfu zhuyi," 1032.

cant part in the Industrial Labor College under Shen Zhongjiu and Bi Xiushao. Anarchists also constituted an important group in the social sciences in China in the late twenties, and they may have played a significant role in the Social Sciences College as well.[32] Led by the Hunanese anarchist Kuang Husheng, they were also active in the elementary and middle schools in the university.[33] Also prominent in the university were foreign anarchists recruited to teach there, conspicuous among them Jacques Reclus, grand-nephew to Élisée Reclus, from whom Li Shizeng had learned his anarchism. Anarchists were also involved in the university in other than official capacities; the radical Sichuan anarchists of the People's Vanguard Society (*Minfeng she*), who opposed collaboration with the Guomindang, were active among faculty and students, encouraging struggle against the Guomindang. Lu Jianbo recalls that a meeting they held to discuss this struggle was attended by "several tens of individuals."[34]

There is less question concerning the curriculum which, in the initial phase of Labor University's existence, was shaped by the anarchists' commitment to the combination of labor and learning. Students were expected to do at least three hours of manual labor every day. Zhao Zhenpeng, who enrolled in the university in 1927, recalled that

> in the morning, students attended classes. In the afternoon, they were led by the directors of practical work to fields and factories to labor; students of the Industrial Labor College to work on machinery in the machine shop or to set type in the print shop, students of the Agricultural Labor College to till the fields or work on irrigation, students in the Social Sciences College to conduct surveys in nearby villages, all of which truly combined mental and manual labor, class work and practise.[35]

There was real incentive for labor; practical work constituted forty percent of a student's grade and was crucial to advancement from one grade to the next. Students in the Agricultural Labor College were notably successful in the cultivation of tomatoes and cauliflower. Students in the Social Sciences College made surveys of social problems and labor strikes; one particularly impressive product was a survey of living condi-

32. Cai Yucong, "Zhongguo shehuixue fazhan shi shangde sige shiqi" (Four periods in the development of Chinese sociology), *Shehui xuekan* (Sociology journal) 2, no. 3 (April 1933).

33. Kuang may have played an instrumental role in the creation of Labor University, and a college he had been operating in Shanghai may have provided an immediate model for it. For further discussion, see Chan and Dirlik, *Fields and Factories*, chap. 2.

34. Jiang Jun, "Lu Jianbo xiansheng," 1016, 1018–19, for these activities.

35. Zhao Zhenpeng, "Laodong daxuede huiyi" (Recollections of Labor University), *Zhuanji wenxue* (Biographical literature) 37, no. 4 (October 1980): 57–60.

tions in Hangzhou.[36] Nor did classroom work and manual labor interfere with social and cultural activities. The school encouraged students to establish clubs and participate in extracurricular activities; each college had its own theater group which, according to Zhao, provided much talent for the Chinese theater in the thirties.

All was not well, however. The number of students who enrolled in the university was below what its founders had originally planned, and those who enrolled were of questionable qualification, at least according to critics. It is possible, as one of the anarchists involved averred bitterly in mid-1928, that the university was undermined by the very stigma attached to labor that it was intended to overcome, which affected both the number and the quality of its students.[37] As Cai Yuanpei's speech in 1930 intimated, the university was under attack from the outside almost from the beginning. Given the emphasis on labor, and the effort to recruit students from underprivileged backgrounds, in strict academic terms Labor University students were not on a par with their peers in regular academic institutions, which deepened envy and resentment over the resources it enjoyed.[38]

This made Labor University an easy target in the politics of education. Labor University was inspired by the French system of education (French was also the first foreign language taught); as Cai and his Francophile colleagues saw it, it was conceived as a step in reorganizing Chinese education along a French model. It was also a radical educational institution modeled after socialist education, which took education not as an end in itself but as an instrument of social reform. According to Zhao, among its chief critics were American-educated educators who did not share the anarchists' views on the place of labor in education. So long as Cai Yuanpei and the Guomindang anarchist elders held sway in the educational system, the critics could be resisted. In 1928, however, the Guomindang decided to revamp the Chinese educational system to bring it under its own political and ideological control.[39] The decentralized, regionally based university system that Cai had spearheaded was to be

36. For this information, see ibid., 58. The Hangzhou survey was published in a special issue of *Laoda yuekan* (Laodong University monthly) 1, no. 7 (October 1930).

37. Lu Han, "Zhongguo qingong jianxue." Lu complained bitterly about the bureaucratization of the university as well as the unwillingness of the students to labor. Peasants and workers were too poor to attend, he charged, and most of the students at the university were radical intellectuals hoping to escape political terror.

38. Ming K. Chan, " 'Zhishi yu laodong,' " 74.

39. Zhao Zhenpeng, "Laodong daxuede huiyi," 58, for the problems with American-educated educators. Duiker gives an overview of Guomindang efforts to bring the educational system under its control (*Ts'ai Yuan-p'ei*, 89–91).

replaced by a centralized system of education under the supervision of a
ministry of education, which replaced the University Council. While
supporters of the university retained important positions in the Guomindang, the changes in the administration of education undercut their
ability to fend off critics of the university. Labor University would remain in operation until early 1932, but after 1930 (when Wang Jingqi
took over the presidency) its access to funds and resources was severely
curtailed.

As far as the initial anarchist mission of the university was concerned,
however, more important were the intentions underlying the Guomindang conception of Labor University, which had already compromised its mission by 1928. Anarchist activists were quite open by mid-
1928 in pointing to the fundamental contradiction between the anarchist
premises of Labor University and its official ties to the Guomindang. The
author who complained about the unwillingness of the students at the
university to engage in labor complained also about the increasing bureaucratization of the university. These developments were products, he believed, of the contradictory goals of Labor University which were implicit
in its very name: a "national" (*guoli*) university with anarchist aspirations was a contradiction in terms.[40]

The contradiction was not between anarchists and an external force,
the Guomindang, but was internal to the anarchists themselves with their
simultaneous loyalties to anarchism and the Guomindang. As anarchist
criticism of the state of Labor University intensified in 1928, it was
extended not just to the Guomindang but to the Guomindang anarchists
who had founded the university. The contradictions had been there from
the beginning, but rose to the surface in response to Guomindang policies
that took shape as the party consolidated its hold over political power.
One development was the emergence of an official version of the Three
People's Principles that did not tolerate alternative interpretations of the
kind anarchists proposed; the Chinese educational system, as it was re-
vamped, was converted into an instrument for the propagation of this
official ideology, which increased official pressure on the university. Another development was the official suppression of mass movements in
1928, which made clear to the anarchists the futility of efforts to organize
mass movements of an anarchist nature under Guomindang auspices.
The contradictions presented by these developments were articulated in

40. Lin Yi, "Sinian qian Zhongguode laodong daxue" (The Chinese Labor University of
four years ago), *Geming*, nos. 29–30 (December 1927): 285–88, 305–8.

the conflicts among anarchists themselves over the meaning of their participation in the Guomindang, which were to result in the suppression of anarchist activity in 1929.

IDEOLOGICAL CONTRADICTIONS:
ANARCHISM AND THE THREE PEOPLE'S PRINCIPLES

The premise of anarchist activity in the Guomindang was "using the Three People's Principles as a means to achieve anarchism." As the editorial to the first issue of Geming explained, Sun Yat-sen's Three People's Principles were quite broad in scope and, therefore, flexible in meaning, which allowed different interpretations with changing circumstances. Anarchists should interpret them from an anarchist perspective and propel the Chinese revolution in a direction consonant with their goals.[41]

What distinguished the anarchists was not that they sought to interpret the Three People's Principles in accordance with their own goals, but the frankness with which they stated their intentions. In 1927 the Three People's Principles served as an ideological battleground on which different factions within the Guomindang sought to achieve a victory for their own particular ideological orientations—from the Guomindang Right, which viewed the national struggle exclusively in terms of the conquest of state power for the party, to the Marxists of the Guomindang Left, who thought that class struggle was an unavoidable component of the struggle for national unity. The Three People's Principles, moreover, were as broad as the anarchists claimed and justified multiple interpretation. Anarchist claims on the Three People's Principles were not as vacuous as they might seem from a perspective that emphasizes Sun's nationalism. In his lectures on the Three Principles before his death in 1925, Sun had on occasion downplayed the differences of his revolutionary ideology from those of the social revolutionaries on the Left, as when he had stated that the ultimate goal of the Three People's Principles was "communism, and anarchism." Even the idea that the Three Principles might serve as a means to achieve anarchism was implicit in his statement that "my distinction between People's Livelihood and communism rests upon this: communism is the ideal of People's Livelihood, People's Livelihood is the realization of communism; the two are distinct only in method." To

41. "Fakan ci" (Opening statement), Geming, no. 1 (July 1927). According to Bi Xiushao, this editorial was written by Shen Zhongjiu, the editor of the journal for its first five issues (thereafter Bi himself assumed the editorship). See "Wo xinyang wuzhengfu zhuyi," 1030–31.

clarify what he meant by method, he had added that "Marxism is not real communism, real communism is what Proudhon and Bakunin advocated."[42] These statements were to provide a textual basis in the anarchist effort to appropriate the Three People's Principles for anarchism.

What anarchists overlooked, however, was that the appropriation of the Three People's Principles for anarchism also made possible the appropriation of anarchism by the organizational ideology of the Guomindang as that took shape with the consolidation of party power. The use of anarchist concepts to "read" the Three People's Principles required adjustment of the concepts themselves to bring them to closer correspondence with the text at hand. This likelihood was reinforced by an imbalance in power; lacking institutional power of their own, indeed having incorporated themselves into the Guomindang, anarchists had to make their particular reading of the Three People's Principles palatable to those who controlled the Guomindang. That anarchist leaders such as Li Shizeng and Wu Zhihui were divided in their loyalties almost guaranteed the ultimate subjection of anarchist to Guomindang goals. This fundamental contradiction, present in the anarchist collaboration with the Guomindang from the beginning, would in the end divide the anarchists themselves and doom their undertaking even before the Guomindang actually stepped in to bring it to an end.

Li Shizeng was in many ways the guiding spirit behind anarchist collaboration with the Guomindang in 1927–28 (even though it was Wu Zhihui who by 1928 drew the fire of opponents as the symbol of an anarchist "takeover" of the Party). Li viewed himself at the time as a defender of "the sacred term revolution."[43] An essay he published, beginning with the first issue of *Geming* and continuing for the next few issues, "The Meaning of Present-day Revolution" (*Xianjin gemingzhi yiyi*), which reads in retrospect like an agenda for anarchist activity in the Guomindang, provides a point of departure for a close examination of the contradictions in anarchist-Guomindang collaboration.[44]

42. For these statements, see Sun's second lecture on people's livelihood in *Guofu quanshu* (Complete works of Sun Yat-sen) (Taibei: National Defense Research Center, 1970), 264–71.

43. Li did not use the words, but the journal he sponsored, *Geming,* stated this to be its goal. See "Fakan ci," where the journal's goal was stated to be the defense of the "sacred term revolution" (*shenshengde geming mingci*). By the mid-twenties the word *revolution* had such prestige that all groups wanted to claim it. The Guomindang itself suppressed revolution in the name of revolution. For a critical discussion of this tendency, see Hu Hua, "Shehui mingci shiyide xiezi" (Preface to the explanation of social terminology), *Geming*, no. 28 (December 1927).

44. The version used here is the reprint in Lang Xingshi, ed., *Geming yu fangeming* (Revolution and counterrevolution) (Shanghai: Minzhi shuju, 1928), 1–19.

Li's essay was intended to provide a metahistorical justification for an anarchist interpretation of the Three People's Principles. Since his earliest writings on revolution in the *New Era* (*Xin shiji*) in Paris, Li had perceived in revolution the key to progress, which he viewed in biological terms as a universal and natural endowment of humankind in history. He now explained that "present-day revolution" meant nothing more than "present-day progress." Revolution, as progress, signified the evolution of humankind from bad to good, simple to complex.[45]

Such progress was manifested in history in the evolution of humankind through a number of political stages, of which Li identified four: "monarchical revolution" (*junzhu geming*, which he identified with a "palace revolution," *gongting geming*, and a "revolution of despotism," *zhuanzheng geming*); "revolution for people's sovereignty" (*minquan geming*, which he identified with "national revolution," *guojia geming*, and "political revolution," *zhengzhi geming*); "class revolution" (*jieji geming*, which he identified with "property revolution," *caichan geming*, and "economic revolution," *jingji geming*); and, finally, "revolution for people's livelihood" (*minsheng geming*, which he identified with "social revolution," *shehui geming*, and "a revolution for great unity," *datong geming*). These revolutions took several thousand years and followed a certain order. The establishment of the Shang and Zhou dynasties in China (the origins of the Chinese state three millennia earlier, in other words) belonged in the first type (stage) of revolution, the American and the French Revolutions as well as the 1911 Revolution in China belonged in the second type, and the Marxist revolution of Lenin in Russia belonged in the third type. In the fourth type of revolution, a revolution for world unity (*shijie datong*), belonged the revolution for a new era (*xin shiji geming*) advocated by P. J. Proudhon and the revolution for people's livelihood advocated by Sun Yat-sen.[46]

Much of the discussion that followed consisted of a criticism of Bolshevism and of Marxist influence in China. Of interest here is that, as Li perceived it, what rendered Marxism undesirable was that at the present stage of revolution it was a regressive force because revolution had already moved past the third stage in which Marxism belonged (conveniently overlooking that China had not yet gone through that stage). As stages of historical development overlapped, however, the present still required a struggle to eliminate the influence of Marxism. Worldwide,

45. Ibid., 1.
46. Ibid., 2–3.

the struggle was between Proudhonism and Marxism, corresponding respectively to the left wing and the right wing in prevailing ideologies of revolution. In China the corresponding struggle was between Sun's Three People's Principles and the Communist party.[47]

In earlier days Li's anarchism had been derivative of P. Kropotkin. By 1927, however, he had come to view Proudhon as the last word not only in anarchism but in social theory in general. During the next two years Li would emerge in the Guomindang as the foremost advocate of a "federalist" reorganization of China that drew directly upon Proudhon's Principle of Federation. The switch may have been a consequence of the greater "practicality" of Proudhon's ideas, since Proudhon had directly addressed the question of a new political organization. It is also possible that as an added attraction Proudhon's scheme was more moderate in its implications and therefore more palatable to the Guomindang, whereas Kropotkin had rejected the state and called for a total social transformation of life at the quotidian level. Proudhon's scheme retained the state, albeit in a reorganized form that allowed for greater local autonomy and therefore liberty.[48]

Of immediate relevance here, however, is that Li established a direct correspondence between anarchism and Sun's Three People's Principles. As he put it in a footnote to the essay, "The unification of the followers of the Three People's Principles and of anarchists to make war upon Communists in the present stage of revolution follows from the close correspondence between the Three People's Principles and anarchism in their fundamentals."[49] He would sound a similar theme in other essays published in *Geming*. In his "Schools of Political Philosophy" (*Zhengzhi zhexuede dangpai guan*), published in late 1927, he not only further stressed the affinity between anarchism and the Three People's Principles, but also made an attempt to bring both into correspondence with premodern schools of thought in China. In this essay, he divided political philosophy into three major schools: advocates of "naked force" (*qiangquan*, which anarchists also equated with "authority") who recognized no morality in politics; advocates of humane politics (*renzheng*) and peace who sought to combine morality and politics; and advocates of humanitarianism (*rendao*) and morality who repudiated politics. In China, Legalists, Confu-

47. Ibid., 9.
48. P. J. Proudhon, *The Principle of Federation*, tr. Richard Vernon (Toronto: University of Toronto Press, 1979). An added attraction might have been that Proudhon saw in federation not just an answer to tyranny but, pointing to mass agitation in France, also a way to save the people "from their own folly" (62).
49. "Xianjin gemingzhi yiyi," 19.

cians, and Daoists (as well as Buddhists) embodied these three schools respectively. In the contemporary world, Fascists and Communist despotism partook of the spirit of the first; Sun Yat-sen in China and Rousseau in the West partook of the spirit of the second. Chinese anarchists and Tolstoy and Élisée Reclus in the West partook of the spirit of the third. Different groups displayed some overlap in their beliefs but used the alternative arguments to their own ends (for example, Communists used the second and third to create the first). Sun's Three People's Principles partook of the spirit of all three but sought to achieve the third, which provided a basis for anarchist cooperation with the Guomindang.[50]

Referring in their study of Chinese anarchism to a tendency of Chinese anarchists early on to utilize the past as a reference for anarchism, Robert Scalapino and George Yu have observed: "As long as Chinese traditionalism was enlisted, selectively, in the service of Western radicalism, as long as that radicalism could be buttressed by reference to the Chinese past, the political pendulum for some radicals could always swing back under certain conditions, causing them to revert to orthodoxy. The considerable staying power of Chinese traditionalism were never more clearly illustrated than under such circumstances."[51] The point is well taken but misleading in its vagueness because it does not specify the "circumstances" of the reference to the past. Li's reference to the past to rationalize anarchism and "demonstrate" an affinity between anarchism and the Three People's Principles ultimately had a clear ideological goal: to make anarchism palatable to the Guomindang Right (he and the other anarchists were opposed to the Left, as we shall see), which was already engaged in a traditionalistic interpretation of the Three People's Principles to justify the suppression of social revolution. Much less than an illustration of the hold of tradition even on radical minds, it illustrated an anarchist effort to incorporate anarchism into an emerging hegemonic interpretation of the Three People's Principles. But in its implications for anarchism, it was indeed a "swing back" of the pendulum.

Out of Li's elaborate reasoning would emerge two themes that informed the contradictions in anarchist ideology in 1927–28. One was the advocacy of federalism through which anarchists hoped to shape the future of China under the Guomindang. The other, of which Wu Zhihui would become the most vociferous advocate, was the idea of "a revolution of all the people" (*quanmin geming*). In "The Meaning of Present-

50. *Geming,* no. 24 (December 1927): 97–101.
51. Robert A. Scalapino and G. T. Yu, *The Chinese Anarchist Movement* (Berkeley: Center for Chinese Studies, 1961), 33.

day Revolution" Li had criticized the "Russified Wuhan government" (*Wuhanzhi Ihua zhengfu*), referring to the still legitimate Guomindang Center under the Guomindang Left in Wuhan, which continued to co-operate with the Communists past the Shanghai suppression in April; contrasting Shanghai and Wuhan, he stated: "The Party Protection Movement in Shanghai now stresses the people's livelihood–based revolution of all the people (*quanmin geming*), which is a revolution that is relatively new and superior, to replace the revolution led by Wuhan."[52] At first directed against the Communists for their advocacy of class struggle, this idea would emerge by 1928 as a weapon in the attacks on the Guomindang Left. Unlike the other anarchist advocacy, a federational re-organization of China, which represented a radical anarchist input into political debate, the notion of a "revolution of all the people" had counterrevolutionary implications and would ultimately undercut anarchism itself.

Judging by currently available discussions of the problem, Li's advocacy of "federation" was radical not because he conceived it in particularly novel ways, or because he called for an immediate anarchist reorganization of Chinese society, but because he counterposed it to the preoccupation with centralization that dominated the Guomindang (Right and Left) in the late twenties. Li spent more time defending the legitimacy of "federation" against its critics than in describing with any precision what he himself meant by it, but the outlines of the idea may be gleaned from his references to it as well as discussions by his supporters. Li made no secret of the anarchist origins of his advocacy of "federation" in Proudhon's Principle of Federation. The particular term he used for "federation," *fenzhi hezuo* (literally, divided-governance co-operation), he traced to a combination of (in the French original) "régionalisme" and "fédéralisme."[53] In practise this meant a combination of local and central government: as in Proudhon's original scheme, a hierarchy of units of government that in China would extend from villages or districts (*xian*) to provinces, regional councils, and finally the central government. The basic purpose was to decentralize power by distributing sovereignty to regional units, which would then associate freely in a rising hierarchy of government. Some of the anarchists acknowledged that this was a temporary compromise, a means to limit central power until the conditions

52. "Xianjin gemingzhi yiyi," 6. It is noteworthy that Li also identified Proudhon's attitude toward revolution as a "revolution of all the people."
53. Li Shizeng, "Jiquan yu junquan" (Centralization and the equal distribution of sovereignty), *Geming*, no. 61 (September 1928): 3.

were realized for the abolition of government altogether. When anarchism was achieved, federation would be worldwide, and the nation-state would become just another local unit in a worldwide hierarchy of governing units. Until that condition arrived, however, anarchists were willing to lodge considerable power in the hands of the state, including, in addition to military power, the disposition of finances and the management of heavy industries.[54] Li himself suggested that his idea of federation was quite flexible and that the exact location of governing units could vary in accordance with the demands of the three-stage (military, tutelage, and constitutional government) revolutionary program of the Guomindang.[55]

While acknowledging the anarchist inspiration and intentions of his advocacy of "federation," Li spared no effort in representing it as an idea that had been consistent not only with much of the Chinese political thinking since 1911, but also, and more important, with Sun Yat-sen's emphasis on local government and confederation (*lianbang*); while the terms were different, the spirit was essentially the same, since Sun too had believed in the distribution of sovereignty (*junquan*).[56] What had given the idea a bad name was the warlords' manipulation of federation to perpetuate their own regional power; his idea of *fenzhi hezuo*, however, was very different from the warlord advocacy of "provincial federation" (*liansheng*) and very close to Sun's idea of *junquan*, because its goal was to achieve local self-government (*difang zizhi*). Li believed local government to be consistent not only with the inclinations of the Chinese people and the best interests of the masses, but also with the most advanced thinking in politics. In a statement that may have aroused the ire of his critics in the Guomindang, he observed that the Guomindang had been for local government since its origins, and only in recent years had turned to "centralism" (*jiquan zhuyi*) because it had been poisoned by Bolshevik centralism, which was nothing but a modified czarist "despotism" (a reference to the Guomindang Left, which opposed the scheme). At the

54. For the sources of these comments, see Li Shizeng, "Fenzhi hezuo wenti" (The question of divided-governance co-operation), *Geming*, nos. 31–32, 36 (February–March, 1928); Han Nan, "Shehui sixiang shi shangdi liangda zhengzhi sichao" (Two great currents in the history of social thought), *Geming*, no. 37 (March 1928); Han Nan, "Fenzhi hezuo yu Zhongguo" (Divided-governance co-operation and China), *Geming*, no. 66 (October 1928); Xiu Ping, "Fenzhi hezuo yu zhuanzheng jiquan" (Divided-governance co-operation and despotic centralism), *Geming*, no. 35 (March 1928); and the citation in n. 56. These ideas were significant enough to provoke a prolonged controversy, which was published as *Fenzhi hezuo wenti lunzhan* (Controversy on divided-governance cooperation) and which I have been unable to locate.

55. Li, "Jinquan yu junquan," 3–5.

56. Li, "Fenzhi hezuo wenti." The version used here is from *Geming yu fangeming*, 20–24. Li also acknowledged that the term *fenzhi hezuo* was originally Zhang Puquan's (22).

same time, "co-opting" Sun Yat-sen for his position, he observed that Sun ("the father and the mother of the Guomindang") had been well aware of the anarchist origin of his ideas but had not found them in any way objectionable.[57]

Li did not seem to notice any contradiction in an anarchist's adopting the leader of a political party as his "father and mother." Not all anarchists were happy with his confounding of the anarchist idea of federation with Sun's and other ideas of federal government that had been current in Chinese politics especially in the early twenties. One contributor to *Geming* observed that *fenzhi hezuo* or "fédéralisme" (in the French original) was a revolutionary anarchist idea because it was derived from Proudhon, who had been a champion of the common people (*pingmin*).[58] But on the whole, there seemed to be common agreement among the anarchists on this issue, and on the surface at least, the controversy provoked by the idea of "federalism" was not among anarchists but between anarchists and others in the Guomindang.

This was not so with the idea of a "revolution of the whole people," which was to divide the anarchists themselves. There was little ambiguity concerning the meaning of a "revolution of all the people," or *quanmin geming*. As the statement by Li cited above expressly put it, a "revolution of all the people" was the Guomindang anarchists' answer to the advocacy of class struggle by Bolsheviks and "Bolshevized" members of the Guomindang, that is, the Guomindang Left, which continued to insist even after the suppression of the Communists that the Guomindang represent the interests of the oppressed classes in Chinese society (which included workers, peasants, and the petit-bourgeoisie) against capital and landlords. The term would gain currency in 1928–29 in the polemics Wu Zhihui conducted against theorists of the Guomindang Left, in particular Chen Gongbo and Shi Cuntong (who had been among the founders of the Communist party in 1921, before they changed their allegiance to the Guomindang). Its express intention was to repudiate class struggle and to unite all the people of all classes under the Guomindang umbrella to complete the tasks of the Chinese revolution. As Wu Zhihui put it, "Mr. Sun Yat-sen did not agree with Marx's class revolution; revolution is not just for one or two classes but for all the common people (*pingminde quanti*), including the intellectual, worker, peasant, and merchant classes. This is clearly stated in the declaration of the First Congress. . . . It counts as a revolution of all the

57. Li, "Jinquan yu junquan," 5–6.
58. Ji Ying, "Guanyu fenzhi hezuo" (On divided-governance co-operation), *Geming*, no. 45 (June 1928): 136.

people (*quanmin geming*) if it clears away the harm to all the masses (*quanti minzhong*), if it unites all four hundred million people in a revolutionary army in which not even one is missing."[59]

In the polemics that ensued, Wu (and some of the anarchists who supported his position) repeatedly referred to the phrase *pingminde quanti* as the textual justification for his advocacy of a "revolution of all the people" (*quanmin geming*). Nevertheless, there was a significant difference between "all of the common people" (*pingminde quanti*) and "all the people" (*quanmin*), which he conveniently ignored. Ambivalent as the Guomindang revolutionary strategy after 1924 had been on the question of classes, until 1927 a revolution of the "common people" had justified a mass-based revolution whose foundation had been the "revolutionary masses." The idea of a "revolution of all the people" abolished all distinctions among the "four hundred million" people of China and made the Guomindang the representative of all the people; a bulwark, in other words, of the existing social status quo. In the transformation of the terminology was expressed the transformation of the Guomindang in 1927 from a revolutionary party to the ruler of the Chinese state, which is what concerned theorists of the Guomindang Left who did not view the social tasks of the revolution as having been completed. Indeed, within the context of the political language of the 1920s, the term "revolution of all the people" (*quanmin geming*) not only was antirevolutionary but had a clearly counterrevolutionary signification. As Wu's critics pointed out (and he could not possibly be unaware), *quanmin geming* was the term that the ultranationalist Chinese Youth party (*Zhongguo qingniandang*) had used to criticize the Guomindang-Communist strategy of revolution in 1924–1927.[60] In adopting the terminology of a counterrevolutionary party that had opposed Sun Yat-sen's social program, indeed any social program, in the national revolution, Wu in effect assented to the repudiation of social transformation as part of the process of a national revolution, which, to say the least, was peculiar for an anarchist. Peculiar, yes, but not entirely unexpected, for though Wu may have carried the idea of a "revolution of all the people" to a counterrevolutionary extreme, he was not alone in advocating it. Li Shizeng shared the idea, as we have

59. Wu Zhihui, "Shu Wang xiansheng zuijin yanlun hou" (Response to Mr. Wang (Jingwei)'s most recent speeches), in Tao Qiqing, ed., *Quanmin geming yu guomin geming*, 1–3.
60. See Xiao Shuyu, "Womende guomin geming yu Wu Zhihui xianshengde quanmin geming," in ibid., 17. The discussion here is based on the essays in *Quanmin geming yu guomin geming*.

seen, and other anarchists would rush to Wu's defense when he came under criticism from the Guomindang Left.

Although it would be unfair to hold anarchism responsible for the counterrevolutionary implications of a "revolution of all the people," the idea itself was consistent with anarchist views on revolution. Wu carried to a logical extreme a suspicion of class struggle that had long characterized the thinking of Chinese anarchists. Not all anarchists were opposed to class struggle; indeed, radical anarchists who believed class struggle to be a necessary component of revolution had refused to join the Guomindang and continued to criticize those of their fellow anarchists who did so. But even they were suspicious of class struggle as an expression of partial interest in society (that is, the interest of a single class) and believed that the task of revolution was not to articulate class interest but to abolish classes and put an end to the class-based thinking that divided people. Such thinking had been a major source in the mid-twenties of anarchist opposition to communism.

There was a fundamental contradiction in the practical pursuit by anarchists of the cause of laborers and peasants, and their opposition to class struggle as an expression of "selfish" interests and an obstacle to the realization of a humane society; this was nowhere more evident in 1927–28 than in the contrasts between the work they carried out in conjunction with Labor University and the ideological struggle in the pages of *Geming* against Communists and the Guomindang Left for *their* advocacy of class struggle. As Bi Xiushao wrote in 1927, when the Labor University was still in the process of establishment:

> The Labor University will be the heart of the peasant and labor movement in China in the future. Its goal, and the responsibility it has assumed, are to plan for the welfare of workers and peasants. It seeks to overthrow all thinking that aids the bourgeoisie, and to help peasants and workers appreciate the true value of labor. It seeks to eliminate the evils of capitalist society, encourage workers and peasants to overthrow all thinking that aids the bourgeoisie, and help peasants and workers appreciate the true value of labor. It seeks to eliminate the evils of capitalist society, encourage workers and peasants to overthrow it by means radical or moderate, and to replace it with a social organization that is more rational and consonant with human nature. It seeks to guide the course of the labor movement, stir up the ideals of laborers, raise their level of knowledge, train them in group life (*tuanti shenghuo*), and cultivate their ability for self-government.[61]

61. Bi, "Laodong daxuede mudi yu shiming," 265–66.

Yet the same Bi was opposed to Marxist ideas of class struggle, denied that class struggle was an important datum of history, and perceived the most basic goals of revolution to be "moral" and "spiritual," for which he was criticized even by the more radical among the anarchists.[62] The contradiction may not have been apparent to the anarchists, who believed that, unlike the Communists, who "used" workers and peasants to their own political ends, their sole goal was to help workers and peasants "cultivate their ability for self-government." And yet they seem to have overlooked, at least initially, that so far as the bourgeoisie was concerned, it might not make any difference that their goals were different from those of the Communists as long as these entailed the privileging of workers and peasants over other classes, or that the Guomindang under whose umbrella they worked might not appreciate the undermining of its power by peasant and worker "self-government." In other words, whether or not they promoted class struggle, their promotion of the cause of workers and peasants might actually issue in class struggle.

The twist Wu Zhihui gave the idea of a "revolution of all the people" represented one resolution of this contradiction, one that was consonant with the goals of the Guomindang (and Guomindang anarchists), which allowed anarchist activity in the party, not to foment struggle among classes but to bring to an end the class conflict that had appeared with the revolutionary movement in 1924–1927. The Guomindang's goal in supporting a Labor University had been to train leaders for a labor movement subservient to it, not an independent labor movement of the kind that anarchist activists had envisaged.

The contradiction was brought out into the open with the decision of the party in the spring of 1928 to terminate mass movements, which, the reasoning went, were no longer needed now that a "revolutionary" party was in state power. The suppression of class struggle, which the anarchists had favored so long as it had been directed against others, now became an issue for the anarchists themselves. While they continued to oppose class struggle, some of the anarchists began to complain in mid-1928 about the betrayal of Labor University's mission and quickly extended the complaint to a criticism of the Guomindang's policies on labor and peasants. Among their targets was Wu Zhihui. A "revolution of all

62. Bi Bo (Bi Xiushao), "Women shi shei?" (Who are we?), *Geming,* nos. 16–18 (August 1927), for a comprehensive discussion of Bi's ideas on revolution, and "Jieji douzheng" (Class struggle), *Geming,* no. 18, for his views on class struggle. Bi was the editor of the journal by this time. For an anarchist response to his views on class, see (Mao) Yibo, "On 'Class Struggle,' " *Geming,* no. 21 (December 1927).

the people" may have been a logical conclusion of anarchist opposition to class struggle, but carried to its logical conclusion, it rebounded against the anarchists themselves and brought into the open the contradiction that had been implicit in the anarchist involvement with the Guomindang from the very start.

THE SUPPRESSION OF ANARCHISM

The larger context for anarchist complaints about the management of Labor University was the apparent suppression of mass movements by the Guomindang, which deprived the Labor University of the meaning anarchists attached to it. It is not surprising that criticism of the course Labor University had taken was joined by an increasingly audible criticism of Guomindang policies toward the masses.

Throughout the summer and fall of 1928, *Geming* took up the question of the Guomindang's relationship to the masses. At first the emphasis was on specific incidents, such as the killing of striking laborers in Shanghai in June 1928 where the murderers went unpunished, proof to anarchists of a collusion between capitalists and the existing political system.[63] Anarchists also observed with dismay that warlords, local "despots," and the gentry, who had been the targets of the revolution, had now joined the revolution and, masquerading as revolutionaries, were busy massacring real revolutionaries who had now been labeled counterrevolutionaries.[64]

Such criticisms gradually took a more analytical turn, tracing incidents such as the above to the Guomindang's betrayal of revolution. As anarchists saw it, the revolution had after all taken a purely political turn, abandoning its social goals. As a consequence, its success was now identified with the good of the Guomindang. When the people called for freedom and the improvement of their lives, they were labeled counterrevolutionaries by the government, which sought merely to preserve its own power and that of the bourgeoisie. The only solution, some concluded, might be for the masses to arise and take their fate in their own hands.[65]

63. Han Nan, "Sizhiye gongchao yu Jiang Axingzhi si" (The labor tide in the silk industry and the death of Jiang Axing), *Geming*, no. 43 (June 1928).

64. Lu Han, "Dadao Beijing yihou" (After the taking of Beijing), *Geming*, no. 54 (September 1928); Yi Mo, "Tuhao lieshenzhi yanjiu" (Investigation of local despots and evil gentry), *Geming*, no. 106 (August 1929); Lu Han, "Dangzhi xiade tuhao lieshen" (The local despots and evil gentry under party rule), *Geming*, no. 108 (August 1929).

65. Xu Sheng, "Geming yu minzhong" (Revolution and the masses), *Geming*, no. 56 (September 1928); Zhuang Xiang, "Shei shi fandongzhe" (Who are the counterrevolutionaries), *Geming*, no. 101 (June 1929); Shen, "Geming shi weiminde bushi weidangde"

An open letter to *Geming* in September 1928 by a "melancholy" Chen carried the criticism to Li Shizeng and Wu Zhihui. Chen, who described himself as a student turned worker, observed that even as counterrevolutionaries joined the Guomindang and turned it against the revolution, Li and Wu seemed to be increasing their official positions; Wu in particular, he noted, could not seem to tear himself away from the powerful and spent his time following Chiang Kai-shek around, while militarists all around the country engaged in terror against revolutionaries. He had long idolized both Li and Wu, he stated, but was now full of doubts about their commitment to revolution. The only way they could redeem themselves in the eyes of revolutionaries was to relinquish their offices and cease their political activities.[66]

The editorial response to Chen's letter was to blame the Guomindang Left for the rumors concerning Li and Wu, but criticisms did not stop. In 1928–29 *Geming* was already proscribed in certain parts of China. The journal was finally shut down in September 1929, by which time it had exhausted its usefulness and become an embarrassment to the Guomindang anarchists. Its final issue bade a touching farewell to its readership. The editorial stated with irony that while "we" (that is, the anarchists) had survived the Communists and the Northern Expedition, the journal finally succumbed to the Guomindang, which had promised freedom of speech to all. It gave five reasons for the journal's closing; foremost among them was the degeneration of the revolution into a political revolution. As in all political revolutions, in this revolution, too, the leading party had made all kinds of promises to the people, which it betrayed as soon as it had achieved power for itself. It was not coincidental that *Geming* had been born during the period of military struggle only to perish under Guomindang "tutelage." With reaction on the upsurge, not only was it no longer needed but its struggle against counterrevolution had become undesirable.

The other reasons all had to do with anarchist opposition to government. The journal had refused to bow to the government, which was despotic by its very nature. Opposition to the government's quest for power and its handling of the people was the final straw. Anarchists who

---

(The revolution is for the people not the party), *Geming*, no. 52 (September 1928); San Yu, "Zhengzhi geming yu shehui geming" (Political revolution and social revolution), *Geming*, no. 53 (September 1928).

66. "Fanmende Chen Yuanshuang gei Wu Zhihui Li Shizeng xiansheng yifen gongkaide xin" (An Open Letter to Messrs. Wu Zhihui and Li Shizeng from Melancholy Chen Yuanshuang), *Geming*, no. 55 (September 1928): 148–57.

had been advocating peace were now charged with seditious activity against the government, and the journal had to close down.[67]

There was some grain of truth in the latter charge, but only a grain. As was noted above, anarchists who had refused to join the Guomindang continued to conduct radical activity in Labor University, and their declarations advocating the overthrow of the Guomindang found their way into charges of an anarchist conspiracy to take over the party.[68] Ultimately, implications by radicals of anarchist activity within the Guomindang were responsible for the proscription. Anarchists, who had been among the foremost enemies of communism for the previous two years, now found that they were labeled "Communists." Bi Xiushao recalls that Li and Wu were warned by party authorities to keep their "wards" under control.[69] Radical anarchists had become not only a thorn in the side of the Guomindang but an embarrassment to the Guomindang anarchists themselves.

Labor University was to survive *Geming* by another two years even though it had lost much of its original anarchist intentions by 1928. The resurgence of student activism following the beginning of Japanese aggression against China in 1931 affected the students in Labor University as well. It was already closed down by the authorities in early 1932 when the Japanese attack on Shanghai in January 1932 dealt it the coup de grace by destroying much of its physical plant.

67. Benbao tongren (Members of the journal), "Yu duzhe gaobie" (Saying so long to readers), *Geming*, nos. 109–110 (September 1929): 257–61.

68. See the 1928 anarchist manifesto cited by Xu Deheng as proof of an anarchist conspiracy to overthrow the Guomindang, " 'Qingdang' yu 'quwu' yu?" ('Purging the party?' or 'Getting rid of anarchists?'), in Meng Ming, ed., *Wu Zhihui Chen Gongbo bianlunji* (Compilation of debate between Wu Zhihui and Chen Gongbo) (Shanghai: Fudan daxue, 1928), 53–62. According to Xu, the manifesto issued from a group in Zhejiang that called itself the "Black Youth Association" (*Heise qingnian zuhe*). The manifesto advocated the overthrow of the Guomindang, the Communist party, the Nationalists (Youth party?) and the Research Clique, with armed force, using "the power of the proletariat"; proposed a social revolution to "return factories to the workers and land to the peasants"; and concluded with the lines, "Long live anarcho-communism" (59–60). According to Xu, it was proof of the anarchist intention to take over the Guomindang (56). The group was probably associated with the Federation of Young Chinese Anarcho-communists (*Zhongguo shaonian wuzhengfu gongchan zhuyizhe lianmeng*, or *Shaolian* for short), a conspirational group established by the radical Sichuan anarchists around Lu Jianbo, who were active in Shanghai at this time. A journal that Lu had published earlier had been called *Black Billows* (*Heilan*). For the activities of this group, see Jiang Jun, "Lu Jianbo xiansheng," 1015–19, and "Fangwen Fan Tianjun xiansheng," 1041–45.

69. Bi, "Wo xinyang wuzhengfu zhuyi," 1034. In spite of Wu's pro-Guomindang activities, he helped his fellow anarchists escape the police. Ibid., 1033.

EPILOGUE

The suppression of 1929 did not end anarchist cooperation with the Guomindang completely. In the south, Liu Shixin and others continued to cooperate with Guomindang-led labor movements. Bi Xiushao, who had been the editor of *Geming,* continued to cooperate with the Guomindang well into the period of the war with Japan (1937–1945). Other anarchists followed the Guomindang to Taiwan after 1949.

Anarchist cooperation with the Guomindang, unlikely as it appears theoretically, made some sense in 1927. Shen Zhongjiu had been correct in predicting that joining the Guomindang would be suicidal for the anarchists, but within the context of anarchist desperation in 1926–27 over the increasing irrelevance of anarchism to the revolutionary movement, even he was unable to resist the promise of Guomindang anarchists that here was an unprecedented opportunity for anarchists to shape the future of the Chinese revolution.

Although the anarchist collaboration with the Guomindang was the high point in anarchists' involvement in the party, as the cases of Li Shizeng and Wu Zhihui suggest, the collaboration was not restricted to this period of despair. Li and Wu had been involved with the Guomindang all along and continued their involvement throughout their lives; and they were not the only ones.

Anarchist political involvement with the Guomindang may be traced to the important role personal relationships played in the Chinese revolution, which frequently overrode ideological differences. The personal relationships of the Paris anarchists with Sun Yat-sen and, in later years, with Chiang Kai-shek was an important factor in their involvement with the party. Nor were they the only ones among Chinese anarchists who, in spite of their formal repudiation of politics, found themselves flirting with political authorities. In 1912 Shifu had criticized Wu Zhihui and the Paris anarchists for their activities within the Guomindang. Shifu's own anarchist group in Guangzhou, however, retained for a decade after 1912 a close relationship with the Guangzhou militarist Chen Jiongming with whom Shifu had been associated before 1911 in the China Assassination Corps.

Important though personal relationships were, they should be viewed within the context of a revolutionary environment characterized by profound ambiguities in revolutionary goals and ideology where revolutionaries, even though they made alternative ideological claims upon the revolution, also shared in a common revolutionary discourse that could serve as the basis for common activity (of which the most prominent example surely is the Communist cooperation with the Guomindang on more than one occasion). While different revolutionary groups identified themselves with different, often conflicting, ideologies, they were also bound together by this discourse of which their ideologies were at once constituents and products: constituents because the revolutionary discourse in its unfolding drew upon different, and disparate, ideological sources as it sought to define a revolutionary strategy that could meet the challenge of the multifaceted problems that faced Chinese society; and products because the revolutionary discourse as it emerged provoked redefinition and reconsideration of revolutionary priorities, which called for a less ambiguous delineation of ideological positions within it. Anarchists such as Wu Zhihui owed their radicalization to nationalist resentment against foreign encroachment on China, which ironically issued not in a parochial nationalism but in a moral utopianism, which made revolution itself a utopia and found an answer in anarchism. Sun Yat-sen, whose first loyalty had been to the revolution against the Manchu monarchy, was also the first advocate of socialism in China because he believed that the national revolution could be secured only through social revolution that would prevent the emergence of class conflict under the future republic that he envisioned. Shifu and Chen Jiongming had started their revolutionary careers (under Revolutionary Alliance auspices) as members of the China Assassination Corps, which sought to topple the Manchus through violence; the one was to end up as a militarist, the other as an anarchist. The militarist Chen also had a reputation for social progressivism. In 1919–20, when he was in control of the Zhangzhou region of Fujian province (where he had been forced to move under pressure from other militarists, accompanied by anarchists of Shifu's group), the area under his control was known as the "Soviet Russia of southern Fujian," and a hotbed of anarchist radical activity (which was confused at the time with Bolshevism). He was one of the first Chinese leaders contacted by the Comintern emissary Gregory Voitinsky when he arrived in China in the spring of 1920 to initiate a Communist movement. In all of these cases, while revolutionary experience (not to say social interest and ideological proclivity) led to identification with different ideologies, the discourse shared by the revolutionaries also provided a basis for cooperation and some blurring of boundaries between different ideological positions.

In the case of the anarchists, there may have been an additional element embedded in the anarchist philosophy of revolution (and not just for the Chinese anarchists). Ironically, the very repudiation of politics by the anarchists may have made it easier for them to collaborate with other political parties, so long as they were not called upon to subscribe exclusively to the political ideology of the party (something that precluded cooperation with the Communist party, with its Bolshevik organization and ideology). Conflicting political interests, which might have divided political parties with their own interests, were not an issue for the anarchists, who claimed that they had no political aspirations of their own and who viewed their own revolutionary goals in exclusively social terms, which in the case of Chinese anarchists appeared primarily in the guise of the education and cultural transformation of the oppressed. This, it will be remembered, had characterized anarchist activity in the early Republic. Wu Zhihui had suggested to his anarchist critics in 1924 that since anarchists had no political aims of their own, there was no reason why they could not work for the revolution under the Guomindang umbrella. And, in hindsight, it is clear that anarchists were willing and able to do so in 1927–28 so long as they could work with the Guomindang *as* anarchists. It was only when the Guomindang imposed its own demands upon the anarchists that the contradiction between anarchists and the Guomindang became apparent and forced upon the former a choice they had been able to avoid earlier.

The Guomindang suppression of anarchists in 1929 did not bring the history of anarchism in China to an end. During the early part of the war with Japan, Lu Jianbo and other Sichuan anarchists were even able to publish in Sichuan (where the Guomindang government had moved in retreat from the Japanese armies) an anarchist journal that advocated a popular war to resist Japan. Other anarchists published short-lived journals, were active in the labor movement, or pursued their activities individually, mostly as teachers in colleges and universities. Anarchist ideas would live on in the Chinese revolution, but anarchism as a movement had ceased to exist.

CHAPTER EIGHT

Aftermath and Afterthoughts

For more than two decades in the early part of this century, anarchism nourished Chinese radicalism. Before the May Fourth Movement in 1919, anarchists virtually monopolized the social revolutionary Left. Having reached the apogee of its popularity in the early May Fourth period, anarchism in the twenties declined before its new competitor on the Left, Marxian communism. Following the attempt to reassert an anarchist presence in the revolution through the Guomindang in the late 1920s, anarchists once again dispersed to their regional bases, and anarchism ceased to exert any significant influence on the course of the revolution. Anarchists did not vanish, but they no longer exhibited the vitality that had opened up new directions for the revolution earlier. Indeed, they had become irrelevant. Whether anarchism became irrelevant to an understanding of the course the Chinese revolution would take in later years is another matter.

The vitality of anarchism in 1905–1930 was bound up with the orientation of the Chinese revolution in these years. The Chinese revolution had its sources in a new national consciousness; but, as I have argued above, national consciousness involved a new consciousness of the world and a new conception of the relationship between state and society. Anarchism voiced the urge to a utopian cosmopolitanism and a sense of an autonomous social existence outside of the boundaries of the state, which were the dialectical counterpart to the demand in nationalist consciousness for an organic unity between state and society to ward off the world that threatened to engulf China. Anarchists, too, sought an organic society; but they believed that such a society could be created only out-side the realm of politics, on the basis of free individuals who could assert their "natural" inclination to sociability only if they were liberated from the crippling consequences of social and political authority. Their rejec-tion of politics was accompanied by a call for a cultural revolution that would release individuals from the hold on their consciousness of authori-tarian institutions and enable them to achieve a genuine public conscious-ness. What gave credibility to their argument was a revolutionary situa-tion in which social mobilization opened up the imagination to thinking of the future in new ways, and the degeneration of authority into corrup-tion and oppression that confirmed the necessity to social survival of a total social reorganization—as well as faith in its possibility.

Anarchism was a beneficiary of this revolutionary situation, and it also provided a social imaginary that gave it conceptual if not organizational direction and a language to voice the nascent urge to social liberation. For two decades anarchists served as the source, or the most consistent expo-nents, of ideas and practises that were to play an important part in shaping the course of the revolution. Among these were the call for a cultural revolution against not just political authority but authority in general, most significantly the quotidian institutions and language of authority; innovations in educational practises that reflected this concern for cultural revolution; a social revolution from the bottom up, which led them to labor and rural organization as well as to the reorganization of work and to experiments in new ways of living; an early concern for the liberation of women, of which they were among the most consistent advocates; and even ideas of political reorganizatiòn. Anarchists were also responsible for introducing to China the literature of modern European radicalism in which these ideas were embedded. Their critique of Bolshevism in the 1920s rings especially true in our day when the fate of a socialism that has abandoned its democratic roots has become poignantly obvious.

Anarchism was most prevalent in China at a time when a revolution-ary movement and a revolutionary discourse were assuming recognizable form. Not only did anarchists contribute to the emergence of this revolu-tionary movement, but anarchist language and practises infused the radi-cal culture out of which this discourse emerged. Anarchism may have disappeared from sight by the 1930s, but it is possible that in spite of the formal repudiation of anarchist ideas, their traces survived in the revolu-tionary discourse, which may account for some of the peculiar features that the revolution would assume under the leadership of the Communist party—traces that may have been all the more powerful because they entered the discourse not as ideas but as cultural practises. If these practises in their consequences appear contrary to what the anarchists had intended, that too may have something important to tell us. Anarchists argued all along that a revolutionary society could be only as good as the revolutionary process that produced it. The revolutionary process in China would ultimately take a course different than the one anarchists had envisioned, which was accompanied by the repudiation (or the indefinite postponement) of the vision that had informed the anarchist conception. The Chinese revolution, for all its practical successes under the leadership of the Communist party, has had a price to pay for abandoning this vision. So has socialism.

THE DISPERSION OF ANARCHISM

After 1927 there was an important change in the conditions of revolution in China. For two decades the revolutionary movement had drawn its power from a social mobilization that, if not quite spontaneous, had been the product of autonomous social activity. After 1927 the revolution would take the form of organized conflict between two forces, each the product of earlier years, one of which had now established itself in government while the other had escaped into the countryside to regroup and *organize* a revolution: the Guomindang and the Communist party. It was social conflict still, but it was organized social conflict, in which organizational ability took priority over social vision in determining the outcome of social struggles.

In this situation anarchists, who had been much better at social activity than at social organization for political conflict, had little to contribute and quickly became irrelevant to the revolution. They did not abandon their activities; but those activities were now restricted to the barely visible social niches that remained within the structure of political power. Some in later years would join the Communist party or take refuge with it; the majority of those about whom we have information continued their activities within the Guomindang framework, some in direct service to the Guomindang, others in resignation.

Education provided the primary area of anarchist activity in the thirties. Guomindang anarchists such as Li Shizeng and Wu Zhihui survived the debacle of Labor University and continued to work with educational programs similar to earlier ones; in later years they would take celebrated places in the Guomindang pantheon as party elders who had made significant contributions in education and culture to the revolution. The Guangzhou anarchists by the mid-thirties held an important place in the Guangzhou educational establishment under Guomindang auspices. In 1936 Liu Shixin was appointed head of the Bureau of Social Affairs in Guangzhou; Huang Yibo, Huang Lingshuang, and Ou Shengbai all held educational offices under him. Anarchists elsewhere may also have engaged in educational activities, then and in later years, judging by the few memoirs that have become available recently.[1]

Anarchists had been deeply concerned all along with the problem of culture, and in the 1930s some of them turned to the pursuit of cultural problems, though now the concern with culture was less as a problem of revolution and more as an abstract problem. Hua Lin, whose approach to anarchism had always exhibited an esthetic orientation, turned to writing about art and literature. Huang Lingshuang, who had returned from the United States in the late twenties to become a university professor, became the advocate of a discipline that he described as "culturology" (wenhuaxue). As he explained it, a systematic elaboration of culture was crucial to national existence; the goal of his "culturology" was to formulate a sociology of culture that was not bound by European ideas but brought into the study of culture a Chinese sociology, in particular the ideas of Sun Yat-sen. Similarly, Li Shizeng sought to create a new field of studies, which he described through a neologism (consisting of a Chinese and a Greek component), "Kiaologie," broadly conceived as a study of the émigré experience in history, whose goal was to contribute to world cooperation and greater cosmopolitanism. Li was probably the foremost voluntary émigré in modern Chinese history, and it was appropriate that he should seek to derive from his personal experiences a world outlook to guide a new way of looking at the relationship among peoples. Like Huang Lingshuang, he sought to bring a Chinese presence into the study of society. This could be viewed as a return to parochialism of the formerly cosmopolitan anarchists. Such a view would be erroneous, however; more important, in either case the urge was to create a genuinely cosmopolitan world outlook by bringing a Chinese voice into a sociology of human development that had hitherto been dominated by European

1. Information for the Guomindang anarchists is available in works cited in the bibliography. For the Guangzhou anarchists, see Jin Zhongyan, "Wo suozhide wuzhengfu zhuyizhe huodong pianduan" (A brief account of what I knew of anarchist activities), *Guangzhou wenshi ziliao* (Historical and literary materials on Guangzhou), no. 1 (1962): 22, and Liu Shixin, "Guanyu wuzhengfu zhuyi huodongde diandi huiyi" (Remembering bits and pieces of anarchist activity), in *Wuzhengfu zhuyi sixiang ziliao xuan* (Selection of materials on anarchist thought), ed. Ge Maochun et al., 2 vols. (Beijing: Beijing daxue chubanshe, 1983), 2:929–39. For the Sichuan anarchists, see Jiang Jun, "Lu Jianbo xiansheng zaoniande wuzhengfu zhuyi xuanchuan huodong jishi" (An account of Mr. Lu Jianbo's early anarchist activities), in *WZFZYSX* 2:1009–22.

conceptions. If there was anything anarchist about these undertakings, it was a continued commitment to such a cosmopolitanism.[2]

Anarchists also continued with their efforts to spread the use of Esperanto, but here too the changed situation was evident. The Esperanto school that Ou Shengbai conducted in Guangzhou under Guomindang auspices after 1930 had to teach courses in party ideology. Ou and Huang Zunsheng also undertook as part of their duties to translate into Esperanto works by Sun Yat-sen (including the *Three People's Principles*) as well as important party documents.[3]

In Guangzhou anarchists also continued with labor activities. In 1927 Liu Shixin and others established a Federation of Revolutionary Workers (*Geming gongren lianhehui*). Guangzhou anarchists had a history of collaboration with Guomindang-related labor unions and, as we have seen, anarchist unions themselves for the most part sought to resolve the problems of labor through reeducation of both labor and capital rather than through class conflict. Like earlier anarchist unions, however, this one also sought to establish a union of workers, which brought it into conflict with the Guangdong General Labor Union (*Guangdong zong gonghui*), which was dominated by employers. As part of their activities, they established a Labor Movement Training Institute (*Gongren yundong jiangxi suo*) in June 1927. Even though they wanted to bring the federation under Guomindang auspices (with Wu Zhihui's help), the federation was shut down following the Guangzhou insurrection (the Commune) by Communists in December. In ensuing years anarchist labor efforts remained wedded to the Guomindang.[4]

2. For "culturology," see Huang Wenshan, *Wenhuaxue lunwen ji* (Collected essays on culturology) (Guangzhou: Zhongguo wenhuaxue xuehui, 1938); for "Kiaologie," see Li Shizeng, "Qiaoxue fafan" (Introduction to Kiaologie) (1942–43), in *Li Shizeng xiansheng wenji* (Collection of Mr. Li Shizeng's essays) (Taibei: Zhongguo Guomindang dangshi weiyuanhui, 1980). *Kiao* (*Qiao*) is the word for émigré, the same word used in *huaqiao*, or "overseas Chinese."

3. Wang Yan, "Wuzhengfu zhuyi yu shijieyu" (Anarchism and Esperanto), in *Guangzhou wenshi ziliao*, no. 1 (1962): 42. Esperanto schools may have been a means in the 1930s (as earlier) for anarchists to survive and spread, although this is merely a surmise. According to the Communist educator (and product of the work-study movement) Xu Teli, who occupied a high post in the party propaganda apparatus during the Yan'an Period, Esperanto schools flourished in the thirties; he mentions schools in Wuxi, Shaoxing, Ningbo, Qingdao, Nantong, Taiyuan, Loyang, Xian, Kunming, Guilin, Hong Kong—in other words, all around China. See "Zhongguo shijieyu yundong jianshi" (Brief history of the Chinese Esperanto movement) (1938), in *Xu Teli wenji* (Essays of Xu Teli) (Changsha: Hunan renmin chubanshe, 1980), 180–82.

4. Liu Shixin, "Guanyu Wuzhengfu zhuyi huodongde diandi huiyi," and Huang Yibo, "Wuzhengfu zhuyizhe zai Guangzhou gao gonghui yundong huiyi" (Recollections of anarchist union activities in Guangzhou), in *Guangzhou wenshi ziliao*, no. 1 (1962): 1–15, especially 5–7.

Finally, anarchists continued with publication activities in the 1930s, though in highly subdued form. As far as I can tell, of the journals the anarchists published in the 1930s, only *Jingzhe* (Spring festival), published in Chengdu during the war against Japan, had a clear identity and an anarchist position. Most of this journal was devoted to translations from Spanish anarchists or news on the civil war in Spain. It is interesting that anarchists for the first time supported the war against Japan as a war against oppression and advocated popular mobilization as a way of fighting it.[5]

Following the war and the victory of the Communist party in 1949, some anarchists went on to Hong Kong, Taiwan, or the United States, while others chose to stay on in China. The tone of available anarchist memoirs (from Taiwan or the People's Republic of China) suggests that even where they confess to the errors of their youthful days, the original faith derived from anarchism has not been lost, though on occasion the faith finds expression in a highly metaphysical language that has little to do with concrete problems of social change and revolution but is reminiscent of the language of Chinese anarchism in its earliest days.[6]

Whether those anarchists who stayed on in China have had anything to do with the occasional appearance of anarchist ideas after 1949 or with the recent revival of interest in anarchism is difficult to say. It is also difficult to say whether there is a new generation of anarchists *in* China, or what anarchism might mean to them. During the last two decades there have been Chinese anarchists in Hong Kong, Paris, and possibly elsewhere. Also, some clandestine literature has appeared on occasion in mail received in China, advocating a social revolution that is more reminiscent of anarchist than of Marxist (at least in the Communist party version) notions of revolution.[7] I am not familiar enough with the numbers or the activities of Chinese anarchists abroad to say whether such literature emanated from them or from disgruntled radicals from within China who had escaped abroad. The content of this literature does not provide sufficient evidence to determine that it is indeed of anarchist origin, for it may owe more to an anti-Communist-

5. *Jingzhe*, 1938. For information on this journal and its background, see "Lu Jianbo xiansheng zaoniande wuzhengfu zhuyi xuanchuan huodong jishi," 1020–21. I am grateful to Julia Tong of the Hoover Institution East Asia library for locating this periodical.

6. See, for example, Mo Jipeng, "A Memoir of Shi Fu." Unpublished ms. Huang Lingshuang, who it is rumored spent the later years of his life in Los Angeles, went beyond other anarchists that I know of in turning to the more esoteric currents in Chinese philosophy, such as the *Yijing* (Book of Changes).

7. I refer to literature smuggled into China, usually in foreigners' mail. I have a few samples, but so far as I know, no one has undertaken systematic study of this literature.

party democratic Marxism (where it overlaps with anarchism) than to anarchist inspiration.

Anarchistic ideas, however, have appeared repeatedly in the People's Republic of China, not in any open advocacy of anarchism, but in the counterposing to the existing political system of an alternative principle of revolutionary organization, namely, the principle underlying the Paris Commune of 1871.[8] The most celebrated instance may be that of the group in Hunan province that called itself the Shengwulian (an abbreviation for the Federation of the Provincial Proletariat), which appeared in fall 1967 at the height of the Cultural Revolution. While the group declared fealty to Mao's thought and the Cultural Revolution leadership, unlike the latter it declared its commitment to the creation of a "People's Commune of China," modeled after the Paris Commune but also claiming the inspiration of the Soviet of Petrograd in 1917, in which "the masses should rise to take control of the destiny of their socialist country, and to manage the cities, industry, communications, and economy."[9]

The Shengwulian was born of the struggles in 1967 between a revolution from the bottom, which would carry the Cultural Revolution to a new higher stage, and a revolution stage managed by the Communist party, which already sought to reassert its control over the revolutionary process. According to the group's manifesto, "Whither China"? published in early 1968, similar groups had cropped up elsewhere in the country since the January revolution in Shanghai in 1967, which had been the first to declare a mass revolution from the bottom. Mao himself had encouraged mass revolution and communal organization, in the early stages of the Cultural Revolution, but was to turn against it when the revolution seemed to be getting out of hand. By 1968 the party in its efforts to restore "democratic centralism" had already launched an attack on the "anarchist" theory of "many centers," to which neither Mao nor the Cultural Revolution leadership was prepared to lend support.[10] Groups such as the Shengwulian were suppressed in the process.

8. For an extensive discussion, see John B. Starr, "Revolution in Retrospect: The Paris Commune Through Chinese Eyes," *China Quarterly*, no. 49 (January–March 1972): 106–25; and Maurice Meisner, "The Chinese Communists and the French Revolution: From la commune insurrectionelle (1792–94) to China's People's Communes," unpublished paper presented at the annual meeting of the American Historical Association (December 27–30, 1989).

9. "Whither China?" in Harold C. Hinton, *The People's Republic of China, 1949–1979: A Documentary Survey* (Wilmington, Del.: Scholarly Resources, 1980), 4:1854.

10. For an example, see "The Reactionary Nature of the Theory of Many Centers," *Liberation Daily* (Shanghai, 14 August 1968). In Hinton, *People's Republic* 4:2158–59.

Anarchists abroad have claimed groups like the Shengwulian for their own.[11] The advocacy of the commune as a principle of revolutionary organization certainly points to the repudiation of the Bolshevik principle of "democratic centralism" that the Communist party upheld; whether it suggests prima facie that such groups were consciously anarchist is another matter. The declaration of fealty to Mao and the Cultural Revolution leadership in late 1967 and early 1968 seems peculiar if the group was indeed anarchist, since by then they had made clear their opposition to the commune form of organization;[12] at the very least it is evidence of deep political naiveté. Moreover, the model of the Paris Commune may be claimed as easily for a democratic Marxism as for anarchism and does not in itself point to anarchist loyalties. The commune principle was to reappear in later years, during the Democracy Movement of 1978–79, when once again it served as an inspiration for antiparty leftists. I suggest that in either case it was the experience of the revolution, rather than any formal anarchist commitments, that played the crucial part in reviving it as a revolutionary ideal.

In light of what I have argued above, it may be a moot question whether a group such as the Shengwulian, or the Democracy Movement, was anarchist or not. Anarchist ideals, embodied in such notions as the commune, were integral to the revolutionary discourse, which they had helped structure at its origins, and were present in it as "traces" long after the revolutionaries had repudiated an anarchist identity. And while as "traces" they had no identity of their own and could not serve as the basis for an explicitly anarchist position after 1949, their disruptive presence made itself known (and served as a beacon for radical dissatisfaction with the betrayal of the revolution) every time the revolution ran into serious trouble. For the present, at least, more significant in the legacy of anarchism in China may be those elements in revolutionary discourse that may shed some light on the twists and turns of the Communist revolution after 1949.

11. John Welsh, "Shen-wu-lien (sic): China's Anarchist Opposition," Social Anarchism 2, no. 1 (1981): 3–15.
12. In response to the Shanghai Commune (and later advocacies of communal organization), Mao supported an alternative organizational form, the Revolutionary Committee, which also emerged in early 1967 and represented a "three-in-one" combination of masses, the military and the party, thus opening the way to the restoration of party power (and also bringing the revolution under military control).

REVOLUTIONARY DISCOURSE
AND CHINESE COMMUNISM

Those radicals who established the Communist party in 1921 and have dominated it since were without question products of May Fourth radicalism, in which anarchism played a central part both as an ideology and vision of social revolution and as cultural practise. Many of them also turned to Marxian communism after going through an anarchist phase, including most prominently Mao Zedong. Deng Xiaoping, the last major figure from that era, was himself a product of the work-study program in France that had been organized by anarchists.

What this means is difficult to say. Anarchism was not the only element in revolutionary discourse that might have contributed to the form Marxism would take in China (aside from nationalism, which in different guises was common to all Chinese revolutionaries). Maurice Meisner has argued plausibly for a populist strain in Chinese Marxism that may have gone a long way toward shaping the Marxism of Mao Zedong, which was to play *the* central part in giving direction to the Chinese revolution.[13] More important have been the material circumstances of the Chinese revolution. The communism that emerged victorious in 1949 was more directly a product of the revolutionary circumstances of the 1930s and 1940s than of the May Fourth period. The demands of a rural revolution and the "guerilla socialism" it produced are sufficient prima facie to account for some of the most basic ideological and organizational features of Chinese communism: the suspicion of an organizational isolation from the people at large that characterized Mao's thinking, a related suspicion of bureaucratism, emphasis on organic ties between intellectuals and the people, and concern for integrating rural and urban development.

May we ignore these features of Chinese communism as being central to the anarchist vision of social revolution? It is arguable that they can all be traced to Marxism and Marxist texts, but the Chinese revolution has been unique nevertheless in its urge to put them into practise. And though the Chinese revolutionary experience may have been responsible for bringing them forward in revolutionary practise, they existed as ideas in revolutionary discourse prior to the 1930s and possibly helped revolutionaries deal with the exigencies of a novel revolutionary situation.

This is *not* to suggest that Chinese communism was shaped by anar-

13. Meisner has argued this in a number of publications, most prominently in *Li Ta-chao and the Origins of Chinese Marxism* (Cambridge: Harvard University Press, 1967).

chism, or that we may describe Mao Zedong as an anarchist. While some Chinese writers in their frustration with the Cultural Revolution, or with the demands for democracy in the aftermath of the Cultural Revolution, have placed the blame for such "deviations" from Marxism on persistent anarchist influences in the party, such charges amount to little more than a vulgarized misuse of anarchism to defend a Bolshevik conception of the party. For all his "deviations" from Bolshevism, Mao was committed to the Communist party. The closest we have to a statement on anarchism is when in 1967, in response to the declaration in Shanghai of a Shanghai commune, he peevishly queried of Zhang Chunqiao and Yao Wenyuan if China was to be turned into a federation of communes.[14]

The point here is not to capture Mao, the Communist party, or the Chinese revolution for anarchism—to which, to make an informed guess, anarchists would be the first to object. Rather, the question is whether we understand better the course communism took in China if we view it as part of a broader revolutionary discourse in whose formation anarchism played an important part historically and therefore introduced dissonant elements into the Bolshevik conception of revolution. That the ideas anarchists introduced into the discourse were not exclusive to anarchism but overlapped with Marxism in later years enabled Communists to disassociate them from their anarchist origins and to claim them for communism. More precisely, the very ideas that appear "petit-bourgeois" when they are associated with anarchists have become part of the Communist party's revolutionary tradition to the extent that they can be claimed for Marxism or identified with Communists, in the process of rewriting the history of the revolution around the Communist party.

The fact remains, however, that while there may be textual grounds for claiming such ideas for Marxism, historically they entered the revolutionary discourse in China through anarchist ideological activity and were initially identified with an anarchist vision of social revolution. We have no reason to assume that, because they were disassociated from their anarchist origins once they had become integral to the discourse, they were purged of all association with the anarchist vision of revolution that had initially informed them. On the contrary, it is possible that these associations lived on in revolutionary memory in spite of their formal repudiation. We must remember that the history of the Communist revolution in China coincides with the lifetime of the generation that estab-

---

14. Mao Zedong, *Chairman Mao Speaks to the People,* ed. Stuart Schram (New York: Pantheon, 1974), 278.

lished the Communist party and has dominated it since. This generation experienced anarchism as part of its political coming-of-age—not merely as an intellectual abstraction but as a set of cultural practises. Anarchist ideas, if they did indeed live on as integral moments of a revolutionary discourse, did so not as intellectual abstractions but as an endowment of crucial moments in the biographies of those who made the revolution. This was not the biography of a single individual, Mao Zedong, with whom we have tended to associate the peculiarities of Chinese communism. Indeed, future research may yet reveal that some of those phenomena in the Communist revolution that have been identified with Mao involved many others who had shared his experiences in the course of their radicalization; some of the foremost names in the Chinese Communist leadership, especially educational leadership, were products of the work-study program in France. The vocabulary of that program persists in China to this day.

According to Zhang Guotao, the populist strain in Chinese communism represented by the slogan "Go to the people" (dao minjian qu), which entered Chinese Marxism with China's "first Marxist," Li Dazhao, found its most fervent advocates in the May Fourth period among the anarchists, from whom Li originally derived the idea.[15] Most important, however, were two ideas that anarchists introduced into revolutionary discourse early on: the idea of integrating agriculture and industry in China's future development, and the idea of labor-learning, which played a crucial part in radical culture during the May Fourth period.

The integration of agriculture and industry was in practise a product of revolutionary experience, especially during the Yan'an period, when the exigencies of rural revolution under wartime conditions forced Communists to establish basic industries to meet subsistence and military needs. It may be no accident, however, that the Communists chose "mutual aid" (huzhu) to describe the small agrarian collectives they established during the Yan'an period and after 1949. More significant was the structure of the people's communes established from 1958, when there was no such need, which were to remind Colin Ward, editor of Kropotkin's Fields, Factories and Workshops of Tomorrow, of Kropotkin's "industrial villages." It is also significant that when the people's communes were established, they were part of an emerging program of development that was to constitute a distinct Chinese way of develop-

15. Chang Kuo-t'ao, The Rise of the Chinese Communist Party, 1921–1927 (Lawrence: University Press of Kansas, 1971), 50–51.

ment that would differ from both capitalist and socialist alternatives that then existed. While they were idealized as organic units of development that would integrate industry and agriculture and provide a cultural (as well as a military) world of their own, it was also important that the program of modernization they articulated had an antimodernist aspect to it, which glorified the countryside at the expense of the city and was suspicious of technology (or of the "fetishism" of technology) as well as of the professionalism that was a by-product of modernity.

It may not be fortuitous that the establishment of the people's communes coincided with a renewed demand for integrating labor and learning. Labor-learning, in its radical interpretation, had been linked in earlier years to "mutual aid" and communal existence; it was the cultural counterpart to the social organization represented by communes, which sought to abolish the distinctions between mental and manual labor that inevitably obstructed social unity. The official insistence on the need to combine "redness and expertise" is familiar and need not be elaborated here; the insistence on making professionals and intellectuals "redder" by demanding that they engage in manual labor, and on making laborers more "expert" by educating them, was to be a cornerstone of radical policy for the next two decades and to reach a crescendo with the Cultural Revolution.

Most striking about this insistence on labor-learning has been its effect on intellectuals and professionals. But it would be simplistic to view it merely as a means to the suppression of intellectual rivals to the party elite (which by the time of the Cultural Revolution would in turn find itself in fields and factories) or as a function of Maoist anti-intellectualism. A Party Work Conference in 1957 signaled a shift in educational policy by calling upon schools at all levels to apply the "principle of combining work with study." The vocabulary was even more revealing. The titles of publications in 1958 on the progress of the new policy included the concept of "diligent-work frugal-study" (*qingong jianxue*).[16] It may also have been no coincidence that some of the more elaborate memoirs of the work-study program in France were published at this time, or that the party should have mobilized graduates of that program to urge youth to "integrate manual and

16. See *Qingong jianxue biandi huakai* (Diligent-work frugal-study is flowering everywhere) (Shanghai, 1958), and *Qingong jianxue gaibianle xuexiaode mianmao* (Diligent-work frugal-study has transformed schools' visages) (Shanghai, 1958). These were published by different district committees of the Communist party in Shanghai. For an explanation of the Party Work Conference decisions, see Lu Ting-yi, *Education Must Be Combined with Productive Labour* (Peking: Foreign Languages Press, 1958).

mental labor, and use both hands and brains."[17] That same year a Communist Labor University (*Gongchan zhuyi laodong daxue*) was established in Jiangxi to promote "both a technological and a cultural revolution."[18]

While it coincided with the renewed radicalization of Chinese society with the Great Leap Forward of 1958, and was represented for the next two decades as the key to the creation of new socialist individuals (and socialism), the call for labor-learning also had a practical side: "to increase the possibilities for universal education." The labor-learning ideal from the beginning had an ambiguity to it in anarchist thinking: as the means to create a new anarchist individual and as a practical means to promote education. A similar ambiguity has characterized the promotion of "diligent-work frugal-study" since 1958. During the Cultural Revolution years, the revolutionary promise of labor-learning overshadowed its practical aspects. Since Mao's death the ideal of "diligent-work frugal-study" has appeared once again. A conference in 1982 called upon the nation to promote "diligent-work frugal-study."[19] In keeping with the practical orientation of the post-Mao years (and with the personal experience of Deng Xiaoping, whose participation in the program in the 1920s had been motivated by practical considerations—he apparently did little "work" in Paris), the emphasis now is almost exclusively on the practical benefits to be derived from students working to support their education.

Further research is necessary before we may state with any confidence whether consciousness of the revolutionary vision associated with these ideas of anarchist origin played any part in their application after 1949— at least for the older generation of revolutionaries. The persistence of the vocabulary provides prima facie evidence of their integration into a revolutionary discourse that transcended political ideologies and suppressed their origins in an anarchist vision as well. Recalling those origins is

17. Xu Teli, "Laoli yu laoxin bingjin, shou he nao bingyong," in *Xu Teli wenji*, 585–87. Xu here presented "diligent-work frugal-study" as an ancient Chinese idea going back to the Han dynasty. He Changgong's *Qingong jianxue shenghuo huiyi* (Reminiscences of diligent-work frugal-study life) (Beijing: Gongren chubanshe, 1958), one of the most elaborate memoirs of the movement, is an example of the publications I refer to. These publications, and the role French-educated party leaders involved in educational work, such as Xu Teli and Wu Yuzhang, played in the movements of the late 1950s and the 1960s might yield fruitful insights into the ideological developments of the time, which have, too simplistically I think, been identified with Mao and a few other major political leaders.

18. *Gongchan zhuyi laodong daxue* (Nanchang: Jiangxi jiaoyu chubanshe, 1960).

19. *Quanguo zhongxiaoxue qingong jianxue jingyan xuanpian* (Experiences with diligent-work frugal-study in elementary and middle schools around the country) (Beijing: Jiaoyu kexue chubanshe, 1982).

significant not only for remembering the important part anarchism played in the formation of the discourse: That perspective is a reminder, in turn, that those ideas were not products of peculiarities in Mao's Marxism, or of the turn the Communist revolution would take in China in response to circumstantial contingencies, but represent ideals that are as old as the history of the Chinese revolution.

This revolutionary discourse had a radicalizing effect on the Bolshevik structure the Communist party had established after 1949, opening up the ideological closure that an organizational ideology had imposed on the discourse, returning Chinese society to the path of social revolution to fulfill the uncompleted tasks that its underlying vision demanded. The consequences, however, were to be vastly different than what the anarchists had anticipated of their revolutionary strategy, because the circumstances of the revolution were vastly different and so, therefore, was the function of the strategy.

Whether we speak of the communal reorganization of society, or of the labor-learning ideal, their purpose in the anarchist conception had been to achieve a social revolution outside of the sphere of politics and against it. They were intended, not to establish a revolutionary hegemony over society, but to abolish all hegemony. Crucial to the process was the liberation of individuals from social and cultural authority so as to reestablish society on a voluntary basis.

Implementation of these ideas under the Communist regime, whether during the Mao years or under Mao's successors, has been anything but voluntary; rather, the premise has been the enhancement of the power of the Communist party—and of its hegemony over society. Liu Shipei might have recognized in the people's communes something akin to the rural reorganization he had advocated. For all its antimodernism, however, Mao's revolutionary policy was guided by a commitment to rapid national development and organic political power. As a consequence, the people's communes came to serve not as the nuclei for a new society but as a means to social control, faster economic development, and the efficient exploitation of labor that this demanded—rendered all the more ruthless for having been attached to the symbols of revolution. I have referred to the fate of the commune principle during the Cultural Revolution. Within the context of a political system dominated by the all-powerful Communist party, the model of the Paris Commune served, not the purposes of democratic revolutionary organization, but as a political imaginary that, under the guise of popular revolutionary control, perpetuated and enhanced the political penetration of society. And when it was transposed against the existing political system by those who took it seriously as a radical principle of a *social* democracy, it was suppressed without hesitation. It may be a tribute to the power of the revolutionary discourse, however, that the party itself is prepared to revive this political imaginary whenever it needs it, and can revive it on its own terms. Following the violent suppression of the dissident movement in 1989, the Communist party has once again revived the idea of a commune as the best means for organizing China democratically, this time because the commune's combination of "executive and legislative powers" makes it the most viable "socialist" alternative to bourgeois democracy.[20] In the presence of an all-powerful "executive," needless to say, this means, not the extension of any democratic powers to society, but the usurpation by the state of any possible assertion by society of some measure of control over its own fate.

Similarly, while Communist party leaders have continued to speak of "producing fully developed human beings" (now quoting Marx) as the goal of education, national and party power have been the condition of education as they have seen it. Lu Dingyi, then head of propaganda work, wrote in 1958: "The combination of education with productive labour is required by our country's socialist revolution and socialist construction, by the great goal of building a communist society and by the need to develop our education with greater, faster, better and more economical results" (the latter a general slogan of the Great Leap Forward). The "all-round development" of individuals, he also warned, "must be under the leadership of the Communist Party."[21] The goal of "all-round development" was not the individual or a new kind of society, but the better functioning of the existing one. Such also was the intention of the conference on "diligent-work frugal-study" convened by Mao's successors in 1982.[22]

20. *South China Morning Post* report on work conference on democracy, 18 December 1989.

21. Lu Ting-yi, *Education*, 20, 17. Lu claimed that the movement had spread from the countryside to the city (1) and included "the establishment by factories of schools and the setting up of schools by factories" (20). He referred to the Communist Manifesto program for establishing socialism, and noted that while the first eight points had been accomplished already, two remained: " 'the combination of agriculture with manufacturing industries; the gradual abolition of the distinction between town and country' and 'the combination of education with industrial production' " (23). He was willing to concede that the idea had initiated with "utopian socialists" (27).

22. *Quanguo zhongxiaoxue*. See the message from the State Council, 2–7.

A CONCLUDING OBSERVATION

The question that has guided this study is not whether anarchists were better, or more consistent, revolutionaries than others in China (which they were not), or whether the anarchist vision is a possibility—anywhere, but particularly within the context of a society struggling for national autonomy or development. Why the anarchist vision should be viewed as more utopian than other competing social revolutionary visions, or what might be wrong with a utopian conception of society, are questions too complex to be entered into here. Suffice it to say that existing society has its own utopianism, whose promise, contrary to all evidence, continues to sustain its hegemony.

Rather, the question is this: What have been the consequences of ignoring or suppressing the anarchist presence in the history of the Chinese revolution, both in a narrow historiographical sense and in a broader political sense? One historian has written that anarchism was appealing in China initially because it provided simple answers to revolutionaries unable or unwilling to deal with the complexities of Western democracy.[23] This study has shown, I hope, that however simplistic anarchist solutions to China's problems may seem, anarchists were probably more aware than many of their contemporaries of the complexities of democracy and responded to it with considerable complexity. Their contribution to the formation of a revolutionary discourse in China is also revealing of the complexities of that discourse which, for all the efforts to contain it, has served as a continuing source of vitality in the pursuit of a revolutionary society.

More broadly, the anarchist contribution to this discourse provides an indispensable critical perspective on the course the Chinese revolution was to take: the suppression in the name of revolutionary success of the very vision that animated the revolution and served as its raison d'être. To appreciate this, we need to rethink what anarchism was about. Aside from the distortions provided by a general cultural and political orientation toward anarchism (which, among all the threatening vocabulary of radical politics, has consistently remained the most threatening), even those sympathetic to anarchism have tended to identify it with opposition to government, which I believe is a simplifica-

23. Mary B. Rankin, *Early Chinese Revolutionaries* (Cambridge: Harvard University Press, 1971).

tion.[24] Though I hesitate to generalize about what anarchism might mean to anarchists, I suggest here that the most important aspect of anarchism is its consistent critique of hegemony—in a basic Gramscian Marxist sense, but with greater consistency and different intentions than those of Gramsci, who among all Marxists has come closest to a democratic interpretation of Marxism. Gramsci's goal, in his analysis of hegemony, was to reveal the cultural roots of hegemony so as to show the way to the substitution of revolutionary for bourgeois hegemony.[25] Anarchists in China, as we have seen, in seeking to eliminate authority from social institutions and language, sought to abolish hegemony as a social principle in general. The coincidence of the problem of social revolution with that of cultural revolution in Chinese society may have dramatically illustrated this antihegemonic thrust of anarchism, but the critique of hegemony is common to most social anarchism. As the Italian anarchist Errico Malatesta wrote on one occasion:

> Someone whose legs have been bound from birth but had managed nevertheless to walk as best he could, might attribute his ability to move to those very bonds which in fact serve only to weaken and paralyse the muscular energy of his legs.
>
> If to the normal effects of habit is then added the kind of education offered by the master, the priest, the teachers, etc., who have a vested interest in preaching that the masters and the government are necessary; if one were to add the judge and the policeman who are at pains to reduce to silence those who might think differently and be tempted to propagate their ideas, then it will not be difficult to understand how the prejudiced view of the usefulness of, and the necessity for, the master and the government took root in the unsophisticated minds of the labouring masses.
>
> Just imagine if the doctor were to expound to our fictional man with the bound legs a theory, cleverly illustrated with a thousand invented cases to prove that if his legs were freed he would be unable to walk and would not live, then that man would ferociously defend his bonds and consider as his enemy anyone who tried to remove them.[26]

The question here is not coercion but hegemony; and it is the thoroughgoing critique of hegemony in anarchism, I would suggest, that has enabled anarchists to think what culturally seems unthinkable, and therefore, to imagine social possibilities beyond the ideological horizons established by

24. See, for example, Michael Albert et al., *Liberating Theory* (Boston: South End Press, 1986).

25. A concise but uncritical exposition of the idea of hegemony is to be found in Chantal Mouffe, "Hegemony and Ideology in Gramsci," in *Gramsci and Marxist Theory*, ed. C. Mouffe (London: Routledge & Kegan Paul, 1979).

26. E. Malatesta, *Anarchy* (London: Freedom Press, 1984), 12.

political ideology. This is also the reason, I think, that anarchists—in China and elsewhere—have devoted more attention than other socialists to problems of quotidian social and cultural practises in which hegemony, at its most fundamental level, is embedded.[27]

As this manuscript was nearing completion in June 1989, tragic events occurred in China when a renewed democracy movement was brutally suppressed by the Communist party under the leadership of Deng Xiaoping, a product of the work-study movement of the anarchists in the 1920s. For a decade Deng had been hailed in China but possibly more enthusiastically abroad as a champion of democracy, partially out of an urge to suppress memories of Mao and the Cultural Revolution, but also because of his policies of once again opening up China to the outside world—especially to a global capitalism. We have yet to understand the nature of this new round in the search for democracy in China; but Deng's reasoning in suppressing it clearly revealed what some historians have known all along: that he has throughout his life been a more consistent Bolshevik than Mao Zedong, who was always uncomfortable with certain features of Bolshevik organization.[28] According to a report in *Asia Week* of May 12, 1989, Deng purportedly said in a party meeting in late April: "The students may be acting out of line but the broad masses of workers and peasants are on our side. Even if the workers and farmers (*sic*) were to join the students, we can still rely on more than three million soldiers to maintain law and order." Fine sentiments to be voiced by the leader of a revolutionary party that derives its legitimacy from its claims to represent the people! In the end, only soldiers were clearly with the party leadership and were able indeed to "maintain law and order." Since then, the party has re-invented the people to once again secure its hegemony.

From a long-term historical perspective, the suppression here is not only of a movement but also of a social revolutionary ideal that is embed-

27. For an anarchist discussion focusing on problems of ecology, see Murray Bookchin, *Toward an Ecological Society* (Montreal and Buffalo: Black Rose Books, 1986). In response to the experience of existing socialist societies, Marxists and other socialists, too, have increasingly turned their attention to the problem of hegemony and quotidian culture. For two examples, which are particularly pertinent for their focus on the question of manual and mental labor, see Alfred Sohn-Rethel, *Intellectual and Manual Labour: A Critique of Epistemology* (Atlantic Highlands, N.J.: Humanities Press, 1983), and Stanley Aronowitz, *Science as Power: Discourse and Ideology in Modern Society* (Minneapolis: University of Minnesota Press, 1988).
28. Maurice Meisner, "The Wrong March: China Chooses Stalin's Way," *Progressive* (October 1986), 26–30. Meisner discusses this problem more extensively in his essays in *Maoism, Marxism, Utopianism* (Madison: University of Wisconsin Press, 1982), especially "The Ritualization of Utopia."

ded in the Chinese revolutionary discourse. Anarchists in the 1920s had already pointed to such an eventuality. When they disappeared from the revolutionary scene in the 1930s, this social revolutionary ideal, too, went into abeyance. Its roots were too deep in the revolutionary discourse, however, for it to disappear completely. Ironically, in using this revolutionary ideal to establish its own hegemony, the Communist party may have contributed to keeping it alive. The ideal has resurfaced repeatedly to challenge the new hegemony, to force a rethinking of the course of the socialist revolution, to pry open the ideological closure that a new political power has imposed on it, and to serve as a reminder of the unfinished tasks of revolution.

The history of anarchism in China may be a history ultimately of political irrelevance, but it provides us with a vantage point from which to rethink the most fundamental problems of politics—not just Chinese or socialist, but all politics.

Bibliography

Albert, Michael, Leslie Cagan, Noam Chomsky, Robin Hahnel, Mel King, Lydia Sargent, Holly Sklar. *Liberating Theory.* Boston: South End Press, 1986.

Anarchism and Anarcho-syndicalism: Selected Writings by Marx-Engels-Lenin. New York: International Publishers, 1974.

Anderson, Benedict. *Imagined Communities: Reflections on the Origin and Spread of Nationalism.* London: Verso, 1983.

Arblaster, Anthony. "The Relevance of Anarchism." *Socialist Register.* Annual. 1971.

Aronowitz, Stanley. *Science as Power: Discourse and Ideology in Modern Society.* Minneapolis: University of Minnesota Press, 1988.

Avrich, Paul. *The Russian Anarchists.* New York: Norton, 1978.

Ba Jin. *The Family.* Translated by S. Shapiro. Beijing: Foreign Languages Press, 1964.

———. *Gemingde xianqu* (Vanguards of revolution). Shanghai: n.p., 1928.

———. *Shengzhi chanhui* (Confessions of a life). Shanghai: Shangwu yinshuguan, 1936.

———. *Yi* (Recollections). Shanghai: Wenhua shenghuo chubanshe, 1938.

Bailey, Paul. "The Chinese Work-Study Movement in France." *China Quarterly,* no. 115 (September 1988): 441–61.

Bakunin, Michael. *Bakunin on Anarchy.* Edited by Sam Dolgoff. New York: Knopf, 1972.

Bauer, Wolfgang. *China and the Search for Happiness.* Translated by Michael Shaw. New York: Seabury Press, 1976.

Beijing daxue rikan (Beijing University daily). Esperanto title, *Pekin-Universitato.* 1917–1921.

Beijing daxue xuesheng zhoukan (Beijing University student weekly). 1920.

Benton, Gregory, ed. *Wild Lilies and Poisonous Weeds.* London: Pluto Press, 1982.

Berkman, Alexander. *ABC of Anarchism.* London: Freedom Press, 1977.

Bernal, Martin. "Chinese Socialism before 1913." In *Modern China's Search for a Political Form,* ed. J. Gray. London: Oxford University Press, 1969.

————. *Chinese Socialism to 1907.* Ithaca: Cornell University Press, 1976.

————. "Liu Shih-p'ei and National Essence." In *The Limits of Change,* ed. C. Furth. Cambridge: Harvard University Press, 1976.

————. "The Triumph of Anarchism over Marxism, 1906–1907." In *China in Revolution: The First Phase, 1900–1913,* ed. Mary C. Wright. New Haven: Yale University Press, 1968.

Bodde, Derk. *Tolstoy and China.* Princeton: Princeton University Press, 1950.

Bookchin, Murray. *Toward an Ecological Society.* Montreal and Buffalo: Black Rose Books, 1986.

Cai Shangsi. *Cai Yuanpei xueshu sixiang zhuanji* (An intellectual biography of Cai Yuanpei). Shanghai: Lianying shudian, 1950.

Cai Yucong. "Zhongguo shehuixue fazhan shi shangde sige siqi" (Four periods in the development of Chinese sociology). *Shehuixue kan* (Sociology journal) 2, no. 3 (April 1933).

Cai Yuanpei. *Cai Jiemin xiansheng yanxing lu* (Record of Mr. Cai Jiemin's speeches). Beijing: Beijing daxue chubanshe, 1920.

Carter, April. *The Political Philosophy of Anarchism.* New York: Harper Torchbooks, 1971.

Chan, Ming K. "Labor and Empire: The Chinese Labor Movement in the Canton Delta, 1895–1927." Ph.D. diss., Stanford University, 1975.

————. "Minguo chunian laogong yundongde zai pinghua" (A reevaluation of the labor movement in the early republic). Unpublished conference paper, 1983.

————, ed. *Zhongguo yu Xianggang gongyun zongheng* (Dimensions of the Chinese and Hong Kong labor movement). Hong Kong: n.p., 1986.

Chan, Ming K., and Arif Dirlik. *Schools into Fields and Factories: Anarchists, the Guomindang, and the Labor University in Shanghai, 1927–1932.* Durham, N.C.: Duke University Press, 1991.

Chang Hao. *Chinese Intellectuals in Crisis: Search for Order and Meaning.* Berkeley and Los Angeles: University of California Press, 1987.

————. *Liang Ch'i-ch'ao and Intellectual Transition in Modern China.* Cambridge: Harvard University Press, 1971.

Chang Kuo-t'ao. *The Rise of the Chinese Communist Party, 1921–1927.* Lawrence: University Press of Kansas, 1971.

Chen Duxiu. *Duxiu wencun* (Collection of works by Chen Duxiu). 2 vols. Shanghai, n.p., 1922.

Chen Duxiu pinglun xuanpian (Selected essays on Chen Duxiu). 2 vols. Henan: Henan renmin chubanshe, 1982.

Chen, Kenneth. *Buddhism in China: A Historical Survey.* Princeton: Princeton University Press, 1964.

Chen Mingqiu. See Ming K. Chan.

Chen Sanjing, *Qingong jianxuede fazhan* (The development of diligent-work frugal-study). Taibei: Dongda tushu gongsi, 1988.

Chesneaux, Jean. *The Chinese Labor Movement 1919–1927.* Translated by Mary C. Wright. Stanford: Stanford University Press, 1968.

Chinese Academy of Social Sciences, ed. *Xinhai geming ziliao leipian* (Materials on the 1911 revolution). Beijing: Shehui kexue chubanshe, 1981.

Chow Kaiwing. *Xinhai geming qiande Cai Yuanpei* (Cai Yuanpei before the 1911 revolution). Hong Kong: Bowen shuju, 1980.

Chow Tse-tsung. *The May Fourth Movement: Intellectual Revolution in Modern China*. Stanford: Stanford University Press, 1967.

Chunlei yuekan (Spring thunder monthly). 1923.

Clark, John. *The Anarchist Movement*. Montreal: Black Rose Publishers, 1986.

Clastres, Pierre. *Society Against the State*. Translated by Robert Hurley. New York: Zone Books, 1987.

Clifford, Paul G. "The Intellectual Development of Wu Zhihui: A Reflection of Society and Politics in Late Qing and Republican China. Ph.D. diss., London University, 1978.

Cohen, Paul. *Between Tradition and Modernity: Wang T'ao and Reform in Late Qing China*. Cambridge: Harvard University Press, 1974.

Cole, G. D. H. *A History of Socialist Thought*. Vol. 1. New York: Macmillan, 1953.

Deng Zhongxia. *Zhongguo zhigong yundong jianshi* (Brief history of the Chinese labor movement). Beijing: n.p., 1949.

Ding Shouhe. *Cong wusi qimeng yundong dao Makesi zhuyide chuanpo* (From the May Fourth enlightenment movement to the propagation of Marxism). Beijing: Renmin chubanshe, 1978.

Dirlik, Arif. *The Origins of Chinese Communism*. New York: Oxford University Press, 1989.

———. "Socialism and Capitalism in Chinese Thought: The Origins." *Studies in Comparative Communism* 21, no. 2 (Summer 1987).

———. See also Ming K. Chan and Arif Dirlik.

Duiker, William. *Ts'ai Yuan-p'ei: Educator of Modern China*. University Park: Pennsylvania State University Press, 1977.

Eltzbacher, Paul. *Anarchism: Exponents of the Anarchist Philosophy*. Plainview, N.Y.: Books for Libraries Press, 1960.

Fan Puqi. "Sanshi nian qiande 'Annaqi zhuyi xuehui' " (The anarchist study society of thirty years ago). *Zhongjian* (The middle) 1, 8 (November 5, 1948).

Feigon, Lee. *Chen Duxiu: Founder of the Chinese Communist Party*. Princeton: Princeton University Press, 1983.

Fleming, Marie. *The Anarchist Way to Socialism: Élisée Reclus and Nineteenth Century European Anarchism*. London: Croom and Helm, 1979.

Foucault, Michel. *Power/Knowledge: Selected Interviews and Other Writings, 1972–1977*. Edited by Colin Gordon. New York: Pantheon, 1977.

Furth, Charlotte. "Intellectual Change: From the Reform Movement to the May Fourth Movement, 1895–1920." In *The Cambridge History of China*, ed. John K. Fairbank. Vol. 12, Part 1. New York: Cambridge University Press, 1983.

———. "May Fourth in History." In *Reflections on the May Fourth Movement*, ed. Benjamin Schwartz. Cambridge: Harvard University Press, 1972.

Gasster, Michael. *Chinese Intellectuals and the Revolution of 1911*. Seattle: University of Washington Press, 1969.

Ge Maochun, Jiang Jun, and Li Xingzhi, eds. *Wuzhengfu zhuyi sixiang ziliao xuan* (Selection of materials on anarchist thought). 2 vols. Beijing: Beijing daxue chubanshe, 1984.

Geertz, Clifford. *The Interpretation of Cultures*. New York: Harper Torchbooks, 1973.

Geming zhoubao (Revolution weekly), 1927–1929.

Goldman, Emma. *The Crushing of the Russian Revolution*. London: Freedom Press, 1922.

Gongchan zhuyi laodong daxue (Communist labor university). Nanchang: Jiangxi jiaoyu chubanshe, 1960.

Gongchandang (The Communist), 1920–1921.

Graham, A. C. "The Nung-chia 'School of the Tillers' and the Origins of Peasant Utopianism in China." *Bulletin of the School of Oriental and African Studies*. Vol. 42, Part 1.

Guangzhou wenshi ziliao (Historical and literary materials on Guangzhou). Nos. 1 (1962) and 1 (1963). Guangzhou: Renmin chubanshe.

Guérin, Daniel. *Anarchism*. Translated from the French by M. Klopper. New York: Monthly Review Press, 1970.

Guo Sheng. *"Wusi" shiqide gongdu yundong he gongdu sichao* (The labor-learning movement and the labor-learning thought tide of the May Fourth period). Beijing: Jiaoyu kexue chubanshe, 1986.

Guofu quanshu (Complete works of Sun Yat-sen). Taibei: National Defense Research Center, 1970.

Guoli Laodong daxue yuekan (National Labor University monthly), 1930.

Hampden, Jackson. *Marx, Proudhon and European Socialism*. New York: Collier Books, 1966.

Harootunian, Harry D. *Things Seen and Unseen: Discourse and Ideology in Tokugawa Nativism*. Chicago: University of Chicago Press, 1988.

He Changgong. *Qingong jianxue shenghuo huiyi* (Reminiscences of diligent-work frugal-study life). Beijing: Gongren chubanshe, 1958.

He Ganzhi. *Jindai Zhongguo qimeng yundong shi* (The modern Chinese enlightenment movement). Shanghai: n.p., 1947.

Hinton, Harold C. In *The People's Republic of China, 1949–1979: A Documentary Survey*. 5 Vols. Wilmington, Del.: Scholarly Resources, 1980.

Hobsbawm, Eric J. *Revolutionaries*. New York: New American Library, 1973.

Hoffman, Robert L. *Revolutionary Justice: The Social and Political Theory of P-J. Proudhon*. Urbana: University of Illinois Press, 1972.

Hong Dexian. "Xinhai geming qiande shijieshe ji wuzhengfu zhuyi sixiang" (The world society before the 1911 revolution and anarchist thought). *Shihuo* (Food and commodities) 12, no. 2 (May 1982).

Hsiao Kung-ch'uan. *A New China and a New World: K'ang Yu-wei, Reformer and Utopian, 1858–1927*. Seattle: University of Washington Press, 1975.

———. "Weng T'ung-ho and the Reform Movement of 1898." *Tsing Hua Journal of Chinese Studies* 1, no. 2 (April 1957).

Hsieh, Winston. "The Ideas and Ideals of a Warlord: Ch'en Chiung-ming." Harvard Papers on China. Vol. 16. Cambridge: Harvard University Press, 1962.

Hu Shi. "Duo yanjiu xie wenti, shaotan xie 'zhuyi' " (More discussion of problems, less discussion of "isms"). *Meizhou pinglun* (Weekly critic). July 20, 1910.

Hua Lin. *Bashan xianhua* (Idle words from Bashan). Chongqing: n.p., 1945.

Huang Liqun. *Liufa qingong jianxue jianshi* (Brief history of the diligent-work frugal-study program in France). Beijing: Jiaoyu kexue chubanshe, 1982.

Huang, Philip C. C. *Liang Ch'i-ch'ao and Modern Chinese Liberalism.* Seattle: University of Washington Press, 1972.

Huang Wenshan (Lingshuang). *Wenhuaxue lunwen ji* (Essays on culturology). Guangzhou: Zhongguo wenhuaxue xuehui, 1938.

Hudson Collection. The Hoover Institution on War, Peace and Revolution Archives. Stanford University, California.

Hunan qu wuzhengfu zhuyizhe tongmeng xuanyan (Manifesto of Hunan anarchist alliance). The Hudson Collection. Package 6, Part 2.

"Internationalist." "The Origins of the Anarchist Movement in China." Pamphlet. London: Coptic Press, 1968.

Jameson, Fredric. *The Political Unconscious: Narrative as Socially Symbolic Act.* Ithaca: Cornell University Press, 1981.

Jiang Kanghu. *China and the Social Revolution.* San Francisco: Chinese Socialist Club, 1914.

———. *Hongshui ji* (Flood waters collection). N.p., 1913.

———. *Jiang Kanghu yanjiang lu* (Speeches of Jiang Kanghu). 2 vols. Shanghai: Nanfang daxue, 1923.

———. *Jinshi sanda zhuyi yu Zhongguo* (Three great modern ideologies and China). Nanfang daxue, 1924.

Jiang Yihua. *Shehui zhuyi xueshao zai Zhongguode chuqi chuanpo* (The initial propagation of socialism in China). Shanghai: Fudan daxue chubanshe, 1984.

Jingzhe (Spring festival, literally "Awakening of Insects"). Guangzhou, 1924.

Jingzhe (Spring festival, literally "Awakening of Insects"). Chengdu, 1938.

Joll, James. *The Anarchists.* New York: Grosset & Dunlap, 1964.

Joll, James, and Apter, D. *Anarchism Today.* New York: Anchor Books, 1971.

K'ang Yu-wei. *Ta T'ung Shu: The One World Philosophy of K'ang Yu-wei.* Translated by L. G. Thompson. London: Allen and Unwin, 1958.

Kannada Huaren gonghui (Chinese labor association of Canada). "Laodong jie jinian hao" (Commemorative issue, Labor Day), May 1, 1922. Vancouver, B.C.

King, Ynestra. "Ecological Feminism." *Zeta Magazine* (July/August 1988).

Kosugi Shuji. "Shanghai koodan rengookai to Shanghai no roodoo yundoo" (The federation of Shanghai syndicates and the Shanghai labor movement). *Rekishigaku kenkyu* (Historical studies), no. 392 (January 1973).

Krebs, Edward S. "Liu Ssu-fu and Chinese Anarchism, 1905–1915." Ph.D. diss., University of Washington, 1977.

Kropotkin, Peter. *Fields, Factories and Workshops of Tomorrow.* Edited by Colin Ward. New York: Harper Torchbooks, 1974.

———. *Kropotkin's Revolutionary Pamphlets.* Edited by Roger N. Baldwin. New York: Benjamin Blom, 1968 reissue.

Kropotkin, Petr. *Mutual Aid: A Factor of Evolution.* Boston: Extending Horizon Books, n.d.

Kropotkin, P. *Mianbao yu ziyou* (Bread and freedom) (*sic*). Beijing: Shangwu yinshuguan, 1982.

Kwan, Daniel Y. K. "Deng Zhongxia and the Shenggang General Strike." Ph.D. diss., University of London, 1985.

Kwok, Daniel. *Scientism in Chinese Thought, 1900–1950*. New Haven: Yale University Press, 1965.

Lang, Olga. *Pa Chin and His Writings: Chinese Youth Between the Two Revolutions*. Cambridge: Harvard University Press, 1967.

Lang Xingshi, ed. *Geming yu fangeming* (Revolution and counterrevolution). Shanghai: Minzhi shuju, 1928.

Laoda luncong (Laodong University essays). Shanghai: Laodong daxue, 1929.

Laoda yuekan (Labor University monthly), 1930.

Laoda zhoukan (Labor University weekly), 1930.

Laodong (Labor). Nos. 1, 2 (1918).

Laodongzhe (Laborers), 1920, 1921. Edited by Sha Dongxun. Reprint ed. Guangzhou: Guangdong renmin chubanshe, 1984.

Larson, Wendy. "Literary Authority and the Chinese Writer." Unpublished manuscript.

Lasky, Melvin. *Utopia and Revolution*. Chicago: University of Chicago Press, 1976.

Lefort, Claude. *The Political Forms of Modern Society*. Edited by John B. Thompson. Cambridge: MIT Press, 1986.

Levenson, Joseph. *Confucian China and Its Modern Fate*. 3 vols. Berkeley and Los Angeles: University of California Press, 1968.

Levine, Marilyn. "The Found Generation: Chinese Communism in Europe, 1919–1925." Ph.D. diss., University of Chicago, 1985.

Li Shizeng. *Li Shizeng xiansheng wenji* (Essays by Mr. Li Shizeng). Taibei: Zhongguo Guomindang dangshi weiyuanhui, 1980.

Li Shizeng and Chu Minyi. *Geming* (Revolution). Paris: Xin shiji congshu, 1907.

Li Shizeng xiansheng jinian ji (Commemorative essays on Mr. Li Shizeng). Taibei: n.p., 1974.

Li Wenneng. *Wu Jingxian dui Zhongguo xiandai zhengzhide yingxiang* (The influence of Wu Jingxian [Zhihui] on modern Chinese politics). Taibei, 1973.

Li Xianrong. *Bakuning pingzhuan* (Biography of Bakunin). Beijing: Xinhua shudian, 1982.

Li Zhenya. "Zhongguo wuzhengfu zhuyide jinxi" (Past and present of Chinese anarchism). *Nankai xuebao* (Nankai University journal). No. 1 (1980).

Li Zhuanyu. *Li Shizeng zhuanji ziliao* (Materials for a biography of Li Shizeng). Taibei: Tianyi chubanshe, 1979.

Liang Bingxian. *Jiefang bielu* (An alternative record of liberation). N.p., n.d.

Liang Zhu. *Cai Yuanpei yu Beijing daxue* (Cai Yuanpei and Beijing University). Ningxia: Ningxia renmin chubanshe, 1983.

Lin Yu-sheng. *The Crisis of Chinese Consciousness*. Madison: University of Wisconsin Press, 1979.

Liu Gih-bor (Jibai). "Wusi qianhoude wuzhengfu zhuyi" (Anarchism around the May Fourth period). *Daxue shenghuo* (College Life monthly) 3, no. 5 (May 1968).

Lu Ting-yi. *Education Must Be Combined with Productive Labour*. Peking: Foreign Languages Press, 1958.

Lu Zhe. *Zhongguo wuzhengfu zhuyi shi* (History of anarchism in China). Fujian: Renmin chubanshe, 1990.

LuOu zhoukan (Weekly of Chinese students in Europe), 1919–1920.

Ma King-cheuk. "A Study of Hsin Ch'ing-nian (New Youth) Magazine, 1915–1926." Ph.D. diss., London University, 1974.

Makesi Engesi lun Bakuning zhuyi (Marx and Engels on Bakuninism). Beijing: Renmin chubanshe, 1980.

Makesi zhuyi zai Zhongguo (Marxism in China). 2 vols. Beijing: Qinghua daxue chubanshe, 1983.

Malatesta, Errico. *Anarchy*. London: Freedom Press, 1974.

Mao Zedong. *Chairman Mao Speaks to the People*. Edited by Stuart Schram. New York: Pantheon, 1974.

Marks, Robert. *Rural Revolution in South China*. Madison: University of Wisconsin Press, 1984.

Marx, Karl. *The Eighteenth Brumaire of Louis Bonaparte*. In Karl Marx and F. Engels, *Selected Works*. Vol. 1. Moscow: Progress Publishers, 1973.

———. *The German Ideology*. Edited by R. Pascal. New York: International Publishers, 1947.

———. *The Poverty of Philosophy*. In Karl Marx and F. Engels, *Selected Works*. Vol. 1. Moscow: Progress Publishers, 1973.

Meisner, Maurice. "The Chinese Communists and the French Revolution: From la commune insurrectionelle (1792–94) to China's People's Communes." Paper presented at the annual meeting of the American Historical Association (December 27–30, 1989).

———. *Li Ta-chao and the Origins of Chinese Marxism*. Cambridge: Harvard University Press, 1967.

———. *Maoism, Marxism, Utopianism*. Madison: University of Wisconsin Press, 1982.

———. "The Wrong March: China Chooses Stalin's Way." *Progressive* (October 1986), 26–30.

Meng Ming, ed. *Wu Zhihui Chen Gongbo bianlun ji* (Compilation of debate between Wu Zhihui and Chen Gongbo). Shanghai: Fudan daxue, 1928.

Metzger, Thomas A. "Developmental Criteria and Indigenously Conceived Options: A Normative Approach to China's Modernization in Recent Times." *Issues and Studies* (February 1987), 19–81.

Miller, Martin A. *Kropotkin*. Chicago: University of Chicago Press, 1976.

Min Yi (Hu Hanmin). "Gao feinan minsheng zhuyizhe" (Response to attacks on the principle of people's livelihood). *Minbao* (People's journal), no. 12 (6 March 1907).

Minsheng (People's voice) (1913–1922). Daian Reprint.

Minsheng zhoukan (People's livelihood weekly), 1931.

Minzhong (People's tocsin). January–July 1927.

Mo Jipeng. "A Memoir of Shih fu." Unpublished manuscript translated by Edward Krebs from the Chinese original, "Huiyi Shifu."

Mouffe, Chantal, ed. *Gramsci and Marxist Theory*. London: Routledge & Kegan Paul, 1979.

National Archives, *Records of the Department of State Relating to Internal Affairs of China, 1910–1929*. Washington, D.C.: The National Archives, 1960.

No. 2 Historical Archives. *Zhongguo wuzhengfu zhuyi he Zhongguo shehuidang*

(*Chinese anarchism and the Chinese Socialist party*). Nanjing: Jiangsu renmin chubanshe, 1981.

National Archives Microfilm Publications. *Records of the Department of State Relating to Internal Affairs of China, 1910–1929; Political Affairs: Bolshevism, Communism and Communistic Activities.* Washington, D.C.: The National Archives, 1960.

Nohara Shiro. "Anarchism in the May Fourth Movement." *Libero International,* nos. 1–4 (January 1975–April 1976).

Ping. "Gongdu zhuyi" (Labor-learning'ism). *Jiefang yu gaizao* (Liberation and reform) 2, no. 3 (February 1920).

Pingdeng (Equality), nos. 20–22 (July–September 1929). *Pingshe* (Equality Society), San Francisco.

Pingxiang gemingjun yu Ma Fuyi (The Pingxiang revolutionary army and Ma Fuyi). Paris: Xin shiji congshu, 1907.

Price, Don. *Russia and the Roots of the Chinese Revolution, 1896–1911.* Cambridge: Harvard University Press, 1974.

Proudhon, Pierre-Joseph. *The Principle of Federation.* Translated and with an introduction by Richard Vernon. Toronto: University of Toronto Press, 1979.

Pusey, James. *China and Charles Darwin.* Cambridge: Harvard University Press, 1983.

Pyziur, Eugene. *The Doctrine of Anarchism of Michael A. Bakunin.* Chicago: Regnery, 1968.

Qian Ye (Wu Zhihui). *Jiu shehui zhuyi yizheng gemingzhi yilun* (Clarifying the meaning of revolution through socialism). Paris: Xin shiji congshu, 1906.

Qin Paopu (Baopu). "A Memoir of Meeting Ms. Goldman in My Early Days." Unpublished letter to Prof. Lu Zhe of Nanjing University (1987?).

Qingong jianxue biandi huakai (Diligent-work frugal-study is flowering everywhere). Shanghai, 1958.

Qingong jianxue gaibianle xuexiaode mianmao (Diligent-work frugal-study has transformed schools' visages). Shanghai, 1958.

Qinghua daxue zhonggong dangshi jiaoyan zu. *Fufa Qingong jianxue yundong shiliao* (Historical materials on the diligent-work frugal-study movement in France). 3 vols. Beijing: Beijing chubanshe, 1979.

Qu Renxia. *Wuzhengfu zhuyi yanjiu* (Examination of anarchism). Shanghai: Zhongshan shudian, 1929.

Quanguo zhongxiaoxue qingong jianxue jingyan xuanpian (Experiences with diligent-work frugal-study in elementary and middle schools around the country). Beijing: Jiaoyu kexue chubanshe, 1982.

Rankin, Mary B. *Early Chinese Revolutionaries: Radical Intellectuals in Shanghai and Chekiang, 1902–1911.* Cambridge: Harvard University Press, 1971.

Ricoeur, Paul. *Lectures on Ideology and Utopia.* Edited by George H. Taylor. New York: Columbia University Press, 1986.

Saltman, Richard B. *The Social and Political Thought of Michael Bakunin.* Westport, Conn.: Greenwood Press, 1983.

Scalapino, Robert, and Yu, G. T. *The Chinese Anarchist Movement.* Berkeley: Center for Chinese Studies, 1961.

Schwartz, Benjamin I. *In Search of Wealth and Power: Yen Fu and the West.* Cambridge: Harvard University Press, 1964.

Schwartz, Benjamin I., ed. *Reflections on the May Fourth Movement.* Cambridge: Harvard University Press, 1972.

Schwarzc, Vera. *The May Fourth Enlightenment Movement.* Berkeley and Los Angeles: University of California Press, 1985.

Shaffer, Lynda. *Mao and the Workers: The Hunan Labor Movement, 1920–1923.* New York: M. E. Sharpe, 1982.

Shao Kelu (Jacques Reclus). "Wo suorenshide Li Yuying xiansheng" (The Li Yuying [Shizeng] that I knew). Translated by Huang Shuyi (Mme J. Reclus), *Zhuanji wenxue* (Biographical literature) 45, no. 3 (1983).

Shehui zhuyi taolun ji (Collection of discussions on socialism). Shanghai: Xin qingnianshe, 1922.

Shifu (Liu Sifu). *Shifu wencun* (Collected works of Shifu). N.p.: Gexin shuju, 1927.

Sima Xiandao. *Beifa houzhi gepai sichao* (Currents of thought after the northern expedition). Beijing: n.p., 1930.

Snow, Edgar. *Red Star Over China.* New York: Grove Press, 1961.

Sohn-Rethel, Alfred. *Intellectual and Manual Labour: A Critique of Epistemology.* Translated by Martin Sohn-Rethel. Atlantic Highlands, N.J.: Humanities Press, 1983.

Sonn, Richard D. *Anarchism and Cultural Politics in Fin de Siècle France.* Lincoln: University of Nebraska Press, 1989.

Stanley, Thomas A. *Osugi Sakae: Anarchist in Taisho Japan.* Cambridge: Harvard University Press, 1982.

Starr, John B. "Revolution in Retrospect: The Paris Commune through Chinese Eyes." *China Quarterly,* no. 49 (January–March 1972): 106–25.

Sun Yat-sen. *Sun Yixian shehui zhuyi tan* (Sun Yat-sen's discussion of socialism). N.p., 1912.

Tai Xufa. *Taixu zizhuan* (Autobiography of Taixu). Singapore: Nanyang Foxue shuju, 1971.

Tamagawa, Nobuaki. *Chukoku Anakizumu no Kage.* Tokyo: n.p., 1974.

Tao Qiqing, ed. *Quanmin geming yu guomin geming* (Revolution of all the people and the national revolution). Shanghai: Guangming shuju, 1929.

Tan Sitong. *An Exposition of Benevolence: The Jen-hsueh of T'an Ssu-t'ung.* Translated by Chan Sin-Wai. Hong Kong: Chinese University Press, 1984.

Tan Xingguo. *Bajinde shengping he chuangzuo* (Bajin's life and creations). Chengdu: Sichuan renmin chubanshe, 1983.

Tang Xiaobing. "History Imagined Anew: Liang Ch'i-ch'ao in 1902." Unpublished paper, 1990.

Thomas, Paul. *Karl Marx and the Anarchists.* London: Routledge & Kegan Paul, 1985.

Thompson, John B. *Studies in the Theory of Ideology.* Berkeley and Los Angeles: University of California Press, 1984.

Tian Xin (Shen Zhongjiu). *Jinggao Zhongguo qingnian* (Warning to Chinese youth). Vancouver: Vancouver Chinese Labor Association of Canada, 1927.

Tianyi bao (Heavenly justice), 1907. Daian Reprint.

Touraine, Alain. *Return of the Actor: Social Theory in Post-Industrial Society.* Minneapolis: University of Minnesota Press, 1988.

Vohra, Ranbir, ed. *The Chinese Revolution, 1900–1950.* Boston: Houghton Mifflin, 1974.

Wang, Richard T. Y. "Wu Chih-hui: An Intellectual and Political Biography." Ph.D. diss., University of Virginia, 1976.

Weiqian nongmin yundong (The peasant movement in Weiqian). Beijing: Zhonggong dangshi ziliao chubanshe, 1987.

Welch, Holmes. *The Buddhist Revival in China.* Cambridge: Harvard University Press, 1968.

Welsh, John. "Shen-wu-lien: China's Anarchist Opposition." *Social Anarchism* 2, no. 1 (1981): 3–15.

Wenshi ziliao xuanji (Selections of historical and literary source materials) (*quanguo*), no. 90. Beijing: Wenshi ziliao chubanshe, 1983.

Willener, Alfred. *The Action-image of Society: On Cultural Politicization.* Translated from the French by A. M. Sheridan Smith. New York: Pantheon, 1970.

Williams, Raymond. *Marxism and Literature.* London: Oxford University Press, 1977.

Wu Zhihui (see also Qian Ye). *Wu Zhihui quanji* (Collected works of Wu Zhihui). 3 vols. Shanghai: Qunzhong tushu gongsi, 1927.

Wusa jinian (Commemoration of May 30, 1925). N.d., n.p.

Wusi aiguo yundong (The May Fourth patriotic Movement). 2 vols. Beijing: Shehui kexue yanjiu yuan, 1979.

Wusi shiqi qikan jieshao (Introduction to the periodicals of the May Fourth period). 3 vols. in 6 parts. Beijing: Sanlian shudian, 1979.

Wusi shiqide shetuan (Societies of the May Fourth period). 4 vols. Beijing: Sanlian shudian, 1979.

Wusi yundong huiyi lu (Reminiscences of the May Fourth Movement). 3 vols. Beijing: Zhongguo shehui kexue chubanshe, 1970.

Wuzhengfu gongchan yuekan (Anarcho-communist monthly) (June 1934). Pingshe (Equality Society). San Francisco.

Xin Ai (Shen Zhongjiu). *Wode Guomindang guan* (My views on the Guomindang). Ziyou zhuyi yanjiushe, 1927. This version pubished by the Chinese Labor Association, Vancouver(?).

"Xinmin shuo." In *Xinhai geming qian shinianjian shilun xuanji* (Collection of essays from the decade before 1911). Beijing: Sanlian shudian, 1978.

Xin qingnian (New youth), 1916–1923.

Xin shiji (New era), 1907–1910. Daian Reprint.

Xu Teli. *Xu Teli wenji* (Essays of Xu Teli). Changsha: Hunan renmin chubanshe, 1980.

Xuedeng (Light of learning), 1924–1925.

Yeh Wen-hsing. "The Alienated Academy: Higher Education in Republican China." Ph.D. diss., University of California, Berkeley, 1984.

Yida qianhou (The period of the first congress). 2 vols. Beijing: Renmin chubanshe, 1980.

Zarrow, Peter G. *Anarchism and Chinese Political Culture*. New York: Columbia University Press, 1990.

——. "Chinese Anarchists: Ideals and the Revolution of 1911." Ph.D. diss., Columbia University, 1987.

Zhao Zhenpeng. "Laodong daxuede huiyi" (Recollections of Labor University). *Zhuanji wenxue* (Biographical literature) 37, no. 4 (October 1980).

Zhongguo xiandai shi ziliao xuanpian (Materials on modern Chinese history). 3 vols. Heilongjiang: Heilongjiang renmin chubanshe, 1981.

Zhu Chuanyu, ed. *Li Shizeng zhuanji ziliao* (Materials for a biography of Li Shizeng). Taibei, 1979.

Zhu Qianzhi. *Huiyi* (Memoirs). Shanghai: Xiandai shuju, 1928.

Ziyou (La libereco), no. 1 (December 1920).

Ziyou congshu (Compendium of freedom). 8 vols. San Francisco: Equality Society, 1928.

Zou Rong. *The Revolutionary Army*. Translated by John Lust. The Hague: Mouton, 1968.

Index

New Life Movement (*xin shenghuo yundong,* May Fourth period), 16, 191–96
"New politics" (*xin zheng*), 103
New Society Movement (*xin shehui yundong*), 168
New Village Movement (*xincun yundong*), 162, 188, 193, 237
New World Society (*Xinshijie she*), 81. *See also* World Society
"New Year's Dream" (*Xinnian meng,* Cai Yuanpei), 66–69
New Youth (*Xin qingnian*), 156, 161, 179, 180, 204; in anarchist/Communist debate, 204–7; anarchist contributions to, 174
Nietzsche, Friedrich, 183
Nihilism, 63, 71, 72
"No-boundaryism" (*wushijie zhuyi*), 124
Nongcun yundong tongmeng (Alliance for an Agrarian Movement, Shanxi), 238

October Revolution, 2, 18; as anarchist revolution, 176–79; and awareness of class in China, 200; and Chinese interest in anarchism, 166–67; and decline of anarchism, 10, 198
"On Equalizing Human Labor" (*Renlei junli shuo,* Liu Shipei), 106
"On Politics" (Chen Duxiu), 204, 212
"On the New Citizen" (Liang Qichao), 60
Oppenheimer, Franz, 204
Oppression: gender and family, 40; Marxist and anarchist explanations of, 9
Organization, anarchists on, 31–32, 233–43
The Origin of the Family, Private Property and the State. See Engels, F.
Osugi Sakae, 25
Ou Shengbai, 15, 18, 19, 20, 208; at Beida, 172, 173, 174; and cooperation with Communists, 203; debate over Marxism and anarchism, 199, 214–19, 221; and Esperanto, 170, 290; fickleness of, 197; in opposition to Guomindang, 243, 255; on revolutionary strategy, 235
"Over-determination," 61

"Pan-laborism" (*fanlaodong zhuyi*), 106, 155. *See also* Tolstoy, Leo
Paris anarchists, 13, 21, 81–100, 116–17, 120; contribution of, to New Culture Movement, 167–69; and Guomindang, 251–54. *See also* Li Shizeng; Wu Zhihui
Paris Commune, 6, 44, 292–93, 299
Peace Society Journal (*Pingshe zazhi*), 175

Peng Pai, 196
Peng Renquan, 21
People's communes: compared to Kropotkin's "industrial villages," 296; and integration of agriculture and industry, 296–97; and integration of mental and manual labor, 296–97
People's Journal (*Minbao*), 125
People's militia (*mintuan*): as revolutionary organs of anarchism, 236, 239–40
People's Tocsin (*Minzhong*), 20, 21, 154, 252
People's Tocsin Society (*Minzhong she*), 20
People's Vanguard Society (*Minfeng she*), 22, 234, 266
People's Voice (*Minsheng*), 15, 126, 155, 175, 195, 214, 223, 228
Perovskaya, Sofia, 74
Pingshe zazhi (Peace Society journal), 175
"Politics of authenticity," 76
Populism, 63, 104, 294
Price, Don, 71, 72, 74
Principles of Social Reconstruction (Russell, Bertrand), 205
Promote Virtue Society (*Jinde hui*), 120, 172, 188
Proudhon, Pierre-Joseph, 21, 26, 270; federalism of, 274–76; Li Shizeng on, 271–72, 274–76
Public (*gong*): vs. private (*si*), 58–60, 96–100, 111, 217
"Pure" socialism, 136; anarchism as, 89
"Pure" socialists, 121, 123–24, 136; criticized by Shifu, 133, 141–42
Pusey, James, 76, 114

Qian Xuantong, 162
Qiangquan (naked force), 68, 124, 204, 205, 212, 272
Qin Baopu, 20, 221, 224; on revolutionary strategy, 233–34, 235
Qing dynasty, 59, 83
Qiu Jin, 73, 74, 89
Qu Qiubai, 195
Quanmin geming. See "Revolution of all the people"
Qunshe (Masses Society), 175

Rankin, Mary, 72
Reality Society (*Zhenshe*), 20
Reclus, Élisée, 25, 81, 94, 243, 266, 273; works of, available in Chinese, 82, 155
Reclus, Jacques, 243, 266
Records of Freedom (*Ziyou lu*), 21, 154, 174
Renaissance (*Xinchao*), 180
Rendao (Humanity), 124, 272

Work-study, 167–69, 188–96
Work-study (Gongxue), 195
Work-study Association (*Gongxue hui*), 193–96 *passim*
World of Society (Shehui shijie), 124
World Society (*Shijie she*), 14, 25, 167
Wu Kegang (Jun Yi), 258, 259
Wu Yue, 94
Wu Zhihui, 14, 20, 70, 75, 81–100 *passim,* 171, 182, 248–85 *passim,* 288, 290; on achieving anarchism, 233; at Beida, 172; on class conflict, 187; in conflict with Shifu, 129; contributions of, to *New Youth,* 174; criticized by young anarchists, 231, 251, 253–55; in defense of Guomindang, 252–53; on education and revolution, 99–100; flexibility with principles of, 121; and Guomindang, 23, 230, 244, 249–50; possible influence of, on Chen Duxiu, 161; and Promote Virtue Society, 120; and "revolution of all the people," 276–78; on Shifu, 124–25, 233; and utopianism, 113
Wuzhengfu gongchan zhuyi tongzhi hui. See Society of Anarcho-Communist Comrades

"Xianzhi gemingzhi yiyi" ("The Meaning of Present-day Revolution," Li Shizeng), 270
Xiao zuzhi ("small groups"), 191, 233
Xie Juexian, 20
Xie Yingbo, 170
Xin qingnian. See New Youth
Xin shenghuo yundong (New Life Movement), 16, 191–96
Xin shiji. See New Era
Xincun yundong. See New Village Movement
Xingqi pinglun (Weekend Review), 155, 169
"Xinnian meng" ("New Year's Dream," Cai Yuanpei), 66–69
Xinshe. See Conscience Society
Xinshijie she. See New World Society
Xu Deheng, 172, 173
Xu Teli, 195
Xu Xilin, 74, 89
Xu Xing, 102, 106
Xuedeng (Light of Learning), 23, 155, 223
Xuehui she. See Sea of Learning Society

Yao Wenyuan, 295
Yi Baisha, 161–62

Yi Peiji, 162, 263, 264
Young China Association (*Shaonian Zhongguo xuehui*), 191
Young Laborers Ten-daily (Laogong qingnian xunkan), 241
Youth (Shaonian), 21
Yu, George T., 273
Yuan Shikai, 122, 126
Yuan Zhenying, 15, 172, 173, 174, 179
Yun Daiying, 191, 195

Zamenhof, L. L., 173
Zhang Binglin, 66, 93
Zhang Chunqiao, 295
Zhang Dongsun, 204
Zhang Guotao, 196, 296
Zhang Ji (Zhang Puquan), 65, 71, 75, 120, 161, 181; criticized by Shifu, 129, 231, 252; as Guomindang elder, 249, 251; and Promote Virtue Society, 120
Zhang Jingjiang, 81, 249, 263, 264
Zhang Puquan. *See* Zhang Ji
Zhangzhou, anarchists in, 15, 150, 171, 183, 284
Zhao Zhenpeng, 266, 267
Zhejiang anarchism, 21, 24, 196; and collaboration with Guomindang, 255; in syndicalist federation, 257
Zheng Peigang, 15, 17, 21, 125, 195, 201
Zheng Xianzong, 205, 206
Zheng Zhenheng, 20
Zhenshe (Reality Society), 20
Zhiping, 20
Zhongguo qingnian dang (Chinese Youth party), 169, 191, 277
Zhongguo shaonian wuzhengfu gongchan zhuyizhe lianmeng. See Federation of Young Chinese Anarcho-Communists
Zhongguo shehui zhuyi dang. See Chinese Socialist party
Zhou Dunhu, 21
Zhou Enlai, 14, 21, 195
Zhou Fohai, 208, 210–14 *passim,* 217; "Seizing Political Power" ("Douqu zhengquan"), 212; "Why We Advocate Communism" ("Women weishemma zhuzhang gongchan zhuyi"), 212
Zhou Zuoren, 162, 179, 193
Zhu Qianzhi, 173, 179, 219
Ziyou lu (Records of Freedom), 21, 154, 174
Ziyou ren (Free People), 21, 241, 253
Zou Rong, 63, 114

www.ingramcontent.com/pod-product-compliance
Lightning Source LLC
Chambersburg PA
CBHW020335270326
41926CB00007B/191